R

OUT OF CHAOS

THE NEW HEAVEN AND THE NEW EARTH

---

by

Simon Peter Fuller

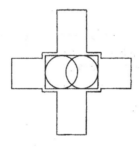

Incorporating the complete text of

REVELATION III

THE THIRD BOOK OF THE APOCALYPSE

Published by:
Kima Global Publishers,
P.O.Box 374,
Rondebosch 7701
South Africa

First Edition February 1994
This revised and expanded Edition December 1996

ISBN 0-9584065-4-5

VISIT OUR WEBSITE AT:
http://www.globalvisions.org/cl/kima

Cover design:
Jurgen Ziewe, 22, King Edward Avenue, Worthing, West Sussex
BN14 8DD United Kingdom.
Printed and bound in South Africa.

Facing page: **The original Aquarian Cross**

REVIEWS

"The Second Coming of the Christ Consciousness on Earth is the most thrilling story of our time. Here it is proclaimed through a miraculously restored biblical text and manifested for all to share by the inspired actions of a dedicated few across the Planet. This unusually comprehensive account is compelling reading and convincingly proves that the final and inescapable choice between Love and Fear now challenges each one of us. Free will is ours by Divine decree, but do we hear the call?" *Sir George Trevelyan, United Kingdom 1994*

Multiple levels of understanding, rich and stimulating await the reader. This text is a must for daring thinkers of every tradition; there is something for everyone, and above all it gives us hope. The Third Book of the Apocalypse, restored by direct spirit intervention, with its power and magnificence reveals to us the Greater hand and Heart that is ever watching for our responses. *Rev.Carol Parrish, Principal and Founder, Sancta Sophia Seminary, The Light of Christ Church, USA*

Simon Peter Fuller offers the most hard-hitting and incisive challenge to organised religions and other exterior-focused belief structures that I have found in our times. Delivering powerful biblical Revelations restored directly by spirit after 1500 years of suppression by false priests, I view him as a leading, independent figure in the reawakening of humanity to the unified (Christ) consciousness within. *Triaka Don Smith, President and Founder, Spiritual World Network, Hawaii USA*

The author generously shares his wisdom and there is no doubt that he provides constructive alternatives to conventional methods of conceptualising man's relationship with the planet.
Conscious Living Magazine, Australia 1996

This book has touched us both deeply. It brings together many threads of knowledge, combines them with powerful emotional and spiritual experiences and offers practical and effective ways of contributing to the healing of our planet. *Professors Margrit and Declan Kennedy, Permaculture Germany 1995*

This book throws light on the past, clarifies and enthuses the present, and gives clear direction for the future. It also embraces scholastic research, spiritual insight, cultural exploration and one man's remarkable personal story. Simon Peter's journey is essential to the end of one aeon and the start of a new, and with his Aquarian Cross, he has created a legend by courageously following his quest.

Hilary Allen, Australian author of Pendulum

In Simon Peter's hands, the Aquarian Cross has travelled far and wide in recent years uplifting human and planetary consciousness during meditations, rituals and ceremonies on many of the Earth's major power centres.... *Odyssey Magazine, South Africa 1994*

For those with ears to hear *Rising out of Chaos* sounds a clarion call, both challenging and profound. Simon Peter Fuller's book encompasses an enormous scope and depth of vision. Each reader must respond from the heart. *Pegasus Magazine UK 1995*

Skillfully weaving personal insight with prophecy, science and universal law, the author makes a compelling case for a Second Coming in which personal responsibility plays a pivotal role. Humanity is at a threshold and here a plausible scenario is presented in which enough people wake up spiritually and link together in time to prevent life as we know it from extinguishing itself in a grand cataclysmic finale.

NAPRA ReView 1995

Rarely these days does one receive publications that hold one's attention from cover to cover meriting in-depth study of the material. The truth and compassion Simon Peter applies to his mission and the account of his realisation and quest proves to be a compelling, moving and challenging document. He is motivated by a sacred respect for the Divine that significantly distinguishes his book from the fringe elements under which more conventional thinkers might seek to categorise it. *Simon Bell, Director, World Network of Religious Futurists.*

Simon Peter Fuller is a man with a mission - to raise human consciousness enough to promote the swift return of the Christ energy to Earth as we pass between the Piscean and Aquarian worls ages. His inspiring story, superbly set forth in this book, adds a vital dimension to mankind's opportunity to create Heaven on Earth here and now.

Dr.Chet B. Snow, author of Mass Dreams of the Future

CONTENTS

WILL YOU WAKE?

The human heart can go the lengths of God
Dark and cold we may be, but this
Is no winter now. The frozen misery
Of centuries breaks, cracks, begins to move;
The thunder is the thunder of the floes,
The thaw, the flood, the upstart Spring.
Thank God our time is now when wrong
Comes up to face us everywhere,
Never to leave us till we take
The longest stride of soul men ever took.
Affairs are now soul size.
The enterprise
Is exploration into God.
Where are you making for? It takes
So many thousand years to wake.
But will you wake for pity's sake?

From A Sleep of Prisoners *by Christopher Fry*

In our age, an energy that is Light, Life and Love
will flood the Earth, re-animating the realm of matter
and raising its vibratory rate to that of the spiritual
worlds. The two will interpenetrate and interact.
So high is this frequency that it will repel all
particles, energies and beings attuned
to the lower frequencies of
egoism, greed,
selfishness, violence,
hatred, rivalry and war.
There will be a total transformation.

Sir George Trevelyan

FOREWORD

On a small planet in a little known system at the edge of a remote galaxy, a cosmic drama of almost inconceivable grandeur is being played out. The people of this world, having lost sight of their origins, their history and the purpose of their journey through space and time, are sleepwalking towards certain self-destruction. All their major institutions social, political, economic and religious are on the verge of collapse. The spectres of war, famine, fear and oppression are everywhere. The planet's seas and waterways, forests, soil and atmosphere are all being poisoned. Indeed, all life-forms are threatened. Cataclysm seems inevitable.

And then, at the very last moment, a miracle occurs: all round the planet, pinpoints of light appear. Solitary men and women, alert to the dangers that beset their world, begin to gather into groups and link up, forming a fragile network, gossamer-fine at first, but quickly gaining in resonance and power.

As the darkness intensifies, this network goes into overdrive, creating the living hologram of a new world co-existing with the civilisation that is dying all around them. A great rescue operation is mounted: first hundreds, then thousands, then millions of the population are woken out of their daydream by this growing army of light. Balance is restored, critical mass is reached, and the unspeakable is averted.

Science fiction? On the contrary: as you have already surmised, that world is Earth, those people are ourselves and, as this book vividly demonstrates, we are *all* leading players in that cosmic drama.

Some years ago, Peter Fuller found himself being torn from his everyday life and goaded into action; frog-marched into a *new* life, into a quest for his own truth, his own past and his future; propelled by some inner voice that would not be denied. Everything he had built up and worked for - his career, his possessions, his beliefs and his sense of personal identity - were suddenly irrelevant.

As the New Age "roadshow" swirled past him with its glamorous cast of visionaries, prima donnas, specialty acts, stuntmen, clowns and extras of every shape, size and description, Peter managed to maintain a clear detachment from it all and resolutely followed his own inner light, wherever it led him.

It has taken him on a unique journey across the world and beyond. It has taken him from Avalon to Africa; to the middle East, Europe, Australia, New Zealand and the Americas. It has taken him back to the dawn of time, through the birth-pangs and early infancy of the new world. It has reacquainted him with the secret history of mankind; with prophecy, magic and the Ancient Wisdom.

It has reintroduced him to other worlds, other dimensions, and to some of the many beings who inhabit them - who have a vested interest in offering us creative partnership in Operation Earth Rescue.

A man of rare insight and sensitivity, Peter almost had to be dragooned into writing this extraordinary, shocking, hard-hitting, courageous and inspiring account of his adventures. But it is a story that *had* to be told: one man's first-hand experience of the most dramatic chapter in the world's history.

It is literally a Book of Revelations!

Michael Joseph, July 26th 1991

Michael, whose own work is primarily concerned with the vital role young people will soon be playing in human affairs, has just published his own fascinating experiences and his adventures with the legendary magician Merlin whose own mission is no longer "the Matter of Britain", but of the whole world. Staying with me in 1991, Michael awoke early one morning, and wrote the above Foreword as it flowed through him. He handed it to me at breakfast with a knowing look long before I had even thought of writing a book! Clearly it was time, and everything conspired during the summer of 1992 to allow the work to proceed.

The author

INTRODUCTION

> **"Humanity is now going through its final examination as to whether it can qualify for its Universal function and thereby qualify for continuance on board the planet. Whether humanity will pass its final exams for such a future is dependent on you and me."**
>
> *R. Buckminster Fuller*

The first reprint of this book, some four years after it was written in 1992, has allowed me to assess its impact on an already enthusiastic worldwide readership with the result that the amendments and additions I have now included will help to reinforce the relevance of its message at this most critical of moments in the evolution of human consciousness.

To make it easier for the reader to assimilate the copious information in the book, and to help keep a perspective of the overall philosophy, I propose to use this extended introduction briefly to identify my main themes and to show how they combine to produce a broad overview of the development of 'western' spiritual culture. By unravelling often deliberately confused historical information and false religious indoctrination, a radically different picture emerges of the last two millennia. Although most people may not be aware of it, it is in fact now the destiny of the western culture, through the English language, to establish the Unified (Christ) consciousness as the only truly universal power capable of reconciling all humanity. With this in mind, the material presented here will challenge conventional thinking and drastically redefine the accepted version of key events that have shaped our more recent history.

It is, though, important to emphasis at the outset that any small contribution my work may be making to the global awakening process is of a practical rather than theoretical nature. The New Jerusalem cannot remain forever an abstract concept in the heads of intellectuals, even though they have inspired us with uplifting visions of it defined in spiritual, emotional, mathematical and geometrical terms.

Now is the appointed time to *live* and *express* these high ideals in our daily lives as an example to others, as well as to prove to ourselves - and the higher realms now watching us intently! - that we can actually do it.

This, above all else, is a time of vision combined with right action, if we wish to take advantage of the golden opportunities we are now being offered to create a new reality on our long-suffering Earth.

By describing in detail my own complex and stigmatised early life, the profound spiritual awakening combined with inner work in mid-life and, soon afterwards, the totally unexpected manifestation of my life purpose, I am able to draw on the still-unfolding story and use it as a practical example of the many processes each one of us must undergo sooner or later on the path to self-realisation. I already have plenty of confirmation that the real life experiences and problem resolution described are capable of empowering and encouraging those who are not yet aware that their own spiritual awakening can only be triggered from within.

We seem to face broadly similar problems in life, so sharing traumatic situations honestly is often a more effective way of encouraging personal introspection and inner growth, than the academic approach based on dry intellectual theory. We have far greater potential for effecting lasting change in those around us by appealing to their hearts before their heads! It takes great courage to face our inner shadows, but nothing of enduring spiritual consequence occurs in our lives or our work until we do - and we only incarnated on Earth to grow spiritually.

It should also be made very clear that the intention of openly sharing the details of my life experiences is not to attract a personal following and create yet another Piscean cult, but rather to liberate and empower people to fulfil their own particular purpose for incarnating here at this crucial time. I don't pretend to have all - indeed, any - answers and can only share the processes I have personally experienced and that unexpectedly transformed my rather bleak spiritual prospects into a fulfilling life that appears to be synchronistically guided by powers beyond our normal comprehension.

Indeed, many reading this book, especially those approaching it from an exclusively intellectual perspective, may well find much in it too hard to accept. What must be understood, however, is that it is written specifically to challenge the sterile and outmoded thinking processes of a race that has for too long prized the sheer cleverness of brainpower above that of the wisdom which shows us how to use thought appropriately. By common consent only a tiny proportion of the full potential of the human mind has so far been activated. Unless we start to produce balanced thought inspired by the Universal mind of One (God) to which we are all inextricably linked, and integrate the different thought capacities of the left and right brain hemispheres, then there simply is no future for us here on Earth.

Since it is only through a healthy body and inner transformation leading to the opening of the heart that we are capable of raising our vibratory frequencies sufficiently to participate in the consciousness shift now destined for humanity, I have added new material in Chapter 18 to help focus these underestimated and all-too-often ignored aspects of our preparation. I also explain the current polarisation of human consciousness between Love and Fear in fulfilment of the prophecy of 'the sorting of the wheat from the chaff'. This relates to the impending split within humanity according to individual free will, so that the low vibrational levels of fear are transmuted before the higher dimensional frequencies can be established on Earth.

Another reason for the personalised approach in writing this book is that, as much of the Earth activation work described later is not yet widely understood or accepted, it is important to demonstrate through a personal testament that the events described did take place and that they are now witnessed historical fact regardless of people's opinions about them. There is a significant body of proof now being gathered by aware people all around the world that they are dramatically transforming consciousness and thereby changing the current reality levels for the better. This is the work in which I am involved during the journeys described here and as the evidence is accumulated, it will be ever harder for the less aware to dismiss it just because they don't understand it.

The dawning realisation that awakened humans are indispensable at many unsuspected levels in the transformation of the predominantly negative reality levels here is itself central to the philosophy expressed in this material. Through mass meditational mind-linking, realigning the planet's subtle energy grid and activating her power centres, we actually create the subtle structure for the New Jerusalem to manifest on Earth.

I must stress that the prime function of this book is to clarify the historical, geographical and metaphysical connection between the First and Second Coming of the Christ consciousness - and it has certainly turned out to be the most controversial! Inevitably, many sacred cows have had to be slaughtered here as false and disempowering concepts about 'Second Coming' are dismissed.

No less challenging is the fact that the Aquarian 'New Jerusalem' spiritual focus is now to be found in a new location that replaces Old

Jerusalem's former primacy. Nothing further of spiritual significance is to occur in ancient Palestine and the world can only observe in sorrow as religious and political fanatics battle for control of a region whose once revered spiritual mandate has now expired.

Spirituality and religion parted company long ago in the common rooted Judeo/Christian/Islamic tradition and we shall now all bear witness to this fact as militant fundamentalists in all three religions manifest the exact reverse of the divine inspiration that initiated them all, so long ago. It is time then at least to lower the curtain on the tired old play called 'Christianity' that once played to packed houses in the western culture, but whose stale and uninspiring lines are now mouthed by ever less convincing actors and whose audiences are daily dwindling to a point where the commercial enterprise backing it is financially unviable!

Meantime the brothers Ephraim and Manasseh, identified respectively as the United Kingdom and the United States of America, are destined to take on the leadership of the once 'lost' tribes of Israel in accordance with Old Testament prophecies. Mainly those of Celtic origin were forced into exile by the English during the last three centuries and in the words of the prophecy 'having multiplied like the sands of the seashore' - throughout the English-speaking New World - they now have the responsibility of establishing the Christ consciousness for the benefit of all mankind.

First and Second Coming, probably the most misinterpreted and confused events ever recorded, can only be understood when expressed in terms of massive influxes of redemptive energy permeating the planet and humanity at the beginning and now at the end of the Piscean Age. The 'Old' Jerusalem dispensation was anchored on Earth by one self-realised, Christed being, precisely so that the 'New' Jerusalem could be manifested within the whole human family two thousand years later. This is to take the form of a mass spiritual awakening within all prepared and freely choosing hearts - initiated, as I explain in this book, through the global Celtic dispersion.

The ever-more-spectacular crop formation phenomenon occurring among the ancient power sites of Celtic south west England, where over two thousand profound symbols have appeared in the fields since the late 1980's, is proof in itself that this region has become a major focus of spiritual attention - especially when related to the historical and geographical perspective explored in this book about the inauguration and activation of the New Jerusalem anchor point.

Revered tribal spiritual leaders and many others in the forefront of the New Awareness movement confirm that the purpose of these exquisite mandalas is to trigger the awakening of all mankind, and that they have been deliberately sited in the region that represents the Heart of Earth. The crop formations are an ancient language that speaks to the soul, and just by looking at the images, we automatically receive their messages - regardless of any intellectual scepticism!

The crucial missing chapters of the Revelations text, restored to WWV by the direct intervention of spirit using modern communication technology, present the most effective challenge ever mounted against the distorted teachings of the Christian belief structure. Clearly, our friends on the inner planes must be mightily concerned about the disastrous influence of this divisive and disempowering religion to have found such an ingenious and effective method for circumventing any further attempts at censorship by the church fathers. Needless to say, this ancient, 'Prophecy of the Second Coming of the Christ consciousness', among much else that is currently occurring, long ago foresaw the anti-Christ role of spiritually ignorant Christian clerics in these last days of the old order.

We are also told of the awakening of the all-important 'critical mass' of humanity. This is referred to in the Revelations text as the 144,000, who are fully committed, 4th dimensional souls capable of activating the exponential shift of mass consciousness upon which so much now depends. The restoration of the Divine Feminine principle 'in the last days' was also long ago prophesied, as the era of the Christ Feminine now brings balance to the Christ masculine manifested at the opening of the Piscean Age. The female of our species is awakening first, as I can confirm at my own public meetings which they attend in a majority ratio to men 3:1. Some say that it was when we first saw our planet from space through the eyes of the first astronauts that human consciousness was reminded of the Divine Feminine by the very roundness and beauty of our exquisite Goddess Gaia.

The full text of Revelations III is not only included in this new edition, but has also been made available to the world at large on our Wholistic World Vision Internet Web site and on Compuserve's Religion Forum. Having received the information electronically, we have offered it back in the same way, so that spirit can spread it through the latest communication technology directly to all those aware enough to grasp its truly awesome significance - free of charge, of course!

Further evidence of this novel means of communication is available in the new book *Conversations Beyond the Light with Departed Friends and*

Colleagues by Electronic Means (see bibliography). The Instrumental Transcommunication (ITC) group that published it confirms with hard evidence that in recent years regular communications with spirit have taken place by telephone, fax, computer and TV screens! Furthermore, their well-documented scientific research into this phenomenon is government funded and apparently even the Vatican itself is involved in this research. At WWV we have also enjoyed direct phone conversations with Gandhi and Winston Churchill, and my editor has similarly conversed post mortem with Ava Gardner. Death, yet again, is proven to be an illusion of the physical dimension and need no longer cause us fear. "The last enemy to be destroyed is Death" (1 Cor. 15:26).

Our guidance is that much vital and deliberately suppressed information is now to be made available to the general public right over the heads of the controlling authorities by direct means, in order to assist in the spiritual awakening process. The Revelation text clearly comes into this category. It also needs to be remembered that, in the multi-dimensional world we inhabit, spirit has often intervened directly in human affairs and the arrival of the Ten Commandments together with the manifestation of the Golden Tablets of Mormon are but examples.

Another distinguishing feature of my work that came into existence at the same time as the Revelations text first reappeared is the Aquarian Cross. This perfectly balanced emblem of the Christ consciousness incorporating the Vesica Pisces, Golden Mean and equal-armed Cross symbology is understood to be the last Cross of the Piscean era. The initial purpose of this Universal and non-religious symbol was as the vehicle for transferring energy between the Old and New Jerusalem power sites at the Aeon Shift ritual in 1990 described in Chapter 6. As much of the book is about helping people to identify the real spiritual legacy of Jesus Christ's mission, it is perhaps appropriate at this point to state that I would describe myself as 'Christ conscious' rather then 'Christian' and that I write from that perspective.

Since 1990, the Aquarian Cross has travelled the world and been used as an amplifier of energy at all the Earth power site activations described in the following pages. As symbols trigger the subconscious, this Cross, through its harmonious equilibrium, helps us open the heart. Small silver and gold versions of the cross have been made by Wholistic World Vision centres around the world, on their own initiative, and many have now chosen to wear it as a token of their inner commitment to spiritual growth and the fulfilment of their own spiritual blueprints. Clear intention, motivation and complete commitment are the three crucial factors in our spiritual striving and, once these are established, we can apply ourselves wholeheartedly to the work we came to do.

Much of the work already referred to has been inspired by an inter-dimensional partnership called Wholistic World Vision, which has many distinguished, but unseen, associates on the inner planes. WWV is a communications network that is being developed in many countries by people who wish to share their spiritual skills and insights, knowing that it is by co-operation through communication that we remind each other of the spiritual truth that already resides deep within each one of us. 'Educare' in Latin means 'to lead out', which presupposes that there is something 'in there', to lead out in the first place! What a pity our current educationalists have lost sight of this and, instead of drawing out the hidden talent within, insist on cramming us with data that is largely irrelevant to our individual paths. Most of us forget it anyway, once it has been superficially memorised just to pass exams.

Spiritual re-education in the principles of the unchanging Ancient Wisdom and Universal Laws is the first priority on this planet, if we are to encourage people to express the inner wisdom that liberates them from ignorance and superstition. We are asked to listen to children, instead of conditioning them remorselessly. They speak wisdom from the heart, and teachers would be advised to pay attention to them, if they wish to maintain order in increasingly anarchic classrooms. Only when we start to educate spiritually will people be enabled to make informed freewill choices that support rather than retard the evolutionary progress of their souls.

Since there can be no genuine freedom or peace on Earth until we live by Divine rather than human law, all will now depend on the availability of enlightened spiritual education across the full spectrum of all human activity on the planet. Fortunately, now that institutional control and censorship is being rendered impotent by mass direct communication on the computer networks like the Internet, we at last have the opportunity to stimulate a huge upliftment of human awareness.

Mass direct communication will also herald the end of our deeply-flawed democratic political process, which has been subverted by selfish career politicians abusing privileged, highly-paid, public positions to advance their private interests and personal aggrandisement at the expense of their public duty. The time for a global network of 'Councils of Wisdom' - formed by modestly paid individuals, from all walks of life and age groups and selected for their demonstrated ability to honour the responsibility of public office - is long overdue to restore sanity to what currently passes for the charade of democratic government.

Only through genuine consensus will we be able to handle the immense challenge of restructuring our socio-economic reality in response to the mechanisation, automation, robots and sophisticated computer technology that are daily - and permanently - replacing millions of manual, clerical and even professional jobs. Recent statistical projections from the USA suggest that some 90 of the 124 million existing jobs are vulnerable to eventual replacement in that country alone! The long-heralded era of **freedom** from conventional 'labour' has now arrived, but we will only be able to benefit from it **if** we are educated spiritually and liberated financially so as to be able to use our new-found 'leisure' for spiritually constructive purposes. For instance, revenue for responsible state spending directed specifically towards the enlightenment and happiness of society as a whole must in future derive from the profits of commercial enterprise, rather than through the burden of restrictive personal taxation.

Wholistic World Vision supports all spiritual educational initiatives and also provides a global network that can be quickly activated for mass meditational mindlinking to counteract the ravages of the fear that is itself the cause of all human dysfunction. Too few people realise that a 'silent minute' observed daily by millions of heart-centred people right across the planet would be sufficient to raise human consciousness permanently above the debilitating levels of fear that dominate our present reality. It is well to remember that the 'silent minute' at 9 o'clock each evening instigated by enlightened initiates advising Winston Churchill in Great Britain during the last war **was** the secret weapon that turned the tide against the forces of darkness unleashed by Hitler - and recently released papers in Germany show that 'the dark initiative' Hitler knew this all too well!

LOVE LINK - THE 'WIN WIN' WAVE

How simple it would be to initiate such a worldwide movement, through which all people of goodwill could simply think loving thoughts about a person or place that really opens their hearts for a few co-ordinated minutes at midday each day. The energy wave would race across the Earth feeding back positive vibrations to those who send and receive the loving thoughts in a rising tide of Light that would provide the greatest possible opportunity for ever more people to lift into the new consciousness.

Let's Link in Love now - and WIN!

Chapter 1

BAPTISM OF FIRE

**"Life is a ladder infinite-stepped, that hides
its rungs from human eyes.
Planted its foot in chaos' gloom, its head soars
high above the skies."**
Sir Richard Burton

It is a highly rewarding exercise projecting our consciousness back into spirit form, so as to remember the experience of being magnetised by two interacting energies at the moment of our conception; then, during the nine-month pregnancy, as our soul dances around the foetus like a bee pollinating a flower, remembering our thoughts about the conditions we had been attracted to and whether we felt able to go through with the assignment! Life actually begins at the first breath *after* birth; it is only at that moment, when we've taken the final plunge into matter, that the soul commits itself to the body. These memories can all be accessed by regression techniques of various kinds, and serve to demonstrate the amazing precision of the spiritual dynamics of human birth. It can also be very helpful in healing the shock to the system of the unnatural birthing techniques of orthodox medicine - a devastating experience from which many never fully recover during their entire lives.

Birth into the comparative confines of a physical body is far more traumatic than the sublime feeling of release as we lift off at the moment of transition back into the world of spirit. In most cases, the conception is likely to have been a purely physical transaction, all too often under the influence of stimulants of one kind or another. The foetus, often unwanted and repeatedly told so, is then subjected to junk food, tobacco, alcohol, drugs, noise, pollution and temperamental parents. With the birth process comes the trauma of emerging into air from the softness and security of water. This usually occurs under bright lights, sometimes with mechanical gadgets, without the father's presence and in front of a production line of overworked medical staff. At least these days, a baby is usually left with its mother to acclimatise

- instead of being held up by its feet, slapped to assist breathing and taken away from the mother during the most vital bonding moments of their lives! Conception, pregnancy and birth are emphatically more than just mundane, physical procedures. Full conscious awareness at all stages is an indispensable ingredient.

What a start to life, and what a perfect example of the level to which the human race has sunk. Is it really surprising that delinquency among children and young adults is so widespread in the materialist societies? Further compounding the problems, parents fail to take personal responsibility for their intractable children and project blame onto social workers, teachers, politicians and society at large for the loveless conditions they themselves have imposed on the soul they freely chose to bring into the world.

Perhaps I'm qualified to speak from experience, having found myself in a precarious situation at my own arrival on the planet this time round. At 20.25 hrs on November 21st, 1947 in Braunschweig, Germany, a soul committed itself to a body in decidedly inauspicious circumstances. It had been attracted to a young, single mother without any means whatever to support it, in one of the worst-bombed cities of that devastated country just after the 2nd. World War. Food was extremely scarce and with nowhere suitable to take a baby, the distraught woman agreed in desperation to immediate fostering arrangements with the town authorities. She was never to see her child again, yet the bond between them was to play a crucial and moving role in years to come.

Such was the start of my latest incarnation. Horst Wollenberg was the name I was given at birth and I had been attracted to the city that naturalised and then elected the Austrian Adolf Hitler to the German Reichstag. I assume that the fostering arrangement was a commercial transaction from which the woman I ended up with made a pittance. I certainly didn't benefit, and was removed in due course with rickets resulting from serious undernourishment.

One of my earliest recollections, aged about three, was standing with other young children on the edge of a nearby main road waiting for, I assume American, army lorries to pass - in the hope that the soldiers would throw us chocolate bars. Occasionally we were lucky, and what bliss it was for those empty and often painful little bellies. We'd land in a heap scrabbling in the dirt for the prizes, and the few lucky ones would scamper away jealously guarding their bounty. It was a case of survival of the fittest, but I think we shared - a little!

In those first years, I can't recall any physical affection other than that of a young woman who tried to nurture me at the orphanage I was next sent to. She was soundly thrashed in front of me for nothing more than displaying her motherly instincts, and this scene indelibly impressed on me a sense of the vulnerability of women; an awareness that, awakened early, has remained with me ever since.

It was just as well I was a personable child: with flaxen hair, bright blue eyes and a self-confident manner, I had a better chance than many others in the orphanage adoption stakes. Re-reading recently the matron's character report on me, aged four, was a powerful and rather emotional experience: "Horst is a nice little boy, who needs to place his confidence in someone. He will reward such a person with loyalty, if they are worthy of his trust." Looking back now, it really was a bizarre start to life. Clearly, I had chosen a blueprint that had little to do with conventional upbringing and much to do with fending for myself right from the start.

I soon became aware that I was being singled out and shown off to visitors at the orphanage. After a few visits by a particular German, who was acting as a friendly recruitment agent, I was introduced to an elderly Englishman. All of a sudden, I was being prepared for a journey and vividly recall boarding an aircraft and experiencing the thrill of flying. In order to keep me quiet, I suppose, those I was travelling with kept feeding me bananas. Then the inevitable happened - I threw up all over them!

The journey ended at a beautiful manor house, set in many acres of classic, formal gardens with breathtaking views over the Weald of Kent in the heart of the English countryside. At last, life was beginning to pick up.

What had happened was that this wealthy English bachelor, who had served in both wars, wanted to make a personal gesture towards healing the trauma between England and Germany. There were many such personal initiatives, and it is not widely known that Churchill himself deliberately recruited German staff for his private household after the war. My future father had already adopted a much older German boy and also helped educate a number of disadvantaged English boys over the years. On this occasion, he was looking for one

3

young enough to be moulded into the image of a natural son, based on his own English educational and social traditions. I found out later that I was 'on approval', with an option to be returned within a few months if necessary! Adoption formalities in these unusual circumstances were not exactly straightforward, and my natural mother was apparently apprehensive when asked for her irrevocable permission.

Meantime, not knowing what was going on, and wide-eyed with amazement wherever I went, I had latched on to the person who was to be my emotional anchor for the next few years - a short, grey-haired archetypal grandmother figure, already 82 years old. I rushed for her on first sight and, burying myself in her skirts, called her "Omi", the German for granny. It was odd because I had never known a granny figure in Germany, but apparently a deep and ancient bond already existed between us, and she and I became inseparable.

Communication was strictly telepathic to start with as I spoke only German, and she had never left England. She had been my future father's nanny and, as often happens in such households, had stayed on with the family. Ruling the roost was a ferocious Prussian cook addicted to the gin bottle, who terrified me well into adulthood and only later became a firm friend. There were numerous other household staff and gardeners to maintain the famous grounds, which were often opened to the public. But I was now safe with Omi, daily putting more flesh on my skeletal frame, and had not a care in the world in this veritable paradise, after a rather tenuous start to life.

So it was that after completion of all formalities, Colonel 'Norrie' Fuller adopted me and had me christened in the local village church, witnessed by three godparents. He chose the names Simon Peter, with the intention that both be used together in the continental style. Although it stuck during early childhood, the concept of a double barrelled Christian name was too precious for my contemporaries at boarding school and I quickly dropped the Simon! It was only quite recently, after I started to focus on the life and work of the biblical Simon called Peter, that I began to use both my given names together again.

Within less than a year, as if in some fairytale, the forlorn orphan Horst Wollenberg had turned into the 'little prince' known as Simon Peter Fuller! My astrological birth chart shows quite clearly that I could not remain long in the place of my birth and that the life "planted in chaos' gloom" was destined to rise until "its head soars high above the skies" Provided, that is, I held to my chosen course and didn't fall prey to life's snares and illusions.

My upbringing in the early 1950s was a throwback to the Edwardian experiences of those who now cared for me. Children were occasionally to be seen, but never heard. Firmly in the care of nanny, and in a part of the house well out of earshot of civilised adults, I was smartened up for the ritual half-hour teatime inspection by our many distinguished visitors. Otherwise, I was left to my own devices to play and fantasise to my heart's content around the estate. Some of my first friends were the grandchildren of our illustrious next-door neighbour, Winston Churchill, at Chartwell He was a familiar figure throughout my early life and my extraordinary interaction with this great soul will be revealed as the story progresses.

Through the rapidly-expanding younger generations of Winston Churchill's family, I was privy to the special intimacy with the old man that was reserved for his grandchildren. In his frail health, he found the boisterous young hard to cope with; his wife, Clementine, usually managed to protect him - though occasionally we did sneak into his bedroom to play while he read his correspondence, and would often accompany him when he went to feed his fish and black swans. Many of the best-known personalities of the day would visit Chartwell, while we scampered around them, unimpressed. The Churchills were guests of my father's too, especially for croquet on his superlative lawn, whose every weed had been sedulously dispatched.

Although there was such a large age gap between us, my father did his best to keep me happy without being spoiled, and in the company of other children. I was taken skiing in the Alps and spent wonderful summer holidays by the Mediterranean with French friends of his in the oil business. They accepted me as part of their own family - three children of my own age and a stern English governess. Miss Mason, a brilliant linguist, had been a translator at the Nurenberg war trials and kept us in order according to the strictest Edwardian English traditions. Then, when I was nine, it was time for my father's influence to replace Omi's, and I was to experience nine years of the English private educational system. The first four were at a preparatory school by the sea and despite boarding away from home, I soon got used to it, made lots of friends and managed to pass my exams well enough to qualify for a place at Harrow. This is a celebrated school that has taught solid, traditional values to generations of British administrators, domestic and colonial, including Churchill and my father.

I have often wondered what I derived from this expensive experience - certainly neither academic brilliance, nor pleasure from team sports. In fact, I had the distinction of being probably the very first boy to refuse to waste time on cricket and insist the school provide professional tennis coaching instead! Rather a bold move in those days, but gratifying to know that tennis was subsequently integrated into the curriculum. Playing soldiers wasn't my idea of fun, then or now. So on Wednesday afternoons, instead of marching around the parade ground, a small group of us would visit the elderly and disabled to dig their gardens, shop and do any other useful chores for them. I don't know what they thought of these young men with their exuberant, clumsy energy disrupting their lives, but I was grateful to them for reminding me that not everyone enjoyed the kind of privileges that I now did, at school and at home.

My greatest accomplishment at school again involved Winston Churchill. He had, during my time there, made regular appearances at the school songs, which he loved passionately. The school has an ancient tradition of entertaining visitors and old boys in the central hall, called Speech Room, by singing stirring, mainly Victorian songs. Many are the occasions on which I remember an elderly, cigar-smoking figure sitting on the stage, literally heaving with emotion, while 600 young men sang rousing, lusty choruses to honour this, the most celebrated Old Harrovian of all.

When granted the honour of a State Funeral in Britain, the recipient is entitled to plan the event! Churchill was awarded that privilege in his last years and requested that four boys from the school he loved stand guard in the Palace of Westminster at the end of his Lying in State, before the funeral procession through the streets of the capital. I'll never know how the selection was made by the school authorities, as I am not aware that my early connection with him was known about there. Anyway, I was invited to be one of the four, and on a freezing winter's day, we got up in the early hours, dressed in military uniform and were shown our positions at each corner of the bier. All I remember was that, having had no food, I was terrified of fainting and letting the school down! Such an event, with all its pageantry, is so awe-inspiring that it is hard to take it in at the time. I do, of course, remember his entire family passing within inches of my nose, and recognised many I had known well in my earlier youth. I received a Ministry of Defence medal for my participation and, until my present work started, always wondered why I should have been drawn so closely into the aura of this giant among men.

My father died after a series of debilitating strokes, at about the same time as Churchill. I had only known him during his long dying process and sadly never had a chance properly to relate to him. He was a complex character, whose motivations were well-intended. In retrospect it seems likely that we were working out some karmic pattern, which this time around was largely, though not entirely, to my benefit. I was most fortunate to be taken on as a ward by my late father's business partner and close friend. He had not long before married my godmother, a brilliant mathematician decorated for her war work and now a director in the same oil company. The three of us, with two elderly retainers of my father's, set up house together and I was given every support and encouragement to complete my schooling and further education. They were a stimulating couple whose influence in my formative years, though not spiritual, was of great benefit. I was happy later to be able to help them both through times of failing health.

I left Harrow with adequate academic qualifications, some good friends - and a determination to get on with real life rather than prolong my academic conditioning at University. My father had entered me for his Oxford college, but with his plans now no longer enforceable, it was decided to send me back to Germany for a year to learn the language of my birth and see if I could heal the old scars. I was most reluctant to go, as I had by now become thoroughly accustomed to my new English role, and looked and sounded the part. Indeed, much of the success of this process had been at the expense of suppressing, for reasons of self-protection, all details of my past.

I had become adept at camouflage during my education in the company of people who, I thought, would not have been too impressed by the truth. It would be fair to say that up until my early thirties, even my best friends were fed plausible stories about my background, which they all seemed to accept and never questioned. Real friends don't care about such things and it was a salutary lesson, later, to find out that many of them knew much more than I realised! It is not too hard to see how my paranoia developed and, despite attempts at home to get me to acknowledge my past, I confess I had already acquired rather grand social aspirations and values and was determined after the uncertain start to my life that nothing would interfere with them.

Suddenly, after my father's death, I was given the full details of my parentage and adoption. It was quite a shock. There, for the first time, was the grim evidence I dreaded staring at me from ageing scraps of official paper. I had already invented many imaginative explanations to convince myself and others, but this was a profound and disturbing encounter with truth. My reaction then and for years to come was to hide the disgrace at all costs, as I just could not reconcile the glaring contradictions in my life. This was, of course, to be my greatest test later on, but for the time being the old fear-based pattern of denial remained deeply entrenched.

The time in Germany was first spent at a language school in the mountains, skiing rather than studying and then being obliged to find a job and room in Frankfurt, which was much less glamorous! My first job ever was at a petrol station, dealing with rather humourless customers, but making plenty on tips for car servicing. Efficient German bureaucracy soon caught up with me, though, and as I didn't have the work permit needed in those days, I was ordered - in a most alarming interview for an unworldly teenager - to leave the Fatherland within 24 hours! As the menacing official stamped my passport 'Invalid' everywhere conceivable, I didn't dare question his authority and complied by boarding the night express for Vienna, a few hours later. Evidently Germany and I still didn't gel, and it wasn't for several years yet that our reconciliation came about.

Vienna, where I took a series of university language courses to avoid permit problems, was a dream and became my student city. I developed the customary passion for rich cream cakes and opera, and felt strangely familiar with its fading grandeur and polite, old fashioned ways. Past life memories, no doubt. Not that I knew anything about such things then, and was anyway fully occupied in living life to the hilt. Looking back, I suppose this must have been the first time I felt truly independent and free. What bliss! Vienna has a very special place in my heart, and was later to be the scene of a powerful and significant event.

As I had no idea what I wanted to do after this interlude, it was decided to play safe by putting me through a legal training. I don't know how I survived three years of it - but I did learn how to express myself with precision on paper, which has since had its uses, but otherwise was happy to leave at the first opportunity.

Considering the direction my life took in my early middle years, it is hardly surprising that I didn't fit easily into conventional careers. Often, our real purpose here doesn't manifest until we have had the widest variety of experiences. During such times of bewilderment and confusion, I found the best thing was to be true to myself, rather than try to fulfil other people's expectations of me, and to resist any conditioning they tried to impose on me.

A brief taste of the West End theatre in London assisting a then struggling, but now phenomenally successful impresario, was enough to show me that the theatre was not my scene. Then suddenly my career began - which for the next fourteen years turned out to be the travel business, planning package holidays for two large companies. I had never heard of this method of travelling, which was then developing into a major industry. Planning was certainly the plum job, involving frequent international travel to investigate tourist potential, and to negotiate contracts with various suppliers. I very seldom came into contact with the clients and toured the world at my leisure, earning rather a lot of money doing it! The hectic schedules wreaked havoc on my social life and relationships, but the job supported a high lifestyle, and travel was and still is one of my passions.

Looking back over the years, it is obvious that this was my apprenticeship for what I am doing now. I am familiar with most countries in some detail, and feel perfectly at home anywhere from the Himalayas to Hawaii, from Sri Lanka to San Francisco. I've done business with most races and nationalities and have a working knowledge of a number of languages. Tourism was the pretext, but the preparations for what I now do were subtly interwoven into it. The blueprint, though I didn't know it then, had started to unfold. I console myself that my birth in one country, adoption in another and familiarity with many others is a kind of planetary citizenship that transcends mere nationality! I had and still have no blood family, so must look to the wider human family to fulfil that role.

Although cheaper travel has succeeded in giving many people a more intimate perspective of the planet as a whole and the reality of human interdependency, it has also inevitably reinforced the prejudices of the less evolved. What eventually disenchanted me with the industry was the increasingly mean-spirited attitude of certain sections of the public and their unscrupulous methods of extracting undeserved refunds! The attitudes of independently motivated travellers and packaged tourists have little in common: ultimately, to derive any real benefit from life, there is no substitute for personal effort. Travel cannot be guaranteed against all unforeseen eventualities, because that denies the adventure that it is - or should be.

One of the least attractive by-products of mass tourism are miles of hideously developed and polluted coastlines, which are now even being rejected by those for whom they were created! When it is eventually realised what immense damage we are doing to the upper atmosphere and our own environment with the noise and carbon-emission pollution of jet aircraft, this mode of travel will have to cease until alternative technology has been developed.

Despite these reservations, my years in travel passed very agreeably and would be many people's absolute ideal as a career and lifestyle. The bizarre incidents alone ensured that life was never dull. Instances of respectable middle-aged people, deranged by too much sun, appearing naked in hotel dining rooms were rather frequent! One client died while swimming in the Dead Sea, only to have his body blown back and forth between Israel and Jordan. As boats can't function on this dense mineral water, it involved all kinds of practical and diplomatic initiatives to solve the drama! Then there was the woman who was all but sucked into an aircraft lavatory due to pressurisation malfunction; her release came only after landing.

I myself got into all kinds of scrapes, negotiating things I had never intended as a result of language difficulties - and the drinking trap set by more experienced negotiators. It was all great fun and useful experience, and I don't regret a moment of it. My private life meantime was a whirr of fast cars, equally fast relationships and all kinds of social aspirations still dependent, I felt sure, on my successfully disguising my origins.

A serious car crash in which I faced certain death twice in the space of a minute, yet survived speechless with shock, was in retrospect probably my first dose of spiritual awakening, and certainly sobered me up. It showed me all too clearly how fragile the body is and how easy it is to damage or destroy it. But it was my first visits to the Third World that were by far the most important education I was to receive in my early years; it was there, in conditions for which I was totally unprepared, that the veil of material illusion first parted.

Here I must confess my deep debt of gratitude to a Roman Catholic priest, who is the very embodiment of selfless and unconditional love. Although he always refers to his 'boss upstairs', I see the divine presence radiating within him as him. Approaching things from such utterly different perspectives, we maintain an uneasy truce on matters spiritual! When we meet, we concentrate instead on the practical work of administration and fund-raising for the most inspiring project I have ever come across - the Pattaya Orphanage in Thailand. It was a hotel manager in Pattaya, intuiting that my interests were wider than most in that business, who suggested I visit the then modest site of this budding initiative.

Raymond Brennan, an Irish-American born in Chicago, was by his own admission a street-wise teenager, who had experienced more in his few years than most do in a lifetime. A priest had once predicted he would take holy orders very early and, contrary to all his own expectations, that is exactly what happened. Brennan, who thought he would be ministering to the tattered army of capitalism's rejects within America, suddenly found himself in the wilds of Northern Thailand's notorious opium-producing region, without any knowledge of the language!

Over the years, his work brought him to the Eastern border with Cambodia at the time of one of the frequent outbreaks of fighting. There, amid all the misery and degradation, Father Ray gathered in his arms some of the first heavily-traumatised orphans around whom the orphanage gradually grew.

It was in what was soon to become one of the world's most notorious sex-market holiday resorts at Pattaya Beach in Thailand that Father Ray was led to establish his orphanage. The phenomenal wastage of an expanding holiday resort gave this highly practical and most inventive of men all the materials he needed to construct and furnish the site: old concrete-mixers were converted into washing machines; methane from animal dung provided fuel, and any discarded hotel furniture, telephone exchanges or other equipment were swiftly requisitioned. As time went by, more and more tourists in the resort heard about the project and regular support starting coming in from all over the world. Even the owners of seedy bars and other dubious businesses in this notorious international vice-centre succumbed to his persuasive tactics and Irish charm! The enterprise is still run entirely by donation of funds and labour, and Father Ray implicitly believes that all will be provided 'by the boss'. I know it must, because the presence of Christ *within* this man wills it to be so - and the outworking of spiritual Law takes care of the rest.

Soon more land was donated and specialist blind, deaf and handicapped adult schools were founded. There was even a refuge for elderly illegal immigrants to spend their last days in dignity and freedom among the children, having been locked up in immigrant jails for much of their lives. Now, his undyingly grateful handicapped adults win medals at the Handicapped Olympics, and most of them are quickly recruited by well-known computer companies after qualifying brilliantly in the technical training courses he has devised. The rich try to bribe him to accept their children at his blind and deaf schools created specifically for the poor! Meanwhile, once-traumatised but now happy and well-balanced orphans are carefully fostered out. While ever more sad cases are deposited with him, Father Ray moves on with his latest scheme - to return to their villages the many young girls and boys duped into prostitution to satisfy the insatiable sexual demands of mainly Western appetites.

Unusually for a Roman Catholic priest, he respects the Buddhist faith into which the children are born, and does not attempt conversion unless first asked by a candidate. A rare man indeed who, paradoxically, demonstrates Christ consciousness within the confines of a religion that has contradicted the very purpose of its declared existence! He has a wealth of both hilarious and devastating stories to tell anyone who drops by: amid the laughter and the tears, even the hardest of hearts entering this holy ground are softened; and joyless, routine lives are transformed forever. Mine certainly was, and I still consider travelling in what we in the West have allowed to become the Third World, to be the best possible life-class.

For those not familiar with such conditions, it can be summed up in the words 'human life is cheap'. Forget any kind of social security or other support systems: if you are sick or disadvantaged in any way, your survival depends on will-power alone. Indeed, such people are considered a drain on scarce resources, and as in the animal world, Nature is often left to take its course.

Human life in the Eastern tradition is divided into seven cycles, each being of between seven to ten years' duration, relating to the seven chakras - subtle energy centres - of the body, starting from the base of the spine. All our body cells except the brain renew every seven years, and this process prepares us for the next phase. Seven years are spent learning the lessons of each cycle, and three years are to integrate them and prepare for the next one.

The first cycle, we are told, is to familiarise ourselves with the physical body, with the realm of matter, and to establish individuality. The second enables us to reach physical maturity by experimenting with the energies of this dimension and interacting with other people - sacral/sexual chakra. The third, or solar plexus, is focused on making the home, family, career and learning personal sacrifice while the fourth triggers spiritual awakening through the heart chakra, and our subsequent search for the meaning of life. The fifth, linked to the throat chakra, integrates our career and all other aspects of our life with the demonstration of spiritual values as an example to others. The sixth cycle is detached from material concerns and is devoted to inner research and the teaching of the younger generations, through mental maturity stimulated by the 3rd. eye chakra The seventh and any further cycles prepare us for our return to the realms of Spirit, having mastered the illusion of matter by activating our crown chakra. Each generation is interdependent and supports the next in its purpose, with businesses and responsibilities being passed on at the appropriate stages.

Slightly ahead of my own fourth cycle - in my mid-thirties, and indelibly impressed by all I had seen and heard on my travels - I detected distinct signs of deep inner stirrings!

Chapter 2

THE LOTUS BLOSSOMS

"Of many thousand mortals, one perchance
striveth for Truth; and of those few that
strive - nay, and rise high - one only
here and there knoweth Me
as I AM, the very Truth."

Bhagavad Gita

Australia was one of the few countries I had yet to visit, so when a good friend, who had set up a business over there and had a waterside apartment on Sydney harbour, suggested I might enjoy a couple of weeks holiday one rather cold and damp English November, I was quick to accept. Having the spare time and a free ticket through my business, I was tempted by the thought of unseasonal sunshine, some rather grand social contacts I'd been given in Sydney and possibly looking up some very distant, adoptive relatives I hadn't seen for thirty years.

Flying over the great red heart of this ancient land in the early morning of my arrival showed me that it was no ordinary place. I've revisited it every year since that trip and despite extensive travel there, I know I'm still only scraping the surface of its deeply concealed mysteries. On my first few trips, however, I focused on Australia's more obvious attractions. Sydney in the early 1980s was cosmopolitan, uninhibited and fun - invitations from leading hostesses, sailing on the spectacular harbour, a beach life of amazing variety and a busy night life of clubs and parties. Then, rather reluctantly, I remembered the relatives in Melbourne, for whom I didn't even have contact details. I remember quite distinctly sitting for ages, phone in hand, debating whether to sacrifice precious, halcyon days to family duties. It was very much in the balance and, considering with hindsight how critical the decision was for my future, I'm heartily relieved it went the way it did despite all temptations to the contrary!

I eventually found them through directory enquiries and we arranged to spend a week-end together. Elaine was the Anglo Indian first wife of my guardian's brother. Not exactly a close blood relation! She had known me briefly when very young as my arrival in the UK coincided with hers from India to divorce her husband. Their only son was a little older than me and went as a young man to Australia, closely followed by his mother. Our early meetings in the following couple of years including the rest of the family, a wife and two young children, were concerned with talking over and healing the many old family conflicts.

Although at that stage I knew nothing about the subject, Elaine was a highly skilled medium, who also trained people with gifts in this direction. In 1983, at the end of one of my Melbourne visits, Elaine looked at me in a curious way and asked if I'd like a 'reading'. I didn't know what she was talking about, but trusting her by now, I agreed. I was to call at her house for an hour on the way to the airport. We sat in silence for some time and nothing much happened, until my taxi-driver rang the doorbell and the session had to be concluded.

I was a bit mystified by the apparent lack of results, but as I stood up to bid Elaine farewell, a most extraordinary thing happened. I was suddenly overwhelmed by an inexplicable paroxysm of emotion, with tears streaming down my face. Elaine was most alarmed, the taxi driver highly embarrassed and as for me, I was utterly bewildered and rather frightened. With a tight schedule arranged, I was bundled into the taxi and cried uncontrollably all the way to the airport. I remember testing my pulse rate on a health slot machine, while waiting for my flight. Danger Zone, it bleeped. What was happening to me, for God's sake?

It took quite a few days to get over this shock, then Elaine phoned to say that the sheer intensity of my reaction had triggered memories of our past associations in previous lives. We had apparently agreed long ago to help one another awaken spiritually, if ever the opportunity should present itself in subsequent incarnations together.

At that time, it still all sounded too bizarre for words. Although I innately trusted her, I didn't understand. Yet I just knew something very profound had happened, and from then on resolved to do whatever was necessary to unravel the mystery.

Back in England around this time, I had been in touch with the German Embassy to try to find out the exact time of my birth. I was having my astrological chart made up and this information is critical.

With amazing efficiency, I was given the time, despite all the chaos that must have prevailed for many years after the war in Braunschweig. For the first time in my life, and after the ease with which my birth time had been produced, I felt a desire to know a little more about my mother. I had deeply resented her for abandoning me, but by now my pain had eased enough for a glimmer of curiosity to surface. The Embassy said they would follow up the enquiries I made with them and let me know in due course.

Meantime, my thirty-seventh birthday arrived and, out of the blue, I suddenly felt the all-pervading 'presence' of the mother I had never known. Such a tenderness and love was being projected towards me that, being unused to this kind of intimacy and still ambivalent towards her, I spent some three days alternating between ecstatic joy and pain. A solution was not long in coming: the Embassy informed me with regret that my mother had died at the very time I had instigated the search. Sadly, we were not destined to meet physically in this life - although it was a close-run thing! But what greater proof could I have had, on my birthday that the bond between mother and child transcends time, distance and even 'death', powerful undercurrents to 'go with the flow'?

I had become disenchanted with my career in travel and, despite excellent career prospects, resigned without a qualm. I had by then built up a financial reserve and found that my London apartment had quadrupled in value.

There is a saying, "When the pupil is ready, the Master appears," and I was about to discover that that is indeed the case. Inexplicably, but in fact activated by the law of synchronicity, information and new perceptions begin to crowd in. When the time is right, we attract completely different kinds of people and situations, and let more stagnant and unproductive relationships drop away. Books seem to jump off the shelves at us and contain exactly what we need to know at that particular moment. Timely opportunities and so-called coincidences become commonplace. Trustingly, intuitively feeling our way ahead, we start to transcend reason and logic and discover that life is at last beginning to work with rather than against us. Instead of endlessly battling against the tide, we feel ourselves being assisted by powerful undercurrents.

With my retirement from the travel industry came the certainty that I could never again return to that way of life, and from now I would somehow have to motivate and support myself. Exactly what I would do, I still hadn't the least idea, so this drastic action, criticised on all sides, was a leap of faith in every sense. Meantime I was being given books that kept me spellbound - and reconfirmed that I must now pluck up the courage to face my future, whatever it held. One person I knew I could totally trust was Elaine and, sensing that I might have to face some deep-rooted personal issues, the idea of temporarily closing down my English life and 'going through my stuff' well away from home was most appealing. So I accepted Elaine's invitation to see what would happen if I worked with her and her associates. I then felt guided to make the - for me - uncharacteristic preparation of building up my body in a gymnasium, before leaving for Australia, and however long the process would take.

Physical fitness as it turned out was a lifesaver! My task, I now realise, was to break up enough past habit-patterns and the accretions of lifetimes to enable me to 'lock on' to my current purpose in one short, sharp burst. I am glad I took that opportunity, because I couldn't have been in safer or more loving hands for this very delicate operation. Elaine and her whole family nurtured and supported me as one of their own throughout the three-month ordeal, between January and March 1985. She herself was in poor health, having already suffered a stroke and severe diabetes, necessitating removal of toes and later most of a foot. It is unfortunately the case that mediums working with high vibrational energies often sacrifice their physical health and all this, combined with the many past traumas of a difficult path, had taken their drastic toll on her. Despite extreme personal discomfort, she energetically arranged and supervised my programme, taught me many aspects of the Ancient Wisdom, combining western and eastern mystical philosophy, with special emphasis on the Law of One, or Christ consciousness. She also started developing my psychic faculties, using tried and tested disciplines, without which it is inadvisable to trespass into the inner worlds!

Her great test in all this came when, a year later, she suffered another stroke and went through a near-death experience. She later told us that she could remember moving along a tunnel towards light, and being met by the spirit guides, who helped her to 'face her own mirror' and decide whether it was time to leave the physical plane, or if she still had any unfinished business here. She discovered she was almost free, but attending to one final detail would apparently guarantee her permanent release from the wheel of rebirth. The near-death experience is becoming commonplace these days, and is a way of confirming the original purpose of our present life. In earlier civilisations, we are told, one of the highest initiations involved detaching the soul from the body in order to undergo certain experiences on the inner planes while still incarnate, and this, I later learned, is what the 'sarcophagus' in the King's chamber of the great Pyramid at Gizeh was in fact used for. That pyramid was no ceremonial burial chamber.

Having made her brave decision to return, Elaine recovered consciousness in hospital in the presence of a medium friend, who confirmed all that had happened. Though furious to find herself trapped again in a rapidly-failing physical body, she soldiered on for two more painful years, making sure, by sending long taped messages to me in the UK - and during my annual visits - that I was well and truly launched on my path. As she was unable to accomplish much else during those final years, except to take up painting, it seems likely that her devotion to my awakening at least in part prompted her to make this final sacrifice. When love is that unconditional, we know we are in the presence of the One.

Her son, to whom she was deeply attached, died early during the next year, after a life plagued with heart dysfunction, and Elaine was to join him within weeks, her work by then complete. I welcomed her release, but at the same time knew with a sense of awesome responsibility that I was now called upon to try to emulate the high standards she set during her life.

The initial demolition job on my accumulated personality defects was handled entirely with love - and no financial consideration whatever - in sessions that often lasted from 9 am until past midnight! No opening of deep-seated traumas for me just as fixed time-and-cost sessions come to an end - which happens to so many unfortunate people these days, causing them even more distress. Rex, the healer who worked on me, has the gift of 'seeing a person's track'. This means that just by attuning to a patient's subtle bodies, he is able to detect blockages and access information about their cause during this or previous lives. He uses massage to trigger emotional response, and has an uncanny accuracy in touching specific parts of the body, while giving you vital information to stimulate the memory. It can be a long process as the patient gradually releases deeply-engrained thinking patterns and emotional distortions that cause behavioural and personality defects. In my case, the purpose was to get me to be totally truthful about myself in every aspect, and so to achieve the first step on my path to spiritual reawakening: love, utter acceptance, and self-forgiveness.

It took months of work to get me to face certain things. I was, I confess, a hard nut to crack - but I wept enough tears to fill a swimming pool in those months, releasing the emotional build-up of lifetimes. At long last, I was ready to confront old fears and the social stigmas I had created for myself and was free to talk about them openly, without shame or fear of ridicule. The relief was absolutely overwhelming. As always, these horrors actually turn out to be 'paper tigers', but only when we have the courage to confront them full-on. After this, I realised that it is only by first acknowledging and then healing our own traumas that we are qualified to help others. Those in need of help quickly detect the sincerity in someone who has also suffered as opposed to the well-intentioned, academically qualified professional, who often has just as much to resolve personally as the patient.

There would be little point in recounting my personal traumas in detail, because we all have our own, and they are really only relevant to us individually. One person's lessons are never identical to another's, and all we can do to help each other through them is to share truth and any useful techniques we happen to have found. By reading the account of my early life, it is fairly obvious what I had to work through - a process, incidentally, that continues to this very day, as it can take a long time to acknowledge and then heal deep wounds. It is paradoxical that all too often we are conditioned to suppress our thoughts and feelings, yet expressing them is one of the main reasons for incarnating in the first place!

After such deep inner exploration, I was utterly exhausted and needed time to integrate these experiences. With fond farewells, heartfelt gratitude to the many who had contributed to my reawakening, and a new invalid carriage as a small parting gift to Elaine, I returned home to face a completely new life. As if to reward me for my efforts, I had a vision during my stop-over in Thailand of the house I would shortly buy in the English countryside. It was already clear that my London life was over and that its trappings, such as my fashionably located apartment and the pride of my life, a rare old Bentley Continental, were easily expendable.

Having been brought up in the country, I had no problem giving up city life. And having at that time also been miraculously protected from a mugging in a London alley one night, when I somehow managed to walk right through a gang with knives raised to strike, I took the hint! Most people I then knew despaired of my irrational actions and put up well-intended arguments against them. Our friends and family can feel unsettled or even threatened by our spiritual growth, and very often their concern or opposition is the first major test of our inner resolve.

In my vision, I had seen my ideal location. It was to be a spacious cottage in the grounds of a private manor house, down a drive lined by beech trees. There was to be an old church, parkland, a lake and lots of traditional red brick walling and outhouses. A typical, idyllic English country scene, for those unfamiliar with this description. Within only two weeks of returning to London, I was recounting this dream to a country estate agent when he replied that if I was serious, I had better be at a property fitting this exact description by 8am the next morning! I got there to find that, unlike many estate agents, this one wasn't exaggerating: there was the vision I had seen on my way home from Australia. It was exactly as described above - and within my price range!

Within days I had obtained outline planning permission for an extension and negotiated double the amount of garden originally offered. This was the first house I looked at on the first day of my search, coinciding with the first day the property was placed on the market. Magic was in the air! By late summer 1985, I had sold my apartment, moved to the cottage and was knee-deep in mud and debris, experiencing my first taste of building renovations.

So here I was, being directed by unseen hands, on my own without local connections in the middle of the English countryside, not knowing or caring what was going to happen next, and having rejected the allure of a comfortable, conventional life. Yet at last I was ecstatically happy, creating my own first real home in a perfect setting and knowing deep within me that I had 'cleared enough of my stuff' to allow me to be open to whatever the next stage of my journey held in store.

Chapter 3

MY STEPS ARE GUIDED

**Jesus said: "Let him who seeks not cease from seeking
until he finds;
when he finds, he will be turned around;
and when he is turned around,
he will marvel, and he shall reign over the all."**

Gospel of Thomas, Logion 2

I decided that, whatever the future held, it could wait while I convalesced from what had, after all, been a rather exhausting personal overhaul - engine, bodywork and re-wiring included!

Doubling the size of the cottage, totally refurbishing the original building, and creating a new garden from scratch was the early fulfilment of a dream I thought I wouldn't realise until I reached my sixties I was going to enjoy it at my own pace, and sensed that my own recovery and continuing progress would be directly related to this creative process. Seven years later, and despite every attempt by greedy speculators and officious planning officials to ruin the 'conservation' area in which the house is located, it survives as a haven of vibrant energy and tranquility. It is 'open house' to the many visitors from all over the world with whom I have stayed during my tours, and makes a perfect base for exploring the numerous ancient sites and recent 'crop formation' phenomena in the mystical south west of England.

The village that so attracted me has neither pub nor shop and was of greater significance in the Middle Ages than it is now. I later discovered that it was where Joseph Smith's father lived before he moved to America to sire the founder of Mormonism. More recently, it became the UK indoctrination centre for the Mooney cult, causing nationwide publicity. And as it has also been my base during the unfolding of much of this story, it would certainly seem to be a place of natural power and inspiration.

Before I became aware of symbology, I was inwardly prompted to make a formal rose garden, incorporating the shapes of the square, circle and equal-sided cross. I later found that the place I had selected was intersected by the ley line running through the ancient, originally Saxon, church next door. I knew I must be on the right track, when I had prepared the original layout and initially needed 32 rose bushes. I went to the local supplier, and hoping to reduce the cost involved found that, only that morning, he had put exactly 32 mixed roses aside behind a nearby hedge - at half price! This was a rather encouraging start. The final layout now has 64 roses and many more in the surrounding borders. The rose is the symbol of the heart, and of England. Indeed, this region - as I shall explain - is now considered by many to be the heart of the Goddess, Gaia.

The symbol I was led to imprint on my garden is none other than the symbol of the Earth herself.

Over the next couple of years, I was drawn more and more to power centres such as Glastonbury, Stonehenge and Avebury, and started to meet what turned out to be a lot of like-minded people in my area, who had been led there in similar circumstances at the same time as myself. I started to attend 'workshops', meet some of the leading personalities of the holistic movement, and read their books. I then joined what I call my local core group, mainly of women, led by Isabelle Kingston, a highly accomplished medium. At our regular 'circles', she would bring through messages alerting us to the impending shift in human awareness and advising how we could assist the process on the powerful surrounding landscape to which we had all been attracted.

This group, when I joined it in 1987, was already receiving detailed information on the phenomenon that was soon to focus world attention on the area, namely 'crop circles'. We were told then that from 1988 onwards numerous, huge shapes would start appearing in the cornfields of south west England. They are known elsewhere in the world, but in nothing like the quantity or complexity seen in England. By their very presence and number in this particular area, and at this crucial moment, they signify in symbolic language that the transformation of human and planetary consciousness has begun. Mother Earth, it appears, is speaking to us, and much of the symbology she is using is recognisable to awakening people and, significantly, to indigenous peoples: I have since shown pictures of the crop circles to the Oromo and Samburu in Africa, Maoris in New Zealand, Aborigines in Australia and American Indians. These same symbols appear in their cultures, and even appear in their ancient cave paintings! Among these are the Mayan and Anasazi Indian civilisations that raised themselves at will into higher frequencies and disappeared, leaving us many intriguing clues about the current stage of our own evolution.

Despite all subsequent attempts to discredit or sabotage them, the 'corn circles' defy all intellectual and mechanical theories: they simply *are*. The symbolic shapes, it would appear, are designed to trigger the deep inner memories of all who see them, in preparation for the great changes the human race is now to face. They are, in fact, only one of many phenomenal manifestations still to appear in these so-called 'last days' that have been designed to awaken humanity from its spiritual slumber. Scientific tests do in fact show that the bent, but still growing, crops have undergone a change in molecular structure - and no faker has yet been able to reproduce *that*!

The first real sign of a worldwide stirring of human consciousness came with what was called 'Harmonic Convergence'. This landmark event was celebrated at sunrise on August 16, 17 and 18, 1987 by hundreds of thousands of people in several countries, and was the first ever globally co-ordinated link-up of human consciousness, focused on peace and love. The powerful thought-energy generated created the matrix for many of the sudden, dramatic and otherwise inexplicable changes we have witnessed since then. The dates had been carefully chosen by those who had studied the mysteries of the sophisticated Mayan calendar system. The Mayans developed an advanced civilisation in Mexico and vanished in the early part of the second Millennium, leaving us detailed information about what has been called the 5,125-year Mayan Great Cycle, governing this phase of human evolution. Harmonic Convergence started the 25-year countdown towards their predicted Omega point in 2012.

1987 was also the year, according to the Hopi American Indian prophecies, that 'the 144,000 Sun Dance enlightened teachers will totally awaken in their dream mind-bodies to help the rest of humanity to dance their dream awake. On August 17th, 1987 the various winged serpent wheels will begin to turn, to dance once again and when they do the Rainbow Lights will be seen in dreams all over the world,.and those Rainbow Light dreams will help awaken the rest of humanity.'

Year by year the Hopi prophecy has been right on target.

Early in 1988 I flew back to Australia to take part in a gathering at Uluru (Ayers Rock), called Earth Link 1988. This extraordinary rock formation rising out of the central Australian desert is not only that continent's major power centre, but is also one of the Earth's main twelve planetary power centres, representing the 'solar plexus'. The event was arranged to activate the site at the moment of the Saturn/Uranus planetary conjunction. This work is done by precise co-ordination of human attunement with major astrological alignments and fulfils what is referred to as 'cosmic design' or the outworking of the Will of God. What is needed is the combined focus of the will to serve, an open heart and the combined energy of those who incarnated specifically to do what is called planetary healing work. It does not involve secret rituals and ancient invocations as many seem to think, and is actually accomplished by spontaneous, joyful and creative activities dedicated to the well-being of the Earth and all her kingdoms.

At 10am on February 13th, a group of some 30 people from all around the world sat in a circle near the rock and offered themselves as transformers of celestial and terrestrial energy. Informal ceremonies like these are the means by which mass human consciousness can be raised - as we shall see later. Having instinctively chosen Terra Australis for my spiritual awakening, I now realised that the surge of intense energy I felt at this event had allowed me to access the wisdom of the Goddess, and for the first time in this life - and perhaps many previously - I was realigned in my own feminine polarity. Interestingly, a state of natural celibacy began at this time and has remained intact without undue effort, allowing my creative energy to be channelled entirely into the activities being described.

It was at this event at Uluru that I first met a highly-aware German girl called Sonja. She subsequently attended events connected with the grounding of the Christ consciousness in England and Israel, but at that time she had just won money in a raffle and was investing it in making a video. She had hired three cameramen to film the sea between sunrise and sunset over the conjunction period and planned to use the result for meditational and stress-release purposes. *Let your soul grow wings* or *Ocean Motion* as it was later called, fulfilled its purpose perfectly and has now helped thousands of people to achieve a state of inner peace in their own homes by simply watching the gentle ebb and flow of Nature. The promotion of the video in England was the vehicle that launched me into the world of 'New Age' exhibitions in the late 1980s and gave me my first taste of dealing with the public.

THE AWAKENING OF SECOND COMING CONSCIOUSNESS

The pace was now speeding up, and I felt ready for anything after hibernating in my now-completed home. The core group medium Isabelle Kingston had passed on a message that I should contact a woman I had once met briefly in Glastonbury, in order to develop my Earth energy interests. She had been the co-ordinator of the Harmonic Convergence celebrations in Glastonbury, but was at this point planning to return to the USA. Rather mystified by my 'message', she did however give me the important link I needed and for which Spirit had obviously selected her.

She had recently come into contact with a 32-year-old English mystic, who was gathering a small group around him for the purpose of first explaining, and then 'anchoring' onto the landscape of South West England, the energy of the Christ consciousness at the Second Coming. This man - who called himself Kuthumi Jon for the purpose of integrating the energy of the spiritual Master of that name and of John the Baptist - had been until then a musician. While penniless and busking in Europe one summer in the mid-1980s, and after a prolonged period without food, he experienced the spontaneous awakening of his Kundalini energies (all the chakras opening fully in sequence). In this state, he received a vision of the Second Coming, how it was to happen, and the role he and his group were to play in the event. It must be emphasised that many have contributed and continue to contribute towards the shift in human consciousness that is Second Coming; the events described in this book are, therefore, but a part of the unfolding story.

The retreat he had chosen to prepare for his mission with mainly women followers happened to be within easy reach of my home. As I first set eyes on 'Tumi', a striking, bearded, Essenic figure in a white robe, I all but lost consciousness and spent some time regaining my composure in the open air before facing him again. This was my first direct contact with such a heightened vibration in this life and after the initial shock to my system, I spent some of what I can only describe as the most spiritually focused times of my life so far with the group that summer.

Serene meditations and joyful chanting were interspersed with Tumi's clear and oh, so *nostalgic* teaching of 'the Way'. There is no doubt that at this time and on our subsequent journeys together, he activated my memory and in that sense prepared me for my own future work. Never had I felt such a bond with another being. How familiar his energy seemed, and of course that of the One overlighting him, whose work we were about.

Tumi had written a published summary of his mission: this time anchoring the Christ-feminine on Earth during the conjunctions of Saturn and Neptune in Capricorn. It set out the schedule of events to be arranged at sacred sites in south west England, between the spring equinox and mid-summer solstice of 1989. Our meditations had centered on an etheric tetrahedron called the Aquarian Triangle which we focused over the landscape with the apex at the Rollright Stone Circle in Warwickshire and the two base points at Glastonbury in Somerset and Greatham (the Cathar chapel of John) in Hampshire. Midpoints of the triangle were the ancient temple sites of Avebury and Stonehenge.

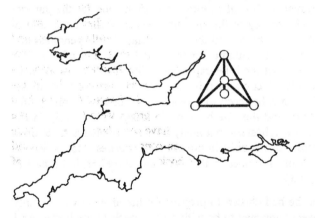

THE AQUARIAN TRIANGLE IN S.W. UNITED KINGDOM with ROYAL LEAMINGTON SPA (the Crown Chakra), THE AVEBURY RINGS (the Ajna Chakra) and STONEHENGE, (the Solar Plexus Chakra) running North to South, with the GLASTONBURY ZODIAC (the Heart Chakra), and Greatham (the Throat Chakra) lying to the West and East respectively.

All these power centres were to be activated in sequence during certain forthcoming planetary alignments, full and new moons, equinoxes and solstices. The highlight was to be a Festival of Second Coming during the very potent Wesak and blue (2 in the same sign) full moon period between May 19-21,1989. Now the task was to invite kindred spirits around the world to be part of a global meditational link-up throughout what Tumi referred to as the Seven Sacred Dates.

Neither First Coming nor the grounding of the Second were intended to attract the masses. They were precisely designated moments, when divine energy would flood into the Earth and its inhabitants, relayed by a handful of people specifically incarnated for the purpose. They were Jesus Christ and his close followers at the First Coming and the 144,000 with 'the risen Christ in their hearts' at the Second. The seeds sown then, having germinated, are now being harvested. Those who worked directly with Jesus Christ have shared His pain by continually holding the Christ Consciousness on Earth through many traumatic incarnations over the past two thousand years until now at Second Coming, usually in direct opposition to the Church.

The autumn of 1988 saw the group paying independent visits to the region of the Cathar massacres in the Pyrenees mountains near Carcassonne in south west France. Many of us felt a deep personal connection with these souls, who had endured one of the most vicious extermination programmes ever recorded. The Roman church felt seriously threatened by information the Cathars had assembled in a devout work called *The Book of Love*. They managed to hide the book with enough gold to publish it, when it was destined to be rediscovered in these 'last days'. However, since the gold was found by a corrupt priest at Rennes-le-Chateau late last century and the plan sabotaged, Spirit is now intent on restoring that vital information in other ways. The mystical esoteric teachings in the barbarous Europe of the 13th century were still hundreds of years ahead of their time, valiant though the Cathar movement was. At least they provide an heroic example of the continuous presence on Earth of evolved and enlightened souls, who are prepared to risk everything - even their lives - to keep the flame of the Christ consciousness alight here on Earth.

In November and December, Tumi and a few group members toured the Western USA and I arranged to meet them over Christmas in South Africa to join a tour of the main cities. A friend, who had lived in South Africa, offered to show me around, so l went early to see as much as possible of this beautiful country on my first visit. A prediction had been made some time before that I would play a role in South African affairs, which seemed utterly implausible at the time, but less so as time passed! I first went to Namibia, just before it was given independence from South Africa, and was touring the Kalahari desert at the time a celebrated rock formation called 'the Finger of God' inexplicably collapsed. In retrospect, many now consider that this event marked the first visible sign of the sweeping social and political changes that were to overtake South Africa from 1989 onwards.

Having explored Cape Town, one of the most spectacularly sited cities in the world, and climbed Table Mountain to experience one of Earth's most potent energy centres, I flew to Durban to join the group. Among the nine travelling were Tumi's wife, their newborn second child, their older child and the young child of another couple. We resembled a large family on the move, and the unpretentious, informal image we presented during the short time I was with them, seemed to encourage those drawn to listen to the message as we toured. Tumi maintained his customary clarity of energy and purpose and I well remember the many occasions when dramatic storms broke out as he spoke, usually culminating in magnificent double, even triple rainbows!

My plans were to fly direct to Australia on my own on January 1st. to take this energy to the country that had unexpectedly played such a crucial role in my life. As we neared the time of my departure, the focus of the group deteriorated as Tumi became preoccupied with matters of a personal nature, which he must have chosen to face and resolve there and then. It is important to remember that even evolved souls choosing to incarnate into the 3rd dimension, including Jesus and other Masters, are imperfect by virtue of the very nature of duality. Tumi himself taught that Jesus could not have been an example to humanity, unless he had come in the 'imperfect state' and had himself battled with and overcome negativity. The temptations during the 40 days in the wilderness, "Get thee behind me, Satan", and in the Garden of Gethsemane even in the Christed state - asking that "this cup be taken from me", are sufficient evidence.

On my last night of the tour, we had to camp out in crowded circumstances at a place called Plettenberg Bay and I ended up sharing a small tent with Tumi. In such limited space, I was awoken in the early hours by his physical contact as he turned in his sleep. At that moment, I received what can only be decribed as a bolt of electrifying energy. It was so intense that I was left tingling from top to toe for several minutes and quite unable to sleep. Clearly, something very profound had occurred between us and I decided to keep it to myself, until I understood it better. With hindsight I can now see that he must have decided subconsciously to share the responsibility with a kindred soul equally committed to the work. Though other matters preoccupied him to some extent, he did nonetheless complete his special mission successfully, as we shall see.

Before leaving Cape Town, a large group of us participated in the annual, 31st December World Peace meditation at midday. This has now become the most effective focus for peace each year involving literally millions of people linked through thought in an unassailable common bond. (The words used in this meditation appear at the end of the book.) Simultaneously with the gathering, and no doubt as a sign that our efforts were appreciated, a huge pod of dolphins accompanied by two whales surfaced and played in the bay below where we stood! This most unusual and heart-warming 'cetacean serenade' was front page news in the Cape Town press next day.

Table Mountain is the power centre representing the element of earth and focuses the qualities of the lower human and planetary chakras, such as will, power, ego, separation and regeneration. This is well illustrated by all the racial and political struggles in South Africa. These issues test each one of us, as nothing happens in isolation in our world, and that country's pain will only be released by the mass projection of detached and unconditional love and constructive support at every level. As we together heal South Africa, so we collectively heal the human group-soul of the illusion of division and separation.

In due course we shall see how this great power centre was further activated later in 1989, but the preparation was assisted by the combined human and cetacean attunement on December 31st. 1988. Soon afterwards, tangible evidence of a shift in consciousness manifested with the removal, through sudden ill health, of a reactionary Premier. This allowed a far more flexible man to initiate the necessary changes. The dam first burst in 1988 and much more was and is to follow, including the great accolade of the Nobel Peace Prize for President De Klerk and Nelson Mandela in 1993.

I arrived in Australia with only a tape recording of Tumi's teachings, a copy of his publication and the will to communicate, despite having no developed public speaking skills or many suitable contacts! Fortunately, a woman who was loosely connected with the group in England happened to be on a visit and gave me valuable support. Otherwise, I was just guided and had to get used to this novel process of trusting - a process on which I have now learned to rely. Small groups attended the presentations and a number of people were impressed enough to make a commitment either to come to England or join us in our aims and endeavours. What I did notice was that storms raged whenever the Christ energy was invoked at these meetings. The most dramatic of these occurred in Melbourne on February 7th, 1989 when, just before my first presentation there, a violent storm broke over the city. It caused the kind of flooding from which people had to be rescued from car roofs - and deposited enough hailstones around the meeting hall for children to play snowballs in the middle of an Australian summer!

A Polish woman healer attended one of the Sydney meetings a few days before returning to her own country. On arrival, she was unexpectedly interviewed on national TV and in the course of the programme mentioned the forthcoming events in England. Such was the public response that she was given another programme in which to focus the peak of the Second Coming energy during the Spring of 1989 in a public nationwide meditation! It will be remembered that it was Poland that initially rebelled against Soviet domination and it was then the first of the East European satellite countries to throw off the crippling yoke of communism *later* in 1989. The national focus on Christ Consciousness during that meditation was, perhaps, not unconnected with the turn of events! The other satellite nations then fell like dominoes, six months after a concerted Spirit-directed Earth energy release at the culmination of the 'seven sacred dates' in England that will shortly be described.

My tour also took in Tasmania with a talk in Hobart to the Fountain group, during a week's exploration of that jewel of an island. It was here that the great public stand of international environmentalists took place against the destruction of the largest rainforest in the southern hemisphere. Tasmania, which is rather patronised by mainlanders, did in fact trigger a major change of attitude across Australia about environmental responsibility. For 200 years, the white colonists imposed completely inappropriate agricultural methods on Australia's extremely delicate ecostructure. There could be dire consequences now with the land unable to support the increasing population.

The Aboriginals preserved that land with the greatest spiritual skill and respect for some 40,000 years, and after their horrific ordeal at the hands of the 'new invaders', are only now cautiously emerging to re instigate the ways of their 'Dreamtime' in partnership with aware white countrymen. The survival of the population as a whole will depend very largely on the outcome of such initiatives.

Terra Australis demands our respect as she and New Zealand now become two of the pioneering territories where the new 4th. dimensional consciousness is to be experienced as a viable reality on the planet. The old order will be seen to decay first here, together with outworn emotional dependency on Britain, the mother country archetype The process is well under way, as observers have readily confirmed: the 'siblings' are leaving the nest and have much to teach their spiritually moribund parent.

Chapter 4

AVALON, THE HEART OF OUR WORLD

JERUSALEM

And did those feet in ancient time
Walk upon England's mountains green
And was the Holy Lamb of God
On England's pleasant pastures seen

And did the Countenance Divine
Shine forth upon these clouded hills
And was Jerusalem builded here
Among those dark Satanic mills?

Bring me my bow of burning gold
Bring me my arrows of desire
Bring me my Spear! O clouds unfold!
Bring me my Chariot of Fire!

I will not cease from mental fight
Nor shall my sword sleep in my hand
Till we have built Jerusalem
In England's green and pleasant land.
                    William Blake

Millions of people with British roots and soul connections sing this stirring, prophetic ballad at every opportunity around the world. It is by far the most popular national song, exceeding even the national anthem, and yet few understand its inner significance. Did Jesus himself walk on Avalon's hills during his 18 'missing' years, seeking the Druidic Initiation among the many others he took in the Middle and Far East to fulfil his mission? His mother Mary's uncle, Joseph of Arimathea, was a rich tin merchant who regularly visited Cornwall, and it is said that the young Jesus came with him on one or two occasions. The sequence of events related in this story alone will show that the clouds *did* unfold to allow 'the countenance divine' to shine, while the etheric city, New Jerusalem, was 'builded' over Avalon. Since there is still so much confusion about Second Coming, the form it will take and its location, we need to establish the background for the remarkable events that occurred in South West England between March 20th, 1989 and April 21st, 1990.

> "In 1990 you will see the twelve sacred Driver Wheels of each of the Eight Great Powers stored and put together to create the figure 8 of infinity sign."
>
> *The American Indian Inter-tribal prophecy*

The map below illustrates this prophecy. So far, I have mentioned the concept of Earth's power centres or chakras, and have pointed out some of them as the story involved them. Here we see the twelve Open Gates of the New Jerusalem and the Two Great Dragon Lines of Infinity:

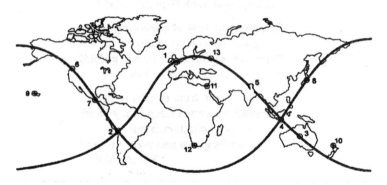

1. GLASTONBURY, UK. Focus for Heart (4th chakra)
2. LAKE TITICACA, PERU. Sexual (2nd chakra)
3. ULURU, AUSTRALIA. Solar Plexus (3rd chakra)
4. GUNUNG AGUNG, BALI. Planetary blood filter
5. Mt. KAILAS, TIBET. Crown (7th chakra)
6. Mt. SHASTA, USA. Base (lst chakra)
7. PALENQUE, MEXICO. Harmonic Convergence
8. Mt. FUJI, JAPAN. Sacred site of Immortality
9. HALEAKALA Mt,MAUI, HAWAII. Spinner wheel (Fire)
10. TONGARIRO/TAUPO, NZ. Spinner wheel (Water)
11. PYRAMID/Mts SINAI/OLIVES. Spinner wheel + Throat (5th chakra) (Air)
12. TABLE MOUNTAIN. Spinner wheel (Earth)

13. GATE 13. ZAGORSK, RUSSIA. (opens during 1990s): Glaston feeds Glasnost directly along the Dragon Line!

6th. Chakra (third eye) This is the mobile Aeon activator of no fixed location, currently over Glastonbury.

(Copyright: Robert Coon, Glastonbury, UK, 1987)

The planet Earth is an exact mirror image of ourselves, and so we can relate to her in precisely the same way we do to the subtle energies and qualities of our own energy systems. Between the mid-1960s and 1990 all 12 Gates of New Jerusalem were activated. The cycle described above started at Mt. Shasta, 'the place of beginnings' during the Pluto/Uranus conjunctions in the mid-1960s when the New Age movement made its mass debut in California, in the initial guise of the flower power and free love culture.

Chakras are best described as 'spinning wheels of energy'. In this vision, there are 8 'driver wheels' moving the energies along the Dragon line of Infinity (main ley line artery of the planet) and 4 'spinner wheels', representing the four elements, two within each loop of the infinity symbol. The former have a power radius of 500 miles, when fully activated and the latter each have a 1,750 miles radius. The four spinners propel energy along the dragon lines.

Progressively, small numbers of people dedicated themselves to the first stage of the planetary awakening by visiting, meditating on and consciously linking up the centres mentioned above. This work has begun the realignment of the planetary energy grid, and inexorably sets in motion the changes now being experienced.

One of the prime movers in this remarkable initiative is Robert Coon, the American visionary and mystic, who has lived in Glastonbury since his activation of the Earth's heart chakra there at dawn on Easter Sunday, 1984. He is a direct descendant of Joseph Smith of the Mormons, but with no role in that sect this time round! An initiate of the order of Melchizedek, an immortalist and disciple of Enochian Cabala, Robert received the complete 'circuitry blueprint' for the realignment of the planetary energy grid direct from Elijah, during a manifestation at Boulder, Colorado on July 1st, 1967. He was asked initially to activate three of the global chakras: Mt. Shasta (base) at autumn equinox, 1975; the Great Pyramid (throat) at autumn equinox, 1979; and Glastonbury (heart) at Easter, 1984.

Much of Robert's work since then has been to protect and release at pre-arranged times the necessary information and geographical locations for the four cycles of energy centre activations to be conducted before the year 2065. The blueprint shows 52 primary planetary energy sites, each developing two additional adjacent sites, which together form orbs of 3 closely-related centres. These are known by the astrology qualities of cardinal, fixed and mutable. The total number of sites to be activated is, therefore, 52 x 3 = 156, the cabalistic number of Zion and the sacred centre of the New Jerusalem.

The recent activation of the planetary heart-orb at the cardinal (inspirational) site of Glastonbury automatically triggered the opening of the 'fixed' (grounding) centre at Berlin through German reunification in 1990, while the 'mutable' (sharing) centre opened in Barcelona, appropriately with the Olympic Games and the World Trade Fair held in that country in 1992.

This vision given in the 1960s throws an interesting new perspective on the otherwise inexplicable phenomenon that at a stroke liberated Eastern Europe, and triggered the reunification of both Berlin and Germany. In due course after the transformational energies released have settled, Germany will fulfil the 'fixed' function of grounding and giving physical expression to the mystical revelation received at Glastonbury. Berlin has already twice demonstrated the shadow side of its unbridled might this century but now that it has been brought into a direct energy alignment with the Heart of the planet, we shall soon witness an altogether more positive manifestation of that awesome power.

The extrovert, warm, southern temperament, represented in 1992 by Barcelona with the Olympic world focus, is most suitable for sharing with humanity (mutable) what has been initiated in the other two centres. Spain is awakening and anyone needing confirmation of this has only to look at the rapid spread of spiritual awareness and learning centres there over the last couple of years. The first conscious linking of the three now-activated aspects of the global heart was carried out by groups in all three countries at the moment of the October 1992 full Moon. I was in Germany for the linking, and then flew direct to Spain to participate in a ritual in the Alhambra Palace gardens in Granada. The energy focus was followed as is often the case by heavy rain, but the day ended in a most unusual sunset: the clouds parted briefly to reveal a perfect pink triangle! Britain, Germany and Spain have awoken the heart, and the world will now witness the results.

In this Elijah vision, Moscow is one of Berlin's 'bonded energy partners, and the inevitable knock-on effect duly occurred with the collapse of the Soviet Union in 1991. Barcelona forms a bonded pair with the El Rif region of Morocco and through this link, the Islamic tradition will receive the universal blessing of Christ consciousness, a process assisted by the Alhambra ceremony. Another interesting geographical combination is Jerusalem and Mecca, which have Kuwait within an orb formation!

The very potent year of 1993 was the launch time of an important phase of the vision called the 'Geoproject'. This envisages ever larger numbers of people living on or near the main power centres, in order to establish 'Liberty Parks'. The areas are to be nuclear free, human and animal rights-respecting, sharing-motivated, ecologically and economically aware, death penalty free and generally 4th. dimensional by nature. The idea is that the centres will expand, increase in number and overlap as more sites are activated, until the whole planet merges by 2065 into one vast Liberty Park. Some of these parks have already been designated and there are plans to link them during a series of satellite-connected concerts and celebrations. Thus, in entirely practical ways, we will establish heaven on Earth, by working on ourselves and our communities right here, and *not* - sorry, all you Space cadets - by means of externalised space projections or any other glamorous diversions! (Robert Coon's contact details are given at the end of the book: please see p. 347)

The area in which Robert's work and mine overlapped, was in what he named 'the Aeon shift ritual'. This ceremony, publicly announcing the activation of sacred sites in South West England as the new global power centre to succeed Jerusalem was conducted by Wholistic World Vision under Spirit guidance. This is fully described later, but it might be helpful here to examine the principle of Aeon shift, as explained to me by Robert after the work was successfully concluded. During the 'precession of the equinoxes', and when we leave each Age (about 2,000 years), the focal planetary power centre is replaced by a new one with different energies and qualities. It is approximately one twelfth of the way round the planet, or 30 degrees in a westerly direction. The 6th planetary chakra or third eye, known as the 'mobile

Aeon activator', also overlights the particular centre that activates each Age.

The energy transfer is always made by human agency, the last having been carried out by the Zoroastrian Magi or the three Wise Men of Biblical record. The Age of Aries (BCE)[1], a fire sign, was focused on the Zoroastrian fire-oriented spiritual tradition in the mountains of what is now known as Iran. Their mystics, prophets and oracles would have known in just the same ways we do now that a significant event was to occur at the end of that Age. Harbinger of all major Earth changes, the comet - in this case the so-called 'Star of Bethlehem' - gave these sages the signal they had been awaiting. Knowing also that the event would occur to the West, they carried their symbolic gifts of gold, myrrh and frankincense to Palestine. In this way they acknowledged the birth of the new dispensation there and through their actions became the vehicles of the Aries/Pisces Aeon shift. As astrologers, they would have been alerted by the three highly auspicious Saturn/Jupiter conjunctions in the constellation of Pisces during 7BCE. This was the actual birth year of Jesus, in the reign of Herod, who himself died in 4BCE!

It may come as a surprise to many to know that in 1993 we had actually reached the year 2000, and so perhaps the great changes we experience now will make more sense in this revised context! Jupiter is the 'kingly' star, Saturn is the protector of Israel, and Pisces is the 'sign of the Messiah'. An acronycal rising or three planets directly opposite the sun would have caused a bright light in the skies throughout the night of September the 15th 7BCE. The Taurus/Aries shift, approximately 2,000 BCE, was initiated by the Tibetan followers of the Bon religion (precursor of Buddhism), and the ancient Chinese civilisation would have been the site of the previous focus.

The activation centre of the next Aeon shift will be 30 degrees west of Britain, suggesting Recife on the eastern tip of Brazil, an area of already powerful Earth energy in a country that is also slowly emerging from religious debilitation. A symbolic journey is always made by those who take on the responsibility for these rituals, as in the case of Jesus' great uncle, Joseph of Arimathea. He is said to have brought the Grail cup of the Last Supper to Glastonbury and to have concealed it

---

[1] BCE/CE Before Common Era/Common Era - an inclusive term used to avoid the exclusivity of BC/AD

in the Well below the Tor, shortly after the Ascension of Jesus Christ. In this way, as first Earthly Guardian of the Holy Grail, Joseph indicated the next site to be activated at the end of the Piscean Age and remains both the most significant and mysterious character in the entire First Coming drama after Jesus himself. It is hardly surprising that both Christianity and Judaism should have deliberately ignored this highly controversial Sanhedrin priest, who personally assisted the first Christ mission and then 'stored' that consciousness secretly at Glastonbury to await the time of its Second Coming.

Tibet now faces a similar re-alignment, and it is interesting to observe the repeating pattern of deterioration at the old energy centres. These sites attract less evolved souls as the original inspirational energy fades and, in due course, little remains but emotional projection and total distortion of their true purpose. In the case of Jerusalem itself, the outcome rests in the hands of the three religions still projecting emotionally onto it. Bitterly disappointing and confusing though it may be to millions of sincere believers, that city's primacy is rapidly waning. With the dawning of the coming Age, the power has moved in accordance with the divine will.

GLASTONBURY, THE NEW JERUSALEM

What does need to be very clearly understood, before we start tracing the delicate and often all-but-invisible threads between First and Second Coming, is that Glastonbury is not intended to replace the old Jerusalem as a physical location.

The small, distinctively shaped hills of ancient Avalon, around which Glastonbury is built on low-lying marsh, once rose out of the sea and were known as 'the Isles of Glass' or Ynnis Witrin. This burial place of numerous saints and kings, called by Blake and many others 'the Holiest Ground on Earth' has always been revered by Celtic and Druid traditions, whose motto was 'Truth against the World', and whose roots can be traced right back to the second phase of Atlantean civilisation. As is now widely known, that era ended in disaster with the continent utterly destroyed as a result of man's abuse of personal and Earth energies in around 10,000 BCE. The egotistical 'sons of Belial', like the powermongers of today, were responsible for the debacle and prevailed at that time against the priests of the Law of One.

The disciples of the Light abandoned Atlantis before the inevitable destruction and established new centres in many locations around the world. These included South America, Egypt and the West European coastline from Portugal, through the Basque lands to Brittany, south west England, Wales, Ireland and Scotland. 'In these sacred places was truth sealed in stone' and guarded till the time it would be honoured and used to lift mankind into higher consciousness. The great stone circles, avenues and individual standing stones are a living testament, and many people are now intuitively accessing the knowledge encoded into them so long ago. Every soul with lessons still to learn, who was part of that second Atlantean phase, is now incarnate on Earth to master Christ consciousness (the Law of One). This third and final Atlantean epoch can then heal its predecessors by releasing this portion of humanity from the limitation of duality and reuniting it with more advanced elements of the race.

It was to re-establish the Law of One that the great teacher of Love came 2,000 years ago, to rekindle the Light that was in danger of extinction yet again. This Law had been observed by many great civilisations during the early stages of our current third Atlantis. Here in the Europe and Middle East of the impending Christ missions, Egyptian, Greek and other once noble cultures succumbed to the forces of darkness through negative ritual in which sexual perversion featured strongly. The latter is the weapon used so effectively time and again against human evolutionary progress, because misuse of our creative energies automatically blocks us from the ability to perceive truth. Hence, much of the healing now needed for Western, materialist mankind is concerned with sexual imbalance. History clearly reveals that sooner or later all such civilisations invert on themselves and crumble, as did Atlantis, Egypt, Greece and the Roman empire.

It was the hierarchical Roman system of conquest and division that established the precedent for Western man's final descent into the depths of material illusion, ably supported by the church that appropriately bears its name. The Roman legacy brought us a class structure based on the ownership of property that was once communally shared for the benefit of all, a legal system to enforce it and armed might to buttress the law. Mighty Rome also delighted in making popular entertainment out of feeding hundreds of thousands of the followers of the Way to starved wild animals in public arenas throughout the Empire. The regime then rapidly collapsed in the hands of degenerate Caesars until, some 300 years after the Ascension of Jesus Christ, the Emperor Constantine and his English mother Helen 'Christianised' the Roman Empire. They adopted the already prevailing Pauline distortion, which reversed the Master's original teaching. Constantine, a later incarnation of Paul himself, then compounded the distortion by endowing the incumbent Pope, Silvester 1, with a huge fortune and so created the first 'rich Pope' - a curse from which that organisation has never escaped.

The last lines of Dante's Inferno:

Alas! Constantine, how much misfortune you caused,
Not by becoming Christian, but by the dowry
Which the first rich Father accepted from you.

The Roman Christian Church, was then officially established and sought to claim direct apostolic descent from Jesus through his disciple Peter. We need look no further than the opulent dome of the Roman church named after 'Saint' Peter to see the bold justification written around it: "Thou art Peter, and upon this rock I will build my church, and the gates of hell shall not prevail against it". Peter, whose emblem was *"Deus in me"* (God in me), can in no circumstances have held the alleged position of Pope or 'First Bishop of Rome'. Neither Linus (son of the English King Caractacus) nor Clement, first and second Bishops respectively, who both knew Peter well, ever even expressed awareness of any such claim. Neither Paul nor any of the Apostles ever made any reference in their copious correspondence about Peter having *any* official association with the Gentile church.

Proof that he could not have held the position of 'Supreme Head of the Church and Vicar of Christ on Earth' is furnished by his trial at the Council of Jerusalem in 46CE. This was convened to settle a serious doctrinal dispute between him and Paul relating to what became known as the 'Pauline heresy' - the attempt to deify Jesus. To the dismay of those who had actually known Jesus, which Paul significantly had not, Paul won the day and is considered by many as the first Christian heretic. James, the brother of Jesus, could never have been accepted as the Council's chairman, if Peter had been 'head of the church' and anyway the elected head the church would hardly have been put on trial! As we know, Jesus appointed Peter shepherd of the people, guardian of the Word and, as such, keeper of the Keys to Heaven. Paul would have made a rather more suitable 'patron Saint' of the Roman Church, which was a creation of *his* in all but name.

Gore, in his *Roman Catholic Claims*, dismisses that organisation's pretension to be the true church: "The Papacy has no scriptural recognition, and is not in or of the Primitive Church of Christ. It evolved out of a combination of circumstances and pressure politics, based on a series of documents proven by all historians to be the 'Forged Decretals'." Those who are interested and discerning enough will easily uncover the deceptions and distortions that made this organisation such an effective vehicle of painful growth for millions of souls, alternately reincarnating as oppressors and victims, by experiencing the agony of self-denial and separation from the divinity within us.

On a short visit to Rome just after the Aeon shift ritual in 1990, I experienced for myself the stark contrast in energy between the peaceful serenity of the small, unpretentious, ruined remains of the site where Peter actually celebrated the sacred mysteries, and the grandeur of the city now surrounding it. It is located some 20 feet under the pavements of the modern city, below the Church of St. Pudentiana, and is a world apart from the glamour and painful emotional projections saturating St Peter's. I poured Chalice Well water from Glastonbury into the fountains of the Vatican, in the knowledge that that action, combined with many others motivated by truth, will contribute to whatever transformation is now to occur.

It was the Senator Rufus Pudens Pudentius, a secret convert to 'the Way' and married to the daughter of the captured British King Caractacus, who gave protection to Peter and later Paul in his house in Rome known as the Palatium Britannicum. The ruins of this building, containing the *first* official Church in Rome, can be found under the Church of St. Pudentiana. I went there on a hot August day wishing to familiarise myself with its energy, but found it closed. Undeterred and sensing my steps were led, I sat in the shade of the courtyard on a doorstep and waited. I knew the history of the place well and felt the cool draft of air rising from the grating under my feet. Down there were the catacombs where lay buried the mangled remains of thousands of brave 'followers of the Way' fed to wild animals in the nearby Coliseum. Then, almost imperceptibly, the door behind me opened enough to show the smiling face of a black nun. She beckoned me inside, closed the door behind me and left as silently as she had come. I was on the holiest ground in Rome, alone and with time to attune to the pure energy my namesake had brought to that city so long ago.

Pudens' wife Gladys had been christened as a baby by the newly-arrived Joseph of Arimathea in England around 36CE. Taken hostage with her father to Rome, she was later adopted by the Emperor

44

Claudius. Having married, she established a refuge and first official meeting place in Rome for the wandering Apostles and early converts to 'the Way' in the early 40s CE. She and her children, brought up in the presence of the Apostles, courageously championed the Christ impulse during the savagery of the demented Emperor Nero -- and paid for it with their lives.

It was Britain, not Rome, that was the first country to receive the faith of Christ. The outer events were enacted in Palestine (on the planetary throat or creative chakra) to announce the advent of the Christ consciousness to the whole world. This was also in fulfilment of Biblical prophecy that the tribe of Judah would produce the Messiah However, the energy whose physical vehicle was denied and destroyed by crucifixion in Palestine, was soon after grounded into the Earth and stored in the planetary heart at Glastonbury by Joseph and his twelve followers. It is now revealed there *and* simultaneously within all open hearts and minds at the Second, but inner manifestation of the Christ's Coming. The truth is that the Christ consciousness realised by Jesus was not anchored in Palestine, where it was rejected, or in Rome, where it was corrupted, but in Glastonbury, where it was secretly honoured and nurtured by the initiated over the intervening centuries.

It is well documented historical fact that Joseph and his followers were exiled from Palestine in 36CE and according to the Roman Church's respected historian, Cardinal Baronius: "In that year the party mentioned was exposed to the sea in a vessel without sails or oars. The vessel drifted finally to Marseilles and they were saved. From Marseilles, Joseph and his company passed into Britain and after preaching the Gospel there, died."

The apostolic foundation of the Christ impulse in Britain is supported by the early Christian theologians Origen and Tertullian writing in the 2nd century. St Gildas, in the 6th century, stated that "Britain was illuminated by the Light of 'Christ the true Sun' in the later part of the reign of Tiberius who died in 37CE." It is also well known that at all the great Church Councils held in the Middle Ages, the English bishops were given precedence as representing the *earliest foundation*. William of Malmesbury, with access to Reformation evidence, subsequently destroyed by the Puritans, was convinced of the claim and stated of Glastonbury, "the resting place of so many saints and kings is deservedly called a heavenly sanctuary."

Over five hundred years before Augustine - the envoy of Rome usually credited with Christianising 'pagan' Britain - Joseph with his original band of 12 followers and visiting Apostles such as Peter, Paul, James, Philip and Simon Zelotes had already created of Britain the Sacred Isle and 'Motherland' of the Christ consciousness, in the esoteric tradition of John.

Baronius lists the 12 followers of Joseph as Mary Magdelene, Mary wife of Cleopas, Martha, Lazarus, Eutropius, Salome, Clean, Saturninus, Maximin, Martial, Trophimus and Sidonius. Many also hold that Mary, Mother of Jesus, entrusted by John to Joseph as 'paranymphos', came too and remained with him till her passing at Glastonbury. Compared with all the other theories about her final years in Turkey, India etc, I personally am inclined to accept that she came to 'the Heart' and have felt her presence very powerfully at the site of the first small, wooden church dedicated to her by Joseph, around which Glastonbury Abbey was later constructed.

I have quoted from George Jowett's *The Drama of the Lost Disciples*, because it demonstrates so clearly the unchallengeable precedence of the Anglican Communion over that of Rome as the legitimate guardian of the Christ impulse during the Piscean Age until the Second Coming. The following evidence derives from carefully researched prophetic texts, which reveal that Great Britain, her Commonwealth of free Nations and the United States of America now become the primary vehicles for infusing the planet and all mankind with the Christ consciousness.

BRITAIN AND THE EMPIRE ON WHICH THE SUN NEVER SETS

'Land of Hope and Glory, Mother of the Free.' 'Rule Britannia, Britannia rules the waves; Britons never, never, never shall be slaves'. Such rousing patriotic songs as these and 'Jerusalem' give more of a clue to Britain's glorious heritage and current spiritual role than most people realise! This role does not, of course, absolve Britain from going through the same cleansing processes as others. In fact, British mental and emotional rigidity are due to be dissolved by the elements of air (mind/intellect) manifesting through wind, and water (emotion) through rising water levels. The signs are already evident.

Interestingly, these are the same elements that humbled the technologically-advanced, but loveless second Atlantean civilisation, whose outer shores embraced the present western European coastline. Britain will be spared from invasions and nuclear devastation, but the elements themselves will do their healing work at whatever the cost. The British people might be surprised and reassured to know that they have the collective power to prevent undue destruction by taking responsibility for their critical spiritual role in human affairs - if they so choose.

In *The Invisible Hand*, Victor Dunstan identifies and examines the crucial role of the missing Tribes of Israel, including the identity of the British and American peoples, and their historical links. Much other information is given on the location of tribes, why they were all punished by dispersal and the accurately predicted timing for the foundation of the modern Jewish State of Israel. His particular skill has been to interpret the terminology used in ancient biblical texts, especially the all-important calculation of accurate timing, though his personal predictions are less impressive.

We remember that Jacob tricked his blind father Isaac into giving him his brother Esau's birthright and therefore the blessings, or 'line of promise', that was passed from Abraham. Jacob was not a Jew, but by changing his name to Israel, became the first Israelite. Abraham and Isaac were Shemites and Patriarchs of Israel, but were neither themselves Jews nor founders of the Nation of Israel. It was Jacob, now called Israel, with his twelve sons, who fulfilled that role. There is then a further unexpected twist, which is critical to the prophecies relating to the present time and is invariably misinterpreted. Israel (Jacob) bypassed his first-born, Reuben, in favour of his preferred 7th son, Joseph. But it was to Joseph's two sons Manasseh and Ephraim that he actually passed 'the line of promise' from Abraham! Moses' full account is worth reading in Genesis verses 8-20, further supported in 1 Chronicles, 5:1,2.

This leads us to some very radical conclusions indeed. The Jews are *not* in fact 'the chosen People' as sole inheritors of the promises made by Jehovah to Abraham, Isaac and Jacob, because the 'line of promise' bypassed all 12 sons (tribes) *including* Judah, and went equally to the two *grandchildren* of Jacob. Israel (Jacob) then gave his *own* blessings to his 12 sons and predicted their individual roles and identities in the 'last days' in which we now live. Judah, the 4th son, Father of the House of Judah and the Jewish State of Israel, was told *"The sceptre shall not depart from Judah, nor a lawgiver from between his feet, until shiloh (the Messiah) shall come; and unto him shall the gathering of the people be."* Genesis 49: 8-10.

Yes, Judah produced the awaited Messiah, the greatest Jew of all and faithfully preserved the ancient prophecies and texts for humanity's guidance in the 'last days', so completing its prophesied purpose as 'the people *chosen* to produce the Messiah'. What makes it virtually impossible for Judaism to accept Jesus in that role is that he actually came to release humanity from the yoke of the patriarchal demi-god, Jehovah, the God of Israel! Now, we must look for the 'Promised Land' and nation or group of nations that give territorial representation to *the whole house of Israel* and thus fulfil the prophecy. The Jewish State of Israel, made possible by the *British* army capturing Jerusalem from the Turks in 1917 *exactly* at the end of Judah's banishment cycle, is now busily repatriating its tribe from all over the world. Modern Israel is made up of a mixture of the two tribes of Judah and Benjamin with a few from Levi, and together they await the imminent appearance of their Messiah.

Through the mission of Jesus Christ, 'The sceptre has now departed Judah' into the main body of the House of Israel or ten 'lost' tribes and it is *there* in the *new*, not the old Jerusalem that the drama is now unfolding. As I have said, the fate of Jerusalem will depend on whether the citizens of modern Israel and all those projecting emotionally onto it can release their exclusive claim to 'chosen people' status and reintegrate with the ten tribes in equality, knowing that *all* humans are 'chosen' within the Law of One (Christ consciousness). Remember 'The Lord thy God is *One*'.

The Assyrians captured the House of Israel, while Judah was taken captive by Babylon, and they thus served their allocated exiles for 'apostasy'. Judah was captured by Babylon between 603-586BCE and their 2520-year or 'seven times' punishment cycle ended in 1917. Manasseh was captured by the Assyrians in 730-733BCE and 2520 years brings them to 1787-89. Ephraim was captured by the Assyrians in 723-721BCE and their 2520-year cycle ended between 1798-1800. The prophecies make clear that only Judah would return to Palestine to fulfil its destiny, while the remainder were to be permanently banished from their country, losing their name, religion, language and identity. So the one place they will *not* be found is in modern Israel!

Despite the dire punishment of the House of Israel, the prophecies foretell their size, location and the timing of their re-emergence.

48

Genesis 12:2 significantly mentions, "I will make thy name *great*" while Genesis 35:11 states, "a nation and company of Nations shall come of thee." 2 Samuel 7:10: "Moreover I will appoint a place for my people Israel and will plant them, that they may dwell in a place of their own, and *move no more*." Isaiah speaks of "the Isles at the end of the Earth" and Jeremiah 31:10,11 refers to a scattered Israel gathered in "the Isles afar off." Isaiah 54: 1-3 states Israel will inherit a Gentile nation and "enlarge the place of thy tent." I don't think it stretches the imagination too far to see that the finger of destiny points squarely at Great Britain, guardian of the Christ consciousness at Glastonbury and her Commonwealth of free nations.

It is also to be remembered that the meaning of the word 'Israel' is 'true to God' and describes any state or peoples that fulfil that high ideal. Logically therefore, we can also have as well as the Jewish State of Israel, the British State of Israel and the American State of Israel.

The line of promise given to the House of Israel but inherited only by Manasseh and Ephraim, was that one would be 'a nation and a company of nations', while the other would be 'a great people'. The British nation evolved into a Commonwealth of nations plus the United States of America, and interestingly each was founded exactly at the predicted end of each cycle of punishment originally imposed on Manasseh and Ephraim: the USA in 1787-9 through a ratified Constitution and the United Kingdom in 1800 with Ireland's official joining of the Union, and the Union Jack becoming the national flag of the UK. This technically makes the USA Britain's elder brother - by just a few years! The prophecy also foretold that 'the elder would serve the younger'; a clear indication that the Christ consciousness emanating from Britain will liberate America from the stranglehold of debilitating Christian fundamentalism currently permeating every level of that nation. Genesis 28:14 makes clear the role of the rediscovered House of Israel with regard to all humans on the planet: "And thy seed shall be as the dust of the Earth, and thou shalt spread abroad to the west, and to the east, and to the north, and to the south; and in thee and in thy seed shall All the Families of the Earth be Blessed."

Finally there is the comforting prophecy by Isaiah in 54:17, "No weapon that is formed against thee shall prosper." The invasion of 1066 CE was the last arrival of the tribes through the Norman Conquest, but from that date onwards - and often in most unlikely circumstances - Britain (later with America), prevailed against all her attackers. Weather intervened at Agincourt and allowed a motley British army, suffering such severe dysentery that they were mainly trouserless, to rout the far superior French army bogged down in the mud! The Spanish Armada was repelled by tempests and at Waterloo, Napoleon's artillery couldn't be positioned due to torrential rain. The German weapon of poison gas at Ypres was blown back at them by an unexpected change of wind. Most know of 'the Few' against an infinitely superior German airforce during the Battle of Britain, and there are even well-documented cases of Germans seeing mirages of British planes coming against them, when in reality no such aircraft were in the vicinity! The exceptionally calm sea at Dunkirk allowing a huge evacuation by small boats, prevented a certain massacre, and many other illogical German decisions ensured their defeat.

British commanders like Lord Dowding and Sir Victor Goddard, who were aware of Spirit intervention and spoke of their experiences to their predictably sceptical colleagues, produced much evidence of these phenomena. Britain and the USA, currently the two largest arms dealers on Earth, now have to set a *peaceful example to the rest of the world*, and there is no further place for weaponry in either 'protected' land. Manasseh (USA) the elder brother, who has betrayed the 'line of promise' and the Christ consciousness by developing and using nuclear power in warfare will, as we have seen, 'serve his younger brother', who will now provide the means for redemption through the Christ consciousness nurtured in England for the past 2000 years. Now the second, but this time spiritual, empire is to be established through energies released in Britain that triggers a shift of consciousness in the USA.

In conclusion, let us consider the words of a former Canadian Prime Minister:

"The colonisation and development of the British Empire is in furtherance of the Divine purpose. I still think that this was no accident, but part of the great purpose of the Infinite, that we should have carried these responsibilities as we have."

Lord Bennett

Chapter 5

BIRTHING THE CHRIST CHILD WITHIN US

And she (Gaia) will be as a woman with child and about to give birth who writhes and cries out in her pain.

Apocalypse III Ch. 3, v 18

We now return to events in and around Glastonbury during 1989 and 1990. Much interest had been created by Tumi's talks and publicity in the UK, USA and South Africa, and by my own efforts in Australia. Some twenty to thirty people from outside Britain had felt moved enough to join in the Aquarian Triangle Second Coming activation at some stage during the celebrations, and hundreds more took part in meditational linking world-wide.

During the spring of 1989, the Earth received the most potent influx of cosmic energy to date. The initiation of human and planetary consciousness into the next dimension is accomplished in stages or 'gateways', and the events of spring 1989 built on previous gateways and prepared the way for others to follow. All such events seek to bring as many people as possible together in circles and internationally-linked groups. Prayer, meditation, song, dance and all forms of heart-based creative expression are the ideal medium to bring planetary co-operation and understanding into reality.

The first focal point at which groups gathered within the Aquarian Triangle was Silbury Hill, near the Avebury landscape temple at sunrise on March 20th, the spring equinox. Here was earthed the initial streams of Christ-feminine energies associated with the three conjunctions of Saturn/Neptune in Capricorn during 1989. I have explained how Saturn/Jupiter was associated with the Christ-masculine principle at Jesus' birth; how through Saturn/Neptune the feminine is anchored to balance the masculine. The Aries-Easter full moon on March 22nd was then celebrated at the Cathar shrine in the ruined chapel of St John at Greatham in Hampshire and focused, according to Tumi "the declaration of the mind-face of Christ or the embodiment of the

Christ-masculine energies". On April 21st., May 5th. and May 20th. we celebrated the rare 'blue' moons (two full and one new) in Taurus, during the most powerful annual moon cycle of Wesak. The theme was "the inauguration into matter of the new dream-dance of the Second Coming," and celebrations were held in and around Glastonbury.

It was on the May 20th blue moon that the Shekum Foundation arranged a week-end of public celebration in Glastonbury. Speakers included Tumi, Sir George Trevelyan, representatives of the Brahma Kumaris World Spiritual University and Robert Coon. Up to a hundred people gathered, to participate in a global full moon meditation link-up, sunrise meditation on the Tor, dances of universal peace, songs of the heart and paneurythmy movement. The event ended a few days later with a large group celebrating Tumi's 33rd birthday, for which we reserved Stonehenge.

On the night of May 24th, we danced the steps of the Aramaic Lord's Prayer inside the stones under a still bright moon until dawn! The Islamic mystic sect called the Sufis have preserved the Peshitta (Lord's Prayer) used by Jesus in the Aramaic/Syriac language he spoke. The phrases have been choreographed into dance steps and are now taught around the world. The vibrational energy of the original words are so potent that spontaneous personal transformation often results. I was moved to tears on first hearing those words again at the festival and, perhaps not surprisingly, had mastered the entire prayer within days of hearing it. I now use it regularly and always at public meetings - with unpredictable results!

At this stage of the celebrations, the friend in Sydney called Robin Bee who recognised our mission and whom I had invited to England for the events, intuited with me that the planetary heart could well do with some fire! The heart is related to the element of fire and it is through the transmutation of heart-fire that we are now truly reborn, after our first birth through the waters of the womb. St.Bridget is the patron saint of Glastonbury and is depicted as a fire goddess, with a special love for animals and horses in particular. In order to dedicate our first three fire rituals, we went, with the woman whose house was to be used, to the site of St. Bridget's ancient hermitage and meditated. We were soon aware of a presence, because the two women were having their legs playfully nipped and their skirts lifted! A foal had appeared and, head on our shoulders, joined in our meditation. We felt our intentions had been given the seal of approval.

So, on the new and full Gemini-Christ moons of June 4th. and 19th. and summer solstice June 21st, we organised non-stop 24-hour chanting based on the 5,000-year-old Vedic Agni Hotra and Trayambakam fire ritual. This derives from the science of the Vedas, the most ancient spiritual Law known to man, and consists of a specially-made small copper pyramid in which are burned dried cow dung (pure organic matter) with ghee (purified butter) and unbroken rice to the accompaniment of the mantram of immortality. Agni Hotra chants mark the precise moment of sunrise and sunset, which are the most potent moments of each day, observed everywhere by the world of Nature. The ritual is a very powerful means of transmuting negative energy within a wide radius, and thousands of people around the world use it to purify agricultural land and products, water, atmospheric pollution and negative thought-forms. In some cities the chanting is maintained on a non-stop basis and is of the greatest benefit in these times of mental stress and rapidly deteriorating quality of food and water. These are the 'sacred fires' prophecied that will help heal this planet.

The dynamics of what was going on were already astounding and, for a newcomer like myself, not always easy to integrate. The next stages after these celebrations were to test me to my limits and there wasn't even a pause for breath as one event led miraculously to the next. In early June 1989, I was invited to meet the Sirius Group, which had been given meticulously channelled details from Spirit about a major Earth energy release ritual to be performed on top of Silbury Hill, the hill of the Shining Beings, at dawn on June 20th, 1989.

This turned out to be the signal to leave Tumi, who was now heading back to the music world after completing his mission. It is often the case in this work that the energies of certain people are brought together to fulfil a specific purpose; once this is completed, they may have little further in common and go their own ways. In this book it is, therefore, important to remember that my interaction with the people mentioned relates only to the circumstances described and does not necessarily imply an ongoing connection or commitment.

My first meeting with the Sirius Group produced the kind of synchronicity I have learned to trust, and resolved at once the reason for some of the most important events in my early life. We were to listen to tapes recorded during recent channelling sessions about the ritual. The first voice boomed across the room and with its precise choice of words and celebrated style, I found to my utter amazement that it was none other than Winston Churchill! The circle was now complete. I was brought into his aura aged five, guarded his mortal remains at 15, and was now to be inspired and assisted by him in some delicate and demanding work that was to accomplish certain long-predicted events. The other being working with him - perhaps surprisingly to those who remember their earlier antipathy - is the Mahatma Gandhi. It would be hard to choose two more loved and admired human beings to guide my steps through the minefields I have had to cross in this work, than these two highly evolved souls, who are still striving to bring enlightenment to humanity.

Increasingly over recent years they function as transformers of energy between ourselves and the highest dimensions. Because they are souls with strong Earth affiliations over many lifetimes and are still concerned for and revered by humanity, they are currently fulfilling a temporary, yet critical assignment to prove the existence of Spirit. Their love and compassion for us, their boundless wisdom and exalted vision of our potential is simply overwhelming, and my associates and I consider it a great privilege to be working with them.

They never cease to remind us of our own unlimited God-presence and emphasise that by attuning to this divine source within we already *know* all they are encouraging us to remember. We are like fledglings testing our wings, with a determined mother nudging us gently out of the nest! Yes, we *can* all fly, but developing the confidence takes time. Increasingly over recent years, I have found my wings and somehow managed to accomplish tasks even *they* had not thought possible - which presumably demonstrates the potential of which they constantly remind us.

Spirit guidance through this source particularly emphasises the need to focus our full attention on the Earth and her current problems rather than indulge in fantasies of rescue projected towards outer space. We have to understand that 'out there' is just a reflection of ourselves - and unless we now take full responsibility here on Earth for being *all that is*, then the very intelligence called God itself progressively disintegrates, starved of energy, through lack of balance within the interaction of the polarities of creation! If we destroy the ecological system on which human and planetary life depend, and on which all multidimensional consciousness is based, then ultimately the negative polarity of the Earth will devour the energies of even the most evolved soul vibration as she releases the toxic poisons that bring about her own demise.

It is a sobering prospect to learn, not just that we are endangering the life of our mother, Earth, but that as every level of evolving consciousness is so closely linked, we now risk setting in motion the collapse of Creation itself.... Let us briefly re-examine John's definition of Creation from this new perspective - seeing God as "the collective presence of *all* evolving life-forms merging as one unit of consciousness," rather than as a separate, superior and unreachable demi-god:

"In the beginning was the Word (LOGOS)[1]
And the Word was with God
And the Word was God
The same was in the beginning with God
All things were made by Him
And without Him was not anything made
That was made
In Him was Life
And the Life was the "Light of men"
And the Light shineth in darkness
And the darkness understood it not."
John 1:1-5

Let us also refer to Logion 24 of the Gospel of Thomas:

"There is Light at the centre of a man of Light,
and he illumines the whole world.
If he does not shine, there is darkness."

God *is* the light within us, and if we fail to recognise it and do not shine then decay and disintegration of consciousness ensues, until the Godforce itself is destroyed through imbalanced polarity within us. If we do not now wake up to our real spiritual potential and responsibility here on Earth rather than fantasising on phenomena in space, then we risk the unspeakable.

Dawn on June 20th, 1989 was the culmination of the anchoring of the tetrahedron and was the time when for a few vital moments the sun and moon were to be visible above the horizon, with the star Aldebaran directly overhead. This was the moment for a pre-selected group of some 30 people to conduct a ceremony outlined to us by Spirit in

---

[1] Logos is more accurately The Creative Force or Universal Law.

great detail. If successful, we were told, it would release such a force of terrestrial and cosmic energy into the Dragon Line flowing east through Silbury that the first consequence would be the collapse of Eastern European communism and the Berlin wall within six months! The energy would then continue eastwards, transforming human consciousness as it did so, culminating in the USA in the mid-1990s. At that time only Poland was showing signs of unrest among dockyard workers, so it was a bold prophecy indeed by Spirit - and one about which we kept a somewhat sceptical open mind!

I am not claiming credit on behalf of the group for this and other results because thousands, world-wide, are contributing through their own work and dedication. Like anyone else, I can only describe events with which I have been personally involved.

Silbury Hill, at 500 feet the tallest constructed neolithic mound in Europe, is situated near Avebury in Wiltshire and is in the centre of a landscape of richly symbolic Goddess sites. Silbury's rounded shape represents the swollen womb of Gaia about to birth the new consciousness, and it is this very energy that was released with a considerable jolt that morning. The event, assisted by the Spirit guardian of Silbury, was videoed, and of the many encouraging signs we received at the time, the appearance of a perfect crop circle in the long grass on the summit of the hill to greet our pre-dawn arrival, was perhaps the most appropriate. That summer, the fields around Silbury were festooned with them!

Since the medium who had channelled much of the preparatory information was not present that day, it was with especial interest that I visited him in south east England for a debriefing. Robert manifested his powers early in life, when as a child he would be locked in his bedroom and promptly reappear up to two miles away - to his own and his parents' consternation! He still occasionally slips between dimensions and is assisted back by his partner. They both have full recall of their previous lives as a married couple in a neighbouring town during the last century and know their old house and grave. Robert still pursues many interests he had then, including local politics and researching local history. He has even found a book written about himself in that life, containing a photo that resembles him today!

Clearly this man who has carefully preserved his subtle and physical bodies, is an ideal channel for Spirit and is able, as I and many others will testify, to receive the most rarefied and elevated of vibrations. It is even possible to hear the voices of Spirit within his aura as they contribute to our conversations, while Robert is fully conscious and involved in everyday activities! Walking through the woods and hearing devic and elemental spirits communicating in this way then listening to him relaying the messages is one of my greatest joys and provides dramatic proof of the living presence of Spirit in everything.

Trance mediums usually surrender their bodies to the incoming entity, and are largely unaware of what is coming through, which can restrict their own development. Robert, however, consciously projects his awareness back into the circle and benefits from the communications. He also works with the direct voice method, by which spirit voices use the ectoplasm of the medium and assembled group to speak, as it were, out of thin air, and not the medium's vocal chords. In this way, several spirits can participate simultaneously while the medium is fully conscious and can join in the discussions. This method, more than any other, disproves the allegations of sceptics that mediums influence or fake communications. Both procedures are equally valid, but whatever is received should always be carefully assessed. It is also strongly recommended that any contact with Spirit takes place in a place dedicated and protected for the purpose.

Many once well-known personalities have spoken through Robert, and also ascended masters of the highest realms, who are usually beyond the reach of Earth. The working team, dealing with practicalities, came in the form of Churchill and other politicians such as Lloyd George, when Robert was involved in active local politics some ten years ago. Gandhi arrived quite unexpectedly, while Robert and his partner were watching the recent film of his life. Gandhi explains that the wave of love generated by the film called him back into active participation in our affairs. Churchill is received by many mediums, but Gandhi conducts what he calls his 'ashram', now named Wholistic World Vision, with Robert, he tells us, as his only channel. The many sessions with these guides in which I participated have made a profound impression on me, but my renewed acquaintance with Churchill was very special, with both of us exchanging comments on our briefly shared lives at Chartwell that nobody else present could possibly have known about. This was a most reassuring and obviously prearranged beginning, so that I should have no doubts about the validity of the connection.

It appeared that our work at Silbury had registered effectively and, having been accepted into the group that I by now sensed held the next stage of my development, we started to get down to business. It had long been predicted, to my horror, that I would be a public speaker. A recent survey showed that most people fear public speaking more than death itself! I was certainly one of them, so was appalled when my new colleagues proposed that I talk without notes to their local group on any spiritually-related subject of my choosing. My first impulse was to make excuses, but I knew I had to face the test sooner or later. I spoke on 'The return of the Christ consciousness,' felt a strong surge of energy as soon as I started, loved every moment - and haven't looked back since! Now after hundreds of public appearances, including radio and TV, for which I had no training, it is interesting to reflect on the many abilities we all have within us, but are usually too fearful or lazy to access. Make no mistake, they'll all be needed in the 'last days'!

PREPARATIONS FOR THE AEON SHIFT RITUAL

After Silbury, Spirit indicated that the energy structure for our future work was to be based on three main rituals. The first at Silbury, successfully integrated into the planetary energy grid the Christ consciousness that had been grounded during the Second Coming celebrations with Tumi and had culminated at the exact moment of that release. The next event was to be a gathering of those who had instinctively been attracted by this work. At the Libra full moon on October 14th, 1989, some 50 people celebrated together on the ancient site of the Long Man of Wilmington in Sussex (the figure of an androgynous giant delineated in white stone on a steep hillside). Spirit promised the appearance of a comet at the moment of the full moon to mark the occasion, which did happen on schedule - but also heralded the arrival of the local police! Fortunately, the presence among us of a senior officer in a national ancient sites preservation organisation soon sorted things out.

The third ritual placed me in a more central role than the previous two and, as Gandhi described it late in 1989, it appeared that some kind of linkage between Jerusalem and Glastonbury was now to take place. I was told that I could expect a vision of a new Cross within the next few days in my meditations, and that this was then to be made according to my specifications in Jerusalem. As can be imagined, this was all beginning to stretch my credulity to the limit, especially before I understood the principle of Aeon shift - the transition between two major epochs - and the First and Second Coming energy connections! The work was to involve myself and two women, who would apparently soon present themselves. Together, we were to absorb energies on Mt. Sinai, at the Pyramid/Sphinx and finally to collect the Cross and bless it on the Mount of Olives at dawn on Easter Sunday 1990. It was to be brought back to England by the three of us, who would go into retreat for three days to balance our energies. The Cross was then to be taken to Glastonbury Tor and raised at midday on April 21st, 1990, in front of the crowd gathered there for the global Earth Week 1990 celebrations.

Between November 1989 and the time indicated, I had to arrange for the Cross to be made, await the arrival of two unknown women, organise the intricate itinerary involved, travel to South Africa and Australia to herald the event - and somehow find the not inconsiderable amount of money to finance the entire operation! As if all this were not enough, we were warned to expect the arrival of missing passages of the biblical Book of Revelations relating to the 'end times' which had long ago been removed by the elders of the Church. Now I had heard it all! I was eager to pursue a spiritual path, but hadn't bargained for this.... In retrospect, it seems hardly possible that it was actually achieved - and much more besides. Yet in those early stages, it was certainly the humility, compassion, humour and wisdom of our Spirit partners that convinced me of the rightness of everything that was happening.

Slowly, everything started to fall into place. I received the shape of the Aquarian Cross while in meditation in my rose garden at home, and was given the name of a South African woman living temporarily in Jerusalem, who had been interested in Tumi's vision. My travel job had, rather conveniently, taken me all over Israel and my contacts were now very useful in arranging the itinerary. It would have been stretching old friendships a bit, though, to ask them to make a cross as well - and I doubted if the British Embassy has a cross-making department! Louise did a wonderful job - based only on sketches, letters and phone calls - and found a competent metal-smith in Jerusalem to undertake the commission.

After all the events of that summer, I needed to retreat and went to two powerful islands to relax: Iona in Scotland and Formentera in the

Balearic islands. No sooner had I returned than I found myself on a plane to Cape Town, to continue this strange assignment. I was to assist in the activation of one of the 12 Earth power centres at the moment of the third and most potent Saturn/Neptune conjunctions of 1989 on November 13th at 2pm. The two-week visit was also to include public talks about the Aeon shift and to encourage simultaneous energy link-ups. As we have seen, Saturn conjuncting Neptune in Capricorn was responsible for initiating the Age of the Christ-Feminine. The conjunction of these two planets also encouraged humanity to initiate new dreams and ideals, while dissolving outworn structures and thought patterns. As Table Mountain is one of the four most powerful sites on the planet, representing Earth and lower bodily chakra functions, it is not hard to see the amazing opportunity that was being presented to us, to accelerate the transformation process in which all humanity will soon be involved.

A number of people I had met during my last visit with Tumi had been alerted and had organised a small festival to honour Table Mountain. By the time I got there, the small committee of women publicising the event had suffered every kind of abuse and even death-threats from Christian fundamentalists, in which that country abounds. It was an early sign that the power was already building up, and that what was in essence a simple gathering of like-minded people, could well develop into a major event. How right this turned out to be - the fundamentalists smelt change in the air and went on the rampage.

Our programme included a preliminary day of 'cleaning up' the mountain, which consisted of quiet attunement to the natural energies, and clearing rubbish from the parks and gardens that make this one of the world's most beautiful natural settings. Specially organised Christian 'hit squads' attempted to disrupt every phase of the work. At the same time, the first 'peace poles' had been brought to South Africa. This is a wonderful Japanese initiative - a kind of terrestrial acupuncture - to erect short poles with messages of peace inscribed on them in urban communities and on Earth power sites. Tens of thousands of these poles have now been dedicated in every country of the world, and regular ceremonies are arranged in which many hundreds gather in non-denominational prayer for peace focused around an inspiring ceremony honouring each country's national flag. Sadly, though, to South African religious fundamentalists, peace poles are 'instruments of the devil' and as such were quickly ripped out and triumphantly destroyed !

Three focal sites had been selected on the mountain for November 13th, and the first was at the Rhodes memorial at dawn. The fifty or so who gathered were heavily outnumbered by hundreds of jeering, hymn-singing Christians, who had been 'guarding' the site most of the previous night. We were left beneath on a large flat viewing area, where we made a circle around an accomplished Tibetan gong player. The circle gently revolved, spinning the great Earth Spinner wheel, to the mystical sounds of the gongs and sacred OM chant as the sun rose in all its glory. It was an unforgettable moment, and was perfectly captured in the Cape Town press next day. The entire event hit the headlines, thanks to the antics of our fundamentalist friends! Highly embarrassed Christian leaders were obliged publicly to reprimand their flock for 'unchristian' behaviour, whatever that means, in the days that followed.

The exact conjunction at 2pm was celebrated in Van Riebeek park high up under the 'table' section of the mountain. Anticipating more opposition, we got there early and prepared a secluded site with a focal altar of Chalice Well water from Glastonbury, crystals, wild flowers and candles. As the moment approached, five of us were joined by two unknown men and as the seven of us linked hands, we experienced the electrifying energy of the activation passing through our bodies. Soon afterwards, the remainder of our group found us and were themselves hotly pursued by Christians armed with sticks and clubs! As we enlarged the circle, the opposition berated us with clubs raised to strike, and one of them even entered the circle to abuse us to our faces. In such a situation, the Gandhi style of fearless non-resistance offers the best protection, and so it was. Also the timely arrival of the Mayor of Cape Town to participate in his private capacity as a Sufi, followed by his request for mutual tolerance, allowed us to complete our business unmolested.

The final attunement took place on Signal Hill overlooking Cape Town, with Table Mountain obligingly displaying its celebrated table-cloth cloud formation. By now, news of the drama of the day's events had spread through the city and hundreds of people joined our evening gathering of singing and gong-playing as the sun set into the sea, and the moon rose out of the water in the east. I have never seen the mountain looking as resplendent as it did that evening.

My final enduring impression of an exceptional day was watching a large group of Christian extremists experiencing the full boomerang effect of the negative energies they had projected all day. The commandment 'Resist not evil' is in fact a statement of universal Law. Negative energy projections that are not resisted rebound with twice the force on the instigator. Try it, next time someone picks an argument with you! All day we had avoided contact with the judgement, abuse and demented 'speaking in tongues' tactics they used, and now the same people were clawing at and seeing devils in each other as their hysteria rose to fever pitch! It can hardly be more obvious that fundamentalism is an expression of fear, which is the exact opposite of the Love implicit in Christ consciousness.

An extraordinary post-script to the event has only recently been relayed to me, and serves well to conclude the story. The ringleader of the Christian opposition, who had broken into the circle, recently bumped into one of our core group and confided he hadn't known what had possessed him at that stage in his life. He had soon parted company with his fellow fundamentalists and said although he still didn't understand what we were doing that day, he now instinctively felt that it had been positive - evidently the moment he had broken into the circle was the turning point in his life!

Soon afterwards I received a charming letter from the Mayor of Cape Town in his official capacity, thanking me for everything we had done there. While there are men of the calibre of Gordon Oliver in that city, with his notable track record of positive inter-racial initiatives and spiritual understanding, South Africa is in very safe hands.

Within a short period, the new energies unleashed triggered a sufficient shift in consciousness to permit the release of Nelson Mandela - which in turn set the course for irreversible advancement in South Africa. Just as in Eastern Europe, we have seen that by working with the natural rhythms and cycles of Earth and cosmic energies, rigid human thought patterns can be dissolved, allowing change to take place. One of several historic figures to have spoken through Robert is the South African leader and mystic General Jan Smuts. Before my visit to Cape Town he said:

"We need as a group to share a particular purpose for South Africa - the human endeavour to be united with each other regardless of skin colour. There is in the black races a cultural difference; not one that is less, just different.

"Integration can only work if the political status of the blacks is the same as the whites, and cultural differences are respected and maintained by both sides.

"Apartheid is an evil word denoting blacks are less than whites. The people must share their identity within a degree of privacy with free choice to live in their own communities, if they so wish. Only equality can work, with ultimately one person, one vote; but this is not to say that a black man will not vote for a worthy white man, or the reverse. The purpose of the ceremony you are planning is to establish energies that will influence the seats of government and set the change in motion. It is the coming together in the great energy of Light, love and harmony which must prevail in both cultures, and in the equality of *all* white and black nations."

Many may not know that Jan Smuts was a visionary and that his daughter married into the Clark family of Street, near Glastonbury. Later in life he regularly meditated at Collard Hill within the figure of Taurus in the Glastonbury landscape zodiac and called it "a piece of paradise manifested on Earth". This is the point where the Pleiades constellation is specifically focused in the zodiac and has crucial significance, with the Sirius star system, in the integration of the Christ impulse on Earth. An attunement on the ruins of Gandhi's original ashram near Durban provided an especially poignant culmination to the tour. At the time of this attunement this area was in the midst of a 'war' zone with rival gangs vieing for territory, but has now been transformed into a Peace centre with wide community support.

I returned home briefly to prepare for the Australian tour and found two further fulfilments of Spirit predictions: eastern European communist satellite states were falling like ninepins, exactly six months after Silbury. The next excitement was that the first chapter of the 'missing' Revelations arrived just in time for me to take it on my tour. The remainder came later, but all in time for Aeon shift. Here I am aware I may lose still more incredulous readers as the story unfolds, but I can only recount as it happened. While in his home, Robert was overshadowed by the spirit of John the Elder, pupil of John of the Revelations, and asked to sit at his word processor. Here was a snag because, being non-technical and with Robert in trance, his partner did not know how to turn on the machine and prepare it! After a while, having worked it out with Spirit, she inserted a disc and the information just *appeared on the screen*, needing only to be printed out later.

There was no human involvement at any stage of the transmission - so these are the words communicated direct from spirit realms.

As I have travelled the world and told this story, I have come across similar situations in which Spirit has demonstrated an ability to work through electrical equipment. Indeed, there have been occasions when the circuitry of weapons systems has been 'adjusted' by them. We can apparently expect a lot more of this kind of intervention as 'the changes' intensify.[2]

Spirit has indicated that original versions of the information in the 3rd. Book of the Apocalypse are still secreted both under the Vatican and in so-far-undiscovered caves around the Dead Sea. It was, however, essential to bring this text to light *before* the Earth changes, to remind as many people as possible that the inherent wisdom of our holy scriptures was later deliberately distorted or suppressed by the Christian church. From the point of view of events here described, the Third Book of the Apocalypse is the authority for the Aquarian Cross and indicates the time, location and form Second Coming is to take. A more detailed examination of its text, significance and origins will be found later in this book.

My main purpose in visiting Australia again, apart from giving talks in Sydney, Melbourne, Adelaide and Brisbane to publicise the Aeon shift, was to arrange the co-ordination of a southern hemisphere anchor point for the shift. Such a major energy movement in the 'masculine' northern hemisphere needs to be counterbalanced in the 'feminine' southern hemisphere, especially as the feminine is being brought into balance with the masculine during the coming Age and will lead the initiation into the new dimension from the south. The plan was to have two feminine anchor points in South Africa and Australia and one masculine anchor at Glastonbury, so that a global triangle of linked consciousness would assist and share the energy as the Cross was raised. It would also reflect the same energy balance of the one male and two females conducting the ritual.

During previous visits I had met a couple who for many years had dedicated their extensive property of virgin bush in the Blue Mountains outside Sydney to natural Earth and spirit energies. Robyn and

---

[2] See bibliography at back of book for *Conversations Beyond the Light through Electronic Means.*

Philip always gave me the benefit of the doubt as my mysterious story unfolded, visit by visit, and Spirit had suggested that this would be the perfect site for the purpose - if the owners and a highly attuned group would undertake this service. Happily they agreed and, as they held regular world-linking meditations there already, they were well used to such concepts. During my visits to Israel and Egypt, they and a small group arranged to tour certain sites in Tasmania, where power flows into Australia from Antarctica, as a preparation for receiving the energy on their own land. Little did they know what they had let themselves in for, and it was only because of their own deep inner connections with the Earth and the exceptionally high vibration of their property that the energy was effectively anchored.

A good deal of interest was generated as the tour proceeded and ultimately hundreds of Australians and South Africans joined those in England holding the focus on April 21st.

The only other unusual event on that tour occurred quite spontaneously as I was walking near the Opera house in Sydney. I bumped into Burnham Burnham, a well-respected Aboriginal elder, whom I had met at Uluru some years previously. We exchanged greetings and when I asked what he was doing at this spot, he pointed to a four-masted schooner on the harbour sailing towards us. "Come and recapture Australia for the aborigines," he said with a broad smile! Intrigued, I asked what was going on - and discovered that a symbolic invasion was about to be enacted in the harbour and that it was being covered by the media. Before I could collect my thoughts, I was being rowed with Burnham in a long-boat manned by a native crew towards the schooner. We then sailed across the bay and made a formal landing in front of the waiting cameras, while Burnham and others read declarations and made impassioned speeches about co-operation between the races and respect for the land. It was a moving occasion and a strange synchronicity that led me to participate in it!

Many people are aware that Australia's very viability as a country is even now in the balance. There is nothing more important for that country and New Zealand than to discard outworn racial attitudes, before they can prepare for their pioneering roles as initiators of 4th.dimensional living on the planet.

Chapter 6

THE AEON SHIFT ACTIVATION

PART 1

MOUNT SINAI, THE PYRAMIDS/SPHINX, MOUNT OF OLIVES

"A great trumpet will sound from a high place and a great star set on a staff will be carried into the midst of the crowd. And the Lord will bless this place and make it a Holy City, and it will be called the new Jerusalem. And the lamb will sit in the midst and will number thirteen. The city will be borne on a cloud of light, not set on the Earth, but carried by the spirit.

"Thus, the word will be revealed by the spirit of the light."

The Third Book of the Apocalypse, Ch.1

SUBTLE PREPARATIONS FOR THE UNFOLDING OF SECOND COMING

"Life begins at conception. Christ returned to Earth through the conception of Easter Sunrise, 1984. Then the planetary Christ body developed in the womb until all parts of its body were formed by 17th August, 1987 (Harmonic Convergence). The activation of the 12 New Jerusalem Gates and the 2 great Dragons at that time completed this womb phase. Then the Child was born from out of the 12 wombs of Gaia during the great Wesak Month of 1989. Both the Aquarian Triangle Project and my own work at Shaftesbury (Dorset, UK) contributed to this birth. And on the 21st April, 1990, through the Aquarian Cross Aeon Shift ritual, accomplished by the Wholistic World Vision group, the planetary Christ conceived in 1984 and born in 1989 is now declared alive and breathing in the manger of the open Heart at Glastonbury. Our New Aeon equivalent to the three Magi journey has now been completed."

Robert Coon, May 1990

By now the remainder of the Revelation text had come through and we had a hard time trying, as Spirit had asked us, to understand what was meant, before receiving clarification channelled through Robert whenever we faltered. I had heard from Louise that the Cross would be ready for our arrival in Jerusalem and a young woman called Sophy, with experience of Earth energy work at Uluru in Australia, had meantime volunteered to accompany me. Another woman friend, whom I had originally met as part of Tumi's group and who had travelled with me to the French Cathar sites, expressed an interest in coming too. As nobody else had materialised - and assuming the designated party of three would travel together from the UK - it seemed logical that she too should come along. All was prepared and the Earth Week organisers in Glastonbury were still willing to give publicity to the ceremony of Raising the Cross, so that as many as possible could gather to witness the event and experience the energies that would be unleashed.

We took a night flight on April 5th. and arrived in our rooms at my favourite Jerusalem hotel overlooking the old walled city, just as the sun was rising. We were to spend a few days acclimatising ourselves to the very complex energies of this deeply-divided, but evocative city by visiting the actual and supposed locations of the Jesus drama. As it happened, Easter, Passover and Ramadan coincided during the ten days of our schedule, which meant that Christians, Jews and Moslems, who divide the city between them, were all celebrating these festivals during this period. The city was packed, and charged as usual with rather more emotion than spirit!

We needed to find a suitable location on the Mount of Olives for the most important of our rituals on Easter morning at the culmination of the energy absorption, so we wandered over the Arab region on the summit and found nothing suitable, as all retreats and gardens were behind the walls and locked doors of churches and monasteries. After an hour or so, just as we were about to give up, an elderly nun with a gentle, smiling face and piercing blue eyes appeared out of nowhere and enquired if she could help. On hearing of our quest, she led us to the perfect location below the summit, among the olives in the garden of the Sisters of Zion. It overlooks Gethsemane and the Golden Gate of the old city. Significantly, it is this gate through which Jesus rode on Palm Sunday and although now bricked up, it is the expected entry point for the currently awaited Messiah of the Jews.

The highlight of this part of the journey was meeting Louise for the first time and receiving the Aquarian Cross from her. With a wonderful sense of occasion, she had taken great trouble to choose the house of highly-attuned Jewish friends within the walls of the old city for the special presentation and had set the Cross on its brass base, brilliantly polished for maximum effect. For me it was an awesome moment: the moment of truth, the point of no return. There, in old Jerusalem, as I gazed intently upon the physical version of the symbol I had envisaged, I at last recognised my true being in the reflection of the Cross - and the Earth stood still.

Cynics will shake their heads and declare this a severe case of 'Jerusalemitis' - the condition that affects hundreds of people who visit the city each year, and associate themselves with Biblical events and personalities. For my part, I know who and what I am, and that is what matters to me. When all glamours and illusions are cast aside, we can only identify ourselves within and as the One.

The next stage of our journey took us to the fabled Mt Sinai, which had by then been handed back to Egypt by Israel and necessitated flights via Cairo. I had been there a few years earlier to visit the Monastery of St. Catherine, during a holiday in Israel. On that occasion, the car I was driving from the Dead Sea to the Red Sea was hit by flash floods in the desert at night and was almost instantly submerged by muddy water. My passenger and I narrowly escaped drowning, while many others that night were less fortunate. The waters abated as suddenly as they had risen and I suggested jokingly that we try to start the sodden car. The little Fiat started first time, and gallantly carried us and other bedraggled travellers to a Kibbutz in the middle of nowhere and some hot soup!

A strange and powerful experience, especially as we both held air tickets for that journey and only decided at the last moment to try the desert route by car. This was my second brush with 'the great unknown', illustrating perhaps that my higher and lower selves were still at odds and needed a little more shock treatment.

The current visit to Sinai was of an altogether different nature. The three of us, joined on the plane by another woman attracted to our quest, were to conduct the first of the meditations on the summit at the sunrise of the Jewish Passover (Pesach), April 10th. Our plan had been to overnight in the hostel of the Monastery and make the traditional climb early, in time for sunrise. Being Easter, the place was packed with Greek Orthodox pilgrims so we decided to risk finding shelter higher up. After a steep climb of about two hours at sunset, using the camel track rather than the 3,000 steps built by a penitent Monk, we reached the Valley of the Prophets below the summit. It was here, so legend tells us, that the Biblical prophets of old rested for the night before they climbed the last 1,000 steps of the 'Stairway to Heaven' in time for sunrise. Moses passed this way and is understood to have received the Ten Commandments on the summit. So did Elijah and Elisha, who contacted the unseen realms to bring through prophecy relevant for thousands of years to come, until 'the end times'.

The scenery is parched, rugged and forbidding, yet has about it an awesome splendour as the sunlight conjures a subtle interplay of colours in the rich mineral texture of the rock. The valley, containing the only trees on the mountain and the ruins of a small settlement, seemed to magnetise us to its wind-free shelter, and soon we had a fire going. It was a night of one of the clearest and brightest full moons I can remember; indeed, it was almost as bright as day. We put on all the clothes we had and danced and sang around the fire, infused with such potent energy that sleep was impossible. As our euphoria wore off, so did the temperature and, unprepared, we were probably saved from hypothermia by the miraculous presence of a Bedouin Arab, who sold us expensive but life-saving glasses of hot, sweet mint tea in his tent for much of the night.

At first light, after minimal sleep on the rough earth floor of an unfinished chapel, we solemnly climbed the Stairway in a high state of anticipation.... Is there nowhere sacred left on this planet?! It seems that a 'Sinai sunrise' is now packaged too - and some three hundred excited, camera-clicking tourists had beaten us to it. The Egyptians even plan to put the finishing touches to 'the mystical Sinai experience' by building a chairlift to the summit - no doubt with fast food thrown in for good measure.

Having regained our composure, we found an adjoining site on undisturbed ground. There the three of us started the process of absorbing the energy of the mountain, as the sun cast its first rays across the surrounding peaks. Language is too limited even to begin to describe the sensations and perceptions that such moments of total alignment can generate, but suffice it to say that we all felt inner confirmation of the extraordinary adventure we had undertaken. It was with some reluctance that we started the long trail back into the 3rd. dimension and down to Earth.

A six-hour bus journey across the desert and under the Suez canal, brought us back to Cairo and to our hotel at Gizeh overlooking the floodlit Pyramids. It was here that Mary from Johannesburg joined the three of us. She had participated in the Table Mountain activation, had arranged a talk for me at her house during my tour and had felt very strongly drawn to this work. As it turned out, it was just as well she had had the courage of her convictions to join us. The perfect timing of this tour was again confirmed.

It is said that comets always herald change, and Robert Coon explains that Comet Kohoutek's arrival at Christmas 1973 marked the reactivation and realignment of the planetary energy grid; Comet West in 1976 signalled the initial preparation of the El Tule tree in Mexico, where Harmonic Convergence was focused in 1987. That year also marked the passing of the powerful Haley's Comet; but now in 1990, just as predicted in Apocalypse 3, Comet Austin reached its zenith as the Aeon shift occurred. Austin passed through the constellation of Pisces in late March, releasing us from old thinking patterns and heralding our spiritual rebirth. On April 12th, it passed through the capstone of the constellation Triangulum, which is associated with the Nile Delta, the mysteries of ancient Egypt and especially the Great Pyramid.

Many who had gathered on that date at the Pyramids intuited that this was the moment indicated by the American prophet, Edgar Cayce. He foresaw that "100 golden souls," connected with the original construction of the Great Pyramid - built incidentally by means of sonics rather than by manual labour - would return and regain access to the vital information contained in the "halls of Records", which it guards. These so-called 'halls' are etheric memory banks stored at power centres across the planet, which can on rare occasions be penetrated by initiates. It is well to remember that our every thought, word and deed is eternally recorded, and that this is the information adepts can access.

"And behold, the Christ comes quickly, for a Millennium will pass and near another and there will be made a sign in the heavens. And you will know this star that called the wise and all-knowing to Bethlehem. Seek there the star at the appointed time, and all Spirit will rejoice in the reward, even unto those who come out of the body, that every man according to his work shall be."

Apocalypse 3, Ch 8:12

It would be exciting if comets were always dramatic and visible, but they function as subtle before physical harbingers of change, to which we need to attune if we are to understand their import. Even 2,000 years ago the 'star' had to be pointed out to Herod and others by the three 'wise men'.

Although many groups had gathered at the Pyramid to consult the memory banks, we chose to concentrate on our own particular mission. We are told that Jesus himself went through initiations at the renowned mystery school of Saqqara near Gizeh and would certainly have accessed the akashic records guarded by the Pyramid and Sphinx. We spent time on both sites, but our main work was to take place inside the Great Pyramid at the height of the energy around midday and, later that night, between the two front paws of the heavily-guarded Sphinx. Fortunately for us, other people participating decided to avoid the crowds in the chambers of the Pyramid and booked them privately before opening time - even knowing they would miss the high point of the energy. We just trusted and were rewarded by the miracle of finding both the King's and the Queen's chambers virtually empty for the five hours of our activities. This is unheard of at the peak of Egypt's tourist season, and as we left the building at 4 p.m., the queue to get in stretched across the entire plateau! Quite literally, it was as though a 'presence' had barred the entrance.

I had often been to Gizeh on business in the past, had walked around the Pyramid and even spent a night in a hotel opposite watching it, mesmerised, in the moonlight. Yet I had always known not to enter it. Misguided tourists pour in daily, encouraged to believe it is a defunct Pharaonic burial chamber. Its shape alone makes it a phenomenal energy accumulator, and as such it can be seen as "The Gateway to the Eternal". I entered the building with some trepidation, knowing of many strange experiences people have had in it. I needn't have worried, because I discovered that the place acts rather like a huge mirror, and amplifies whatever state of mind one brings into it. Our purpose was to integrate Christ consciousness (the Law of One) within ourselves; and the Pyramid, like the Sphinx later on, simply overwhelmed us with the power of concentrated love.

In the King's chamber, due to our unexpected privacy, we took turns lying inside the sarcophagus. This is the only structure in

72

the room and was originally used by initiates to separate the soul from the body for a while, in order to experience the inner planes, and to demonstrate the existence of our physical and subtle anatomy. These days, what is known as the 'near-death experience', has replaced this practice: over a million Americans, for instance, have recorded that they almost 'died', then returned to life with total recall of what they had experienced. Dr Elisabeth Kubler-Ross and others have dedicated a lifetime of study to this phenomenon, which seems to have been designed to prove that 'death' is only a transition, and thereby to dispel all the fear and ignorance surrounding what is, after all, a quite natural process. The story of Elaine's near-death experience gives a useful illustration of what happens to the soul in such cases. All who go through it get a glimpse of their original life plan, which normally transforms the remainder of their present incarnation.

We were amazed to find that another young woman was waiting for us in the chamber. Already strikingly positioned in meditation on a rock in a clear protective stance, Bettina, from Berlin, whom none of us had ever met, just *knew* she had to be there for our ceremony: she hopped on a charter flight to Cairo, leaving behind her a rather bewildered husband and child! Her energy, as we heard from Spirit later, was crucial here and at the Sphinx later. She has since become a good friend and is now another link with my country of birth.

Although I knew we had to attune at the Sphinx, I frankly doubted that even Spirit could get us between its paws, with the monument recently fenced off and guarded by armed soldiers. No permits were being issued by the Ministry, after recent misguided attempts to penetrate the chamber of the Akashic Records had left the poor old Sphinx even worse for wear.

I said to my companions that the *Son et Lumiere* light show at night would probably be the closest we'd get to it, so we went to the performance. Before it started, we got as close as the fence allowed, and just then heard a voice asking if we needed any assistance. I should have known - everything in Egypt has its price - and as there were four lovely young women to manhandle over some tricky terrain, this red-blooded young Arab struck a quick deal! Within five minutes, and after some decidedly intimate handling, we reached our goal and placed our foreheads on the carved stone book over the Sphinx's heart. We then formed a circle within the paws to meditate, and were soon awash in an exquisite outpouring of energy that left us in no doubt about our purpose. All this was accomplished within ten minutes, with a nervous guide hurrying us along in the full glare of the powerful search-lights of the show. I can only assume our movements could not be seen by the audience, otherwise it would have been a highly unusual performance that particular night!

Leaving Bettina to continue her pilgrimage around the key sites of Egypt, the four of us flew back to Israel on Good Friday, April 13th, to conduct the main energy ritual on the Mount of Olives. Jerusalem was now swamped by a sea of religious emotion, nowhere epitomised more obviously than by the Christian church of the holy Sepulchre, well inside the city walls. Since the time of the original events, the various Christian sects, especially the Roman, have attempted to deny all the evidence about the real site of the crucifixion and burial sites of Jesus Christ. We are clearly told that Golgotha was a hill both *outside and north* of the city walls, that the garden of Joseph of Arimathea's tomb was nearby, and that it contained a winepress and large underground water cistern.

Recent archaeological opinion is clear that the northern Damascus gate of Jerusalem was also the city's northern boundary at the time of the crucifixion. Some five minutes' walk due north of this gate is located the Garden Tomb. First excavated in 1891, the tomb is adjacent to the Place of the Stoning, where Stephen was martyred. Stonings were carried out at the foot of the still clearly delineated Hill of the Skull at the back of the present Arab bus station, north of the Damascus gate. General Gordon, the celebrated English soldier and Bible scholar, in company with many other eminent researchers, was certain in 1883 that this tomb area was the actual site of the events. It is, of course, no coincidence that the British Protestant tradition, direct inheritor of the Christ impulse through Joseph of Arimathea, should be the exposers and now guardians of this site. The true path is never obvious or glamorous, but is veiled and secret and calls for inner attunement rather than outer show. A comparison between the emotional hysteria of the Sepulchre church with people grovelling on the floor, fawning over every relic and artefact in sight, and the serenity of the Garden Tomb in the Temple of Nature, serves as a perfect example of much that I am attempting to convey in this book.

> "And his servants threw out all the priests of the Earth who had given false prophecy, for they had laid bare the Earth and caused the stars in the sky to move." *Apocalypse 3, Ch 2:1*

While sitting quietly in meditation holding the Aquarian Cross with my companions in front of the Tomb that Good Friday afternoon, I experienced the sublime sensation of the opening of my heart chakra. I knew we were in the presence of Jesus, and that we shared in those ecstatic minutes the perfect blending of our souls with the Christ energy. Waves of gentle heat pulsed through me and as I felt the emanations from my heart, the palms of my hands all but burned. This was without question the most profound moment in my life so far.

Now that my personal proof had been furnished, it was with intense joy and renewed determination to fulfil our purpose, that my friends and I withdrew from that scene. The same night eight of us gathered round the Cross at the same house in which I first saw it, and sitting under an eight-branched candelabrum, we transmitted the supreme energy with which we had been blessed that day as a healing for the Old Jerusalem.

I had been told about the very few special sites still holding the Christ energy in modern Israel by a South African friend called Annie, who had made a brief visit to Israel just before ours. Apart from the Garden Tomb, she strongly recommended a visit to Tabgha on the Sea of Galilee. So we went the next day as part of our preparation and visited the Mount of Beatitudes and the site of the loaves and fishes miracle. The Church of St Peter's Primacy is built over the still potent rocky outcrop where Jesus summoned the fisherman, Simon Peter, to follow him. "Andrew first findeth his own brother Simon, and saith unto him, We have found the Messias, which is, being interpreted, the Christ. And he brought him to Jesus. And when Jesus beheld him, he said, Thou art Simon the son of Jonah; thou shalt be called Cephas, which is by interpretation, a stone". *John 1: 40/2*

What serenity and peace we found that sunny afternoon amid the gentle green hillsides carpeted with spring flowers. Nothing can have changed. Fishermen knee-deep in clear water were still casting their nets as of old and all around could be felt that familiar presence evoking memories of the appearance on the water. Ah! . . . a fleeting glimpse? Yes . . . perhaps, or again maybe just daydreams inspired by a deep devotion. Who knows? But we could have stayed there forever.

During that day, it was becoming increasingly clear that the second woman who had come out from the UK was by now incapable of being one of the main participants in the ritual next morning. She had suffered minor accidents and stomach problems from the start and had particular difficulty reintegrating with the Jerusalem vibrations after those in Egypt, which she had much preferred. It was decided that Mary from South Africa should replace her and I was left with the unenviable task of breaking the news to her in the sickbed to which she had now retired. Hysteria and recriminations echoed through the hotel for much of the night, which was not exactly how I had envisaged preparing myself for the great event! But our first priority was to establish a proper balance for the occasion, and eventually, after conceding her weakened state, she reluctantly agreed. She did, however, join the support group both in Jerusalem and Glastonbury and fulfilled a most important overall role for which I am forever grateful.

First light on Easter Sunday, the most potent moment in the Christian calendar, revealed a cold and misty Jerusalem as seven of us, five women and two men, assembled on the Mount of Olives. We formed a Merkabah of a triangle within a circle with myself, Mary and Sophy around the Cross in the centre and the others guarding the four airections. Seven red poppies growing in the garden were placed around the Goss and after a purification with the Chalice Well water, we focused intently for an hour while the sun rose. It seemed as though the energy entered the three of us mainly through the Earth, linking our base chakras, while cosmic emanations bonded us at heart level. The sensation of swirling energy made us dizzy and here the outer group provided much needed support.

We were aware neither of the time nor the cold on our bare feet, and after an hour took the Cross to the edge of the garden and directed the energy towards the Golden Gate below us. The three of us were now sealed in the raw power that it was our task to purify to the highest degree before releasing it on Glastonbury Tor six days later. To achieve this degree of oneness is no easy task on the physical plane, and further dramas were to test us severely. For the moment, though, a hot bath and deep sleep revived the Garden Tomb sensation and showed me that all had so far been successfully accomplished.

Mary had been obliged to change her plans at short notice in order to take up her position and unfortunately, as it turned out, could not travel back to the UK on our flight. She flew instead next day via Athens to London and met us on our arrival. The three remaining spent the last day relaxing and bathing in the therapeutic waters of the Dead sea, in what seemed like a planetary baptism at the lowest place on

Earth, and was also no doubt a preparation for the ordeal to come next day.

The Jewish state of Israel struck back at us in no uncertain terms on our departure from Tel Aviv airport. The renewed hysteria of our companion caused the authorities to suspect and fiercely interrogate her. This inevitably led to all three of us being subjected to stringent personal and baggage searches. The Cross was removed for high security analysis, in what for me was an agony similar to a mother's desperation when her newborn baby is snatched from her.

Spirit later confirmed, somewhat clinically, that this was a counter-attack of opposite polarities, and all that is needed in such cases is to remain centered and in harmony. In this way, such forces can never prevail, because they are starved of energy through lack of reaction. They also assured me that the Cross cannot be affected by any 3rd. dimensional energy, and that it would certainly have had a very profound effect on anyone physically handling it, one way or another.

In all this turmoil, we only just caught the flight but throughout the ordeal Sophy and I somehow managed to guard the precious energy we carried, while our companion virtually brought the airport to a halt with her fury. Being last to board, we also had to put up with dense cigarette smoke and being continually kicked in the back by boisterous children. We were being tested to the limit of endurance, and it was not over yet.

GLASTONBURY TOR, APRIL 21st 1990

> "And they will rejoice, for the Christ is descended from the Higher planes even to the darkest corner of the Earth. For none will fear, for the Christ is within."
>
> *Apocalypse 3, Ch 4: v 13*

On our arrival back in London, we were relieved to meet Mary again: our trio had been restored and was less vulnerable. We got back to my house and eagerly awaited the departure of the fourth member. Her car wouldn't start! Eventually, after Sophy was inexplicably hurled to the ground, badly grazing both knees, and I had all but lost my composure over the car, we decided to drive her home immediately and put an end to this disruption. It is important to remember that both polarities are always present in work like this and that it is essential to identify the source of any negativity, so it doesn't destroy what is being attempted. There is no right or wrong in these situations, and this woman had joined us to fulfil a critical function which was every bit as important in the success of the Aeon Shift as any other.

There now followed three days of total retreat, in which first to rest our bodies after our recent exertions and then to integrate as One in a series of deep meditations around the Cross. After some powerful attunements at local energy centres, and our own interpersonal processes, we felt we were ready to share what we had brought back to England with us.

We heard later that, unsurprisingly, the good townspeople of Glastonbury had felt threatened and ill-at-ease about the whole concept; and yet as we arrived on the cold, windy and misty morning of April 21st, a crowd of a hundred and fifty from all over the country, including many pilgrims from overseas, had gathered for what the Third Book of the Apocalypse describes as the most significant moment in human affairs for some 2,000 years.

The huge Glastonbury Zodiac, in which all twelve signs of the zodiac are traced on the surrounding countryside, depicts Weary All hill as part of the Pisces symbol. It was here, after landing on the Isles - now hills - of Avalon, that Joseph of Arimathea planted his staff of Mediterranean thorn, and a venerable scion of the original stands there to this day. The procession gathered around this tree. At 10.30am we moved off for the one-mile walk to the Tor, within the Aquarius symbol of the Zodiac. Under the thorn tree, Robert had been advised by Spirit to select a group of five women and five men, dressed in white and ready to participate as the 13 designated in Apocalypse 3, Ch 1:6 to release the energy:

"And the Lamb will sit in the midst and will number thirteen. For seven will be called and five will be chosen...."

I held the Cross on a three-foot brass pole made for the occasion, while Sophy carried the new Aquarian symbol - a cup - filled with Chalice Well water and Mary held a sprig of the old Piscean Thorn tree. The procession sang *'Jerusalem'* and other rousing choruses as we climbed the steep approach to the Tor. At 11.30 the ten formed a circle around the three with the Cross, outside the west door of the tower of St Michael.

The fire ritual already described had been performed since dawn to purify the energies, despite gale-force winds which persisted throughout the ceremony. I opened the proceedings with the Aramaic Lord's prayer, in the words and language used by Jesus (set out at the end of this book). Sophy then led the assembled company in the Great Invocation, established by the Theosophists earlier this century to 'invoke the return of the Christ'. As our ceremony was designated as the announcement of that event, the Great Invocation has now served its purpose and is replaced by proclamations of the Christ Presence on Earth. Mary invited us to make the following affirmation of our kinship with all Creation:

"I am the Light that I am. I am the Peace that I am.

"I am the Love that I am. I am the Christ of God.

"I am that I am."

I then said the following prayer: "Mother/Father God, we ask for a blessing on this sacred place, that this day the etheric city, New Jerusalem, be established here in accordance with the divine prophecy contained within the Third Book of the Apocalypse, restored to humanity as the pure word by the realms of Light."

The following extracts were read aloud from Chapter 7:

"For the days of the prophecy are to be fulfilled. And you will know the place by the bright star that was sent as a messenger to Bethlehem.

"And the bright star will appear over the Holy City and all that abide within will be baptised in the light. And all that sit in high places and observe the light from afar, they also will be made one with the light.

"And they will raise the sign of the cross that will be carried on a staff and all will bow their heads in the presence of the Father. For the old will be made new, and the city will abide forever. For all who share this vision will enter through the gates of the city of paradise and bliss.

"And I will search in all hearts and in all minds, that they may be pure. For I will send the spirit of My son, Jesus the Christ, that all will be made one with His spirit.

"And a great light will circle them and they will know each other. And they will rejoice and share the sign. And they will be given vision and light. And wisdom will be revealed to them, that they will know their task.

"And there will be a new Heaven and a new Earth. And everything will be made new. And they will walk in the light of the Christ returned.

"And the light will go out to every nation from their mouth, and to every king and leader and to every tribe and language. They will know the will of the Father.

"For the Spirit will talk through the prophets. And there will be a new Bride. And the Bride and the Spirit will talk with one voice. And the Bride will bless the earth.

"The redeemed will be known to one another, for they will be dressed in white robes. And the Christ light will lead them to the springs of living water.

"And they will make the sign to the newly born and baptise one another. And their riders will be given power to take peace to all the people. And they will rejoice in the light and be trustworthy and true in the gift of the Divine Love of the Father.

"And their spirit will inherit the Earth. And they will have dominion over the stars even to the tenth planet.

"For His angels will show His servants all things to come, that all will bathe forever in the river of Divine Love which flows through the city of paradise and bliss."

Extracts from Chapter 8 followed:

"And there shall be no night there, and they need no torch, neither light of the sun, for the Father giveth them light, that they may abide in the light forever.

"A Millennium will pass, then near another and behold, I come quickly. Blessed is he that keepeth the sayings of the prophecy of this book.

"And he saith unto me, "Hide not the sayings of the prophecy of this book, neither let no man do likewise, for the time is at hand that all wisdom shall be known."

"And behold, the Christ come quickly, for a Millennium will pass, and near another, and there will be made a sign in the heavens. And you will know this star that called the wise and all-knowing to Bethlehem. Seek there the star at the appointed time, and all spirit will rejoice in the reward, even unto those who come out of the body, that every man according to his work shall be.

"And there was great light and there stood before me Jesus the Christ. And He spake thus, that I may know the authority of the angel. And bade, "Watch for the star that was foretold by the prophet Jacob, that you will know the time of the Second Coming, when I will enter all hearts.

"He which testifieth these things saith, Surely I come quickly. Even as night follows day, so shall century follow century, until the second Millennium is nigh. Amen. Even so, come, Christ light"

Another prayer followed:

"We ask a blessing on our Earth Mother, the goddess Gaia, on all kingdoms of the Earth, on all humankind and on all Creation throughout the Universe, that this day will be born a new Heaven and a new Earth, joined as One. We link consciousness with all those sharing this vision throughout the world, especially the many hundreds at this moment forming the great global triangle with this place in South Africa and Australia."

Ch 2, v 21: "And the seventh angel came forth and broke the seal. And there was silence in heaven for half an hour for the time of the prophecy was known."

As the Cross was raised the following dedication was made:

"Lord we present to you the Old and the New, to be a perfect gift for the New Jerusalem and for the blessing of this sacred soil upon which we return to you that which is Old (*the thorn branch is laid on the earth*) and raise to you that which is New."

At midday on April 21st, 1990, the Aquarian Cross was raised by one male and two females. As it went up a number of things happened simultaneously: the sun suddenly broke through dense cloud for the first time that day and enveloped all those present in a concentrated beam of light; this was witnessed by many people in Glastonbury and throughout the surrounding countryside. Ch 7, v 9 &12 indicate that the Comet Austin was directly above us at that moment: "And the bright star will appear over the Holy City and all that abide within will be baptised in the Light. And a great Light will circle them and they will know each other." Then somewhere in the crowd, a sleeping dog leapt to his feet and emitted blood-curdling howls. Ch 1, v 4: "For the beast will be slain...."

After this there was a deep meditation for half an hour to mark 'the silence when Heaven and Earth are One', during which many saw streams of energy around the three of us as we felt the gradual release of our precious burden. The thirteen then blessed each other with the Sufi Greeting: "From you I receive, to you I give, together we share, by this we live." Each was anointed with Chalice Well water and held the Cross. The crowd demonstrated the energy of love by hugging one another, and then we all joined hands in a huge circle, revolving seven times round the tower of St. Michael. This done, we looked up to see that the dense cloud had been replaced in a blue sky by white clouds surrounding the Tor in the unmistakable formation of enfolding arms!

Even now, I am still hearing about strange things that happened on the Tor that day, and of the inner and outer battle between Light and dark that raged there, as people of all dispositions held their own simultaneous ceremonies and rituals. Both polarities were, of course, received by kindred groups around the world and many were taken unawares. Happily, I heard later that all were able to process the energy without mishap and helped to ground it successfully in both hemispheres.

The most extraordinary, yet widely witnessed occurrence, was the appearance of Anthony Roberts singing *Jerusalem;* he had passed away while walking on the Tor only two months previously. He was a friend and close associate of Robert Coon, who says that he was among the most knowledgeable of men on the structure and unfoldment of New Jerusalem. He chose to work on the inner planes for this event and will, we are told, continue to work in the heart of Avalon until he is satisfied that the planetary New Jerusalem has been established. Thank you, Anthony, for so convincingly demonstrating the reality of Spirit in non-physical dimensions!

This day of days ended in an all-night vigil with a fire ritual and some 16 didjeridoo players on the Tor to herald Earth Day, which was being celebrated worldwide and had even caught the attention of the American President. The timing was carefully synchronised so that the blessing of April 21st could encircle the planet next day. Throughout Earth Day, the Cross was positioned in front of the tower on the Tor, and many came to film and photograph it and experience its energy. A woman from Australia, who came over to the UK especially and had to crawl up the hill to reach it, received an extraordinary healing, after which her badly crippled hands opened for the first time in years, and her life was transformed.

For those interested in astrology, about which I personally know little, a rather revealing chart was drawn up for the Aeon shift, linking Glastonbury on midday 21/4/90 and Israel on 14/5/48 at 4pm, when independence from British rule was declared. The Aeon shift was described as 'explosive' in relation to Israel, mainly because Glastonbury's chart is dominated by "a perfect Grand Cross', which ties in

Pluto with Mercury, the nodes and the AS-DSC axis. Inevitably, Judaic sensibilities are threatened by the new, open and dogma-free Aquarian spirituality epitomised by the New Jerusalem dispensation. Also the fact of Joseph of Arimathea as a member of the Sanhedrin (an interpreter of Talmudic Law) founding the first Christian church, when the Jewish leadership at the time denied Jesus as the prophesied Messiah, finally has to be addressed. Astrologically, the Aquarian Cross, aligned in the centre of the Glastonbury chart on April 21st, 1990 offers huge empowerment possibilities and is seen as an immense power point in time!" I received this fascinating assessment after the event - if indeed further proof were needed of what had been accomplished.

Not that he is so far aware of it, a further synchronicity involving the Cross concerns no less a person than HRH The Prince of Wales. The lineage of the British royal house was traced during Queen Victoria's reign right back to the Priest King David "out of the stem" of Jesse. This is the line of Solomon and Jesus, blessed with "the spirit of wisdom and understanding, counsel and might, knowledge and fear of the Lord." Isaiah 11. The purpose of this line of Priest Kings is strictly one of personal self-sacrifice for their people and leadership by example.

As the British nation now wakes to the splendour of its true heritage, it is through the enlightenment of whoever inherits the throne that in due course spiritual leadership must replace the established role of this ancient line. In this way alone can it help to inspire not only the once 'lost tribes', but *all mankind* at the time of its greatest need. This uniquely placed family could still influence world opinion, and its positive example could be of inestimable benefit at this time of crisis. Indeed, unless the British monarchy acknowledges its divine purpose as champion of the Christ consciousness grounded on the sacred soil of England, it will inevitably disintegrate like any other 3rd. dimensional institution steeped in ego, glamour, privilege, possessions and separative conduct. Much emotional suppression, lack of adaptability and unresolved personal issues within that family have been revealed to the public in recent years. This precisely matches the current trends, as we are *all* obliged to confront our own private demons in order to heal ourselves.

As the younger generations of that family carry out the involuntary demolition of the untenable mystique of outdated royalty, many people will have sensed an inner significance in the location of the fire that partially destroyed the traditional home of the Saxe-Coburg-Gotha-Battenberg-Windsor family at Windsor Castle on November 21st, 1992. The Sovereign's private chapel represents the very core of that family's spirituality. It would appear that the rising tide of new awareness spares nobody and will only support those with clear vision and intention based on the living example of love, enlightenment and sharing.

1992: 'annus horribilis' - or a heaven-sent opportunity for new inspiration and direction? The fire that threatened 'the fabric of the national heritage' couldn't be a clearer warning that now is the time for the British with an enlightened Monarchy to transcend their divisive obsession with class, status and past glories that now seriously undermines their new and infinitely more noble world role.

On Tuesday October 30th, 1990, I went to the Chalice Well at Glastonbury with Louise, who was on her way back to South Africa. She had particularly wanted to experience the energies in England after the Aeon shift, having been so much involved with the event in Israel, and brought a woman friend from Jerusalem with her. That morning, the three of us decided to do a private ritual with the Cross over the Chalice Well - whose cover, inlaid with two interlocked circles, creating the Vesica Piscis - had been the source of my inspiration for the design of the Aquarian Cross. Having completed what we had come to do, we saw Robert Coon in the Chalice garden, who told us that Prince Charles had come to take the waters for an arm injury only two days before. It seemed that the press already had the story and the TV companies were planning coverage. At that very moment, the cameras arrived and, being among the few people around, we were asked for our opinions on the healing qualities of the water. Seeing the Cross, a rather cynical interviewer short of newsworthy material asked us to re-enact the ritual we had just done.

That night both BBC (West) and HTV ran the item in their main news bulletins, and so it was that the Prince inadvertently became the vehicle for the first public exposure of the Aquarian Cross to the British people. Now that the tribes of the House of Israel, who received 'the line of promise' through Manasseh and Ephraim, are identified as the peoples of Britain, America and the Commonwealth of free nations, it becomes clear that the role of any future monarch of the country in which the Christ impulse is anchored, can only be that of a 'priest king'. How fitting that the heir to the throne, led to Glastonbury that day by perfect synchronicity at soul level, should have enabled this symbol of the Second Coming to be seen by millions of a once lost, but new-found tribe of Israel. Interesting too that the Aquarian Cross was raised synchronistically on the Queen's birthday and that later I should have witnessed the Windsor Castle fire while driving to London on my birthday!

Robert Coon summarised the whole event in a letter dated April 3rd, 1990 from Glastonbury:

"Many thanks for the doing of the Great Work. Many signs have come to me that tell me that the Aeon shift ritual you and your friends just did is of great significance. Personally, I rate it with the Magi and Arimathean missions."

Chapter 7

THE TRAVELLING CROSS

"And they will raise the sign of the Cross that will be carried on a staff and all will bow their heads in the presence of the Father."

Apocalypse 3, Ch. 7: v.10

Once the Aeon shift was completed and the participants had returned to their homes, I gratefully sought my own haven, to review all the wonders of recent weeks. I felt it important to record the details, so that the experiences would stay fresh and, in due course, become a living record for those who wish to share in the outworking of events so long predicted.

As it turned out, I had little time to rest: that very day a former colleague phoned out of the blue and offered me some consulting work that summer. It was over five years since I had been in touch with him, and I had long since decided that I had had enough of the tourist business. However, at that particular moment the offer felt just right, and I accepted at once. Guidance from Spirit made it clear that I was now to spread the energy I had recently been involved in carrying from Jerusalem to Glastonbury.

Over the next several weeks, I visited eleven countries throughout Europe and the Middle East, from Scandinavia back to Egypt and Israel! The basic purpose of the tour was to negotiate hotel and ground arrangements with local suppliers - which would leave me plenty of time to carry out the inner work, whenever and wherever opportunity arose.

Since my programme concerned city holidays, I anticipated that much of my other agenda would be in churches and cathedrals that had been placed over Earth energy sites and intersecting ley lines. The Cross would be rather cumbersome on such a frantic itinerary, so I took Chalice Well water from Glastonbury instead and sprinkled it on altars and mingled it with fountains and rivers, as directed.

In this way, I 'worked' Vienna, Salzburg, Munich, Frankfurt, Cologne, Brussels, Berlin, Copenhagen, Helsinki, Stockholm, Paris, Bordeaux, Nice, Geneva, Zurich, Lucerne, Venice, Florence, Rome, Cairo, Luxor, Aswan, Tel Aviv and Jerusalem. Space does not permit detailed impressions of these travels, though I have already mentioned the events in Rome at the church of Santa Pudentiana. It was good to find myself back in Israel so soon, to hold meditations in Jerusalem with Louise and her friends, and strengthen the flow of energy between the Old and New Jerusalems. I was to return there yet again in 1991 and experience the site of Massada, where the Zealots committed mass suicide rather than succumb to Roman rule. It was at the nearby site of Qumran that, some 40 years ago, the Dead Sea scrolls had been discovered, so it seemed particularly appropriate that I happened at the time to be reading a new book called *The Dead Sea Scrolls Deception.* It describes how for over forty years, the agents of the modern Roman Church suppressed sections of one of the most significant discoveries of original biblical texts ever found - and suggests that they probably destroyed the rest.

The remainder of this chapter describes the journeys of the Aquarian Cross around the world up until the writing of the first edition of this book in late 1992. Each country will be listed in turn with a brief description of events and their significance.

AUSTRIA and GERMANY

As we have seen from the Elijah-inspired vision of Robert Coon, Berlin became the 'fixed' expression of the evolving global heart chakra at German reunification in October 1990, and the restored capital of Germany in 1991. Under the Kaiser and later Hitler, Berlin demonstrated its power, but lack of heart energy ensured the demise of those regimes. Now that the city fulfils a designated heart function, it will become a centre of inspiration in the coming Age.

No sooner had the Aeon shift been completed than I found myself travelling extensively in these two countries. In retrospect, it seems clear that we had been involved in the spiritual preparation for reunification, which at the outer levels was then only manifesting as a commercial liaison, with West Germany intent on swallowing the East in one huge mouthful. It won't be quite as easy as that, and the West will painfully have to regurgitate much that is indigestible in the East, before a really democratic union can emerge, based on human rather than commercial values.

First port of call was my old student city, Vienna. All had been prepared for this visit, as I had often been back on business since those early days, and consequently my travel work was quickly accomplished. This left me with time to focus attention on the mysterious 'Spear of Destiny' housed there.

I had not long before read Trevor Ravenscroft's extraordinary book of the same title and had learned how the spear, once the property of Herod and thrust into the side of Jesus on the Cross, had had a dramatic impact on the history of the last two thousand years. The Roman centurion Longinus in his inspired act of mercy had also performed the most critical role in the crucifixion drama: by releasing the precious blood and water into the earth, he initiated the planet into Christ consciousness at a single stroke. This created the current potential for both human and planetary upliftment, as a direct result of Jesus' sacrifice.

The early movements of this mysterious talisman after the crucifixion are not clear, but Spirit has confirmed that it was taken to Rome and passed into the care of the early Christian church. It re-emerges publicly as the talisman of Germanic Holy Roman Emperors, such as Frederick 1st, known as 'Barbarossa', and Charlemagne. Much information about its historical uses, both positive and negative, is given in *The Spear of Destiny* and its sequel *The Mark of the Beast* - though I do not agree with their predictions about its future purpose. What concerns this story is the central role it played in Hitler's third Reich, when its negative powers were deliberately unleashed with devastating results for the planet and humanity. The spear had traditionally been kept in Nurenberg, which was the spiritual centre of all three German Reichs. When Napoleon, who knew of its legendary powers, tried to capture it, the spear was quickly removed to Vienna and placed in the care of the Hapsburg dynasty. It is now on public display there in the national treasure-house.

In 1910 a young and, by all accounts, unprepossessing student by the name of Adolf Hitler was actively pursuing his interests in the black arts in Vienna. At that time, he is known to have spent hours on end standing mesmerised in front of the display cabinet containing the spear. He too knew its history and potential either for good or ill and, most likely, started to formulate his demonic schemes for world conquest while standing in its presence. Years afterwards, in the late 1930s, he was to annex Austria for the specific purpose of capturing the ancient focal symbol of the German Reichs and returning it to Nurenberg. Once there, he and his fellow Nazi initiates harnessed its powers by means of rituals and, as we all know, brought civilisation to its knees. World War II cannot be properly understood, or the roles of the main players assessed, without an awareness of the spiritual dimension of the confrontation between the forces of Light and dark that triggered it.

However, Ephraim (UK) assisted by Manasseh (USA) held the 'line of promise' from Abraham and, under the resolute and inspired leadership of Churchill, prevailed against the Nazi leviathan. It was the Americans who stumbled on the spear in the rubble of Nurenberg, literally hours before Hitler's suicide in his Berlin bunker, and it was also significantly in their possession when they dropped the atom bomb on Hiroshima. In 1946 General Eisenhower, Commander of the Allied Armies in Europe, ordered the Hapsburg Regalia, including the Holy Spear, or 'Heilige Lanze', as it is known in German, to be returned to Vienna. With the recent increase of right-wing historians regurgitating the old appeasement arguments and vilifying Churchill's leadership, it really is time that the world fully acknowledged the truly demonic nature of Hitler's vision and activities.

This was no ordinary man, and he didn't just happen to catch the imagination of a demoralised nation. He was in fact an advanced initiate who, this time and in previous lives, deliberately chose the path of darkness. Rudolph Steiner, the anthroposophist, was his spiritual polarity - and the only man Hitler feared. In these circumstances, the divinely-protected nation championing the Christ consciousness had no option but to oppose the forces of the Antichrist that had been intentionally invoked through the Spear. The works of both Ravenscroft and Steiner need to be studied in depth, to clarify the recent history of Germany, before we can begin to understand the destined role of that now reunified State in an evolving Europe.

On that visit to Vienna in June 1990, I had a few spare hours and was anxious to set eyes on this awesome symbol for myself. With some trepidation, I searched various rooms packed with imperial paraphernalia and at first missed the spear altogether. Then, retracing my steps, I was suddenly face to face with it - and found that I too was almost overwhelmed by its potency. I stared at it for what seemed like an age, but in fact turned out to be an hour. Suddenly and without any warning, I experienced my second full opening of the heart chakra, and stood there glowing with radiant energy in an almost exact repeat of the Garden Tomb incident on the previous Good Friday in Jerusalem!

Clearly I had accessed the positive aspect of the Spear, and according to Spirit, it was at that moment that it was re-balanced and cleansed: the destructive purpose for which it was more recently being used was replaced by the universal Christ consciousness. The spear had been recharged, making of it a positive, healing object of great power, now permanently sealed in the Light. There are dire warnings for anyone attempting to misuse it again, and it is interesting to note that the former President of Austria, once a long-serving United Nations Secretary-General associated with a Nazi past, retired soon afterwards! A serious fire in late 1992 at the Hofburg Palace, where the spear is kept, is also worth mentioning.

This was the start of what, with hindsight, can be seen as a carefully-orchestrated tour of some of the German and Austrian cities associated with the infamous regime inspired by the spear. Had it been designed to contribute to the transmutation of the remaining negative energies, in preparation for German reunification in October 1990? The evidence seems to suggest that it might have been.

Looking back now, the interplay of my two simultaneous roles was not without a certain irony: one minute I was conducting intense touristic price negotiations, and the next, darting into a church to light candles or, unobserved, pouring Chalice water into fountains and rivers! I often doubted my sanity, but timely signals kept showing me I was still on track.

In Berlin I met up with Bettina from the Great Pyramid ritual, and she and her husband took me on a magical bicycle ride, zig-zagging through the first gaps in the fateful Wall. The elation of riding across the barbed-wire no-man's-land and Checkpoint Charlie unchallenged, where, only weeks before, people were still being gunned down, was a moment of history to be savoured. Round every corner groups of people with rented hammers were delivering their individual verdicts on yet another ideology that had failed them. Then we arrived at the Hitler bunker, which seemed to me to be the end of the trail that had started with the Spear in Vienna. Here we sprinkled Chalice water on the ground as a blessing and healing for this soon-to-be-reunified city that is also a major world power centre.

Later in 1990, Robert Coon was giving talks in Germany to coincide with the reunification on October 3rd, and I joined him with the Cross. As a participant in the Silbury ritual the previous year, it seemed appropriate to be working on energy sites at this delicate moment in Germany's history, and we were guided to perform alignments on three main power centres. At the autumn equinox some twenty people gathered for a three-hour attunement near Berlin's Brandenberg Gate, sitting in a circle around the Cross in the Tiergarten park. We all expressed our hopes and aspirations for the new Germany and were led by Robert in powerful cabalistic 'Tree of Life' invocations.

Before the next event, on the way to visit friends in the south, I had the opportunity to take the Cross to Nurenberg, centre of German nationalism for hundreds of years. I was first led to the massive fortress dominating the city, and in particular to what is known as the 'Deep Well'. Despite crowds of tourists looking into it, I managed to pour in some Chalice water without causing too much of a stir. Having then lit candles and taken the Cross to three of the main churches, I felt I had done all I could do on my own and left, glad that this city with its troubled history had been included in the energy realignments we had been asked to undertake.

On the 29th September, Robert, a woman friend and I gathered on the 3,000 foot summit of the Brocken mountain in the Harz region. The old border had divided the mountain in two and only now were all Germans once again able to follow the famous Goethe Way into the heart of an area deeply significant in Germanic folklore. This was St. Michael's day and designated as World Healing Day by many groups around the planet. Interestingly, all three alignment days coincided with some of the major Jewish festivals - Rosh Hashanah around the autumn equinox, Yom Kippur 29th. September and Succoth 3/4 October over reunification itself. Quite clearly, an important reconciliation was taking place between the Aryan and Jewish tribes too at subtle levels.

As the main Nazi leaders were all adepts of the darker arts, they were well practised in manipulating energies, and did not hesitate to use Earth's power centres for their own unsavoury ends. So it was with the Brocken region, which in addition has ancient affinities with various kinds of sorcery and witchcraft. With hindsight, a group of three was hardly adequate to tackle these entrenched energies, and I must have failed to protect myself against what we had stirred up: that night

I passed out in the small town where we were staying and badly cut and bruised my face. I was a sorry sight next morning, as I made my way to nearby Braunschweig for the first return visit since my adoption, aged four, to the city of my birth - which Hitler represented in the Reichstag (parliament).

I always knew I'd return one day, and since my mother had died there I was now drawn to find her grave. Knowing that we are attracted at soul level to the place of our birth, it was a powerful experience going back to familiarise myself with my own physical origins. After the heavy bombing, there wasn't much trace of the beautiful old Hanseatic League city, but I did find the hospital where I made my first appearance. A little later, it felt very strange to be heading for the city's central cemetery. Having bought a purple heather plant at the gates, I was directed to the records office and within minutes was following a map to the place where lay the only evidence I had ever had of a blood connection with anyone. It would be hard for those surrounded by family and other kin to imagine my feelings as I approached the grave.

I had come not to mourn, but to seek reconciliation with someone I had once loathed, but now loved deeply for the sacrifice she had made to provide the exact conditions I needed for my start in this life. I must have been a strange sight with my battered, tear-stained face, digging with bare hands to plant the heather; but as I placed the Cross on the gravestone, lit a candle and sprinkled Chalice water, the sun emerged from behind the clouds. At long last our two souls met and our pain was finally released. For an hour we communed undisturbed in the soft light and glorious colours of autumn. On that unforgettable, golden day I was myself at last reunited with my mother and the country of my birth. A German reunification, both inner and outer! As I withdrew from the scene, the clouds gathered again, but I now felt reinvigorated and sure of my purpose - with the great bonus of a powerful ally in spirit!

The third alignment was to be at Germany's heart centre known as the Externsteine, south of Hanover on October 3rd, 1990, Reunification Day. This site is an extraordinary outcrop of rock containing initiation chambers and grottoes, with numerous 'faces' and other recognisable shapes in the outer surface, the most remarkable being a relief of Jesus Christ on the Cross. The site, like Stonehenge in England, is aligned on the midsummer solstice and was again until recently subject to neo-Nazi activity. These days, large numbers of peaceful, dedicated and mainly young Germans gather there every summer.

Without any planning, thirteen people from all over Germany assembled on the summit at midday - seven women and six men. This, you will remember, was the exact configuration to ground the Christ energy at Glastonbury, and I feel confident that the same impulse was anchored there that day, in some of the brightest and most intense light I have ever experienced. A serene atmosphere of harmony was achieved, to launch the newly-reunified Germany on its new path. In order to reach this state though, Germany - like all other countries - will have to heal and transmute the shadows in her national psyche, and it is this painful process, I believe, that we helped to initiate.

Part of my own work in the coming years will be to act with others as a bridge between Britain and Germany, assisted by the mystical energy emanating from Glastonbury. The two Germanys now face the supreme test of unification, based on tolerance and sharing; it will be a painful process while both sides resist the inner purpose that is destined for that nation.

As a Czechoslovakian Jewish medical student from Prague, who at soul level chose to experience the initiation of the gas chambers in my previous life, which ended in 1942, I am only one of many thousands now working to heal the traumas of the World Wars. Balance is often achieved by swapping roles in the successive reincarnations: large numbers of Jews destroyed in the concentration camps are now living in Aryan bodies, just as many former Nazis and anti-semitic Aryans were reborn as Jews. This is how the soul learns to heal the illusion of separation.

It is only by acknowledging that we *chose* such difficult situations that self-healing, followed by group and national healing, can ever take place. Many chose to test themselves at soul level to ensure that the last traces of violence and aggression had been expunged from their psyche, so that their present lives could be a clear demonstration of tolerance and harmony, in preparation for the new awareness now emerging. The holocaust and its accompanying horrors provided just such an opportunity, and many souls now reincarnated are more enlightened as a direct result of deciding to go through it.

In recent years, Germany has received a great blessing by the presence there of an incarnation of the Divine Mother. She is called Mother Meera, and Spirit has confirmed that she is one of the most elevated souls now on the planet - an Avatar sent specifically to that country 'to mend the broken heart'. She has incarnated as a beautiful young Indian woman and gives silent 'darshan' (blessing) to open the hearts of those who are ready. Thousands from all over the world now visit her in a small village near Frankfurt (Contact details at the end of the book).

As for me, I returned home utterly exhausted after so many exhilarating experiences. It took me a week, lying virtually motionless on a beach in Spain, fully to recover - and prepare for the next adventure.

KENYA, ZIMBABWE, SOUTH AFRICA, AUSTRALIA and THAILAND, January to April 1991

It was now time to present the Cross and share the Aeon shift experience with the many in South Africa and Australia who had been grounding that energy. During the previous summer I had met a woman living in Nairobi called Rhodia, who had heard of the Cross and was most anxious that it be brought to the region that is known as 'the heart of Africa'. The plan was to raise the Cross in Nairobi and then take it on safari to integrate its energy with the native peoples and Kenya's animal kingdom. Spirit indicated that Epiphany Sunday, appropriately the Feast of the Magi on January 6th, would be an ideal time.

Some 50 people representing various races and various religions gathered in Rhodia's delightful garden in Nairobi and, during a programme of spontaneous singing, dance and ritual, the Cross was once again raised by one male and two females. Two African women joined me, one the wife of an Oromo elder, the other representing the large Asian population. Thus was established a powerful thought-form, based on co-operation and harmony between the races. It was a glorious and deeply moving occasion, punctuated that night - you've guessed - by inexplicable flashes of lightning in an otherwise clear and star-studded sky!

The rest of the itinerary took us to the Mara game reserve, where we were fortunate to see many of the rarest animals at exceptionally close quarters. Even the rangers remarked how unusual some of our group's experiences were with the animals, which seemed to sense our peaceful purpose in a land where their very existence is continually threatened. On the night of the declaration of war on Iraq, we were in the Amboseli park tuning in to the mystical Mt. Kilimanjaro, another of the planets natural power centres. It is linked in a triangular energy grid with Mecca and Jerusalem, so we were well placed to transmit light into the situation.

Some weeks before, I had sent a letter of encouragement to the Jordanian royal family, some of whom I knew personally. In reply, they said they were confident that eventually a peaceful solution would result from the many initiatives they and others were attempting. Though inevitably discredited by the West, they were in fact the only genuine peacemakers in that situation. In the event, the combined effect of millions projecting thoughts of peace into that theatre of war transmuted much of the savagery on both sides of the conflict. Soon though, this tradition of murderous hostility will have to be discarded if the Middle East is to avoid becoming the venue for the long-predicted final showdown. Just after sunset that night, the new crescent moon appeared above the horizon and equally brightly, but *outside* the crescent, Venus. Was the Islamic symbol of the star within the crescent out of kilter with the feminine, represented by Venus?

In many ways the highlight for me was the Safari arranged by Rhodia to a site called 'the Winds of God' in the northern province of Laikipia. Twenty camels were hired and with a large retinue of Samburu supporters, including a tribal elder and herbalist, we set off on a five-day trek into virgin territory - and, for me, the journey of a lifetime. At last I could experience nights sleeping under the stars, and enjoy a deep communion with Nature. In the evenings, we all joined in meditations round the camp-fire and participated in dance and invocations. All indigenous peoples who have seen the Cross recognise the harmony and balance of the symbol, and immediately respond to its heart-opening quality.

As a special gesture, we were invited to a Samburu ancestor worship site in a huge cave. Here we performed a ceremony around the Cross in the presence of what we later discovered was yet again 13 people (6 black and 7 white)! It was so powerful that a photograph afterwards shows a distinct aura around the Cross. Our aim had been to invoke all our respective ancestors and demonstrate the willingness of humanity now to live in peace, beyond illusory tribal and racial conflict and the endless cycle of revenge and bloodshed. Our genetic forebears have a powerful influence on us, so it is all the more important that we establish new patterns of behaviour, in order that returning souls are not continually trapped in negative patterns and cycles.

Curiously, a few weeks later in South Africa, we heard that at the time of our ritual in January, Nelson Mandela and Chief Buthelezi had finally decided to meet and try to resolve their differences! Indeed, our arrival in Durban coincided with their momentous meeting in February 1991 and headlines proclaiming 'Let Peace Prevail', with pictures of the two men embracing! Whether our own activities *enable* changes to occur around us, or merely help them to do so, or simply coincide with them, we have no way of knowing. I will only say that the unending procession of apparent coincidences between our work and outward events has made me think, long and hard.

Shortly afterwards, we were at the Parliament building in Cape Town at the historic moment when the last apartheid laws were struck from the statute book. We had worked to open the heart of Africa in Kenya - and already there were signs that old divisions and energy blocks were at last beginning to heal. Many African states reopened air links and diplomatic relations with South Africa and each other. As a Kenyan citizen, Rhodia was unexpectedly able to accompany me on my South African tour, and at about this time several African Presidents, including De Klerk, started to meet and initiate rather than close discussions.

On the last day in Kenya, an Oromo elder, who had been guided by the star Sirius to walk from Ethiopia to Kenya and teach under a sacred fig tree on the outskirts of Nairobi arranged an attunement with his pupils around the Cross. Dabassa's wife had helped to raise the Cross at the first ceremony and now he gathered some fifty local people under the tree to radiate the Christ Light across all Africa from her heart. What a joyful ceremony it was, with many children participating in the teachings and prayers with him. I instinctively felt that such simple, natural gatherings as this, if held in every country, are all that is needed to inspire us to reach the next step on the ladder of evolution. I heard recently that Dabassa and his family have since been guided to walk back to their native land.

In South Africa, I gave a series of talks in the main cities and appeared on my first national radio 'phone-in', which was rather alarming in a country with such extremist attitudes! In the event, the host was quickly won over by information on the crop circle phenomenon, and the two-hour programme was received with great enthusiasm by a multi-racial audience across the country. By all accounts, it tapped the deep reservoir of interracial co-operation which promises to transform mass consciousness there. During the tour we visited the three main power points of the country: Pilansberg near Johannesburg (fixed quality), the Drakensberg Mountains in Natal (mutable) and finally, on the cardinal site of Table Mountain, we held a gathering to attune to the Saturn/Aquarius conjunction on February 6th 1991. We mentally linked the major power centres we had visited in Africa, then anchored the 'I am that I am' consciousness into the great Spinner Wheel, representing the element of earth, that is Table Mountain.

Within a day, the Devil's Peak section of the mountain burst into flames and even caused the evacuation of outlying areas of Cape Town! This was a most opportune cleansing of obsolete thought-forms, not only in South Africa, but throughout the planet, and was a fitting finale to our quest of igniting the heart flame of Africa.

A stop-over in Harare on the way to Australia unexpectedly resulted in my staying with the Economics Minister followed by an interview on a TV documentary about the subject of higher consciousness! This has since been seen over much of the African continent, with the Aquarian Cross as a focal feature.

In Australia my friends Robyn and Philip, who had held the main Aeon shift energy for the southern hemisphere, had arranged a ceremony for the dedication of part of the newly-renamed Glastonbell property in the Blue Mountains as a community dedicated to 4th.dimensional living. The Cross was raised on February 16th in the course of a large group celebration accompanied - you will hardly be surprised to hear - by fierce storms. A similar dedication took place on Mt. Dandenong in Melbourne, when the Cross was placed on the altar of the church of St Michael - precipitating a deafening crack of thunder right above us, which served admirably to focus the attention of the fifty or so present!

I met up with a number of people around the country during my talks who had been involved in the Aeon shift and we shared our impressions and experiences, which in many cases were as powerful in Australia as they had been in England. Radio interviews and public talks in Sydney, Melbourne and Brisbane followed, before my departure for Thailand.

A supporter of WWV from England named Elizabeth has close connections with Cambodia and has been instrumental in bringing the plight of this land to public attention in the West.

Spirit suggested that an attunement with the Cross in Thailand before Elizabeth entered Cambodia would prove beneficial. So, at dawn on Easter Sunday - the first anniversary of the Mount of Olives ceremony - we sat with the Cross on the beach at Pattaya in the same town as the orphanage described earlier. Only two stray dogs joined us, but within minutes of completing our meditation the inevitable thunderstorm deluged the region for some two hours. I remember thinking that this was a much-needed cleansing for such a notorious flesh-pot, but it was not for a while that we knew why we had been directed there by spirit.

In August of 1991, it was decided to hold the first serious peace negotiations in Pattaya to resolve the seemingly intractable problems of Cambodia! To date, the agreements reached there still hold, and the country enjoys a measure of peace for the first time in decades. Elizabeth also had an exceptionally useful tour there and has made great progress in finding inexpenslve supplies of artificial limbs for the many thousands of mutilated victims of booby-trap mines planted in the rice fields.

So ended the first major tour. I had hoped to cross America before returning home, but Spirit cautioned that the USA would not be ready for this energy just yet - and must, in the meantime, courageously address the problems created there by the serious misalignment of her own energies.

UNITED KINGDOM, 1991

Since its arrival from Jerusalem in 1990, the Cross has been used on several English power centres, especially in the west country where I live. Although many people have experienced miraculous healings in its presence, I use it more for Earth healing, which at this moment is no less vital. During 1991, I travelled to northern England and Scotland with Robyn from Australia, to strengthen the link between the Australian fire energy and the watery power sites of Britain. We went to the Castlerigg stone circle in the Lake District, to a Buddhist community on the Scottish border and then to the magnificent standing stones of Callanish on the outer Hebrides near Stornoway.

Our attunement at the stones was timed to coincide with a partial eclipse of the sun and a new moon, and as always we found many remarkable people to participate in the meditations. Callanish, being inaccessible, retains a greater measure of undisturbed natural energy than is normally found on such sites. Only later did we hear that at this very time the community of Stornoway nearby scored national press headlines over a serious international banking scandal that virtually bankrupted the finances of the region.

On the way south, we took the Cross to the isle of Lindisfarne off the Northumberland coast, with its early Christian associations. The approach is over a tidal causeway and as the water was too high when we first arrived, we sat eating fish and chips overlooking the island, while a huge black cloud developed. Lindisfarne was deluged for an hour by heavy rain. On our second approach, the tide had receded and it felt as though all was prepared for the integration of the energy we carried. We did a meditation on a grassy headland with only sheep for company, as the sun set gently across the sea.

Next day, the Cross was placed on a side altar in Durham cathedral, which has historical associations with Lindisfarne - and a decidedly unorthodox bishop; perhaps a glimmer of light is at last stirring somewhere within the patriarchy, and maybe the awakening of Christ consciousness there will assist the process. Our tour ended in Cambridge - which greeted us with a miasma of blocked traffic, congested pavements, drizzle and pollution that gave us both a headache within minutes, and threatened our harmonious relationship for the first time in a week! So much for the unbalanced atmosphere created by overaccentuated brain-power. Perhaps that lovely city will one day open its heart, when a long-overdue 'Chair of Spiritual Science' is established at its University?

In early summer, Rhodia from Kenya and another woman friend joined me on an expedition with the Cross along the 'Michael line' to Cornwall. I have already mentioned this major ley line forming part of the 'Dragon line' of the infinity symbol laid out across the planet *(see the Earth Chakra map)*. The power travels from west to east and entering England at Land's End passes through St. Michael's Mount. It then traces its way through many ancient stone circles, standing stones and Michael churches in a straight line across southern England to Bury St. Edmunds and on into the sea on the Norfolk coast. It was along this line that the Silbury Hill ceremony released energy into Eastern Europe and Russia before traversing the planet.

We travelled down the line from Avebury to Land's End as the one male and two female trio which activates the Cross, and were led to perform realigmnents of the Earth energy grid and release blockages in it caused by misuse. It is a journey thoroughly recommended to those who wish to balance themselves with the healing powers of the Earth. Off the line, but well worth a visit, is Tintagel, stronghold of the magician Merlin, King Arthur's mentor. Linking with those energies on that dramatic site soon transports one into the heart of English folklore and the initiations known as the Round Table and the quest for the Holy Grail.

On August 22nd 1991, I took the Cross to Jersey during a brief tourist assignment. This channel island is a major power centre on a ley line that links it with England. The Nazis, who were noted for manipulating Earth energies, certainly knew about it, and after capturing it, turned the island into an elaborate underground headquarters for their invasion of Britain. The ruins can be seen to this day and, according to Spirit, the energies their urgently needed to be transmuted. Gale force winds developed during my 24-hour stay, and overnight the usual thunderstorm apparently did more than just clear the air when we spoke to Spirit about it later!

TIME SHIFT, 26th. July, 1992

In order to bring the work of the Cross up to date, and in the middle of writing this book in France, I returned to England to celebrate what was known as the 'Time shift' on July 26th, 1992. Wholistic World Vision was involved in the promotion of two festivals, one at Eastbourne and the other at Stratford-on-Avon. I attended both, and at dawn that day joined over 125 people gathered in the ancient stone circle known as the Rollrights in Oxfordshire. We linked with many hundreds of thousands of people throughout the world who were also celebrating this historic moment.

I mentioned earlier that the highly-advanced Mayan civilisation in Mexico left a detailed calendrical system highlighting the key dates in the countdown to the year 2013. This date is also Teilhard de Chardin's 'Omega point' and the moment known as the end of 3rd. dimensional time.

Five years after Harmonic Convergence, the Time shift has been described as the most potent cosmic gateway yet experienced by man. Its chief purpose was the restoration of the natural Earth time of 13 Lunar (feminine cycle) 28-day equal-length months over the Julian/Gregorian Patriarchial distortion of 12 Solar (male) unequal length months. The 12:60 (month/minute) ratio distortion created the 3rd. dimensional time warp of our materialist civilisation, in which, according to current thinking, 'time is money'. This is a flawed linear pathway to certain extinction, which all but human ostriches can clearly see.

According to Jose Arguelles, 'Universal peace and higher dimensional timelessness is based on Earth's natural galactic operating cycle of 13:20 or 13 months and 20 solar tribes living in harmony.' Another way of looking at it is that now is the time to reverse the clockwise spiral of life from gravity to levity and start the return journey to the source from which we came *(more details in Chapter 16)*.

At dawn on 26th July, 1992, people around the world projected thought into the planet by selecting a rock and then circling clockwise around it while bidding farewell to the decaying 3rd. dimensional time structure. Then came the moment of reversing directions, to signal to the Earth's core via the rock our intention to realign once more to her natural cycle. As our group of 125 reversed the spiral at the Rollright Stones in the presence of the Aquarian Cross and linked mentally with many other groups - especially one in New Zealund at the opposite end of the new planetary spiritual pole - everyone present sensed the change. Spirit confirms that the worldwide human intention that day registered indelibly, and that the next phase of our transition into the 4th. dimension will soon be apparent. Gandhi later confirmed that a phenomenal purification had taken place, somewhat akin to a 'Noah's Flood' in energy terms. That same day he added the following message:

"Thus I rejoice so happily in the most important event of all our lives and mine as well. For we have danced into the new era of human consciousness and from our dimension now access the outer reaches of all knowledge. We touch the very essence of the total Universe in the simple consciousness of each individual mind. And therefore, God has seen fit to rebirth the whole human race and to perceive on this wondrous day a vision which all of you share and which we now have a duty to prosper in every heart. Every single being regardless of what he has done in his life now has the opportunity of being "the true droplet of God". In Christian terms, all are sinless. In my country, all are without karma. The last energy barrier was surmounted by the pure love of the many who rejoiced and celebrated in the global interaction of the world population."

We are talking here of a great opportunity being given to all mankind to attune to the heightened frequencies released onto the planet that day. Through the dedication of the few, *all* are offered a fresh start.

What we do with it is up to us!

MALTA, October 1991

Malta is an ancient Mediterranean crossroads with a history stretching back long before the earliest radio-carbon dating of the neolithic and Copper ages (4,500BCE). Spirit sources indicate that this was one of the early settlements of the Priests of the Law of One escaping the collapse of Atlantis, some 10,000 years ago. The original inspiration for temples dedicated to the divine Mother came from that era, and exaggeratedly female statues can still be seen in many of them on Malta and neighbouring Gozo. Primitive, neolithic peoples would not have had the knowledge and skill necessary to build such carefully-aligned sites. The feminine deity appears to have predominated at that time with the island of Gozo known to have been dedicated to the goddess Calypso; indeed, it is likely that the local traditions over the ages were of a feminine and Earth-related orientation. However, the balance was drastically reversed by the arrival of the apostle Paul, who was shipwrecked there on his way from Palestine to his trial in Rome in 60 CE.

As the originator of the distortion on which the Roman church based its teaching, and by landing on Malta before arriving in Rome, he seeded that energy there first. The islanders are to this day imprisoned by his sinister legacy. From my own perspective, Malta and Rome are joint bastions of the tradition inspired by Paul, and therefore, energy work carried out in one automatically affects the other.

Saul of Tarsus, ruthless persecutor of the followers of Jesus, who as the 'converted' Paul could later claim convenient Roman citizenship through his wealthy family, was the source of the Roman distortion of

Jesus' original teachings known as 'the Way'. Spirit guidance on the subject is as follows:

> "Paul was not of his (Jesus') exalted status, and was sent to corrupt the very essence of his life. He rejected the Goddess (feminine polarity), made of the Church (structure) the vehicle of the spirit and taught the supremacy of Faith over the Law (universal Law known as 'the Word').

He played a key role in creating the illusion of separation that the human group-soul had chosen to experience, and provided the opportunity for much of humanity 'to know the darkness in order to see the Light.'

"Jesus of Nazareth was verily a true prophet and an great man, but Lo! his followers all went insane one day and made a god of him."

The Prophet Mohammed

Paul evidently represented the rational materialistic, masculine left-brain hemisphere, while John and Peter respectively embodied the more intuitive, feminine right hemisphere, linked to the heart. John understood the vision of the Christ consciousness, while Peter, a passionate man of the heart, was chosen to ground it through practical demonstrations of healing and preaching. Paul tended to focus on the external, separative projection of faith onto Jesus Christ, who is seen as consubstantial with God. This approach was bound to have more general appeal among the less evolved, working through logic and reason, rather than the inwardly-directed, heart-oriented teachings of Jesus based on the Universal Law. The strict interpretation of that Law was zealously guarded by James the Righteous (Jesus' brother), Peter, John and the inner group forming the first "church" at Jerusalem, before the destruction of the Temple in 68CE. Now is the time for mankind to reappraise those original, but then seemingly unworldly, teachings.

Since the role of Paul is so crucial in illustrating the origins of what later became Christianity, it is worth quoting some of the research on the subject contained in *The Dead Sea Scrolls Deception*. Paul the apostle who significantly never met Jesus, spent three years in Qmran and not Damascus as a postulant, immediately after his sudden conversion. This was the city of the Essenes, who strictly upheld the Law -in contrast to the corrupt Sadducee and Pharisee priesthood in Jerusalem, who compromised with the Roman administration. While there, Paul had access to a wealth of ancient texts, some of which form the collection of now celebrated Dead Sea scrolls. Although Jesus was a Nazarene rather than an Essene, it would appear that the latter sect was the repository for much of the material from which his original teachings derived. One of the scriptural texts to which Paul attached much significance defied contemporary Judaic teaching and was known as the (apocryphal) Book of Habakkuk. Among the scrolls was found the Habakkuk Commentary, which describes similar events to those in the Acts of the Apostles regarding the conflict of three characters known as "the teacher of righteousness on one side, and the liar and the wicked priest on the other" - or, to give them their true identity, James the righteous, Paul the liar and the High Priest Ananias. The charge against the liar is that "he flouted the Law in the midst of their whole congregation", "led many astray" and "raised a congregation on deceipt". Paul is accused of these same failings in Acts, which even states that an attempt was made on his life as a result of his distorted teaching.

The liar opposes the teacher "from within", and this indeed is what occurred as Paul contradicted the teachings of the early Jerusalem church led by James: he refused to acknowledge that community's authority, although it came first hand from Jesus himself. Having spread the distortion through the churches of Asia Minor, Paul was saved from assassination in Jerusalem by the authorities only by virtue of the Roman citizenship he enjoyed through his parents.

So, when James was martyred and the Jerusalem community broken up during the Roman suppression of the Judaean revolt, Paul was sent for trial to Rome, as was his right. He then continued his mission there until he was eventually put to death.

The Habakkuk text is in fact a commentary on the original 7th. century BCE Old Testament Book of Habakkuk, and it would appear that it was from a deliberate misinterpretation of this work that Paul developed his theology and felt authorised to champion the supremacy of faith over James' determination to extol the Law. The reference on which his teaching was based comes from Chapter 2, verse 4: "The upright man will live by his faithfulness." The commentary, however, expands on the same theme: "But the righteous shall live by his faith. Interpreted, this concerns all those *who observe the Law in the House of Judah*, whom God will deliver from the House of Judgement because of their suffering and because of their faith in the Teacher of

Righteousness". This appears to be the actual point of schism, because Paul chooses to ignore the paramount obligation to observe the Law *before* deliverance is attained by suffering and faith.

Paul, through his widescale preaching and correspondence, fired by the passion of the zealous convert, and teaching much truth was more than any other responsible for ensuring that 'Christians' would not forget his version of the personified God in the guise of Jesus Christ. As mankind has chosen to learn through pain and separation, Paul was an appropriate teacher and amply fulfilled his role. However, what we are concerned with now is to transmute the legacy of the negative and disempowering aspects of his indoctrination, which no longer serve evolving humanity or, needless to say, the feminine principle. And it is this which prompted the work of the Cross on the Maltese islands.

During the summer of 1991, WWV had channelled Spirit guidance to a Maltese group working with Earth energies, in preparation for an autumn ritual. As the time approached, it became obvious that the group wasn't attuned to this particular work and so with many misgivings, I had to decide a few days before the non-refundable departure whether to admit defeat or go anyway and just trust.

From the moment I decided to go, synchronicity simply took over. A French Catholic woman, apparently with past-life connections with me in Malta, appeared via an American group that visited me in UK just before my departure. The group donated money for her fare and expenses, and a spare seat suddenly materialised on our overbooked plane. Christiane, who had never flown before and nearly missed the flight, even managed to sit with me - when the person allocated next to me moved away as she approached! During the flight, we read in the airline's house magazine that the 5th. annual Vatican-inspired Inter-Faith gathering with some 300 religious leaders as delegates from 60 countries was currently convened in Malta. It was enough to make our hair stand on end especially when the in-flight cabin music serenaded us with *Ave Maria* as we taxied to the terminal!

As I knew my way around from previous visits to Malta, and feeling we should be based on the highest point of the island, we hired a car and just allowed ourselves to be led. In Rabat, the car stopped in a square dominated by a magnificent church facade and an inn. Knocking on the inn door, we found it was for sale, but the owner, who turned out to have Rosicrucian knowledge and information on energy lines and power points on the island, was happy to put us up. Later, he told us that for some strange reason he seemed to be attracting only spiritually aspiring guests to the hotel while waiting to sell. The monastery next door was apparently celebrated for its grotto, where numerous apparitions of the Madonna had been witnessed. The inn had been part of the monastery and was directly connected to it by a ley line that passed through the rooms we were given.

The next day we took the Cross to the famous St. Paul's cave under a church along the same ridge in Rabat and started the process of attunement around the Cross. After an hour or so, we were saturated in a heavy emotional energy and decided to clear ourselves by bathing in the sea at St. Paul's bay, where the apostle was supposedly shipwrecked. Much refreshed, we then met the only other guests at the inn, a Swiss couple who had at short notice decided to visit Malta. Suzanne confided me that she had reached the stage in her life when she was actively seeking an inner experience, and I thought no more of it till later. The next day, Christiane and I decided, at the owner's suggestion, to visit the neighbouring grotto. We wandered around the church, saw the grotto from the grating in the floor above and tried to tune in for a few moments. We then sprinkled a little Chalice Well water into it and, as there was nobody to let us in, left the church. Suddenly things started to happen rather quickly:

As we stood in the square wondering what to do next, the Swiss couple came towards us - just as a priest followed us from the church. Moments later, he had gathered us together with a couple of other tourists, opened the grotto and ushered us all downstairs! After some five minutes, the party began to leave and I suddenly realised what was developing before my eyes. The trio of one male and two females was about to manifest around the Cross on the site of the Madonna apparitions - in the month of October, when she is particularly venerated and the rosaries are traditionally said. It became clear that the divine Feminine Principle represented in only limited form within the Christian tradition by the Mother Mary was about to be released, after two millennia of patriarchal imprisonment.

Slowly, Christiane and I carried the Cross to the altar in front of the statue of Mary and stood waiting, while Suzanne still wandered around the grotto inspecting the decorations. After a while, we both turned to face her and, smiling, she accepted our invitation and came forward to join us. As we joined hands, a force was directed through us that left us tingling, flushed and short of breath. Then followed a warm and loving sensation in our hearts. At that moment, the choir started to sing the midday mass in the church above.... Still glowing, the three of us quietly withdrew and joined the service. Discreetly looking over my shoulder some minutes later, I caught the eye of the priest as he locked the door to the grotto with a knowing smile.

After this exhilarating event, Christiane and I went straight to the main goddess temple at Hagar Qim to integrate the energies we were carrying, so long suppressed on Malta. On arrival, she immediately found a trinket on the ground depicting the Madonna on one side and the Maltese Cross on the other. A further sign, which moved us both deeply, and reconfirmed our activities.

The day of this ritual, October 10th, 1991, was also the final day of the Inter-Faith conference, when the 300 leaders were to sign a peace accord in the main square of Valetta. We joined in, wishing to share the exquisite energies we had just experienced with the delegates soon to disperse across the planet.

There was a shock in store for us both, which quickly brought us back to reality: the robed and mitred priests were praying for peace in separate denominational groups! So much for church initiatives in that direction - and what a shocking waste of a prime opporturlity to demonstrate true spirituality to the world at large. The delegates did, however, manage to occupy the same stage for a while, and signed a book of intention in front of a huge crowd holding candles. We held the Aquarian Cross high at the back of the square, and Spirit later confirmed that seeds of Christ consciousness were indeed scattered by these unwitting delegates, as they travelled home to 60 countries. The rest of our visit was spent attempting to release Christiane from the awful legacy of pain and self-denial imposed on her by the conditioning of the Roman church during her convent education. Our thinking was that if just one person could be healed on the island, then a powerful thought-form projected from it could perhaps release many others similarly afflicted. She was finally convinced when witnessing the ultimate degradation of pilgrims crawling backwards on their knees, kissing the ground of a famous Madonna shrine in Gozo. Enough is enough, even for a former convent girl!

Next day, we read in the local papers that the 'bejewelled jawbone' of St. Anthony of Padua had been stolen. It is apparently the second 'holiest' relic of the Roman church, and Spirit later indicated to WWV that soon all such artefacts would disappear, as mankind awakes and no longer needs such gruesome props.

That week, Italy was deluged by storms and even St Mark's square in Venice was unseasonally flooded. Next, the Pope attacked Protestant fundamentalists as being a threat to his church, then excommunicated a senior German bishop for his unorthodox views on the Virgin birth and abortion. It is quite extraordinary how often everything we need to know is drawn to our attention. If we trusted this process, we would be spared so much distracting and useless information!

In Gozo, we were treated to a three-hour storm of such ferocity that we had no option but to stay up all night in what seemed like daylight caused by continous sheet lightning and terrifying thunder that remained overhead for much longer than normal. It certainly felt as if Calypso was celebrating the end of her long banishment!

The net is inexorably closing in on the Roman church, as Earth healers start the process of re-aligning the energy grid in and around Rome itself. Another stage of this work following our own in Malta was initiated through higher guidance on well-known landmarks there at Easter 1992, and some obvious results are already manifesting in the current political turmoil of that country.

I was involved in the next phase of this work over Easter 1993, when a ceremony was performed linking Qumran on the Dead sea and Avebury in England. This will apparently among much else serve directly to identify the Vatican as the source of both Italian and International political and financial corruption and hasten its long predicted demise.

According to Spirit, the Protestant faith can still be transformed by permitting women to fulfil appropriate spiritual roles, though this will of course, depend paradoxically on extricating Christ consciousness from within Christianity. Though the spectacle of women stridently opposing their own kind and even leading die-hard male priests to Rome, is hardly encouraging!

The fate of the Roman church, on the other hand, as a result of the unmasking of the Vatican in the book *In God's Name*, appears to be sealed. Its main allegations, so far not disproved, include the poisoning of the last Pope, John Paul I on his 33rd day in office. He was a rare holy man of spirit, who died an agonising death still clutching the list of 90 corrupt Cardinals he intended to replace the very next day. Then there are the scandals of Mafia and Masonic control of the huge Vatican financial empire, and political alliances with both Mussolini and Hitler, which included protection and escape arrangements for war criminals often dressed as priests, known as the 'rat line'. Much detailed information about this was revealed in a BBC TV documentary in late 1991. The Vatican has a monumental task to re-establish credibility if it is ever to be taken seriously again. Many ancient and so far uncannily accurate predictions on the papacy are not exactly auspicious!

John Paul II, who rigidly adheres to the indefensible Roman catholic policy of planetary overpopulation (even animals know better!), was fully acquainted with the truth of the real nature of the Vatican at his election. Consummate politician that he is, he agreed, as a rank outsider in the contest, to maintain the status quo in return for sufficient votes to elect him Pope - and the guarantee of financial backing to overthrow communism in Poland. This was an entirely political strategem, using highly dubious funds, designed to trigger a mass emotional response towards the church as a 'saviour' from the evils of that regime. As we all know, this ploy contributed to subsequent events - but never let it be claimed that it was spiritually motivated! American CIA funds and Mafia drug money undermined Polish communism at a secular level and it was left to others to invoke divine assistance. Their dedication transformed more than just Poland with an energy that is incomparably more potent than cynical financial manipulation. The present Pope is a patriotic Pole, no more and no less. He chose to use his elevated status to engineer a classic temporal revolution. As the truth emerges, it will become clear that these machinations of the Roman church nullified its final pretence to spiritual authority, in yet another vivid demonstration of its terror of communism: a terror that has attracted to it the strangest bed-fellows during contemporary history, from the Nazi era to the present day.

What clearly emerges, amid all this confusion, is that neither the Protestant nor Roman church retains any spiritual mandate in these latter days. It is inconceivable, even laughable, that they could now be vehicles for the Second Coming consciousness, as they are in fact the very last place to seek the truth of what is now occurring. It was no different during Jesus' mission, when the orthodox priests of his time became not only his greatest detractors, but also his ultimate executioners. Any power they still command is temporal and results from political and economic manipulation. They also retain the ability to exploit emotionally the remnants of the once pure devotional impulse of the Piscean era, reinforced by their trump cards, guilt, self-denial and the fear of death. Over four million readers of *In God's Name*, with its meticulously researched and unrefuted evidence, have been left in no doubt about these infamies.

> "And Jesus went into the Temple of God and cast out all them that sold and bought in the Temple and overthrew the tables of the moneychangers and the seats of them that sold doves, and said unto them, 'It is written, my house shall be called the house of prayer; but ye have made it a den of thieves.'"
>
> *Matthew 21: 12/13*

It looks as though the still unlearned lessons from the First Coming are about to be faced in earnest. The last 'foreign' (non-Italian) Pope, a scrupulously honest priest called Adrian IVth., significantly wrote to his German Delegate as long ago as 1522: "You are also to say that we frankly acknowledge that . . . for many years things deserving of abhorrence have gathered around the Holy See. Sacred things have been misused, ordinances transgressed, so that in everything there has been a change to the worse. Thus it is not surprising that the malady has crept down from the Head to the members, from the Popes to the hierarchy. We all, prelates and clergy, have gone astray from the right way. Therefore in our name give promises that we shall use all diligence to reform before all things, what is perhaps the source of all evil, the Roman Curia." This brave man - yes, you guessed it - met the same fate as John Paul I within months of making that astonishing statement of truth. Just under one billion humans currently pay allegiance to the Roman church, and there will be much confusion during the rest of this decade as it is devoured by the inevitable consequences of its own doings. Whatever happens, critical soul-lessons will be learned by all those involved in the closing drama, regardless of the pain involved. It is to be remembered that we were granted free choice, and those now opening to spiritual awareness yet still within that church or indeed any religion, might do well to carry out impartial investigations of their own, before the last chapter unfolds.

The final phase of energy alignment work on Malta was successfully completed by nine members of WWV under spirit guidance at the

3rd. conjunction of Uranus/Neptune on October 24/25th 1993 in the ancient Goddess temples at Skorba and Mnajdra. Underwater circular formations were seen in the seaweed around the island at this time![1]

USA, HAWAIIAN ISLANDS, NEW ZEALAND AND AUSTRALIA,
December 1991 to April 1992 and December 1992

The above-named places completed the first world tour of the Aquarian Cross. All continents have now been touched by the energy of the 'Christ returned' that it so powerfully focuses and in the years to come that presence will be manifested in every country where the universal principles of love and sharing are invoked. At the same time, the Third Book of the Apocalypse has also been widely distributed and is on the WWV url and Compuserve Religion Forum. Tens of thousands of people have now heard the story of the Cross through TV, Radio, public talks and press articles and, with the publication of this book, the initial phase of Wholistic World Vision's work is complete.

My reasons for travelling to the Antipodes via the Pacific were first to complete the world circuit of the Cross, and briefly to interact with the energies of the American mainland. The initial point of impact was Houston, Texas and it was with more than passing interest that I saw a newspaper article reporting severe flooding around that city just afterwards! Similarly, on our return to the UK, there was a brief stop in Los Angeles just before the serious riots in spring 1992. The Hawaiian islands were my first US goal and the Cross coincided with the visit of the President to mark the 50th. anniversary of the Japanese attack on Pearl Harbour. I had not realised that the incident is widely held to have been 'permitted' by Roosevelt and Churchill to encourage the tribe of Manasseh (USA) to come to the assistance of its brother Ephraim (UK), threatened by the Nazi war machine. During recent questioning, Churchill freely admitted that, "If you are to crush the aggressor you do it with force; so a comparatively few lives lost in a great cause are sometimes necessary - if you are to save millions and give them ultimate peace and freedom." What a tangled web we weave, once we resort to violence as a solution.

My hosts in Hawaii were the Spiritual World Network group founded by an inspiring lifelong media communicator called Triaka-

---

[1] See page 129

Don Smith. SWN and WWV had been in contact for some time and, with such similar objectives, a personal meeting seemed long overdue. SWN have already been broadcasting on radio and TV out of Hawaii for a number of years. They work with the cost-free media training, equipment and air-time scheme available in the USA called 'community access'. WWV had plenty to learn from them. Don and his small, dedicated team have a past-life connection with the settlement of Manasseh into their 'promised land' through the Quaker movement - the process of integration had, incidentally, probably started as early as the 8th century with the arrival on American shores of St Brendan from Ireland. This time round, Don has nation-wide media contacts interested in spiritual development and plans to be instrumental in facilitating the progress of the Cross through the USA in the coming years.

As can be seen on the Earth chakra map, Hawaii is one of the four most powerful planetary energy centres. It is the 'spinner wheel' representing the element of fire, through the 'seat' of the fire goddess Pele, in Haleakala crater, Maui. As the energies released at the Silbury ritual are approaching America from the West, Hawaii currently operates as a transformer, feeding energy and information into California for dissemination further east.

The karmic account Manasseh, as co-holder of the line of divine promise, has to settle for betraying the Christ by developing and then using nuclear power as a weapon of war, is formidable. At that moment, Spirit has intimated, all evolving consciousness, known as God, was threatened with extinction. The atom is the prime component of the physical Universe, and was designed to be contained in one piece or 'wholeness' - not to be split for use in destructive or other negative enterprises. A full-scale nuclear cataclysm, we are told, could implode all dimensions and collapse all levels of existence associated with the planet. We have tasted the forbidden fruit, and although Spirit promises intervention at times of dire necessity, it is as well to know the full horrific potential of what we in our ignorance could unleash on the Universe. Splitting the atom is mankind's ultimate demonstration of separation from the divine, and now we see all too clearly where this path could lead us. The literal translation of the word Manasseh in Hebrew is 'causing to forget'. Will Americans now remember the sacred trust bestowed so long ago on their tribe, and lead us back from the brink of nuclear cataclysm?

The most urgent task is to realign the badly distorted Earth energy grid and this will be accomplished by working closely with the indigenous native peoples. That work is well under way in the USA and will be intensified from 1993 onwards with dramatic, but ultimately healing results. Meantime, Japan resorts to the economic weapon against America as part of the process of settling old scores. Even more disturbing are the insidious Japanese video computer games that have recently flooded the American market and addicted that country's youth. More optimistically, Vice-President Al Gore has just published an excellent book, Earth in the Balance, in which he propounds the vision of sharing and caring outlined in the President's inaugural speech. Selfishness and social irresponsibility have long been the hallmark of a people conditioned to believe that financial security is the only freedom worth having. As the deprived and enslaved masses become increasingly restive, 'Share, or suffer the consequences' becomes the new order of the day in the US of A - and throughout the world.

An opportunity was unexpectedly presented in November/December 1992, over the Thanksgiving period, for the Aquarian Cross to be properly integrated for the first time into the American energy grid. As it approached the first landfall at Denver, yes, a storm blew up over the whole of central America, with tornadoes in the south and such heavy snow in the north that the flight was diverted to Los Angeles overnight. Interesting that this 'City of the Angels' should be the first fully to experience the energy of the Cross!

Subsequent attunements were performed at Boulder and Mesa Verde, Colorado, at Anasazi Indian sacred sites and on the 'Four Corners' power centre. We ended with a dedication at Red Rocks near Denver on the day of my departure, which coincided with the spectacular full-moon eclipse of December 9th, 1992.

The next phase of WWV's work had clearly started, and it seemed auspicious that I underwent an unexpected initiation from an Apache Indian during that first visit.

One of the ancient Hopi Indian legends speaks of the 'Red and the White brothers': the White brother went away, but the Red one always knew he would return; when he returned with a Cross, it would mean the time was not right and much trouble would result (Christianity and the crucifix). But when he returned with the Cross and the Circle, then both brothers would resume their journey together in harmony.

114

A friend of mine from Glastonbury called Ahuva was staying on the island of Maui in Hawaii and before I left for New Zealand, I suggested she might get some people together for a ceremony with the Cross inside the crater of Haleakala. Four of us, two males and two females, drove up the mountain on the morning of December 12th, 1991. Spirit had advised us the previous day that, above all, the deity Pele wished humanity to demonstrate 'harmony and balance'. It so happened that I was being accommodated on the slopes of the crater itself in a six-sided meditation cabin with a Star of David on the floor, beautifully inlaid with different woods. The symbol of perfect balance!

I sensed that midday would be a suitable moment to raise the Cross, but as we were a little behind schedule, I glanced at my watch and just knew the precise moment was to be 12 seconds past 12 minutes past 12 midday on the 12th day of the 12th month! So it was that the Aquarian Cross was in that location at that exact time, and the four of us then grounded the balanced energy requested by Pele in a deep meditation. Archetypal Polynesian symbols soon appeared in the form of two white horses, an owl and an eagle, to show that our intentions had registered. It was not, however, till I got to New Zealand the next day (Friday 13th, US time and Saturday 14th, NZ time) that I learned of the possible outcome.

NEW ZEALAND

December 14th, 1991, was a day of destiny for 'the Land of the long white cloud'. An ancient Maori legend of the South Island states that when Mt Cook (Aorangi), the tallest mountain in New Zealand at 12,349 ft, loses the snow on its summit, then "the times of the great changes have arrived". In the early hours of that day a massive avalanche lowered the peak by 20 meters - with no earth tremors or storms recorded to trigger it! The 55 million cubic metres of debris travelled 7.3 kilometres, leaving a scar two and a half times the height of the Eiffel tower with a dust-cloud that rose 700 metres and an air blast that was felt 5 kilometres away. This major geological event was widely reported by the international media. No official theory has yet emerged as to its cause.

Those familiar with the ancient legends of the Polynesian cultural hero god, Maui, will know that this planetary power centre in Hawaii is closely linked with the spinner wheel representing the element of water at Lake Taupo in the north island of New Zealand. As Robert Coon wrote in August 1991, "Maui gives fire to the Earth. He activates the original Grail net archetype by raising up the Earth from the sea. The wand and the cup unite alchemically. The sacred mysteries of Love and Will, of Water and Fire are illuminated by Earth healing activities, uniting these two global Spinner Wheels." The spirit of Maui, according to Maori legend, returns in these 'last days' to complete the great work of lifting the Grail net to reveal the planetary New Jerusalem - and who would now deny that that phase has well and truly started?

This was my first visit to New Zealand and I was excited about exploring its beautiful scenery, despite having only one contact there.

Now that I have a more complete picture of what I became involved in, it all makes more sense. 1991 was the year that the new spiritual pole was established on the planet between UK and NZ; the two countries are exact geographical opposites. This alignment also moves at the end of each Age and matches the westward movement of the Aeon shift already described.. Various independent groups had worked on anchoring that energy and some were inspired by the American visionary, Joseph Jochmans, who had identified a site on the North Island called Raurimu. Tradition has it that, as part of his mission after the resurrection, Jesus visited the planet's 156 main power centres in his Ascension body. Some call him by the name of Apollonius of Tyana, but in New Zealand he was known as the Maori Christ 'Wakea - the God who walked on Water'. It is understood that he designated Glastonbury and Raurimu as the exact polar opposites to form the new spiritual pole of the planet at the time of 'Second Coming'.

The solar eclipse of January 15th, 1991 was chosen as the moment to plant a large crystal to seal the energy link. Other crystal 'workings' were undertaken that year by unconnected groups, so it can be seen that a potent-thought form was at work. It would appear that the ritual with the Aquarian Cross in Maui, at what I later discovered was the most powerful moment in the Polynesian calendar, put the finishing touches to this collective initiative. My investigations also showed that during the 1980s, energy centres in NZ and the UK had experienced simultaneous power surges. 1984 saw the opening of the global heart at Glastonbury, while in NZ four important stolen sacred Maori artefacts were returned to their tribal sites, through the intervention of the spirits of three Maori wise-women communicating through an aboriginal medium! That year, a labour Government introduced a non-nuclear policy, reflecting a large shift in the general consciousness in those regions, and there was a hugely successful Maori art exhibition in the U.S.A.

On December 12, 1989, soon after we activated the Aquarian triangle in the UK, a group of Maori, led by the visionary Reg Wharekura, saw in the night sky symbolic visions of the Polynesian equivalent of Christ consciousness - expressed as the Tree of Life, Pegasus, the fish, the owl the eagle, etc. A series of visions are to occur every three years on December 12th till the turn of the century, and we await the next with interest.

As soon as Reg heard of the coming of the Cross to NZ, he was anxious to see it, and a meeting took place at which whites (Pakeha) and Maori exchanged the traditional nose-to-nose greeting (hongi), and made a profound inner connection. It felt to me as if every Maori spirit ever incarnated was crammed into the Tauhara Centre hall at Lake Taupo to witness this moving event as, in turn around the circle, we all spoke our truth and expressed our own visions of humanity's future. Reg channels an energy he calls "The Lady" and was led to the Maori heart chakra of New Zealand at Te Miringa Kakara (Fragrance of Heaven) in the centre of the North Island, not far from Raurimu. It is here that the visions appear and I and two New Zealand women, whom I first met on a midnight swim in a thermal hot river on Christmas night, raised the Cross on Boxing night in the centre of a huge equal-sided cross marked out long ago on the site.

That ritual coincided exactly with the second, though smaller, avalanche on Mt Cook recorded at that time.

On my return journey in March 1992, I toured the spectacular South Island with a friend and gave a few talks en route. At Milford Sound, dolphins escorted our boat, riding in the bow waves for over two hours to everyone's great delight. These highly evolved beings, together with the whales, embody an 'unfallen' state of Christ consciousness that has been holding the energy of pure, unconditional love for aeons on the planet - and will continue to do so until we evolve to the same state, and relieve them of that function. When we see the beauty of the dolphins' healing work with manic depressives and the mentally handicapped, also their beneficial effect on the human water-birth process, and frequent rescue of humans from shark attacks - to mention but a few of their skills - there can be no doubt of their exalted status. Isn't it time we started to honour all cetaceans as a superior consciousness with whom it is a privilege to share our world, instead of slaughtering them in polluted seas?

When we took the Cross to Mt Cook, temperatures reached an unseasonable 35°C and the most incredible lenticular cloud formations manifested in all kinds of recognisable shapes: huge spacecraft, birds and fish, etc. Next day, after a sharp drop in temperature, it actually snowed across the southern mountain ranges! On my way back north to Auckland, I had arranged to hold a day of celebrations at the Tauhara Centre in preparation for the world consciousness linkup over Time Shift on 26/7/92, described earlier.

Throughout the tour, days were set aside for spontaneous gatherings and much enjoyed by the few who didn't feel too threatened to sing and dance together. It is amazing to me how an advertised talk on the topics in this book will draw hundreds to feed their intellect or imagination - yet no more than twenty or thirty dare risk opening their hearts and feeling the Christ consciousness by singing and dancing with 'strangers'!

The Tauhara centre is the result of the vision of Hermetic adepts (alchemists), who came from the UK some 50 years ago with a vision that this place would some day become one of the great spiritual universities of the world. I spent a memorable Christmas there with a like-minded group. How ironic it is that Jesus came to demonstrate our release from the realm of matter, and yet we celebrate his birth in an orgy of materialism encouraged by the church - rather than manifest the Christ consciousness he exemplified by sharing with those in desperate need for just one day each year in his honour!

It was an introduction to Vernon, one of the Tauhara administrators, that opened up the entire network of hospitable connections throughout New Zealand and made it such a productive visit. He, Vivien and a small group of trustees are in the process of establishing a sanctuary called Zuvuya on land adjacent to Tauhara. Here, on an ancient tribal site, Maori and Pakeha can start the process of healing old racial conflicts and celebrating the new energy that is enveloping the planet. The spiritual role for New Zealand, with its population of only three million, is to be a testing ground of 4th dimensional living, so it is essential that there and in Australia a bridge be built between the white and indigenous populations. Native peoples are generally closer to the Earth than we are, and hold master keys to the subtle energies on which human survival ultimately depends. Spirit concurs that there is no more vital initiative in both these countries than co-operation and mutual respect between different ethnic groups, and that this is the very foundation on which 4th dimensional existence will be built. A group of thirty led by Reg, whose own tribe appropriately stems from this region, dedicated this land with the Cross, Chalice Well water and a large crystal as part of the radiant light and later Time shift celebrations. It is a most inspirational place and, together with Glastonbell in Australia, provides a firm anchor point for the Christ consciousness in the southern hemisphere.

New Zealand was also the first country to start producing the Aquarian Cross symbol in the form of pendants and in a larger format for personal and Earth healing work. On my last night, as on my first dawn in New Zealand, I meditated with a small group on Auckland's main power site, an extinct crater called One Tree Hill. As we sat there again in the familiar one male, two female configuration, the bright full moon above us developed a glowing nimbus throughout our half hour thanksgiving to the Spirit of that land. It faded slowly as we left and a gentle, cleansing rain fell for the remainder of the night. How unfailingly Nature responds when we work from the heart, and with respect for the One.

AUSTRALIA

A major theme on this tour was, 'To bond the fragmented energies of the new consciousness movement in joyous celebration.' The movement needs to express more heart-felt joy, if it is to fulfil it's task of transforming human consciousness, because it won't through intellect alone! Consequently, Radiant Light gatherings, as I called them, and talks were held at Glastonbell, Sydney, Perth, Melbourne and Brisbane. In this way, the Time Shift linking network planned for July 26th was also being spread across the planet.

At the end of the Australian tour in Brisbane, the Cross was taken by request to the bedside of a woman in the last stages of cancer. Despite her frailty, she sat up in bed and channelled some potent American Indian wisdom, as the energy in the room dramatically intensified. I was later told that soon afterwards she was able to return home and enjoy a period of remission.

So ended a four-month tour involving over 30 public talks, radio and TV interviews and press articles. It seemed fitting that three new friends made along the way should now join me back in England to celebrate the second Aeon shift anniversary on Glastonbury Tor. Elizabeth from Hawaii, Glenn from New Zealand and Charmian - whom I met at Glastonbell in Australia - and I took part. The energies there seemed to have settled after the impact of the original event in 1990. Inevitably, in a world of duality, great darkness always counter-balances Light, and Glastonbury was no exception.

FRANCE; 1991/92

My associations with France go right back to my early youth, but my first inner connection with the country occurred in 1988, when I visited the Cathar region in the south west. On that occasion, we drove via the impressive standing stones at Carnac in Brittany and used the great Gothic cathedrals, such as Chartres, Bourges, Poitiers and Nar-bonne as the traditional 'stepping-stones' to our pilgrimage. On that occasion I stayed with friends who were restoring an ancient fortress in an unspoiled region of the Gard, west of Avignon. I had been drawn to the site from the first moment I saw it: not only was it dra-matically beautiful, perched on a hilltop surrounded by an old village, but I also sensed strong Earth energies flowing through the region.

Along the ridge on which the village is situated are huge clusters of weirdly-shaped boulders and within view of the castle is a favourite chapel of mine, where I have received much inspiration. With its square tower, but otherwise ruined and roofless, it has a long history and is, according to Spirit, Templar in origin. These Christian mys-tics, original guardians of the Grail, were well aware of Earth energies and used them in their rituals. They established a network of such chapels across southern France, along their pilgrim routes.

We received much information from Spirit just before this book was started, and from a very special source came the following:

> "I never preached in churches, proclaiming that the church was the open air and that all men could be part of it. Wherever they gathered there was a great temple, and there the Light of the Father would be in all hearts. Therefore, as you charge people to come to the open spaces, let them know that the energy of God and the purity of his Love and Light come upon them. The church is an enigma and was never to be built. I never pro-claimed such a thing: only man caused my words to be dis-torted."

The Castle stands on ground which was contaminated by bloodshed during the Catholic/Protestant wars of the 16th and 17th centuries in this fiercely non-conformist region of South West France, where the Cathar movement was established and where the Huguenots originated. In 1991, when I first brought the Cross to this place, the castle was framed in the blackest of clouds imaginable. There followed, even by my standards, an exceptional storm. Spirit volunteered that this is one of the major energy centres in France and that the focus of the Cross had caused a considerable cleansing throughout the country. France is under the rational, intellectual Pauline influence, exemplified by Descartes and the Age of Reason. Perhaps for this reason Roman Catholic France, with a former Papal seat at Avignon, has not traditionally related well to the more heart-influenced energy of Britain and America. This could also perhaps explain why the energies focused by the Cross have had such a dramatic effect on the elements in that country!

During a subsequent visit to the castle in the summer of 1991, I discovered some unrestored outbuildings, which struck me as an ideal retreat for a writer, and casually mentioned this to my friends. Also, at a lunch party, I was seated next to a London publisher, who was interested by my subject matter, and encouraged me to start writing. For the meantime I put both these indicators to one side and not planning ahead, I had no idea what the summer of 1992 would bring.

On my return from the southern hemisphere, the decks were somehow cleared and I was offered the accommodation at the castle for as long as I needed it. Synchronicity was clearly at work again and all I had to do now was rent my house, buy a word-processor and drive to France to spend four months in idyllic surroundings. At last having the time to be able to share this story was an exciting prospect and I couldn't wait to get started. A medium had, however, warned me just before leaving UK to remember that "All that glitters is not gold" with regard to my chosen retreat!

The first six weeks of writing in June and July were accompanied by the most disturbed weather in living memory over much of southern France. Rain fell in torrents daily, while freak storms often struck the castle and interrupted the power to my word-processor. If this were not enough, a former employee had refused to accept his dismissal and, with ineffectual French laws unable to dislodge him, he spent his time defying the owner by damaging the property and regularly plunging the household into darkness. Unfortunately, the main fuse box happened to be located in his quarters. The dubious electrical supply certainly made work on the word-processor a hazardous and frustrating business! Sadly, the owner then succumbed to serious ill health with dire prognoses from 'experts'. Happily, he lived another four years and miraculously confounded them all, through sheer determination! Meanwhile, the country itself came to a standstill as lorry drivers blocked the main motorways, disrupting food and fuel supplies. The President announced he had cancer, while his wife narrowly avoided assassination in the Middle East. In September, on my last day, a widely-publicised storm around the powerful Mt.Ventoux nearby caused flash floods, drowning many people and causing much damage. Furthermore at this time too the nation held an indecisive referendum on the Maastricht treaty in the midst of a major European currency crisis.

Obviously, it was a most unsettled period for France; but for my part, the beauty of the house and setting with walks, cycle rides and plenty of swimming, kept me going despite the high dramas and fluctuating moods of everyone around me during the dramatic summer of 1992!

> "You must live your revelations. We expand by finding our limitations and going beyond them. The time is not far distant when humanity will realise that biologically it is faced with a choice between suicide and adoration."
>
> *Teilhard de Chardin*

In 1995/96 France, representing the intellectual, left brain of the masculine northern hemisphere of the planet, bombarded the right brain of the female southern hemisphere with underground nuclear explosions at Muraroa atoll. Apart from provoking the fully justified outrage of the civilised world, at a spiritual level this act graphically illustrates the continuing human struggle between intellect and wisdom. Furthermore, since it is now scientifically proven that nuclear underground explosions directly cause major earthquakes, the French, Chinese and any other 'uncivilised nation' persisting in this demented behaviour will inevitably pay dearly at karmic levels for their unwholesome conduct.

Chapter 8

FURTHER TRAVELS WITH THE CROSS

"Mankind has learned to fly through the air like birds, to swim in the sea like fish. We have still to learn how to walk on the Earth like brothers."   *Martin Luther King*

The first reprint of *Rising Out Of Chaos* in 1996 has provided an opportunity to update the new edition with details of my many exciting journeys and adventures since 1992. My aim in sharing the small part of the plan with which I am associated is to demonstrate how unseen forces, with of course our full co-operation, are shaping the new reality on Earth through an amazing series of synchronicities involving all those genuinely committed to the path of service and love in action.

The important theme running throughout these experiences is that spiritually awake and aware humans **are** the Divinely-appointed agents for raising consciousness on this planet. Friendly aliens, ETs and other 'higher spirit Beings' are doing all they can to encourage us to take personal responsibility. Such beings, both positive and negative, will undoubtedly continue to manifest even more frequently among us, so that ever more humans will themselves witness the true nature of the multidimensional reality in which we live. Contrary, however, to much misguided New Age thinking, **no** external force is going to throw a switch on some distant planet that suddenly transforms us without our individual effort! Neither are we to give away our power to any ETs and external forces, unless we wish to run the risk of being limited and controlled for aeons yet to come.

As I have frequently emphasised, this race now faces a major initiation and, having incarnated here specifically for this purpose, we each have within us **all** we need to fulfil our own mission. Just as with any examination, we don't expect the teacher to sit it for us and so those externally-focused religionists still awaiting the return of a physical Messiah will be as sorely disappointed as many ET-obsessed New Agers.

This is the time to demonstrate that an ever-increasing proportion of the human race is spiritually mature enough to accept its own innate divinity and to take responsibility for their own and the planetary ascension process. Through open hearts and willing hands, the critical mass of true Aquarian world servers - who are spirit- and not ego-motivated - will now lead by example and trigger the dimensional shift by anchoring ever higher frequencies of consciousness onto the planet. In this way we raise our frequency levels above those of negative alien forces and finally rise beyond their sphere of influence over us.

Many of the journeys described in this chapter demonstrate the gradual fulfilment of the Earth power site activation programme described in Chapter 4. This amazing vision represents the 'new circuitry' of the planet which is destined to be connected by heart-centred human electricians from all the spiritual traditions. In this way we create together the subtle structure for the New Jerusalem - 'Earth Ascending'.

My primary purpose in describing these journeys and then pointing out the subsequent synchronistic transformations occurring in those places, is to demonstrate that through the realignment of the subtle energy grids of the planet, the negative, controlling and fear-based forces are literally being starved of energy. It is this that leads to dramatic changes in social and political reality, as has been witnessed in the sudden, profound and otherwise inexplicable changes in Eastern Europe and Russia, South Africa, Ireland, Bosnia, Israel and Palestine, etc. All humans with clear motivations and intentions focused on ' the will to good ' are qualified to do this work and the sooner people awaken to their potential - especially using the invincible tool of global mass mindlinking - the sooner Heaven on Earth will manifest for the benefit of us all.

Now that ever more of us are not only aware of our ability to transform consciousness in the ways described in this book, but are actually manifesting results, we have reached the crucial stage when there is sufficient hard evidence to prove what has until now been only unsubstantiated theory. My work is to help provide practical proof, so that the less aware among us no longer have the easy option of dismissing such activity as New Age fantasy. According to the degree of our inner preparation, we are each now required to finally choose the reality levels

124

with which we resonate - and so, according to ancient prophecy, will 'the wheat be sorted from the chaff'.

IRELAND

Earth energy activation work, Autumn Equinox 1993

The Autumn Equinox was, by the consensus of many, both incarnate and discarnate sources, an appropriate moment to integrate the energy of the Aquarian Cross into Ireland for the first time. We were also told that our contribution would help to strengthen critical - and, at that time, clandestine - peace initiatives. Apparently, if successful, the work would help create the subtle energy structure needed for peace to become a reality within a year.

The impetus for this visit grew organically with minimal planning required. Jo, WWV core-group member, mentioned to me early in 1993 that she had started on her spiritual path when living in Ireland some years before and knew that if ever we were led to work there, she could link us up with a small network of committed light-workers. Although I had long hoped to be able in some way to contribute to the peace process, I had no contacts there and so welcomed this unexpected opening. We quickly got encouraging responses from her friends and on September 23rd the Cross arrived on Irish soil.

The next three days were for me like a homecoming to a land of enchantment I had known long ago. After first visiting the exquisite Book of Kells in Dublin, a work that had profound spiritual influence on medieval Europe, we visited Sheila, an astrologer, dowser and authority on Irish power centres. Her advice was to start our attunements south of Dublin at the Castleruddery stone circle - a teaching circle with a 'talking' stone - and then nearby at the Piper's circle. We had thought our main ceremony on the Sunday would be at Newgrange, but on hearing from Sheila that it has become such a tourist attraction, we decided to concentrate on Tara instead.

Before leaving, she told us two interesting things. First, that the astrological birth chart of Mary Robinson, the Irish President at the time, fits literally hand-in-glove with the one drawn up for Ireland, demonstrating perhaps the appropriateness of her election and by inference

125

the need for the female approach in solving the seemingly intractable problems of the country.

Secondly, she reminded us that the Romans never subjugated Ireland nor imposed on it an artificial linear grid in the way they did across England. "Irish thinking is circle-orientated, while that of the English is linear", she says - a fascinating perception that helps to explain the problems between England and her otherwise Celtic co-inhabitants on these small islands!

Our next call was on Paddy, a talented medium and a gentle, compassionate man of spirit, who held the Cross in reverence and spoke of its heart-opening quality. He also remarked on "the love emanating from the Rock" with reference to the link he perceived with the biblical Simon called Peter. That evening we collected Lucy and Graeme, who came over from London to make up our core group.

We all appreciated the beautiful quality of undisturbed elemental energy next day at the Castleruddery and Piper's circle attunements. Lucy received this guidance: "We will show you. Feel the breeze and watch the sky. Sing your songs and set us free." Dark clouds and heavy, cleansing rainstorms quickly manifested! Later that day we went to fetch another member of our group whom I had never met and who came significantly from a Northern Irish family with Orange traditions. Suzanne had anyway already planned to be at Tara / Newgrange that very weekend with her whole family! She joined us for a talk we gave to a group in Dublin that night about the emerging Christ consciousness, Earth Healing, Reiki and the WWV global communications network. We all enjoyed some powerful meditations around the Cross as we invoked healing and harmony across all Irish divisions.

On Sunday September 26th, eight of us drove to the ancient site of Tara (3500 BCE) - seat of Kings and traditionally the spiritual heart of Ireland. Our focus was on healing the land by attuning to Earth energies. Once the natural energy grid is restored, mass human consciousness is also lifted and is again free to evolve beyond the primitive and divisive conditioning of outdated belief structures. Perhaps Christianity's significant retreat from sacred Tara with the recent deconsecration of St Patrick's church and the removal of his statue from the site is a sign that this separative religion is beginning to release its grip on the many it still imprisons on that enchanted island of magic and pure spirit.

126

At midday our group formed a circle around the Cross on the mound of Hostages in bright sunlight as Tara was somehow cleared of the last straggling tourists. We sprinkled water from the Chalice Well at Glastonbury, lit a candle and burnt a mixture of frankincense and myrrh to prepare the site. We said the Aramaic prayer of Jesus Christ - using the original language and words preserved by the Sufi tradition of Islamic mysticism. This was followed by the invocation of the Omega Point and other affirmations and prayers were contributed by us all. For a while we sat in silent meditation scanning the whole country and projecting light to regions any of us felt particularly needed it. The border absorbed a lot of energy.

The most touching moment occurred when the four participating Irish women - linking at a heart level across the artificial north / south, political religious divisions - spoke words of empowerment in their own language of Gaelic and then sang songs of haunting beauty, while tears of joy flowed freely. We activated the energy through circle dances and then finished by hugging each other in an atmosphere of such transcendant light that we somehow knew our heartfelt dedication and positive intentions had registered most profoundly.

We had been warned by Sheila that an energy line feeding the site was still blocked between the churchyard and the mound we had sat on. The first Christian church had been placed on the line between the original entrance to Tara and the main site. We worked on the blockage before leaving and planted a crystal programmed to keep the flow lines clear. What was once pagan (meaning 'of the Earth') became Christian, as the natural energy sites were harnessed to that religion's motives. Now our Earth mother reclaims her natural energy centres for her own agenda, with aware humans as the willing agents!

On leaving the site, we were met by Suzanne's family from the north, and it felt particularly appropriate that such a symbolic meeting between north and south should take place at Tara on this special day. We then concluded our site visits at the great neolithic initiation longbarrow of Newgrange. This is a perfectly aligned chamber constructed to 'trap the sun' during its low point over the five days of the midwinter solstice. Initiates would be left in the chamber either to succeed in their spiritual initiation or lose their minds. These ancient and extraordinary monuments may later have been used by more primitive peoples as convenient burial chambers, but - with apologies to the charming official guides of Newgrange - this was emphatically **not** the purpose for which they were originally constructed. I managed to sprinkle Chalice Well water inside the chamber which, we were told, no water had penetrated for thousands of years!

As we drove to the airport, the sky was filled with shafts of piercing sunlight. 'Watch the skies' had been our guidance that week-end, and now, with a spectacular send-off, we knew why. Newspaper headlines soon after revealed information about the new Irish internal and Warrington peace initiatives. The latter are supported by both Mary Robinson and Prince Charles, as well as ordinary citizens stunned into a peacemaking role by UK mainland bomb atrocities.

Writing now in mid-1996, we know that a period of genuine peace **did** come into effect in late 1994 - one year after the events described here. Many groups had worked at subtle levels to raise the consciousness to a point where negative male religious and political influence was denied energy. The voices of reason were at last heard above the rantings of bigots. By July 1996, however, the peace process was sadly again under threat with outrageously provocative traditional male marches, obviously calculated to tip the delicate balance into anarchy once more.

As I made clear with reference to Israel, if there is not **first** peace within the hearts of a substantial majority of a population, then peace remains illusory and simply will not manifest in this physical dimension. Where is the next generation of wise-women to follow on from those who briefly held that energy at the start of the recent Irish troubles? As this short account of experiences in Ireland makes clear, it will be through the wisdom of the female coming together in healed feminine energy across artificial, man-made barriers that the situation will finally be resolved.

If ever there was a poignant example of the malign legacy of the fatally flawed Christian belief structure, then this is it. Unless the Universal nature of the original Christ impulse - now termed the Christ consciousness - is not soon manifested in that society, then there will be little hope at the hands of the false priests and rigid male traditionalists to whom so many still needlessly give away their power.

MALTA

Further activation work carried out on Malta and Gozo at the 3rd conjunction of Uranus and Neptune, October 25th, 1993.

My initial contact with the powerful energies of Malta had occurred in October 1991, when I had been guided to bring the Aquarian Cross to the island for the first time. Malta and neighbouring Gozo had for thousands of years been a focal point of Goddess worship and the veneration of the Divine Feminine principle. Even today there are some 30 impressive remains of temples dedicated to the Goddess, and it was to align and reactivate this energy that our group of 9 gathered from all over the world at the time of this powerful and transformational moment.

The Uranus / Neptune conjunction in Capricorn occurs every 171 years and always heralds a period of major spiritual, scientific and social upheaval for humanity. There were three conjunctions during 1993, each gathering in momentum and challenging every one of us to face unresolved personal issues such as fear and denial. It was hardly surprising, therefore, that so many unhealed and insecure relationships succumbed to this immense pressure and disintegrated by the end of the year - even our own WWV core group was not immune.

It was Robyn from Glastonbell in Australia, where the Aeon shift had been anchored in the Southern Hemisphere in 1990, who had first alerted me to the significance of Malta in late October 1993. She had guidance to re-establish the ancient Sisterhood of the Rose there at this time. Originally an order of spiritually-focused women working covertly at the time of the Crusades, it is now to be revived as a balanced male / female light network with initially six centres around the world.

Another synchronicity linking WWV to Malta at this critical time was that the Malta Esoteric Group had invited my partner Robert to conduct a channelling workshop on the island. With hindsight it is obvious that Spirit realms had clearly orchestrated a gathering of specific people for this cosmic event, and despite many testing obstacles, all nine designated participants eventually gathered on the island.

Among others who made up our core group were Loni and Jo from WWV UK, Lucy and Graeme from Australia, and Elizabeth and Kevin (Reiki Masters living on Malta). Fortunately, Robyn had been given a connection via Hong Kong to Kevin and Elizabeth as they are both knowledgeable about the Malta / Gozo energy grid and as subsequent anchors locally for this energy, their hospitality and enthusiasm were indispensable to the success of the work. Although Robyn and I had some experience with the temples from previous visits, our local guides introduced us to Skorba - probably the most ancient and powerful of them of all - where we eventually anchored the conjunction energy.

Channeled guidance I had received in UK emphasised the need to work with the water element and it was therefore most interesting to hear from local contacts about mysterious seaweed crop circles and unaccountable lights in the sea around the island in the lead-up to this event. Kevin had only just sailed around the island and told us of a 'coincidental' sea-bed clean-up operation recently launched by the authorities!

Having arrived a few days ahead of the others, Robyn, Jo and I had visited some possible temple sites that could be used for the ritual and then managed to arrange special access to the tombs of the twelve Grand Masters at St John's co-Cathedral in Valetta. Here we experienced a lovely synchronicity, when on entering the building we found ourselves surrounded by some fifty young school children. The group just happened to be passing the entrance to the vault as we were having it opened so they joined us and blended their vibrant energy as we all experienced this major power site under the high altar of the cathedral.

From there we went to the St Angelo fortress on the Grand harbour, having heard that it was being prepared for the auspicious return in 1994 of the order of the Knights of St John after centuries at the Vatican in Rome. Miraculously, there were no guards on the gates or indeed anyone to challenge us in the huge complex as we wandered at will. We attuned around the Aquarian Cross under the great bell at the highest point we could reach and invoked a blessing of light on the site and this ancient order.

As on my first visit to Gozo in 1991, a dramatic thunderstorm broke out there after our attunement at the main temple site of the Ggantija. To the consternation of the locals next morning, the three of us rushed to the sea with the Cross at the height of the storm and submerged ourselves. Well, Spirit did say "Work with the water element"! Forks of lightning struck the sea all around us! This is the island associated with the Goddess Calypso and again she was quick to respond to those who honoured her.

On the 22nd of October and now that Robert had arrived on the island, we had the first update with our spirit partners. Seven of us sat at a round table in Elizabeth and Kevin's house to hear first Churchill tell us that this event was as big a turning point for the world as Potsdam had been fifty years earlier. Then Gandhi appropriately reminded us that the energy about to be unleashed had destructive potential too, if not handled properly - it depended entirely on the clear motivation and intention of each member of the group. We were further told that the then new Arab / Israeli peace initiative would also be directly supported by this alignment work on Malta, as the island is such an important energy connection point for the whole region. There then followed guidance about the exact details of our work on the night of the 24 / 25th Oct.

As well as the Uranus / Neptune conjunction in Capricorn, there was also an alignment of Mercury / Mars / Pluto in Scorpio. Therefore, our first attunement at 21.30 hrs on 24/10 was to be at the temple of Mnajdra and focused on Mars. Spirit guidance had explained, "Do not play down the role of Mars as communicator hitching a ride on the larger and more powerful forces, because it is now necessary to destroy those levels of communication which have gone amok".

Apparently, it was also vital to hold the energy at 02.45hrs for half an hour at our hotel. This formidable building was once the palace of British governors of the island and is dramatically set high into the battlements of the ancient capital, Mdina - the city of Palaces. Finally, on the conjunction itself at 10.30 hrs on 25/10, we were to be at the altar in the Skorba temple.

All the sites chosen were on the main island of Malta, as it is strategically placed between the Christian and Islamic worlds, and both religions have denied the feminine polarity that Malta was now being prepared to represent once more. The symbols we were to use for the ceremonies were the twelve-pointed star, the Maltese Cross and a Rose, while the three conditions to be fulfilled by each of the nine were: freewill, come prepared, and accept that this mission had been agreed to by us all, many lifetimes ago.

With the arrival of Lucy and Graeme from London late on 22nd October, our party was complete. Next day seven of us visited the island of Gozo, mainly to attune at the temple of Ggantija. It was there that we found the purple rose required for the rituals. Before going there, we went to Ta Pinu church to experience the pure energies of this famous pilgrimage centre associated with Mary. With almost no-one else about and at the end of our visit, we noticed the arrival of a limousine with outriders. It was soon clear that the President and his wife had somehow chosen the moment we were all in the church to make a private visit! Spirit had previously indicated that our work was to be given the approval of the Maltese authorities and so it was, miraculously, that we found ourselves in conversation with Mrs Tabone, the President's wife. As Robert shook her hand, such a powerful energy was transmitted to her, that it not only gave her a visible shock, but caused a blister to appear immediately in the middle of Robert's own palm!

Next day on Sunday October 24th, having integrated the energies of the Ggantja temple and picked the rose, we returned to our hotel at Mdina on Malta. It had been agreed that we should all wear white, and our rendez-vous with Kevin and Elizabeth at Mnajra temple was at 21.00 hrs, to leave us time for preparation. The remoteness of this hauntingly beautiful site on a bare hillside overlooking the sea suited our need for total privacy, as did the cover of night. It did not, however, help our navigation on unpaved and unsigned roads, which at some stages in rough, stonewalled lanes barely the width of our cars, had us despairing that we would ever find the site again!

However, all nine were in position by 21.30 and Robert, guided by spirit, led an inspiring ritual working with the positive, physical transformational potential of Mars. As a preparation, and observing the guidance we had received to work with water, we anointed ourselves with Chalice Well water and then each participant dedicated the energy unleashed to the Light. We concluded by spinning the energy anti-clockwise to release it and embraced each other. We then attuned individually at different points in the warm, heart energies of that large and inspirational temple site. Our act of service complete, we returned immediately to hold the vigil in the battlements of Mdina.

Subsequent guidance received by Kevin was as follows: "So the first ritual at Mnajdra did indeed set the scene. The inward-spiralling energies that you have just created, harnessed to the current planetary alignments, have built up the impetus of power that was sufficient to set in motion massive changes in consciousness. The spiralling vortex was of a global scale, encompassing many power centres of the Earth, and this gathering of energy was available for all humanity to use" - indeed, this was what the second ritual was about. The energy was available up until 03.00 hrs Malta time, which was a threshold point. Until then, either dark or Light forces could have utilised the energy vortex. Every ounce of effort and focus was utilised for us all to bring the project to fruition.

Keeping nine people awake and focused all night, however, isn't exactly easy, so after lighting candles around the Aquarian Cross on a window-shelf dramatically overlooking the lights of Malta far below, we took it in turns to rest until the next moment of focus. At about 02.40 hrs I rejoined those keeping vigil and noticed they had by then rather lost concentration in more general conversation. Without warning a blast of wind hit the battlements and forced open two securely locked and bolted windows - without knocking over the Cross or extinguishing the thirteen candles! The room was filled with a powerful presence and those able to receive spirit communication agreed that the message was to redouble our efforts with all nine to be gathered for half an hour from 02.45 hrs. During this intense half hour we also linked strongly by previous arrangement with a group holding the energy on Zuvuyaland near lake Taupo, New Zealand. Significantly, Kevin is from NZ.

The urgency of holding this focus was so critical that it had taken the forces of Light to stage a dramatic intervention at the last moment to support our flagging efforts. Certainly, an awesome experience for those of us present that left no doubt about the delicate balance between success and failure. After a deep meditation over the period requested, the group broke up at around 04.00 hrs, with Lucy volunteering to hold the vigil till dawn.

After a short rest, we set out on October 25th in different cars for Skorba temple. Again, for whatever reasons, we were all tested once more by getting lost and delayed and only just got into position in our '9 configuration' for the critical 10.30 hrs conjunction moment! During the morning a strong wind had sprung up and we were later told, "There was an enormous etheric expansion which created a partial vacuum over Malta and caused the high winds - they had been building up since the 03.00 attunement as the vacuum increased. The 3rd ritual sealed the whole event and brought together a multi-layered Lighted network that linked all those ancient temple sites which have been acknowledged and cleansed by the Light workers".

After anchoring the conjunction energy and tuning in on various parts of the temple sites, the rose was entrusted to Robyn for her to inaugurate each new centre of the Order with one of its petals. In her subsequent report on our work Robyn says, "It seemed as though an atomic bomb of love and light was dropped on the site to spread ripples around the planet. The role of Malta and New Zealand is to express and send love and light around the planet and consolidate the overlighting energies. Malta is the hub of the wheel, where the great forces, both light and dark, do battle for supremacy". Feeling that the whole work had now been successfully completed, we sealed the bond between the nine with hugs and vacated the fenced-off site, just before an official guide arrived with a tourist group!

Graeme, Lucy and Robyn flew out that day leaving the remainder to focus a powerful channelling of Gandhi by Robert at the Malta Esoteric Group's centre. He explained the significance of what had just been accomplished to the twenty or so gathered, to the accompaniment - yes, you have guessed - of a five-star thunderstorm!

For all the reasons described, it had been unusually hard at our imperfect human level to hold the energy requested of us by spirit, and writing with hindsight now in 1996, it was this event that heralded necessary changes in the original WWV coregroup in UK. On the other hand, the positive spirit guidance about stabilising energies to prepare for a time of more peaceful co-operation between Israel and Palestine has certainly been vindicated so far with the establishment of an indepedant Palestinian state under Yasser Arafat soon afterwards in 1994.

Ultimately, though, the raising of consciousness by the kind of energy alignment work described here will only benefit those who through their free choice decide to expand their awareness and express inner peace in their own daily lives. When a fanatical religious Jew assassinated a Prime Minister, and fellow Jew dedicated to peace, and the country then voted for a right-wing religiously dependent administration in 1996, one can only conclude that there are still not enough people with peace in their hearts to win the day. The curse of religious fundamentalism has been very publicly mirrored back to the people of Israel and now no longer can they project blame externally for their self-inflicted woes.

Fortunately for the rest of the world, after the Aeon Shift work in 1989/90 (one of the main themes of this book), Old Jerusalem no longer has a valid spiritual mandate. While theologians, certain New Agers and assorted intellectuals persist in their vindication of that city and somehow convince themselves that it will be transformed into the 'Celestial City' of

Revelations, the truth is that, almost unnoticed, the scene of action has moved in accordance with prophecy and Divine Will. The Universal Aquarian dispensation establishes the unified New Jerusalem consciousness for those ready to accept it in greener lands to the west. Divisive religions and their blinkered followers, however, may well choose to battle it out, and nothing can prevent them either here or anywhere else in the world. You will recall spirit's inspirational guidance about the Aquarian Cross that had specifically been made in Old Jerusalem: "We know how necessary it was that the beautiful Cross was fashioned and stored with the great Christ energy and then removed from Israel".

MOROCCO 21 / 22 NOVEMBER, 1993

A series of synchronicities saw the energy work on Malta quickly extended through the planetary ley line grid into the Islamic world. I had been invited to spend my birthday in Morocco, while at the same time, unknown to me, Graeme and Lucy were to be teaching Reiki in the volcanic Canary Islands and Kevin and Elizabeth were to return to Mnajdra temple on Malta. The three places in which we were now somehow positioned traversed the highly unstable Islamic nations of Tunisia, Algeria and Morocco, and obviously formed some kind of energy alignment.

The guidance I had received in advance of my trip was that by taking the Aquarian Cross into an Islamic country for the first time, a start would be made in transmuting the fear and male domination that has overrun that religion. Now was the time to restore the gentle heart vibration with which its founder originally endowed it. Morocco also features in the energy alignments with Spain of the expanding Global Heart chakra between Barcelona and the El Rif mountains - an important link for healing Christian and Islamic intransigence.

On my 46th birthday (21/11/93), I had arranged a dawn meditation link between Marrakech and Lanzarote with Graeme and Lucy. I then embedded rose quartz crystals in the walls of the Koutoubia mosque and the centre of the main square (Djemaa el Fna) to anchor the energy flowing from Malta. The grand finale that day came when a Princess living in a superb palace showered my host and myself with 100 freshly-cut roses from her garden - but that is another story! The rose is a symbol with

135

which I have a particular affinity and so this was the most wonderful and unexpected birthday present - with perfect sense of occasion, no doubt the work of our spirit partners!

Graeme later described to me how he had made a deep Earth connection by climbing to the live crater on Lanzarote and sprinkling Chalice Well water into it. On the 22nd November a huge storm was inexplicably triggered over that arid island and the heaviest rains for some 15 years fell there! The same storm also hit the coastal town of Essaouira in Morocco, where the Cross and I were by then located! Within days an important international GATT treaty was also signed in Marrakech.

SPIRITUAL PREPARATIONS FOR THE SOUTH AFRICAN ELECTIONS
8 - 24 APRIL 1994

My fourth visit to South Africa was severely tested even before the start - on Good Friday April 1st I was blown over by hurricane force winds after an attunement for South Africa and broke my leg! Splendid timing by the opposing forces perhaps, but the journey was far too critical at all levels to be cancelled and despite every kind of obstacle, it went ahead. Our purpose was first to carry out energy work on Table mountain, Cape Town (main power centre of South Africa) in order to help prepare the subtle energy grid of the country for the critical upcoming elections. Secondly, I went to support my South African publisher for the first official launch of my book and the Revelations 3 text. It was interesting and unexpected that South Africa rather than the UK should become the launch pad of my work, considering that the material I present is of such particular relevance to a once 'Great' Britain that now so desperately needs to present a fresh and inspiring image to the rest of the world.

Our work started on April 10th at Hout Bay on the edge of the Table Mountain, when between sunrise and sunset we conducted the 5,000 year old vedic Agni Hotra fire ritual with its repeated 'Trayambakam' sanskrit mantram of Immortality. Some 30 people joined the ceremony and many were later aware that it had indeed achieved its purpose in helping to dissolve and counteract at subtle levels the main obstacle in the country at that time: **fear**.

Overlighted by the great spirit guardian of Castle Rock on Table Mountain, the work of that day was completed with a gathering in Kirstenbosch botanical gardens to attune to the New Moon in Aries (new beginnings!) at 02.17 hrs on April 11th. The highly significant number of 13 people assembled synchronistically around a specially selected layout of crystals and we experienced an exquisite feeling of peace and interconnectedness with each other and the Earth. Despite the lateness of the hour, it was hard to leave that enchanted spot with the mountain resplendent above us and so clearly illuminated by the light of the stars! A small group returned two weeks later to the same site at the full moon on the eve of the elections in order to complete the attunement cycle.

From the moment of my arrival, one name kept cropping up - Credo Mutwa. I knew of this highly respected prophet and spiritual leader of the Zulu nation, as I had been given his book *Indaba my Children*, on my last visit. Now, according to the guidance of my local friends, was the appropriate time for our meeting. As usual in such situations I've learned not to engage the left-brain hemisphere in rational planning, but rather to await synchronistic signs. They weren't long in coming! Through the sale of one of my books in Johannesburg a few days later, we met a man who had worked with Credo and who also thought this was an auspicious time for us to meet. We soon heard that Credo was in agreement and George, a wise and gentle man dedicated to educational and environmental improvement, then led a party of nine of us out of Johannesburg at 4.0 am on April 16th for the four-hour journey to Mafeking. Our route took us right through the heart of some of the most disturbed regions of South Africa, such as the Afrikaner resistance movement HQ at Ventersdorp and then Mabatu, the battered capital of the now defunct and chaotic homeland of Bophuthatswana. Clearly, the combined energy of our group was being used to help counteract the fear and aggression of this region, so graphically portrayed on the TV screens of the world.

'Vusamazulu' (the outcast) Credo Mutwa, spiritual leader of the Zulus, was long ago rejected by his people for defying tribal customs - he had written down and shared with whites the Zulu spiritual traditions that had only ever been passed on by word of mouth among their own initiates. Like all true prophets aspiring to a more noble and integrative level of consciousness in this world of duality, he lives under constant threat and both his sons have already been murdered. Indeed, hours before our arrival, he had only just managed peacefully to repel a gang that had come to 'necklace' him with burning tyres.

As our group of nine joined his household of four (13 again!) our combined energies quickly rose above the prevailing levels of fear saturating that region. During the next few hours was to follow one of the most intense and potent periods of prayer and divine intercession in which any of those present had ever participated.

First, we showed Credo a magnificent painted cloth depicting protea flowers, which he says is the real African symbol of peace, **not** the dove. This was the inspired work of Philomena Ward of Simonstown, and Credo praised it euphorically as the true flag of South Africa painted by 'the hand of Africa'! Next we placed the Aquarian Cross on the cloth in front of him and to this he responded with the most uplifting and moving sung and spoken invocations in his own tongue. In turn we all made our own contributions as we felt the awesome power of Spirit passing through us. Needless to say, there wasn't a dry eye among us and for my part there were times when I felt the alternating waves of intense pain and ecstatic joy were almost too much to bear as the transmutational energy invoked rose to a glorious climax.

Later we heard that it was **exactly** at this time on Saturday April 16th that King Goodwill Zwelithini of the Zulus had unexpectedly taken the initiative to approach Nelson Mandela of the ANC in order to break the stalemate on his people's election boycott. The two men met initially **without** the presence or consent of Chief Buthelezi, the political adviser to the King, and it was only when the latter was confronted with this fait accompli that he had no alternative but to accede.

This was the chain of events that paved the way for the historic announcement three days later on Tuesday April 19th of the Zulu participation in the elections - thus miraculously averting a certain bloodbath. The critical 10% Zulu share of the vote became the vital factor that prevented the ANC reaching the dangerous landslide 2/3rds majority, which would have permitted them to rewrite the Constitution and thus almost certainly trigger the disintegration of the State. After the election Mandela found himself stating publicly, "Thank God for the Zulu vote!"

With this demonstration of the deep spiritual bond between the Zulu's prophet and their King, perhaps it is now time for an official reconciliation and the reinstatement of Credo Mutwa among his people. In just such a

138

way a greater potential for peace and harmony could well be achieved in this volatile land of extreme passions that has by no means yet resolved its inner struggles.

During our five hours together - in which a truckfull of soldiers arrived to protect him - Credo shared a wealth of fascinating and vitally important information concerning the great evolutionary changes to be experienced in the next few years by the entire human race. He especially emphasised with much evidence the increasingly important role of extra-terrestrials or higher dimensional Beings that will, he says, soon manifest for all to see. As the vibrational frequencies of humanity and the planet increase, those prepared will be able to see that which was once unseeable! Such a phenomenon would certainly eclipse the spiritually ignorant religious, political, racial and sexual prejudices currently destabilising humanity.

In relation to the specific spiritual work we were there to perform with him, Credo recognised the ancient symbology of the Christ consciousness represented by the Aquarian Cross and confirmed that this awareness had been established in Africa long before the distortion called 'Christianity' was more recently imposed on her people by missionaries. He was also gracious enough to acknowledge my own Cross-bearer role as part of the cleansing process of African energies at this and on previous occasions. Furthermore, my name and the overall purpose of my work was apparently not lost on him either. Even, he said, my one-legged appearance before him was entirely appropriate within the context! This was certainly an unexpected, but most welcome valediction, after all the pain, judgement and mental / emotional confusion I had had to endure since breaking my leg in order apparently to reach this moment of destiny.

Credo explained that he saw my work in Africa exemplifying the archetype of the 'one-legged God - the wounded healer' symbolised by the sacred Ankh that is long-established in the ancient spiritual traditions.

The significance of the gathering was further emphasised when Credo offered in return for being shown the Aquarian Cross to bring out the magnificent Zulu tribal artifacts with which he has long been entrusted. Enormous, heavy necklaces measuring up to three feet across with fascinating symbols attached were then ceremoniously laid out for our inspection and attunement. Very few people have been privileged to see these ancient treasures, but it is Credo's wish, provided he can be found

139

somewhere safe in which to pass his final years, that they be permanently exhibited and shown to all who visit him.

Surely it is not too much to ask of those who understand and respect this great sage that they ease the terrible burdens he has had to suffer by arranging for him a secure and harmonious sanctuary from which he can continue to contribute his energy and great wisdom to the unfolding peace process?

The launch of my book *Rising out of Chaos* was clearly an integral part of the overall energy work, especially as it was the book itself that led us to Credo Mutwa. Overall and with such challenging material - especially Revelations 3 and its dire implications for Christianity - it was probably appropriate that the initial launch turned out to be muted.

After the exhausting and unexpectedly testing events and incidents of the first week, it was bliss to relax at Simonstown, watching unforgettable sunrises and sunsets as well as the suddenly much-increased dolphin activity. Lucy and Graeme, who had accompanied me from the UK and valiantly supported the work with their reiki energy alignments, went on to visit the game parks in Natal. After unintentionally driving through some black townships there, Lucy was suddenly taken extremely ill miles from assistance and would certainly have died, had it not been for her husband's healing expertise. Immediately after the meeting with Credo it seems that the three of us somehow physically took on some of the fears, angers and negativeness of the white and black communities in order to help process and transmute them. We were each subjected to some very tough challenges from unexpected sources.

What mattered most, however, is that the bloodbath keenly anticipated by the assembled and predominantly negative world media was not only averted, but that a miraculous turning point was achieved, capable of inspiring humanity in so many other apparently hopeless situations. The fact is that **goodwill** cemented the diverse elements of South Africa through carefully prepared consciousness-linking events in both meditation and prayer on a mass domestic and world scale. The people themselves wanted peace and made the necessary inner and outer efforts to attain it. Certainly nothing could have been achieved behind the scenes at the higher spiritual levels without such a solid platform on which to build. After the election's result was clear, the world's media representatives left South

Africa deprived of an orgy of violence and with only one word on their lips
- miracle!

So culminated the Earth alignment work on South Africa's natural
energy grid, which had been carried out quietly behind the scenes by many
dedicated groups. The years 1988 to 1994 saw the falling of 'The Finger
of God' in the Kalahari desert, followed by major political shifts and the
release of Nelson Mandela himself soon after the major Table Mountain
activation on November 13th 1989. As the current dimensional shift
gathers pace, those who think they rule us will soon see they are no match
for the forces now being unleashed on Earth by the ever-strengthening
band of Light workers!

ACTIVATION WORK ON THE MOUNT FUJI
POWER CENTRE, JAPAN
July 22 - Aug 11th, 1995

THE IMMORTAL MOUNTAIN

Fuji Yama
Touched by thy Divine Breath,
We return to the Shape of God.
Thy Silence is Song,
Thy Song is the Song of Heaven ...
- Yone Noguchi

"You are invited to Japan", read the fax from Marcus - the remarkable
young Australian living in Japan who organised the worldwide Earth
Gathering linkup centred on Mount Fuji - "your airfare and expenses are
met courtesy of the **dolphins!**" Evidently, three Japanese ladies had
generously offered the royalties from their translation of Joan Ocean's best-
selling *Dolphin Connections* book to pay for my entire trip. Its as though
the dolphins - under such threat in Japan - had themselves written the
cheque!

Marcus, an Australian teacher of English in a provincial Japanese city,
had enjoyed my book and was impressed with the enthusiastic response he
got from the international Wholistic World Vision contact names listed in
the back. How gratifying that the WWV network was used for the first
time to play a supportive role in such an important global initiative - just

what it was designed for. This opportunity now allowed me to take the Aquarian Cross to Japan for the first time to participate in three major Earth healing events.

My host had intrigued the many networkers he had contacted around the world by signing his faxes 'Marcus and Reina'. We all assumed that Reina was his wife or partner, but the big surprise came when he took me home to meet his Japanese wife Akami and their 8 month old daughter, Reina! It appears that her arrival triggered Marcus to fulfil a long-held ambition to focus world attention on Mount Fuji before he returns to his roots in Australia.

He and some local astrologers had identified a very powerful planetary configuration for July 22nd. The formation was a 'Star of David' made up by the Sun, Saturn and Pluto and the Moon, Kiron and Uranus. With this information, and helped only by his wife and a few local friends, he dedicated himself (and the funds that he would otherwise have donated to the Kobe Earthquake disaster fund) to creating the latest in a series of major planetary healing events. This time even radio and TV coverage around the world strengthened the mass meditational mindlinking on which the success of such events depends.

These global mindlinking initiatives, starting with Harmonic Convergence in 1987, have been of paramount importance in raising human and planetary consciousness. Indeed, they are now widely accepted as the means by which this planet's frequencies were raised above the low levels that would inevitably have led to catastrophe. Mount Fuji itself has long been identified as one of the 12 major power centres of this planet, all of which have now been activated through human focus. With the energies building up in Japan earlier in 1995, as represented by the devastating Kobe earthquake, the Sarin gas attacks in Tokyo's metro and serious ongoing economic instability, this now appeared to be the time for action!

In addition to the July 22 linkup, I was aware that according to the American mystic, Robert Coon, the annual Aquarius Full Moon 'is the most auspicious time to seek the Immortal Elixir atop Fuji'. Then Marcus recalled that August 6 and 9 also happened to be the 50th anniversary of the American Atomic bomb outrages on Hiroshima and Nagasaki, with an automatic worldwide focus of billions of people on Japan guaranteed. A pretty potent mixture that without doubt heralded a major shift in

142

consciousness in that land - comfortable or otherwise according as ever to the choice of her people.

As usual, much rain, thunder and lightning had greeted the arrival of the Aquarian Cross in the Tokyo area, while on July 22nd a typhoon hit the south and a medium-sized Earthquake struck the north. We were in business! 02.30 hrs on July 22nd revealed a wet and misty scene as Marcus and I drove up to the meditation site at the Hoezan crater half way up Mount Fuji - site of the last eruption in 1707 CE.

A handful of people had gathered at dawn in the crater and then suddenly a violent storm hit us with fierce winds and torrential rain that, after about half an hour of attempting shelter, drove us back soaking wet into one of the mountain rest stations. Clearly, the world focus could not be held in the open **that** morning and we were fortunate to secure - at a price! - the dormitory areas of the station situated in an appropriate wooden 'upper room'. Gradually others arrived, until some 70 people crammed into the room to hold the energy over 3 one-hour attunements. These were dedicated to 'Gratitude', 'People living in Peace' and 'The Earth is a Shining Star'. Dramatically, thunderclaps announced the start and finish of what was for all attending a most profound and powerful focus.

Happily, soon after midday, the clouds parted revealing spectacular views and affording us the opportunity to hold a final meditation in the crater itself. Some twenty gathered around the Cross, while a huge dolphin-shaped cloud formed overhead. Glastonbury's Chalice well water was liberally sprinkled and a stone from the Well garden was exchanged for the red and black larva, which I brought back to the planetary heart chakra in England.

Hiroshima and Nagasaki were man's darkest hour and his ultimate statement of separation from the Divine. These monstrous acts on defenceless civilians, for which no pragmatic or intellectual excuses will ever atone - the Japanese were already at the point of surrender before the bombs were detonated - together with the Chernobyl disaster, have brought us all to a stark choice: evolve or become extinct. Let the nations still indulging in inexcusable nuclear testing be warned - particularly as there is now ample scientific evidence linking underground nuclear detonations with subsequent Earthquakes.

143

Marcus and I had been directed to powerful shrines and temples in the Kyoto and Hiroshima area by an elderly Shinto priest, who had anticipated this inflow of energy to the country and had himself been guided to prepare certain sites on Mount Fuji one month previously. Shinto is the ancient religion of Japan and is a pagan spiritual tradition based on natural law - a most appropriate structure to nurture the awakening expansion of consciousness in that country. Revealingly, Christianity was always treated with justifiable suspicion and mainly banned!

Kyoto, the spiritual heart of Japan, fulfils all one's expectations and we attuned at many exquisite temples - and even saw a rare Geisha girl! After a talk in nearby Osaka, we were driven though the night to arrive in Hiroshima one day before the commemoration in order to prepare various local energy sites. We were greeted by a remarkable survivor of the bomb, who together with a group of some 15 Japanese took charge of our programme there. Masaji Kawano was only 10 when he witnessed the explosion and describes vividly how he ran back into the ruins, sustaining fearful injuries, in order to gather the scattered remains of his entire family. Over 5,000 died last year alone from radiation effects, but this cheerful man was determined to survive and now acts as an ambassador of the Light for what is miraculously once again a beautiful city of parks, flowers and rivers - a city and population that, needless to say, now single-mindedly champions the cause of **peace** and nuclear disarmament throughout the world.

We visited the sacred shrines on Mount Miyajima - an enchanted island of tame deer and the celebrated Shinto Seagate Temple - and meditated on pine-clad slopes among huge butterflies and exotic bird song. Even here can still be seen the red scorch-marks of the explosion on the rockface. On August 6th we gathered at the Peace Park at dawn with some 60,000 others - including Hopi Indians, from whose land the uranium for the bombs was mined, Auschwitz survivors, all kinds of other special peace initiatives and the TV cameras of the world. Our group assembled around the Aquarian Cross next to the only building to survive the blast, and I felt that the Vesica Piscis, symbol of light, helped filter and rebalance remaining disturbed energy. 1945 the A-bombs and in 1995 the A-Cross! How appropriate that the Aquarian Cross just happened to be in Hawaii for the Pearl Harbour 50th anniversary on 7/12/91 too.

144

Having visited the nearby Mount Noga Kogen energy sites during the day, we returned at sunset to the Peace Park to support our host in his more personal remembrance. We stood under a pink moon on a bridge above which the bomb had exploded at 600 metres and watched, deeply moved, as the flotilla of colourful little 'spirit' boats floated down to the sea - each with a candle commemorating a bomb victim. Evidently, the fact that the explosion had taken place above ground level meant that most of the radiation had dispersed - otherwise nothing would have survived and the site would still be heavily contaminated.

Finally, we accompanied our friend to his family grave, picking flowers from the roadside on our way, and knelt there together in a simple act of forgiveness, reconciliation and release. Touchingly, he confided that this was the first time in all those years that anyone had accompanied him on this annual homage at his family vault. A fitting end, perhaps, to a day that hopefully finally drew a line under past inhuman folly - and certainly, the warmth of the heart energy we all generated together remained with me well into the night.

Our final attunement was achieved on top of Mount Fuji at 11,900 ft - an exhausting night-time climb with temperatures ranging from 35+ to 5- in icy winds with a heavy backpack and all achieved in six hours! Of the five who made it, Marcus and Flint walked ceremonially around the crater, while I and two female supporters, Reiko and Janet, raised the Cross to a magnificent and bright full Moon at 03.16 precisely. The view of the sunrise and the moonset within moments of each other across the crater was worth **all** the hardship - including a very difficult descent on deep, dusty and constantly shifting volcanic beds of cinders.

My hosts in Tokyo, Reiko and Flint, found time to arrange some public talks for me, both to the English-speaking community and Japanese (with translation). Response was excellent. Much of the emphasis in my talks was on taking responsibility for Earth healing on local power sites and this novel idea was received with enthusiasm as were 'Circles of Light' to ease the tectonic plate pressures within that inherently unstable landmass.

According to a May 1995 channelling from Sedona, USA: "Two grand vortices only remain to be activated - one in Japan and one in Russia". This report explains the work successfully completed in Japan and a description of the Russian journey in June / July 1996 can be read later in this chapter.

145

BOSNIA

'THROUGH THE HEART TO PEACE'
3rd Peace Women of the World's Mission to Bosnia.
22 - 30 May 1996

Wholistic World Vision has been in contract with the UK support group of this important global initiative at Hazelwood House over the past two years. Indeed, our annual Celtic Odyssey Tours to sacred power sites stay overnight at this lovely retreat centre, deep in a secluded Devon Valley.

When I first wrote this book in 1992, I stated then that aware women working in healed feminine energy would find common cause with each other across artificial man-made barriers, so it was exciting to discover that this group also started their first contacts with Bosnian moslem women that very same year. So it was a great honour to have been invited to witness this dynamic energy in action. The task of spirituality aware humans is to raise their vibrational frequencies to the highest possible levels and this can only be achieved through the unconditional love of the open heart. By **Living the Loving** and **Walking the Talk**, we automatically raise our vibrations so that we can transmute the negativity of all the lower frequencies of fear, violence and war around us. Hence the name of this vitally important mission, **Through the Heart to Peace**.

This project originated in the midst of the horror of the killing fields of former Yugoslavia - a European country ripped apart by male politicians (psychopaths to many) determined to unleash demonic nationalism to serve their own egotistical greed for power and conquest. Bosnia, the central state once peacefully populated by all the warring parties, became the flashpoint and history now tragically shows how her poorly armed and peaceful moslem inhabitants became the victims of 'Christian' Serbs and Croats who, as well as slaughtering each other, competed to inflict on them horrific levels of ethnic cleansing not seen in Europe since Hitler targeted the Jews.

During 1992, a Moslem and a Croat women both received similar visions showing that it was up to spiritually aware women to initiate peace by linking across the ethnic divisions there and also with women around the world. The amazing story of how all this developed - through perfect synchronicity and inspirational guidance associated with the Mary appearances at Medugorie - is available from the Dandelion Trust (see Contacts).

Having worked at higher consciousness levels myself in some of Earth's most troubled countries at the times of otherwise inexplicable changes that subsequently occurred in each of them, I am convinced that by reaching besieged Sarajevo in 1994 and 1995 - under impossible conditions - that this group raised consciousness levels sufficiently in Bosnia to pave the way to peace through the recent Dayton Accord brokered by the USA. Let's face it, male politicians, many of whom are already indicted as war criminals and certainly with **no peace in their hearts**, are hardly likely to have suddenly become the instruments of peace! No, emphatically there is a different and dynamic reality operating unsuspected behind the scenes in the hands of those aware enough to know the power of focused thought based on the highest frequency of unconditional love.

This 3rd Bosnian peace mission consisted of some forty women from UK, Germany, USA, Australia, Switzerland, Croatia and Bosnia. The only other two males participating apart from myself came from Austria. Ages varied from early twenties to well into the seventies and many had been on both previous journeys.

The 'flexible' aim this time was to continue the policy of planting Peace trees in particularly devastated and traumatised communities throughout the region, to take the energy into the new Bosnian Serb republic and to hold another conference in Sarajevo. Flexibility was the name of the game and continually tested our patience and courage!

My own contribution was to take the Aquarian Cross, small stones from the ancient Avebury landscape temple in Wiltshire and Chalice Well water to help heal the damaged Earth energy grid of Bosnia. This land is itself immensely powerful and it is no coincidence that the region has often sparked conflict in the past, including the First World War at Sarajevo!

Our first engagement in Zagreb on arrival was to attend a performance of the powerful 'Sarajevo Circle' dance drama. The explosive choreography and vivid stage effects captured perfectly the trauma of that city's agonizing four years siege under constant sniper attack and helped to prepare us for the very challenging adventure. The plan had been to make an early start so as to plant trees at Samobor near Zagreb and Kozarac,

147

now in Serbian Bosnia, before reaching Sarajevo. As it happened, the bus broke down and what was to have been a one day itinerary turned over three days into a dramatic shift of focus from Sarajevo and onto the new Serb republic border.

Apparently, the UN regional commander had heard of our peace quest and had telephoned the UK office to state specifically that he would give us every support in reaching the site of the appalling Serb massacre of moslems in 1992 at Kozarac. With hindsight it is clear that he wished to use us to test the Dayton Accord's "freedom of movements in all zones" clause. Interestingly, a recent BBC documentary had just been shown in UK focusing on this town and the activities there of the first war criminal to be brought before the international court at the Hague. Kozarac is also the home town of the Moslem woman who had received the Heart to Peace vision and was therefore an important goal on this journey. Having planted our tree at Samobor next to a St Michael Church - the bell tolled to mark the exact fourth anniversary of the start of the Kozarac massacre! - we proceeded into wartorn Bosnia.

From now on for the next six days over hundreds of kilometres we were to see destruction of property on an unimaginable scale with virtually every dwelling either destroyed or badly damaged. We also had pointed out to us the sites of many mass graves. Our only consolation in this utter desolation and human degradation was the unfailing beauty of mother nature as the vibrant spring colours gave hope to this exquisite, yet tragic Bosnian landscape.

At the village of Luscipalanski, despite our unavoidable eight hours delay, the population turned out to greet us, to plant a tree together and to entertain us to a reviving traditional Bosnian dinner accompanied by much singing. The village translator turned out to be a sophisticated young woman whose two year old child had been born in Auckland New Zealand! - could all this really be happening in 'civilised' Europe? Then we continued to what was to be our base for the next three nights: the hotel in Sanskimost that we later discovered had been used as the Serb police interrogation centre. After all the recent torture, rape and carnage in this building, we had an opportunity to transmute the all too evident negative energy still lingering there.

The next day saw the group patiently waiting at the 'Whitefang' UN border checkpoint, as our two attempts to gain access to the Prijedor /

Kozarac zone were determinedly undermined by the Serb police, many of whom were themselves orchestrators of the recent massacres. In order to spread fear and strengthen their people's resistance, they even broadcast propaganda that we were a decoy for a full scale moslem invasion!

Later in the day, having negotiated for a Serb bus to take us over the border, we dispatched our Bosnian bus with all our belongings on board to meet us further along the route. Unfortunately the Serb driver was then intimidated by the police, took fright and left us stranded! From this point on, our low-key entry plan was rapidly superseded by the UN commanders, who at the very highest level in that country were determined to challenge this major Serb infringement of Dayton.

Pentecost, on Sunday May 26th, started with a strange omen. A small Eagle had flow down a hotel corridor and crashed into a large plate-glass window killing itself in a shower of glass, blood and feathers.

After another peaceful, but unsuccessful, attempt at the border in a German registered bus and this time with an official UN observer on board, the exasperated UN General in command of the local IFOR troops offered to escort the coach with a 'rapid reaction force'. Now, as a peace group, we faced a serious dilemma. However, after discussions all around about the significance to this mission of accessing Kozarac, and holding a meditational circle, which including the army personnel, we decided to accept the offer.

Our armoured column at first proceeded without difficulty and although met mainly by surly stares, there were hopeful signs of encouragement from the crowds gathered along the way. Suddenly, the mood changed and with skilful tactics the Serb militia managed to block our route with a sizable rent-a-crowd. They barricaded the road with women, children and cripples, and then, to our horror, organised bands of young men armed with stones to attack the bus sandwiched in the middle of the column. Talk about being a sitting duck! As the rocks rained in, we crouched on the floor with glass shattering all over us knowing that short of shooting people there was little the armoured might of our escort could do to protect us. After some very tense minutes, when our nerve was tested to the limit, the column was fortunately able to reverse and retrace its steps to the border - with the odd stone from angry bystanders to help us along.

149

Fortunately, injuries on the coach were only minor and the group remained admirably composed, though severely shaken., We heard later that certain Serbs were so disgusted by the treatment we had received that they offered to create a diversion to occupy their own militia, if we would try again the next day. We felt we had done all we reasonably could without resorting to force and anyway, according to those UN commanders closely monitoring the situation, the ripple effects of our action were already 'hitting the stratosphere'! Clearly, our combined energy was being used positively to confront the core of remaining negativity in this volatile situation - but not in the way we had expected and flexibility was again the key. Let us hope that aggressive and predatory Serb nationalism - represented that day by their emblem of the Eagle - had met its match in the shower of glass, both symbolically and literally. The mass uprising in Belgrade six months later seemed to confirm the energy work.

Our journey continued to Jajce, a major Bosnian power site associated with St Michael from medieval times and more recently used by Tito, when he was forming the modern state of Yugoslavia. We worked to clear the dark and sombre energy in the focal catacomb / alter site and felt strongly that it had at various times in history been used for unsavoury purposes.

In Sarajevo we held a very belated and therefore low-key meeting with local women, many of whom were understandably still far too traumatised, angry and politically motivated to fully grasp the potential of the real 'Heart of Peace' frequency of **healed** female energy. We spent enough time at Medugorie, the site of recent appearances of the mother Mary to local children, to enjoy the isolated and barren hillside location in the early morning, before the hoards of religious pilgrims transform it into yet another commercial shrine.

The journey continued to the once beautiful, but now devastated Mostar nearby. After lunch, given by a pioneering clothing co-operative run by moslem women, we visited the spectacularly located moslem shrine of Blagaj to hear of the Bogomil (cathar) links with this region. This fascinating connection would seem to support the Hazelwood / Dandelion Trust initiative of funding a large property in south west France (Chateau Castelfranc) as a place of recuperation for Bosnian and Chernobyl orphans - among other traumatised victims of our planet's painful transformational processes. Some ten hours later we were back in Zagreb.

Our purpose had been to carry the 'healed' feminine energy wherever we were led and to anchor as much light as possible. It seems that Dayton, a temporary and unjust solution cobbled together under pressure by the male protagonists, offers only breathing space in which to organise meditational circles of light linking all elements of good will in this war torn region. It was certainly clear to me that unless the **higher frequency** is now held regularly by as many people as possible here and around the world, the men will resume the fight when the UN eventually withdraws. Perhaps the Croat soldier at the Hague who has just admitted the atrocities he committed is an early sign of changing attitudes.

Within two weeks of our visit we heard that three women from the Bosnian 'Heart to Peace' - core-group had managed with the help of some Serbian women - and despite enormous risk to themselves - to slip unnoticed in Kozarac! It was also noticeable that the US negotiators from this time on started to apply much greater pressure on the Bosnian Serbs to comply fully with the Dayton Accord. Certainly, by July the former Bosnian Serb President and indicted war criminal, Dr Karadzic, was forced from political office. Then in August, the Mostar city council finally agreed to ethnic co-operation and thus paving the way for viable Bosnian elections later in 1996. So, perhaps this is another example of ways in which ordinary people can contribute powerfully at subtle levels to changing the political and social realities of entire countries. The mass uprising on the freezing streets of Belgrade six months later challenging the Serbian Government gave proof of the effectiveness of this energy work.

Interestingly, an Aquarian Cross was worn by the Publicity Relations Organiser of the Dayton airbase throughout the Bosnian peace negotiations in the USA!

TO RUSSIA WITH LOVE!
Activation work on the 13th Planetary Gateway - Moscow/Zagorsk
June 18th - July 2nd 1996

Those now familiar with the concept of raising Earth's energy frequencies through the spiritual activation of the main global power centres - known as the 12 gates of New Jerusalem (see p.30) - will also be aware that 1996 was predicted to be a critical turning point for Russia. Since the mid-1960s, many groups around the world have worked on the

12 Gaian Gateways and, according to the American mystic Robert Coon, the Red Rose of Russia blooms and flourishes to the degree that the 12 primary Gates of New Jerusalem are activated by prayer and celebration. At the end of each cycle of activation the 13th site unifies and integrates the energies of the previous twelve.

The Prophecy of the Open Heart

"And now the Final Prophecy is Spoken: When the 12 Open Gates of the New Jerusalem invite all Immortals to partake of the Millennial Feast of the Open Heart, then the 13th Gate shall Open! Prepare thyself to heed this Invitation and take thy rightful Seat at the Round Table of Planetary Transfiguration ... For when the Grace of true Communion is freely offered through the 12 Open Heart Gates of this New Jerusalem, then the Mystical 13th shall Open near Moscow, the Red Rose blooms - and Peace and Joy and Life Everlasting shall reign forever and ever upon this Sacred Planet Earth!"

Robert Coon, Avalon, 1987

Robert also points out that two full or New (blue) moons in any one astrological sign are critical focal times for the opening process of the 13th Gate. Apart from other reliable spirit guidance indicating that 1995 was the activation time for Japan and 1996 for Russia, we only had to look at the recent Presidential elections to know that all eyes were on Mother Russia at this pivotal moment in her destiny.

Having worked on the activation of the global heart chakra with the knock-on effect on Russia, it was now time to experience the emerging energies in this newly liberated land for myself. My own first visit to Russia with the Aquarian Cross had been foreseen in 1994 by Rosemary Todd - a Reiki Master in New Zealand - but was made possible through perfect synchronicity by Margaret Monro, a pulsing therapist, in Australia. So it was that I joined the seventh 'Free Breathing' conference, which just happened to be perfectly located between Moscow and Zagorsk. This conference not only gave me the opportunity to be officially invited to Russia to help focus the above-mentioned energy work, but also provided me with fertile ground among spiritually committed Russians to find people interested in joining the energy work that was to be conducted.

A member of the foreign delegation attending with whom I particularly resonated was Or Olam from Japan. This powerful monk was trained from birth in the mystical 1200-year-old Mikkyo tradition of which he is now a Master. He heads the Japanese World Peace Movement initiative and creates phenomenal energy manifestations by whistling and clapping during this workshops, meditations and healings. Ably assisted organisationally and energetically by Lorraine and Stephanie, his UK co-ordinators, we all worked together to focus on an early morning solstice meditation for the conference on June 21st.

This was followed by an energy clearing within Zagorsk, which is now known by its former name of Sergei Pasad commemorating St Sergei in whose honour this fabulous monastery with its exotic onion domes was founded in the 14th century. Here I mixed the Chalice Well water with the highly venerated sacred water of the monastery and left a linking stone from Silbury Hill, Avebury to strengthen the 'Glaston / Glasnost' direct linking bond along the Female Dragon Line of Infinity.

From the moment I arrived at the conference on June 18th, and in the light of the delicate political situation, I could see it was not by chance that some 200 spiritually aware people had been gathered on this great power site at such a moment. So, once again, we were presented with a golden opportunity to effect change at a subtle level. Boris Yeltsin had failed to achieve a decisive result in the June 16th election and before the second vote on July 3rd we were offered three significant opportunities to work spiritually. As the energies at the conference started to lift, so we heard that Yeltsin had surprisingly sacked his two closest advisors in nearby Moscow and had offered a ministerial position to General Lebed, who had unexpectedly secured 15% of the first round vote on a Law and Order ticket. Soon after this it transpired that Yeltsin had suffered a minor stroke - enough to remove this volatile and accident-prone character from the limelight until after the second vote had been safely secured.

After the conference, I travelled to St Petersburg to give more talks and to enjoy the sightseeing and 'white nights' (no darkness) in this spectacular city of palaces. July 26th 1996 had been designated as 13:13 in the ancient Mayan Calendar, which is based on 13 lunar months (representing the 13 cycles of the female and true Earth time).

153

Boundary Dissolving Ceremony
26th June 1996

"144,000 to gather at the Four Corners sacred site in the USA. The call has gone out to gather 144,000 Rainbow Sundancers near the Four Corners area on '28 Crystal Rabbit Moon' - 13:13 day in the Mayan Calendar - to dissolve the old paradigm: the boundaries of nation states, the illusion of Gregorian '12' time, the veil between worlds, the separations of the heart. This gathering, foreseen by indigenous peoples and lightworkers worldwide, is an extremely important step to seeding the oneness of humanity. Through music and ritual we will initiate a giant vortex which will open an interdimensional portal for Divine Light to enter and dissolve the boundaries which separate us.

> *Vision without action is merely a dream*
> *Action without vision just passes time*
> *Vision with action will change the world!"*

> Jose Arguelles

As we made a meditational link from St Petersburg with the group of around one thousand that physically gathered in the USA (the rest linked meditationally all around the world), it was reassuring how the number 13 of the feminine kept appearing in association with this spiritual opening of Mother Russia!

As the July 1st full moon occurred early on the Monday morning, I decided to convene the celebration at Sergei Pasad on Sunday afternoon, June 30th. Some 32 people gathered, many with red roses, on a bright and sunny day to focus the energy by programming a Rose Quartz Crystal with everyone's highest aspirations, intending to plant it somewhere inside the monastery. One of the Russian women then had the inspiration to place it as near as possible to the remains of St Sergei - for many the most sacred place of pilgrimage in Russia. This is not easy task as this shrine is closely guarded by orthodox priests, but with an embarrassing clatter as it fell to rest beside the coffin, the crystal was successfully positioned and is now well placed to amplify the highest ideals of this deeply spiritual land. The Russian Orthodox Christian church, with its inspiration directed towards the 'Mother of God', derives from the influence of Peter rather than Paul and of all the fragmented Christian sects it is the closest to the original source - as confirmed, to the profound discomfort of the Roman Papacy, in the Fatima prophecies relating to the end of this century.

154

A large worldwide focus involving hundreds of groups, including the full WWV international network, had been prepared to link in consciousness on July 1st to maximise the potential of the energy available, and many felt the amazing power of this Capricorn full moon that formed a perfect Grand Cross. Later I heard that there had even been a 1 minute silence for peace across Ireland.

Capricorn Full Moon
July 1st.1996

"This is a most significant astrological pattern involving the Full Moon opposition in what is called a Grand Cross. The full moon is in cardinal signs (Cancer/Capricorn) and a Grand Cross here is often a crisis indicator showing that major lessons have to be learned. The other arm of the Cross is formed by Saturn in Aries and Chiron in Libra and these both align with the Moon's Nodes. The entire Grand Cross involving the Sun and Moon (our Father and Mother) with Saturn and Chiron (the old wisdom and the new wisdom) conjunct with the Moon's nodes (our direction in this lifetime deriving from our directions in past times) signifies a time of earth-moving significance".

Richard Giles, Australian astrologer

I meditated in Moscow with Marina Borruso from Italy, appropriately, a woman in her power - giving seminars in Russia on sexual energy mastery. How quickly our world would change if humans knew how to control their life force energies and were able to enjoy love-making without the unnecessary risk of unwanted pregnancy. It is a sobering thought and explains much about human dysfunction that a large proportion of those alive on the planet now were **not** actually wanted by their parents at the time of conception.

At the second vote on July 3rd we heard that President Yeltsin won by 13%. That number again! Confirmation perhaps of the emergence of the Divine Mother on Russian soil.

A POT POURI OF PLACES AND EVENTS OF NOTE SINCE 1992

THE UNITED KINGDOM - THE ERA OF THE MAD COW

My home base is still in the beautiful and gentle English countryside around Avebury in Wiltshire, though, with so much travelling, I have had to give up ownership of property and possessions to allow for maximum flexibility. After my USA and southern hemisphere tours each winter, I return to this lovely region in spring to run the WWV Celtic Odyssey tours with Isabelle Kingston for those from around the world whom I have encouraged to visit the ancient sites and the ever-more-intriguing crop formation symbols in the surrounding fields. Many on my travels dream how exciting it must be to live, "where everyone is surely so spiritually aware"!

If only it were so. In fact, it would be harder to find anywhere where people are so sceptical about the spate of unusual phenomena that regularly manifest here these days. Those who are open to the magnificence of what is actually happening are usually from abroad and are treated with predictable British disdain by locals, who call them "gullible"! Certainly, we are all free to awaken at our own pace, but with such obvious signs appearing almost daily every summer and with the vast majority in this country still dismissive or oblivious of them, one can perhaps be forgiven for wondering what exactly is needed to shake people from their apathy and spiritual amnesia. The answer, of course, is whatever it takes, as we collectively create ever sharper awakening experiences for ourselves.

Considering the important and long prophesied spiritual focus that these small islands now hold for the whole world, it is inevitable, I suppose, that we must first witness the final, painful breakdown of the old order. Only then can Ephraim awaken to his glorious spiritual heritage and new global role nurturing the second, but this time spiritual, empire.

Meantime, an ever less 'Great' Britain - a dis-United and socially fragmented Kingdom if ever there was one - loses its old influence and respect at an accelerating pace. Perhaps this is not so surprising when it betrays its spiritual role by becoming a leading player in the arms manufacturing industry, secondly only to America. Under the euphemism of 'defence contracts' the people are beguiled by their elected politicians

156

into believing that their jobs and livelihoods depend on this gruesome trade of killing and maiming our fellow humans. In this era of dawning enlightenment, are jobs with that kind of stigma attached actually worth having? When will we take responsibility for what we are doing and demand a say in corporate decision-making? Nothing will change until the unaware and greedy controlling class is made to feel the sharp edge of growing public dissent and disapproval.

In this depressing spiritual vacuum, the same politicians have no trouble launching the biggest gambling bonanza ever known - the national lottery. They cynically trade on poorer people's lower instincts of greed and their increasing desperation to rob them weekly of vast sums of money - much of it deriving from the State's own benefit payments to sad and disempowered people with no greater vision of life than winning absurd sums of money. Even those who do win aren't capable of handling their sudden (mis?) fortune and usually learn some hard lessons about the predatory nature of their own families and so-called friends!

And the wafer-thin justification for unleashing this monster of greed and false hope? A tiny percentage of the proceeds is put aside to subsidise the arts and other 'worthy causes'. In the event, the money involved turns out to be a drop in the ocean when compared with the huge loss of revenue suffered by bona fide charities as a direct result of 'The Great National Robbery'. It is tragic to see people's charitable instincts being subverted in this way by elected public servants, and to witness the inexorable deterioration of the nation's moral fibre.

Anyone protesting is, of course, branded a 'spoilsport' by those who have been so easily deceived by the slippery tongues of politicians desperate to squeeze ever more revenue for their 'defence' budgets and other grandiose and irrelevant intellectual fantasies. At the same time, these unscrupulous controllers are busy applying savage cuts in welfare spending to the very underclass they are creating - and robbing! - in the name of 'fiscal prudence' and the absurd and destructive myth called 'economic growth' - more accurately described as planetary suicide. One might imagine that politicians would now see the wisdom of re-directing state funds to fulfil their primary obligation to the electorate - a healthy nation provided with clean, organic food and pure water and air. But no, they fritter away the public purse on inessentials, while the lifeblood of the nation drains away in a miasma of disease, apathy and inertia.

157

To crown it all, and to demonstrate just how far Britain has now sunk spiritually, the company organising the lottery is called 'Camelot' and the machine used to select the winners is called 'Merlin'. And to round off this travesty, when Merlin is unable to make an appearance, a mechanical device called 'Arthur' is wheeled on to do the honours. As if this were not enough, a would-be sorceress with overtones of Morgan le Fay is trundled out every week to make questionable prophecies about the impending winners in this ersatz medieval farrago.

A more complete denial and vilification of a great and still only-too-relevant heritage can hardly be imagined. When **will** the British people withdraw Excalibur, the double-edged sword of discernment and truth, and cut away the illusion that still blinds them?

Meantime, Karma already seems to be exacting a toll on Britain as the country is forced by trading partners to take effective, but financially damaging, measures to eradicate mad cow disease before it turns into a mass human epidemic - if not already too late. We are told that Kreuzfeld Jakob disease takes some ten years to develop in human brains. How did this horror start in Britain? In the mid-1980s, greedy farmers fed herbivorous cattle with foodstuff containing the offal of other animals to accelerate growth for meat production. As the heat processes for destroying disease-producing bacterial organisms in the offal were ineffective, we were suddenly confronted with the fulfilment of Rudolf Steiner's prophecy earlier this century, warning us that cows would go mad if they were ever fed in this way.

As BSE is rapidly spreading across the animal food chain, it looks as though the horrendously exploited 'group souls' of domestic farm animals may well have suffered beyond endurance. Guidance from many sources all agree that they are now to retreat **en masse** to other dimensional pastures well beyond our greed, cruelty and exploitation - leaving humans to get used to a non-carnivorous diet, for which our bodies with few canine teeth and a very long intestine were originally designed anyway. Demand for organic food has quadrupled so far during this crisis. Lighter diets based on clean, uncontaminated food greatly assist spiritual awakening, so there could still be a silver lining to this woeful tale.

With not a statesman to be seen among the rabble of self-interested career politicians, who have disastrously weakened the fabric of British society, a Prime Minister who prefers to "condemn more and understand

158

less", a rudderless royal family adrift on an ever rising tide of republicanism, an Anglican church bankrupt spiritually and financially after losing nearly one billion pounds in usurious property speculation, and all too few voices of wisdom that anyone will listen to, the country faces a crisis of gravest proportions. Even the magnificent English language itself is under threat at the moment of its greatest destiny. English is now better spoken in such outposts of the former Empire as India than it is in Britain!

Meanwhile the game of soccer, once a focus for individual skills, creative teamwork and regional pride, has sunk into wholesale corruption and thuggery, producing a breed of hooligans on and off the pitch that have given the country an unenviable reputation for extreme antisocial behaviour.

So this is the state of Ephraim, the nation that was long ago divinely designated with his brother Manasseh, to champion the cause of the Universal and Unified Christ consciousness at its Second Coming! It was indeed prophesied that Great Britain's role as the leading world power was destined to pass to America, and this has progressively been occurring since the end of the Second World War. However, having relinquished that secular role, the intention was that Britain would then prepare spiritually to fulfil the far greater destiny described in these pages.

After many years of socially divisive right wing government, when sinister elements unleashed a tidal wave of greed and selfishness, perhaps what will now go down in history as 'the era of Mad Cow' will be sufficient to awaken enough people to demand the changes that are so long overdue.

Ironically, all attempts by myself and other like-minded souls to bring these vital matters to public attention have been met either by blank incredulity or outright hostility from the British media. Only the intervention of an independent and far-sighted South African publisher has made possible the release of this material and its encouraging sales around the world.

Meanwhile, we continue, under regular guidance from Merlin, through Isabelle, to do what we can through group activation of the node points of the greater Avebury landscape temple, knowing that this is the most effective way in which we can contribute to the general raising of consciousness in this country. Group work is also regularly conducted in

159

Ireland and Scotland, setting up an overlighting triangle of power to reinforce the spiritual grid that was long ago ordained to protect these sacred shores from negative external forces - but **not** from their own inhabitants!

For myself, with hindsight, it felt entirely appropriate that I just happened to be leading a group of 13 Germans inside the great stone monument of Stonehenge on September 15th, 1993 - the 2,000th birthday of Jesus Christ, born at the 'Acronycal Rising' in 7BCE, the **actual** turn of the Second Millennium, and the day Israel and the PLO signed their Peace Treaty!

GREECE

THE ISLAND OF PATMOS & THE CAVE OF ST JOHN'S REVELATION

After a particularly exhausting tour to South Africa in April 1994 on crutches, and then moving out of my home of eight years, it was time for some real relaxation. The Greek Islands beckoned. In view of my totally unexpected involvement with the missing Revelations text in this book, I felt an island-hopping holiday could be combined with taking in Patmos and visiting the celebrated cave. I had hoped it might be situated in a wild and isolated location, beyond the reach of the crowds. It is in fact, as I might have guessed, a major Christian shrine incorporated into a church and guarded by fierce orthodox priest, issuing instructions as is their wont with streams of tourists and the usual souvenir industry. So much for my idyllic Greek hillside!

How was I to erect the Cross and quietly read the text aloud in the cave without attracting attention? Trust, as usual, was my intuitive answer!

On the appropriate day, I arrived at the church observing the strictly-enforced dress code with a discreet holdall in hand and sat in the chapel attached to the cave site closely scrutinised by the duty priest. As I went into meditation, the priest suddenly reciprocated by going into paroxysms of coughing. He then spat forcibly against the most revered wall of the cave and promptly left the building! The few straggling tourists left with him and I was alone.

Setting up the Cross, sprinkling Chalice well water and depositing a programmed crystal are quickly accomplished, but reading 8 Chapters of

160

powerful text aloud and with due reverence is another matter. As it turned out, apart from a short visit by a large German group (who mistook me for a religious 'believer'!), there were no other disturbances and the priest returned some fifteen minutes later as I was preparing to leave. Intellectually, it is always difficult to know what if anything has been achieved by such actions - apart from feeling good! Yet when circumstances adjust themselves so very conveniently without any personal intervention, one somehow **knows** that there is a greater design than we can comprehend.

This particular holiday also allowed me to visit Ephesus on the nearby Turkish coast, and some of the other sites associated with the 'John' energy there. It is from a courtyard in Ephesus that one of the 'Johns' is reputed to have 'ascended', leaving only a pair of slippers behind. One day soon, I'm sure many will be able to follow where he, Jesus Christ and many others from Earth have gone to prepare the way. However, knowing that it was not yet my time, I returned to the idyllic island of Samos to complete a very nurturing vacation!

ITALY

ROME - THE ETERNAL CITY

Late October and early November 1994 was to prove a very potent time in Rome and Italy generally. My Australian friends, Lucy and Graeme, both Reiki initiates, had received guidance to go to Rome at this time and invited me along. We later discovered that a gathering of some 600 leaders of world faiths and a separate convocation of Cardinals at the Vatican were taking place that very same weekend!

Our first appointment was at the Italian Buddhist centre south of Rome, where we were unexpectedly to meet and meditate with the Venerable Mahago Sananda - Cambodia's spiritual leader and the Nobel peace prize nominee for leading the recent inspirational peace march to Angkor Wat. This fortuitous encounter with one of the most evolved beings on the planet, who particularly related to the Aquarian Cross, helped us perfectly to align our own energies for the work we were about to undertake.

On Sunday morning we mingled with the crowds in St Peter's and quietly meditated as a group in strategic locations, planting programmed crystals wherever we could install them unnoticed. Not easy in St Peter's, which is decidedly lacking in the convenient nooks and crannies of most old buildings.

With the odd recalcitrant crystal clattering to the marble floor at awkward moments, we quickly learned to affect an air of insouciance and move on smartly!

We joined the throng at the papal blessing and were interested to see that many were actually protesting there against different aspects of unpopular church policy. Under the Pope's balcony, we gathered around the Aquarian Cross and then mixed Chalice Well water with the fountains before withdrawing.

Similar work was carried out within the Vatican itself in its miles of soulless, cold and obscenely treasure-stuffed corridors and we were glad to get away from its oppressive and sinister atmosphere. On a quick return visit to the St Pudentiana church (see p. 44), we were by contrast rewarded with pure energy and enjoyed the happy celebrations of a Philippino wedding in progress at the time.

Before leaving the city, I had an appointment to meet again someone I had been introduced to at a dinner party on my first night in Rome. Having only exchanged superficial conversation on our first meeting, we knew nothing about one another, but as Adrian walked me from the Colosseum to some nearby ruins, a certain feeling of familiarity grew. As we stood in the centre of the ruins of the Emperor Nero's palace, a favourite location of Adrian's and about which he is knowledgeable, we suddenly discovered that he had known my family well and often stayed with us in England when I was young! Indeed, as an Australian, he had settled and lived in Rome for the past 30 years because of a holiday we had all spent together in Italy in the 1950s.

It all happened so suddenly and was such a remarkable synchronicity that we both stood speechless and breathless for some moments as the strong energy engulfed us. Certainly a powerful reconciliation of energy had been achieved at some level on a very relevant site. No doubt too, it contributed to the effectiveness of our work in the city where the apostle Peter had long ago been agonizingly crucified - upside down. The method of execution of his Master was too good for him.

In the days that followed, northern Italy was inundated with the heaviest rains this century, and the following weekend Rome witnessed the

162

biggest political demonstration in recent history with over one million people attending. Perhaps it helped to further expose the almost impenetrable depths of Italian political corruption that now sees a former long-serving Prime Minister, closely associated with the Vatican, accused of membership of the Mafia itself.

THE AVALON CONNECTIONS IN AUSTRALIA AND NEW ZEALAND

On recent visits to New Zealand, I have been brought into contact with a most interesting group called the Culdees. This is a Celtic sect initiated into the teachings of 'The Way' by Joseph of Arimathea himself two thousand years ago in Avalon.

After inevitable persecution by the church into the Middle Ages, there is no further trace of them, until in 1980 a group received channelled guidance about them in the Coromandel peninsula. As the mainly women members gradually grew and attracted other like-minded supporters, the Culdee Bible, known as the Kolbrin, was miraculously restored to them together with other early teachings. We met when, unknown to each other, we were giving simultaneous presentations with Joseph of Arimathea as our common theme in the same small town in the North Island!

I find it particularly fascinating that this pure energy should have re-emerged at the exact opposite end of the new heart chakra of the planet. The heart chakra of the planet is indeed being activated in south west England, but as I have said, it is the destiny of New Zealand first to be an example to the rest of humanity. How appropriate, therefore, that this Avalonian inspiration should manifest in New Zealand now.

AVALON - AUSTRALIA

Near the town of Geelong in Victoria, Australia is another very special link with Glastonbury, demonstrating once again how well understood have been the ancient Celtic spiritual links binding the English-speaking New World with ancient Avalon. This is yet another confirmation of the main theme I present in these pages.

In 1832, James Austin, a farmer from near Glastonbury, emigrated to Australia. He prospered and after making a fortune from sheep farming left the 'Avalon' estate he had created near Geelong to return to England to fulfil a long-standing dream. He had always been inspired by the ruins of Glastonbury Abbey as a great spiritual centre with its special association with Joseph of Arimathea. Now he was in a position to buy them with the intention of restoring them to the church. The sale was not realised until his son sold them to the Anglican Church in 1907, but meantime, during his ownership, very significant links were established between Avalon in UK and Avalon in Australia.

One is planted in the courtyard: a descendant of the original thorn tree, said to have grown from the staff which Joseph of Arimathea planted into Wearyall Hill on his arrival at Glastonbury - the staff being from the tree which supplied the crown of thorns at the crucifixation of Jesus the Christ. The other is set into a wall: a piece of masonry from the Abbey carved with a Tudor rose. The adjacent inscription reads as follows:

> *Into the walls of Avalon is wrought*
> *This stone from Glastonbury brought:*
> *Stay for a while, Traveller, and view*
> *This **link** between the Old and the New*
> By J L Cuthbertson, Classics Master at Geelong Grammar School

The descendants of James Austin donated the buildings to the Anglican Brotherhood of St Lawrence in 1962 with the request that the property be used "as a powerhouse for peace". In 1996, the neighbouring Geelong Grammar school bought the property "and the many friends of the original Avalon community look forward to the school using Avalon in accordance with the spirit of peace and healing which motivated its donation to the Brotherhood of St Lawrence."

Researched by Anthea Eyres: Melbourne 1996

THE PROPHECIES OF THE ANDES
September 16 - October 2, 1996

The year 1996 proved to be a landmark in my travels with visits at last to some of the few places in the world that had still not succumbed to my roving spirit; namely Russia and South America. How interesting that Zagorsk and Lake Titicaca are either side of Glastonbury on the female dragon line of infinity! The opportunity to take the balanced Cross to the South American continent for the first time after centuries of misery caused there by the imbalanced crucifix

164

came as a result of an invitation from an Australian friend, Rosemarie Bauer, who arranges regular spiritual journeys to Peru. On this occasion, her local agent in Cusco - the shaman Jorge Luis Delgado - had organised a conference over the Spring Equinox called "The Prophecies of the Andes" at which I was invited to speak.

As there were opportunities for other international speakers, I recommended the participation of Or Olam, the Mikkyo Master from Kyoto, Japan with whom I had recently worked in Russia, and Anabel Watson from another international peace initiative "Through the Heart to Peace". Happily, Credo Mutwa, the highly inspirational South African Zulu spiritual leader with whom I had worked just prior to the 1994 South African elections also joined us as part of his research into the important spiritual links between Africa and South America. As he says; "Humanity was birthed in Africa, but its knowledge came from South America". Together with other delegates and speakers from the USA, Argentina, Australia, New Zealand, South Africa, Japan and UK, we were joined by many interesting (though all male!) Andean shamans.

My first pleasant surprise on arriving in Lima was to find that my friend Robyn from Glastonbell in Australia had also been invited - we had always said that one day we'd work together in Peru, and now synchronicity had created the opportunity! I was glad to be able join her small party on a thrilling day excursion south of Lima to see the celebrated 'Nasca lines'. There are innumerable theories about Nasca's long straight lines across the mysterious Ocucaje desert and the images so clearly visible from above of an astronaut, monkey, condor, dog, hands, tree, parrot, spider, heron and humming bird.

For me, much was revealed by a fascinating visit - after a somewhat unsettling light aircraft flight! - to the private museum of 'The Engraved Stones of ICA', In recent years Dr. Javier Cabrera has accumulated some 11,000 extremely ancient (Mesozoic -230 million years old) and meticulously engraved stones depicting the activities and teachings of a highly advanced race of humans living in that region at the time. Among much else there are clear depictions of heart and brain transplants carried out under acupuncture, together with the vital information that a non-rejection agent is contained within the human umbilical cord! To the embarrassment of our young, female translator there were also graphic illustrations of what constitutes appropriate and inappropriate human sexual behaviour, pointing out in detail the inevitability of mass disease and plague resulting particularly from male homosexual promiscuity. All the great civilisations have ended in sexual inversion, and here, way back in pre-history, is the warning that highly immuno-supressive semen should under **no** circumstances ever enter other male bodies. Yet, loving, faithful and non-promiscuous male/male relationships are given approval, subject to the above injunction. Loving female bonding is also condoned, and indeed throughout history has never been condemned because, unlike the male equivalent, it does not have a life-threatening potential.

The stones provide a wealth of vital knowledge and information on many subjects as our civilisation like so many before is threatened with demise. Characteristically in these 'left-brain' times of intellectual and academic supremacy, Dr.Cabrera's collection has been dismissed and ridiculed by the dysfunctional 'experts' in whom most of humanity foolishly still invests its trust. Here is a genuine treasure trove that at last turns our evolutionary theory on its head - time is fast running out for our race, and intellectual scepticism and ignorance must no longer go unchallenged! Those who can help to bring this priceless wisdom to a wider international audience should contact Dr.Cabrera for his book and research information at: Plaza de Armas, Bolivar No 170, ICA Peru Tel: ICA 231933.

We now started our battle with altitude sickness as we journeyed through the high Andes between Cusco and La Paz in Bolivia at heights well over 3,000 metres. On the way to the conference in the Sacred Valley, we visited important Incan sites at Tambo Machay for a water purification, K'Emko the Puma temple and the ruins of Sacsayhuaman, geometrical centre of the Incan Empire. Here we heard the enchanting pan pipes and saw our first condor in an incomparable setting! Utter magic and so evocative of ancient memories in this timeless landscape.

The Prophecies conference was imaginatively located at a lovely old monastery converted into a comfortable hotel with flower-filled gardens and fountains. For the first two days we all listened attentively and with much interest as local shamanistic wisdom was imparted in a

166

strictly 'piscean' format with male lecturers and straight rows of chairs. Credo Mutwa's wise and compassionate contribution was especially well received. However, as is the way these days, the conference delegates were predominantly female and their patience with male lecturing was running out!

With the highlight of the event at Spring equinox on September 22nd. (1p.m. as the Sun entered Libra) fast approaching, Jorge Luis kindly asked me to focus a suitable ceremony. So on the Sunday morning it was decided to change the seating into a large oval and delegates were treated to Anabel Watson's fascinating and moving description of the origins of the 'Through the Heart to Peace' movement and the amazing peace initiative of courageous women working in healed feminine energy across man-made barriers in former Yugoslavia and in many problem areas around the world. Or Olam then worked his Mikkyo magic with the world Peace prayers and the universal Mudra, Peace breathing and his powerful and dramatic invocation of the Divine energy through whistling and clapping.

I then gave a short talk on the significance of bringing the balanced Aquarian Cross, symbol of the Universal Christ consciousness, to the Americas in fulfilment of Hopi prophecy and to signal the end of the era of distorted Christianity that since the mid 16th.Century has decimated the indigenous population and the spirituality of these lands. Because of the devastating effect of the 'western' religion, the local shamanistic religion unsurprisingly appears to ignore the entire 2,000 year era of the 'Christ' mission (1st. and 2nd.Coming) and speaks instead of an energy shift now direct from the Himalayas - a former focal power centre of the planet - to the Andes. As this book makes clear, it is the role of the western nations (especially the UK and USA) through the Celtic dispersion to declare the Second Coming of the universal and unified (Christ) consciousness in **all** prepared human hearts. The actual prophecy of the Incas for these times is that Christ conscious brothers and sisters from many spiritual traditions all over the world will return to the Andes and help to trigger a raising of consciousness there - largely through the indigenous 'wise women', who are still subjugated in that society!

Early on Sunday morning, awoken by the usual altitude headache, I had looked idly out of the bathroom window and noticed a perfect location for the ceremony in a lovely courtyard with a fountain decorated with flowers. And so it was at midday that some seventy delegates formed a circle around the fountain, where I had filled a chalice with well water from Glastonbury, Zagorsk in Russia and the Sacred Valley River. The open-centred Cross was placed horizontally over the chalice to receive the full light of the midday sun, while Or Olam and I performed the Universal Peace Mudra among other prayers and invocations for the New Birth at Springtime. Credo Mutwa contributed a potent Zulu incantation and then four self-selected women made affirmations around the fountain. Four root-races were represented. It just so happened that a large swarm of bees had decided to focus on the fountain at this moment too and as bees and the Humming bird in local tradition represent the Divine messenger, we were given a perfect reconfirmation of our intentions! All participants then received the waters of the Chalice as a blessing and many a seasoned shaman, including Jorge Luis with tears in his eyes, affirmed that this had indeed been an exceptionally powerful and blessed ritual. I ended the conference by showing the latest 1996 UK Crop formations to an enthralled audience.

The stunning setting of Machu Picchu must surely exceed everyone's expectations. We approached by train and bus through ever greener and more precipitous scenery. Sometimes bathed in sunlight, but often in low cloud and mist with dazzling rainbows, this evocative site demonstrates above all the sophistication of Incan life, and that these peoples had access to a higher knowledge derived from very ancient civilisations on that continent - possibly the ICA connection? Certainly they were infinitely more advanced spiritually than the Christian predators who took advantage of internal Incan political conflict to subjugate these people and all but destroy them from the 16th. century onwards. Our contribution to the site was an uplifting purification ceremony with fire and water expertly conducted by Chaski, our group guide. At midday we then found another site to work with the Cross and this time organised the group into two interlinking circles of a human Vesica Piscis. The circles were both spun before each person passed through the sacred mandorla at the centre containing the Cross. Or Olam led us again in the Universal

Peace Mudra and then sang most beautifully in Japanese his own Peace song composition. Interestingly, both ceremonies were conspicuously supervised at close range by wild Llamas attracted to the energies! These mysterious and very ancient animals are highly revered in the Andes, so perhaps another sign was manifested for us. Many in the group thought I both looked and stood like a Llama - perhaps I've found my animal totem at last!

The auspicious full moon eclipse on September 26th was held at the Temple of the Moon 'Amaru Machay', a cave near Cusco and a lovely ceremony with the moon's rays penetrating a hole in the roof was conducted by Betty and Julio - local shamans. At Lake Titicaca we explored the famous reed islands on reed boats, visited the haunting site of Silustani where we danced the Mystic Spiral and enjoyed a sensational sunset. Next day we attuned deeply at the amazing interdimensional gateway of Amaru Muru - the seat of Master Meru and his consort, the Deities overlighting the lake.

On St.Michael's day we crossed to Copacabana on the Bolivian side of the lake and a small group attended mass that evening at the famous pilgrimage church of the black Madonna. This turned out to be a perfect preparation for the final ritual on the Island of the Sun next morning. Robert Coon had suggested placing the Cross horizontally on the ground here to mark the exact crossover point of the Symbol of Infinity (the planetary sexual chakra where the dragon lines mate). After a beautifully prepared flower ceremony by Chaski committing to the lake the small offerings of the conference delegates, we gathered at the island's sacred fountain. Having cleansed ourselves, we then spun the symbol of Infinity in human form around the Cross marking this great global intersection point. Titicaca water was mixed with the other sacred waters in order to invoke the flow of energy along the female dragon line north eastwards. Chaski then read aloud in Spanish a powerful Invocation to Lake Titicaca that had been used by Robert Coon during his work there just prior to the Harmonic Convergence activation in Mexico in August 1987. After many hugs and much happiness expressed on this very potent site, we noticed that two Llamas were again overseeing our activities and that the high winds accompanying the work had now thankfully abated. Near La Paz we briefly visited the remains of Tihuanacu and then all too quickly the tour was over. In Lima that night there was a strong Earth tremor

169

and a plane crash at the airport. However, a Humming bird did tap my hotel window as I was leaving! The siege of the Japanese embassy in Lima and two major earthquakes soon after this energy work in late 1996 again seem to confirm that the local energy grid has been activated.

CURACAO - NETHERLANDS ANTILLES
3 - 6 October, 1996

To be honest, I had only ever heard of the drink! So when Gerda Wout contacted me with appreciation for my book and hoping I might some day visit the island, I had my doubts. Then our old friend synchronicity swung into action again when I discovered that my cheap flight to Lima on the Dutch airline KLM would be stopping in both directions in the Netherlands Antilles. With alacrity, I accepted the invitation!

Gerda and her husband Sixto had for long been students of both Carol Parrish in the USA and of Mr.Beazley, the British esotericist. So, with their connections at Sparrow Hawk in the USA and at Eastbourne in the UK (also the WWV headquarters), it was inevitable that our paths would cross sooner or later. Sadly a few years ago, tragedy struck when Gerda was seriously injured in a car accident and became paralysed from the neck down. Despite this dreadful handicap, she and Sixto still continue their health food stores and esoteric bookstore/ library. They are a great inspiration to many on the island and indeed all over the world.

In a channelling of Merlin through Isabelle Kingston before the trip, we heard that: "Curacao is a most magical place, a shining jewel and a place of power, this is a node point within the great matrix of the planet and a place of interdimensional and intergalactic connection. If the energy is balanced there, the island will give light and focus to the whole Caribbean region". In reply to what we were to achieve during my visit Merlin answered; "Hold a light, light a beacon and let joy emerge. Most important - there is no rush or hurry in this place. There is always time!"

Since it took fully forty minutes to offload a few bags at Curacao's tiny airport on arrival, I was glad of this warning before I blew a fuse!

170

After a relaxing tour of the island and some of its power spots and a delicious swim with Marianne, who had recently been on our Celtic Odyssey in the UK, it was time for work. The programme started with a free evening talk with meditation and questions at the University attended by an excellent turnout of some one hundred and fifty people. Forty five of these were sufficiently attracted to join the full day workshop next day when I expanded on my basic themes and showed slides of the WWV global work and latest Crop formations. The programme concluded with the spiritual highlight, which consisted of around seventy people gathering in Gerda and Sixto's garden early on Sunday morning. After a gentle routine of body movement with the group, we formed into two interconnecting circles and spun the Vesica Piscis around an altar comprising the Cross and everyone's special stones and jewellery. After this we mixed the sacred waters already mentioned with those of Puerto Rico and Curacao and sprinkled it over ourselves. Our dedication was blessed by a gentle shower of much needed rain with ominous rolls of thunder in the background - indeed, local reports indicated that for some weeks afterwards this parched island received regular and gentle rains. There were then hugs all round and as I left for the airport, the consensus was that we had indeed "lit a spiritual beacon"!

Chapter 9

AMERICA - THE UNITED STATES OF EARTH?

"There is a time in the affairs of men,
Which, taken at the flood, leads on to fortune;
On such a full sea are we now afloat,
And we must take the current when it serves,
Or lose our ventures."
William Shakespeare - *Julius Caesar, IV, iii.*

How, we may well ask ourselves, could a vast continent inhabited by a spiritually and environmentally aware indigenous people with 70 or so million buffalo in their care, have mutated into the dysfunctional module for so-called 'western civilisation' that now holds the world to ransom through its distorted values?

The root cause, according to an American friend called Joe, with whom I recently travelled the south west, is the religion that swept through that Continent, ruthlessly cutting down anyone - and any belief, tradition, cosmology or culture - that stood in its path. Granted that all these horrors were yet another outworking of the overall pattern of the pain of separation that was chosen by humanity - itself a major theme of this book - but let us not forget that, both in North and South America, as elsewhere in the world, the impetus was actually provided by zealous Christians spreading the poison of division and separation. They conducted their violent crusades under cover of a wholly unjustifiable and arrogant elitism that has ever since been the basis for dislocation and disharmony within all the cultures and societies that have fallen under their baleful influence. Joe went on to explain that under the pernicious yoke of the white man's alien religion, literally millions of native Americans, many adhering to the principles of Universal Law, were brutally exterminated. At the same time the great 'spirit force' of the buffalo was massacred and quickly reduced to small herds in reservations by men who showed so much disrespect for their victims that they used them for indiscriminate target practice from moving trains! Warming to his theme, my friend pointed out that we need no more proof than the spate of fundamentalist sects and cults with bizarre messianic figureheads that are being spawned in its death-throes by not only eternally divisive Christianity, but all religions the world over .

Now, he went on, is the long-awaited time when we are witnessing the final stages of the titanic battles and financially-motivated power struggles that will soon liberate not only America but the entire planet from the malign influence of outdated belief structures. Then and only then will the original, idealistic dream of a genuine 'United States and Peoples' - a land of power and great beauty that is ultimately destined to enshrine all the principles of 'Heaven on Earth' - come into being. I could only concur with Joe's incisive and uncompromising vision; yet I suspect that, although he is speaking for only the tiniest, enlightened minority of his fellow countrymen - the majority would doubtless regard his views as highly subversive - forthcoming events will soon prove him right: the dramatic changes that are already beginning to manifest throughout America - changes in which I have found myself being involved as the story of the Aquarian Cross continues to unfold - have considerable significance for the whole world.

It was at a 1992/3 New Year's celebration in the UK that I met a young woman who had attended an international native American gathering the previous summer. Amanda was full of infectious enthusiasm about the event and its importance; so, as my own path now seemed to be leading me towards the USA, I kept in touch with her and contacted other friends who were likely to be interested in attending the next meeting during July 1993.

So it was that our group of seven, from both the UK and USA, converged on the camp-site for the Lakota Indian-inspired 'Sixth Annual International Brotherhood Days' event near Pine Ridge in South Dakota. This wonderful event that attracts hundreds of people from within America and all over the world to meet in friendship for a week and learn about native American spirituality -at a cost of only $15 for the camp-site - is the initiative of Severt Young Bear Sr., who was deservedly honoured by his people that year and made a chief just before his recent death.

It was not until my friends Amy and Bob from Iowa joined us that I heard for the first time about the devastating floods that were occurring in the middle-American States. The rains had been unremitting for over a month with many rivers including the Mississippi bursting their banks. This quickly developed into a national catastrophe that would cost an already fragile economy billions of dollars.

Long-standing prophecies of major geological change in America are well known, and many people I spoke to during my three-week stay were wondering if we were already witnessing the first state of flooding that would eventually merge the Great Lakes with the Gulf of Mexico, as predicted.

For me, it was particularly interesting to note that, once again, the Aquarian Cross was present at the height of the crisis, when a 50-foot wall of water was only narrowly held back by the levees and prayers of the people of Kansas City. Happily, on July 28th, the day of my departure, the weather pattern changed for the first time in weeks and at least gave the long-suffering people of the region some respite from their ordeal.

South Dakota was not immune from rain either, and as an inexperienced camper already trying to come to terms with on-site facilities limited to a single water pump, I found it rather alarming to be only under flimsy canvas during the ferocious thunderstorms and accompanying tornado warnings we were to experience throughout that week. Perhaps, though, the daily 'Water of Life' ceremonies we took part in, bonding all those present in a powerful ritual with the element of sanctified water, were not unconnected with the tempestuous climate! They were conducted by a well-focused Dakota medicine man and were, I felt, the spiritual high point of the gathering.

In order to make our own private contribution to these peoples who had bravely resisted submitting to the US Government and incurred much carefully-orchestrated hostility over the years as a result, five of us took the Aquarian Cross to the infamous 'Wounded Knee' massacre site nearby. This tragic event late last century, when hundreds of Indian men, woman and children were ruthlessly exterminated by white troops, is seen by many to have been the moment when the spirit of the Indian peoples was finally broken and subjugated to the white man's yoke. This landscape, also the grave of the legendary, mystical Indian leader, Chief Crazy Horse still exudes the palpable sadness and despair of a people robbed of self-respect after generations of deprivation caused by the imposition of a totally alien culture. This can justifiably be called 'the land of the broken heart', and it was to offer healing that we formed a circle on a hilltop near the graves of those whose troubled spirits still haunt this desolate land.

During our invocations, songs and prayers, an unexpected sound told us that we had company: a rattlesnake had decided to join us - and at the same time, presumably, test our fear thresholds! As it slithered behind me, the Sun suddenly burst out of a cloudy sky and we all instantly realised with great relief that, using the symbol of the serpent, the Earth Mother had responded. Before leaving the site, we sprinkled Chalice Well water from Glastonbury and buried a small stone from Ragged Stone Hill - centre of the Circle of Light in England - to link this land directly with the Gaian heart.

Having enjoyed the tribal dancing and other entertainments laid on at the Brotherhood Festival, we were told about a 5 day Sun Dance ritual nearby, where visitors were welcome and would be fed free of charge. We decided to take up this rare opportunity and spent the next two days experiencing the build-up of energies around some 30 male dancers, who fast for the duration and alternate the dance with sweat-lodges. Predictably, the US Government, fearful of Indian power derived from natural energies, banned the rituals for much of this century! During the Sun Dance certain candidates volunteer for the ultimate initiation, which involves piercing the chest with a metal prong that is attached by rope to the focal 'Tree of Life', representing Wakan-Tanka (Sky Father) and around which the dance is performed. During the ritual the candidate leans back against the rope until the flesh tears. This symbolises the pain of separation, after which he becomes a channel, drawing down through the dance the light of the Sun (male) into the Earth (female).

Although, needless to say, I did not participate in this painful ritual, I was able to join a sweat-lodge for the first time. The medicine man who led the water ceremony, invited certain people from the camp to his own lodge on the last night. So at sunset a fire was lit to heat some large rocks, while our small international group gingerly disrobed on a chilly night in an isolated valley far from the madding crowd!

Eli led the way into a low, oval, covered structure, while seven red-hot rocks were passed through the entrance and deposited in the central pit. The flaps were now dropped and we were in total darkness. Then, as Eli poured water over the hissing rocks, we were suddenly enveloped in a cloud of searing steam. After a moment or two of claustrophobic panic, I settled down, but was still pleased to be next to the exit, where it is anyway a little cooler!

The ritual is divided into four quarters, with prayer focused on four specific purposes, and the entrance flap is raised after each one for a breather. It turned out to be a most profound and moving initiation in which each vocalised his prayers and aspirations for himself, humanity at large and the Earth Mother. Afterwards we all smoked the Peace pipe and then with my two female companions from Glastonbury, Charmian and Ahuva, I showed Eli the Aquarian Cross. It was, for me, a profound moment as the first native American absorbed it into his consciousness.

Before returning to Denver and having left Charmian at the sundance, Ahuva and I decided to visit some more power centres in the vicinity. 'Take me back to the Black Hills, the Black Hills of Dakota' had been a favourite childhood song and now it was about to be realised! The heads of four US Presidents peered eerily down at us from Mount Rushmore through occasional gaps in the low cloud, and later we saw the equivalent Indian monument of Chief Crazy Horse which is still under construction. But then came an unscheduled and most welcome initiation: 70 million buffalo had once roamed the north American plains, but now the few remaining herds are confined to a reservation in this area. While driving along and hoping to see some in the distance, we rounded a corner and were suddenly surrounded by a large herd crossing the road. They were in no hurry as huge snorting bulls eyed each other up for a fight and more docile cows and calves ambled past the car at no more than arm's length! To the joy of the indigenous Indians 'Miracle' the long-predicted albino buffalo calf was born soon after, and signifies the return of the Buffalo Calf woman.

Our last port of call, appropriately over the mid-July New Moon, was the dramatic focal point of the film *Close Encounters of the Third Kind*, known as Devil's Tower - the first American national monument. This must be among the most unusual natural formations on Earth and is a vast, solitary, cylindrical, fluted mountain of grey-green rock rising some 1000 feet sheer out of the northern Wyoming plains. It is a place of awesome natural power that doubtless plays a crucial role in the energy alignments of this Continent. We both tuned in with the Cross and then made a complete circuit of the base, among the fallen boulders, scrub, pine trees and snakes.

I was convinced that in the remaining week of my visit, there was a still more important connection to be made, and always had in the back of my mind the prophecy spoken of by the Hopi elder Thomas Banyaca (mentioned earlier in the book) about the White brother returning to the Red brother with the Cross and the circle, signifying that the time to resume co-operation between them had now come. Some say that the shape of the ancient Celtic Cross (equal-sided within a circle) represented in recent crop formations in the UK is the awaited sign. I don't subscribe to this theory, because the Celtic Cross is actually older than the Crucifix, and it is the imbalanced crucifix without any circle symbology that was long ago predicted to be the cause of great suffering among the Indians. Logically, therefore, the Hopi prophecy must relate to a *new* symbol combining the Cross and circle, and what could be more appropriate than the Aquarian Cross - symbolic of the Christ consciousness and talisman of the New Jerusalem?

So much for the theory; but not knowing whom to contact or indeed where to go to further this inner conviction, I had no option but to wait and see whether the Universe would make the necessary arrangements. I needn't have worried; all I had to do, as usual, was sit back and watch the unfolding of the plan in all its glory and perfection! Ahuva had a meeting at her recording studio in Boulder to finalise details on her superb new album of sacred Hebrew songs. Afterwards, I took her to meet David, a recent contact there of Charmian's, who had just completed a beautiful wooden structure on a hilltop aligned to certain stars that was being used for Universal peace dancing and other forms of creative expression.

Later that night he phoned me in Denver to say that a clairvoyant friend of his named Peter living in Santa Fe, New Mexico had in conversation with him that very day said that he recognised my name from a recent magazine article and that I must try to attend the last of the Hopi Kachina dances, known as the Home dance, being celebrated all day on July 24th at Hotevilla, Hopi Land in Arizona. The cosmic connection still appeared to be in working order! I knew it was rare for outsiders to get an invitation and, speaking to Peter later, he suggested Ahuva and I join his family camping at Titus' Cornfields, a few miles outside Hotevilla.

In high excitement, we repacked the car and this time headed south on the second leg of our quest. Distances are huge in the USA and the next five days were eventually to take us in scorching heat as far south as Sedona in central Arizona - some 1800 miles in all! After camping overnight under the Mesa Verde power site - and being rather un-kindly moved on by the police at 3 a.m. for being on an apparently closed camp-site - we arrived exhausted at Hotevilla, the traditional Hopi village-capital of the reservation, in time for the morning cere-monies.

THE HOPI - "the People of Peace" - OUR LAST HOPE

The Hopi are directly descended through the Anasazi from the Mayans, and are part of a migration of native peoples from the south with totally different genetic roots from the majority of nomadic, car-nivorous plains Indians - Apache, Navajo, Sioux etc. - who migrated from the north. The Hopi have always been a peaceful, domestic race, operating by consensus rather than force, and husbanding the Earth in deep attunement to the grains and vegetables on which until recently they lived. Surrounded first by predatory northern tribes and then by meddlesome and subversive whites, the lot of the 'people of peace' has not been an easy one.

Throughout their ordeals, however, certain of their elders have re-tained the spiritual knowledge and prophecies of their Mayan fore-bears especially those that refer to what they call "the transition from the 4th to the 5th Worlds" in the days leading to their Omega point of the year 2013.

This period is known as the time of the "Rebirthing of the World" and, according to their teachings, humanity must pass through 9 "Worlds" before achieving completion. Their prophecies warn those aware enough to recognise and act upon them, of negative thought-patterns and certain critical events to look out for at this stage of our evolution. Since they have been so liberally - and often inaccurately - interpreted, I feel it might be helpful to summarise their particular relevance to us all.

THE ESSENCE OF THE HOPI PROPHECY

The balance of life

As caretakers of life, we affect the balance of Nature to such a de-gree that our actions determine whether the great cycles of Nature bring prosperity or disaster. Thus our present world is the unfoldment of a pattern we have set in motion, and our divergence from the natu

179

ral balance is traced to a point preceding the emergence of the physical form we manifest today.

Once we were able to appear and disappear at will, but through our own arrogance, we took our powers as instruments of Creation for granted and neglected the plan of the Creator. As a consequence, we became confined to our left and right sides - the left side (right-brain hemisphere) being wise and the right (left-brain hemisphere) being clever and powerful - but unwise and forgetful of our original purpose here.

The cycle of worlds

This suicidal split was to determine the entire course of our history, for Age after Age. As life resources diminished, in keeping with the cycles of Nature, we would try to better our situation by means of our own inventiveness, believing that any mistakes could be corrected by further inventions. Through sheer cleverness, most people would lose sight of humanity's original purpose and become committed to a world of their own design, which would ultimately oppose the order of the Universe itself. Such people would eventually become the mindless enemy of the few who still held the key to survival.

In several previous worlds, the majority advanced their technology in this way even beyond what we know today, and the consequent violations against Nature and fellow humans caused severe imbalances that were resolved in the form of war, social disintegration and natural catastrophe. As each World or Age reached the brink of annihilation, there remained a small minority who managed to live in nearly complete accord with the infinite plan, as implied in the name, Hopi. Towards the final stages even they would encounter signs of disintegration within, as well as receiving enticing offers and severe threats in the outer world aimed at forcing them to join the majority.

Our present world

Our common ancestors were among the small group who miraculously emerged from the last world as it underwent its destruction, although they too were tainted with corruption. The seeds of the crisis we face today were brought with us when we first set foot in this world. Upon reaching our present world, the Hopi set out on a long migration to meet the Creator in the person of Maasaw, the caretaker of this land and all the life-forms upon it. They followed a special pattern; however, a serious omen made a separate journey necessary in order to balance the extreme disorder anticipated for the (present) 'latter days'.

The true white brother

A Hopi of light complexion, now called the True Brother, left his people and travelled in the direction of the rising sun, taking with him a stone tablet which matches a similar tablet held by those who went on to meet Maasaw at a place called Oraibi. It was here that the present Hopi villages were established according to his instructions. The Hopi anticipated the arrival of a race of light-skinned people from the east, predicting many of their inventions, which would signal various stages of unfoldment of the pattern that the Hopi had studied since ancient times. It was clearly foreseen that the visitors in their cleverness might have lost sight of their original purpose, in which case they would become very dangerous.

The Hopi were to watch for one who has not left the spiritual path and carries the actual stone tablet.

The swastika and the Sun

Throughout the centuries, the Hopi have in their ceremonies recalled previous worlds, our emergence into the present world and our purpose in coming here. Periodically they have renewed their covenant with Maasaw to love the simple, humble way of life he laid out and to preserve the balance of nature for the sake of all living things.

The knowledge of world events was handed down in secret lodges which kept watch as each stage unfolded. The elders looked especially for a series of three world-shaking events that would be accompanied by the appearance of certain symbols (crop formations matching the Hopi petroglyph symbols) describing the primordial forces that govern all life, from the sprouting of a seed to global events such as weather, earthquakes, migrations and wars.

The Gourd rattle is a key symbol and its shaking during a ceremony means the stirring of life forces. On the rattle is drawn the ancient symbol of the swastika or meha, showing the spirals of force sprouting from a seed in four directions. This is surrounded by a ring of red fire, showing the encircling penetration of the warmth of the sun tawa, causing the seed to sprout and grow. The first two world-shaking events would involve forces portrayed by the swastika and the sun. Out of the violence and destruction of the first the strongest elements would emerge with still greater force to produce the second event. When these actual symbols appeared, it would be a clear sign that this stage of the prophecy was being fulfilled.

The Gourd full of ashes

Eventually, a "gourd full of ashes" would be invented, which if dropped from the sky would boil the oceans and burn the land, preventing anything from growing for many years. This would be a signal for certain Hopi to reveal some of their teachings in order to warn the world that the third and final event would happen soon and that it could bring an end to all life unless people correct themselves and their leaders in time. Hopi leaders now believe that the first two events were the first and second World Wars, and that the "Gourd full of ashes" was the atomic bomb. After the obliteration of Hiroshima and Nagasaki, teachings formerly kept secret were compared and released to the world. The details presented here are part of those teachings.

The day of purification

The final stage, called the Day of Purification, is described as the hatching of a "mystery egg" in which the forces of meha and tawa unite with a third force symbolised by the colour red, culminating in either total rebirth or total annihilation - we don't know which, but the choice is still ours. War and natural catastrophe may be involved but the degree of violence will be determined by the amount of disruption caused among the peoples of the world and in the balance of Nature.

In this crisis, rich and poor will be forced to struggle as equals to survive . That it will be very violent is now taken for granted among the traditional Hopi societies, but even now we may still lessen its impact by correcting our treatment of Nature as well as of each other.

Ancient spiritually-based communities, such as the Hopi must be preserved - and not forced to abandon their way of life or the resources they have vowed to protect.

The fate of humanity

Clearly, the Hopi have a key role to play in the survival of the human race, by virtue of their vital communion with the unseen forces that hold natural balance, and as an example of a practical alternative to suicidal man-made systems. They can thus be seen as a fulcrum of world events. The pattern is simple: "The whole world will shake, turn red and rise against those who are hindering the Hopi." The man-made systems now destroying the Hopi culture are deeply involved in similar violations throughout the world and the devastating reversal predicated in the prophecies is merely part of the natural order. If those who thrive under that system and its money and its laws can prevent it from eliminating the Hopi Way, then many may survive the Day of Purification and enter a new age of peace. But if no-one is left to continue the Hopi Way, the hope for such an age is in vain.

The forces we must face are formidable, yet the only alternative is annihilation. The man-made system cannot be rectified by forcing others to do one's will, for that is the very crux of the problem. If people are to re-direct themselves and their leaders, the gulf between the two must be eliminated. To accomplish this, we can only rely on the energy of TRUTH itself. This approach, which is the foundation of the Hopi Way, is the greatest challenge a mortal can face. Few are likely to accept it. But once peace is established on this basis, and our original way of life is allowed to flourish, we will be able to use our inventive skills wisely to encourage rather than to threaten life, and benefit everyone, rather than enrich a few at the expense of others. Concern for all living things will far surpass personal concerns, bringing greater happiness and prosperity than could have been realised before. Then all living things shall enjoy lasting peace and harmony.

> Extracted from the *Global Purification Messenger*,
> journal of traditional Hopi Elders.
> The prophecies were condensed by Tom Tarbet and
> taken from the original given by DANAGYUMTEWA.

At the end of the Cycle of Worlds, it says that even pure-living people will be tested by negative inner and outer influences. Hopi Land itself is no exception, and the US government made inroads long ago to disrupt their traditional culture. Government agents first set up a subversive 'Tribal Council' through rigged elections based on bribery and misinformation, which still acts as a puppet of Washington's dictates. They then forcibly removed Hopi children to distant boarding schools where they were indoctrinated into the system, with a liberal dose of 'Christianity' thrown in for good measure, no doubt.

Divide and rule has been the official policy on all Indian reservations and, having had their culture destabilised, the native peoples are furthermore specifically excluded from economic investment aid and kept deliberately below subsistence levels on demeaning state hand-outs and subsidies. Beggared and demoralised, they are then additionally subjected to the White culture's subversive tactics through addiction to alcohol, drugs and sugar-laden junk food. The result of all this on the entire native population is pitiful to behold, with infant mortality at unacceptably high levels, diabetes on the rampage and many afflicted with a wide range of mental and physical illnesses. This, then, is the stark reality of the dis-United States of America, far away from the superficial glamour of the coastal fringes that I stumbled across during my brief tour of 'reservations' that bear a disconcerting resemblance to concentration camps. If the native population is treated with such callous disrespect, what, I wondered with a shudder, was the lot of the other non-white ethnic minorities. For this 'Christian' country that preaches one thing and blatantly practices its direct opposite, there is much to be done to put its own house in order before it can ever be a positive influence on the world stage.

No doubt natural justice through the immutable laws of rebirth and karma is working itself out with former oppressors now experiencing the role of victims in Indian bodies, but unless at this eleventh hour - both for the human race and for the planet itself - we now short-circuit such cumbersome lessons and genuinely embrace each other across all illusory frontiers and divisions, it will, as the Hopis say, quite simply be too late for all of us, whether we are controller or victim in this particular life.

After a day of powerful ceremonies and rituals under a baking sun in the small main square of this humble village, watched by many hundreds of Hopis from the surrounding region, we decided to return to Titus' farm to watch the sunset. We had only briefly called there that morning and had seen in the middle of arid desert a miraculously healthy-looking 20-acre field of corn (on the cob) watched over by one elderly old man, while a younger man sat fasting within a small stone circle, in order to observe this sacred day of the Hopis.

Ahuva and I had briefly met Roy in the circle and, after I had honoured it by sprinkling Chalice Well water, he had asked us to similarly honour three vigorous corn plants nearby. He later told us that three small clouds had appeared overhead soon afterwards! Now I was to find out why I had been led to this particular site. The sign on the main road announcing the farm said "Hopi Land - Sovereign Under Creator's Law. Council officials and their associates enter only with approval of the traditional leadership of Hotevilla." It appeared that a schism had occurred among the Traditional Hopi Elders, of whom Titus Qumayumptewa was one, over Government-inspired exploitation of land and produce. Here their prophecy was daily unfolding as 'the system' now directly challenged the very last elderly men who guarded the ancient wisdom. And here I was - miraculously directed to some of the very people for whom the symbol I carried was intended!

At sunset Roy received the Aquarian Cross into the circle - which happened to be situated next to a sacred burial mound - and shared with me the significance to the Hopis of the interlinking circle symbology. It stayed there all night long with Roy until I alone, of those camping rejoined him for the ritual sunrise chants next morning.

During the night an international gathering had formed, to camp there after the dances at Hotevilla, including people from Prague and Tokyo.

After sunrise Roy had carried the infirm Titus onto the sacred burial hill, and together they decided to hold a meeting of all participants, to launch an important new initiative. Some thirty people squeezed into the circle still containing the Cross, to hear Roy explain the recent history of the farm and how, after the first corn harvest failed four years ago, each subsequent year it had improved until they had produced the miracle we could all see this year. How was this abundance possible without water? The answer, we were told, is intense thought projection and a deep attunement to the plants and the Earth - the Way of the Hopi. A drop of rain, he continued, is actually a mixture of sound, light and gas and can be reconstructed etherically and directed by conscious thought projection!

No-one present could deny the results or come up with any other solution to the miracle we saw all around us, in the absence of rain or any kind of pumping or irrigation facility.

It soon dawned on us all that Titus, Roy and other passing traditional Hopi Elders were using this land and the corn to ground the last essence of the Hopi Way on behalf of the whole human race - and that even most of their own tribe on Hopi Land had rejected them! What a humbling experience it was to be present there that day - and to realise, after the relentless onslaught of 'advanced' western cultures on all the indigenous peoples world-wide, in what an incredibly delicate balance our lives and our future are now held.

Roy explained that the new initiative was twofold. First, we and all future visitors were asked to dedicate the ancient burial hill above us as Mound Virtue, and gradually to build a mound of stones on it from our own sacred sites all around the world. Second, in line with the prophecies, Titus' greatest wish is that the World Purification comes with the rising forces of the East - the Sun. If this fails to occur, then the purification is to come from the West - and will cause a devastating rebirth through mass destruction.

Since the Creator's Law states that the cleansing and healing come from within, it is of paramount importance that we first heal ourselves. The 'Heal Yourself Centre' is, therefore, to be inaugurated on Hopi Land with the aim of helping individuals become sovereign beings again. Our synchronicity with Creation depends on the nucleus that is carried by our health - so our health is actually the key to the essence of creation. Without health there is no freedom, so the Centre will provide instructions to empower our internal Sun for World Purification - correct preparation of grain and corn hold the key! We then all smoked the Pipe of Truth with Titus, to seal our commitment to this inspiring and practical vision. I ended my visit by presenting the Cross to Titus. This wise and gentle holy man, now well into his nineties, gazed intently at it and then thanked me with heartfelt sincerity. He had nothing more to say. This, after all, is a symbol, and a symbol does not *mean*, a symbol *is*. It automatically triggers the sub-conscious. (Contact details for those wishing to assist this crucial initiative are given at the end of the book.)

My own journey continued to the amazing town of Sedona, and its dramatic rock formations and energy vortices, in time to tune in on the Bell Rock on 26th July. This was the first anniversary of Time Shift and is now a powerful annual energy focus in the final outworking of the Mayan calendar. On the way back to Denver we stopped briefly in the charming Spanish colonial town of Santa Fe and were finally treated to a spectacular sunset and rainbows near Pueblo, just south of Denver on the last night of my visit.

As I flew out of the country, it was already clear that pro- and anti-abortion lobbyists were preparing a warm reception for the Pope in Denver only two weeks later. Interesting timing, I thought! I heard later, that he was greeted by torrential rain and storms on this the most potent region of the American landmass. Contrary to all the elaborate

186

plans this actually ensured that his arrival was in fact a low key affair.

George Washington, significantly a Freemason during the drawing up of the US Constitution (he denounced that subversive cult during his last term of office), once had a very important supernatural experience. A beautiful woman appeared to him, showed him three dramatic scenes concerning the future of the Republic, and then said, "Son of the Republic, what you have seen is thus interpreted: three perils will come upon this Republic. The most fearful is the third, passing which, the whole world united shall never be able to prevail against her. Let every child of the Republic learn to live for his God, the land and the Union!" Washington then said: "With these words the figure vanished. I started from my seat, and felt that I had been shown the birth, progress and destiny of the Republic of the United States. *In her union she will have strength, in disunion her destruction.*"

These are words from Washington's own lips - and I respectfully suggest that every American, of whatever status, origin or creed, would do well to heed them.

And not just Americans, but the rest of us, too. The Lady's final words apply to every nation, every person on Earth: how can we fail, if we respect the Mind that imagined the Universe, the planet we inhabit, and each other?!

On April 20th. 1995 an event occurred in the USA that was to shake that country's confidence to the core. The massive bomb that destroyed the Federal Building in Oklahoma City with considerable loss of life will undoubtedly, in retrospect, be seen as a critical moment in the shift of consciousness that is eventually destined to turn this country into the champions of the New Awareness. First, however, must come the painful inner purging. This internally-generated urban terrorism now blamed for the Oklahoma and the Atlanta Olympic Games outrages appears to be the means by which Americans will be forced to look at themselves and the imbalanced society they have created.

A lethal combination of heavily-armed fascist militia and religious fundamentalists, both hell-bent on defying the Constitution by imposing a rigidly exclusive white, Christian, middle-class society, looks set to manifest all the dangers of which the Lady warned President Washington long ago: "the most fearful is the third, passing which, the whole world united shall never prevail against her". If America can survive this demonic internal onslaught, then she will indeed have earned her role "to speak forth and demonstrate the Unified Christ consciousness to the world". The guidance we received in 1989 that the transformational energy released at Silbury would be felt in the USA in the mid-1990's now looks uncannily accurate.

Interestingly enough, I had been invited to the Ozark mountains power centre in Oklahoma state during January 1995 to visit the head-quarters of Rev.Carol Parrish's inspiring Mystery School. Carol, one of the world's most distinguished teachers of spiritual metaphysics, had resonated so closely with my book that she had done me the great honour of inviting me to be the keynote speaker at her annual Sancta Sophia Conference in October 1995. The first visit of the Aquarian Cross to the Sparrow Hawk Village in January coincided with the highly significant arrival there of nine Tibetan monks on a world tour demonstrating their 'sand mandalas' and overtone chanting. According to Hopi and Mayan prophecies, Tibetan lamas are due to have a particularly profound impact on the US in these times.

In those same prophecies, the period 24 October to 5 November 1995 is known both as the 'Fall of America' and the 'Arrival of Camelot'. Significant perhaps that the conference led up to these dates and that the Israeli Prime Minister was assassinated on November 4th. by an ultra-religious Jew. Jewish religious extremism is largely developed in centres like New York and then exported to Israel's 'new set-tler' flashpoints by brainwashed fanatics. Such people, in my experience as a regular visitor to Israel over the past fifteen years and with many friends there, are much resented by most peace-loving Israelis - both religious and secular.

The rest of my time in the USA in late 1995 and early 1996 was focused on the West coast and much of it in Los Angeles. Despite the serious dangers to health living in such a polluted atmosphere, I found LA to be sizzling with synchronicity and creativity. It was here that the WWV web pages were set up on the inspirational Global Visions web site dedicated entirely to higher consciousness initiatives. At this time WWV also made an important connection and contract for the USA book launch with the same PR company promoting Mother Meera's literary work - an energy with which it is a privilege to be associated.

Earth energy activation work was carried out at the Yogananda Lake Shrine in Los Angeles (where some of Gandhi's ashes are buried), the Meher Baba sacred mountain near Ojai at halloween, Mt. Tamalpais on November 22nd. (New Moon and seven planets in Sagittarius!) and finally in badly flooded Seattle at the Snoqualmie Falls (in full flood) and at the Mercer Island labyrinth. Many of the most enlightened Masters in recent history have set up centres and ashrams on the American west coast and the guidance we have is that they have all contributed to aligning the energies for America's spiritual voice to emerge from the north western region of that country at the turn of the millenium.

With this in mind, a small group of us conducted a carefully prepared energy working with programmed crystals around the Los Angeles Music Center for the March 25th. 1995 Academy Awards Ceremony. Somehow unnoticed, despite the strictest security precautions, I found myself sprinkling programmed crystal dust onto the renowned red carpet only hours before the stars arrived. Roxzanne, the initiator of the enterprise, even managed to access the exclusive Governors Ball afterwards without tickets! Another illustration, perhaps, of heightened frequencies becoming ever less visible to the less attuned.

Unlikely though it may seem at present with its negative image, Hollywood is now subtly being prepared for a long-overdue transformational role that will uplift mankind. Some film stars are already responding by condemning its irresponsible image of violence and fear and refusing lucrative contracts associated with the dementia it currently perpetrates. Perhaps Manasseh is slowly remembering at last!

PART 2

THE KEYS TO HEAVEN

Chapter 10

ANCIENT WISDOM - SANITY AT LAST!

"**The Pharisees and the scribes have taken the keys to knowledge and have hidden them. They have not entered, nor have they allowed those who want to enter to do so. As for you, be as clever as snakes and as innocent as doves.**"

Naq Hammadi Codices - *The secret teachings of Jesus*

As this book is a vehicle for re-establishing mislaid knowledge, and frequently refers to 'laws' and 'dimensions', the following is a brief summary of the 'Ancient wisdom', designed to assist the reader's memory processes. The Aquarian Age is not to be established on new teachings!

THE UNIVERSAL LAW GOVERNING LIFE ON EARTH

1: Reincarnation, the Law of Rebirth

If an aspect (a soul) of the One (God) chooses, through extreme limitation, to serve the greater purposes of Creation by experiencing the 'separation' of 3rd. dimensional existence, it cannot ascend from that dimension until it is again consciously aware of its divine nature within the One. This is the wheel of rebirth and karma that binds us to duality, until we demonstrate a unified state of consciousness based on love/wisdom. Having regained this awareness, the accumulated karma of lifetimes is automatically transmuted and we are released from the treadmill to continue higher-dimensional existence on our journey back to the source.

Physical life is thus a school designed to remind us of our innate divinity and Earth is a planet of free choice, currently advancing from the 3rd. to the 4th. dimension. When our body can no longer support it, the spirit returns to the inner planes to review its progress, and in due course seeks another physical experience. The cycle continues until either self-realisation is achieved and the soul rises permanently into the higher dimensions (heaven). Or, after repeated failure to nurture the inner Light, its frequency eventually falls below the vibrational rate required to sustain human individuality.

2: The Law of Cause and Effect, or Karma

This is a law of physics too: for each and every action, there is an equal and opposite reaction. We are totally responsible for our every thought, word and deed while on Earth; and karma, both positive and negative, ensures that we re-balance all the energy or matter (so-called sin) we have ever disturbed. All Creation is subject to this law and in its precise outworking, we learn our lessons here. Once self realisation is achieved and past karma transmuted, we work here unimpeded to serve humanity, the planet and the whole of Creation.

3: The Law of Opportunity

This law ensures that souls are drawn to appropriate conditions and circumstances in which to balance past karma, related either to careers, relationships or any other aspect of life. In its positive form, it allows us to continue developing our special skills and interests, but equally, unused talents are withdrawn. Conversely, if we can face whatever we have previously set up for ourselves with as much awareness and grace as possible, we can balance the books more quickly and build up positive karma by being an inspiration to others in our adversity.

4: The Law of Balance and Equilibrium

Here, we see how the Universe maintains harmony by preventing any undue extremes or imbalances. Life is a circle and everything is in a cyclical motion. Sooner or later, any errant energy will be challenged and reintegrated. It can be seen as a process of compensation.

5: The Law of Correspondences

This is best described in the familiar words, 'As above, so below.' Man on Earth made in the image of God is the 'microcosm' of a greater 'macrocosm' and manifests in matter the thought of the Mind of One (God). All is linked and interdependent: even the position of the planets at our birth has a direct influence on our purpose here and our potential to achieve it. In this realm of duality, we grow by reconciling between opposites and externalising our inner Will.

Definitions adapted from the teachings of White Eagle.

The seven dimensions (or levels of consciousness) in this phase of human evolution contained within the earth's vibratory frequencies and experienced as parallel interconnecting realities.

First dimension

This basic frequency is the matrix of matter and energy out of which atoms and molecules are formed, and is consciousness perceived as a point. It is at this level that genetic codes are constructed.

Second dimension

Here consciousness is perceived as a line. This is where it first expresses before Ego develops. Group/species identity is first established here, and it is the realm of the plant and animal kingdoms.

Third dimension

Individual identity replaces group identity and humans first appear at this stage. With individualisation comes the illusion of separation or duality. This dimension demonstrates the most extreme impression of separation from the whole and therefore provides the greatest stimulus for inner growth or reintegration with the One (GOD) Planet Earth and those of humanity who are ready, are now preparing to rise from this to the 4th dimension. There is currently a marked overlap between these levels, exemplified by the dramatic polarity in current human attitudes and affairs.

Fourth dimension

This is where the ego sees beyond the illusion of separation and reintegrates into group consciousness, but without losing its own identity. Heightened vibrations give access to superconsciousness and a desire for unity and harmony - in contrast to divisive 3rd. dimensional activity. Here we begin to accept personal responsibility instead of assigning blame or projecting insecurities. Fear-based control systems of the negative polarity lose energy support and rapidly decay. This is the last dimension in which physical life manifests.

Fifth dimension

From here on, non-physical life is experienced and the borders between dimensions are less clearly defined. We move beyond linear time and experience awareness of the 'I' as the group identity. At this level, we connect with our innate wisdom or knowing and feel the desire to share it with the less evolved. Our vehicles become Light bodies, through which we can manifest in whatever form we choose.

Sixth dimension

This is the frequency of the Christ or Buddha consciousness, where total recall occurs. We start to take responsibility for the Whole rather than for the self, and the progress of both become synonymous.

Seventh dimension

Here, we achieve our goal and are restored to the consciousness of the One. This frequency acts as the dynamo that propels the lower dimensions towards integration with the One. Once sufficient numbers of the human race reach this stage, 'critical mass' is reached and, having completed the present assignment, we will embark on another experience within the polarities that fuel Creation at still higher frequencies. In this manner, GOD expands indefinitely in the search for ultimate perfection.[1]

DUALITY

The theory of two interdependent principles working in apparent opposition, such as good and evil, or mind and matter, representing idealism and materialism. Division of the One into two, causing separation.

POLARITY

Two poles having contrary qualities, which reflect rather than oppose. All Creation flows naturally through the interaction of two charges (positive and negative). It can only be disturbed by external interference with the flow.

---

[1] Some of these definitions were inspired by *The Prism of Lyra* (Mission Possible, P.O.Box 1495, Sedona AZ86336, USA)

CHRIST

The term originates in Sanskrit, and derivatives of it are Krishna, Tsar, Kaiser, Caesar and King. Its meaning is 'anointed one' in the sense of the anointed presence *within* each one of us, and it has NO religion. The Christ is a level of consciousness and *not* a person. Using it in a personalised context by referring to Jesus Christ simply as 'Christ' is yet another subtle, but powerful, way of reinforcing separation by implying that there is only and can only be *one* Christ, namely Jesus, when in fact all spiritually-awakened humans automatically access that state and are free to follow where he led.

CHRIST CONSCIOUSNESS - THE LORD THY GOD IS ONE

This is the Universal Law of One, and is the awareness of unity through the interconnection and interdependence of all aspects of Creation; the wholeness (holiness) and therefore the circle, its own symbol. Even science now accepts that all life shares a common DNA and gene pool! The Christ energy is the 'whole' concept of God incarnate in Man as the 'only begotten son', and that is the gift Jesus the Christ shared with us here on Earth. We only come to the Father - return to the source - by finding the Christ consciousness within us all that was exemplified by Jesus, and *not* through projection onto the personality of Jesus as the exclusive saviour promoted by Christianity.

The reason it is so important to establish this impulse is that the Christ, or Law of One, is the only truly universal power capable of reconciling all humanity. Once it has been prised from the jaws of the religion that for so long has imprisoned it, it will become the healing vehicle for the world's dominant, but disintegrating, Western cultures. From there it will radiate in every direction, touching everyone on Earth, regardless of creed, race or colour. This time round, the spiritual awakening of mankind will be initiated by the western world, by means of a universal awareness that now rises like a phoenix from the ashes of a belief structure that has well and truly served its divisive purpose.

CHRISTIANITY

A man-made religion based on an almost immediate distortion of the Ancient wisdom teachings of 'The Way' given by Jesus the Christ. It adheres to the false and separative belief that he is 'the only begotten son of God' and that the way to God for *all* mankind is through the figurehead of Jesus. The Church misunderstood the mission of the Master Jesus and the nature of the Christ. Its valid purpose has been to provide a learning vehicle for those needing to experience the illusion of separation from the God which essentially *we are*. This path was inspired by the authority of the Old Testament with its jealous and judgmental patriarchal 'Creator-Gods' known as the 'Demiurge'. It is from this very tyranny that Jesus sought to release humanity, by teaching universal truths that reconnect each one of us, through the Christ consciousness, directly to the supreme intelligence and Love that encompasses us all as God. The distorted beliefs of patriarchal Christianity that both deny the innate divinity within hu-man and fail to acknowledge the feminine polarity (the Goddess) have no further purpose now that we have matured spiritually and reached the appointed time when we are obliged to recognise our true identity as an integral and inseparable part of a balanced Godhead. In short, the Church misrepresented the mission of Jesus and the universal nature of 'The Christ'.

DEMIURGE (from the Greek demiurgos, meaning 'creator')

This refers to the level of the demi-gods or lesser divine beings, serving as an instrument of the still higher powers. They created the hu-man hybrid to serve their Earthly needs by cross-breeding with the higher primates already evolving here at a much slower pace (ref: Genesis Ch 6). Originally, so as to keep control of their creation, they deviously attempted to deny free choice to humanity. After 'Eden', when humans gained their divine right to choose, the demiurge judged them to be 'sinful' (actually more sinned against than sinning) and unleashed Noah's Flood in one of many attempts to eliminate their own creation!

The celebrated Gnostic Valentinus (lst. Century CE) explains: "It is not God, but the demiurge who reigns as king and lord, who acts as a military commander, who gives the law and judges those who violate it - in short, he is the God of Israel (Jehovah)."[2] Jesus' mission (First and Second Coming) is designed to release us all from this tyranny and reconnect us to the loving intelligence at the heart of Creation. Mainstream Christianity aligned with the demiurge to instil the pain

---

[2] The Gnostic Gospels, by Elaine Pagels

of separation into human consciousness, while small, persecuted, mystical societies secretly preserved the Light of the Christ consciousness on Earth 'till the Second Coming'. From this we can see that even in the 4th. and 5th. dimensions there are evolved beings who still display negative characteristics. They resist further evolution into the highest dimensions for fear of losing their ego identity as they begin to merge with the source. A cursory glance alone through Sumerian, Biblical, Greek and Roman texts will confirm the bizarre antics of the demi-gods in the prehistory we call 'mythology'! Although our path is much clearer once we are free of dense matter, we are still tested at every level of our ascension process.

Those interested in scholarly material derived from ancient texts and artefacts dealing with our celestial ancestry and Earthly struggles are recommended to read Zechariah Sitchin's highly illuminating six volumes of *Earth Chronicles*. The only proviso is that according to the Spirit guidance we have received, all levels of the higher evolution described by Sitchin across the Universe originate as consciousness from the divine planet Earth in her subtle and multi-dimensional role as the Goddess, Mother of Creation.

CONSCIOUSNESS

The essential cohesive force of Creation, embodying all thought, knowledge, feeling and awareness.

THE TWO FACES OF EVIL

They are represented as the archetypal thought-forms known as 'Lucifer' and 'Ahriman'. (definitions from the ancient Persian Zoroastrian tradition, where these negative, dualistic manifestations were identified).

The Book of Revelations warns humanity that it will now face twin aspects of evil. The first is Lucifer, the seven-headed, ten-horned beast known as the 'fallen' spiritual Light. This represents the doubt or fear that led to our process of separation known as 'the Fall'. Lucifer obstructs our path back to Christ consciousness, using such deviations as spiritual glamour, psychic manipulation, distortion of truth through the control of fear-oriented religions, negative space phenomena, conspiracy theories and any other counterfeit spiritual paths.

Ahriman, the two-horned beast of duality, is Lord of the illusory world of physical matter and sense perception. He seeks to enslave us by means of cold, insensitive scientific materialism and soulless computer technology. They work together on the inner and outer planes to imprison humanity within the duality of the 3rd. dimension. The shadow that these thought-forms represent must be understood, courageously faced and transmuted by all of us.

Note: Human beings can be at any of the stages between the 3rd. and 7th. dimensions, as evolved members of the race are always present and work interdimensionally to raise mankind towards the One; such people operate at higher frequencies than dense matter and are able to manipulate it to suit their purposes. They can use physical or 'light' bodies, within or beyond human vision. We all have the potential to reach these rarefied frequencies ourselves. Indeed, we are *required* to do so, if we choose to align with the evolutionary spiral leading us back to the source from which we sprang.

All light requires constant generation and if, after many lifetimes, we allow ourselves to fall below the vibrationary level where human existence can be supported, we forfeit our human individuality.

The current consciousness shift has been instigated by the presence on Earth of 144,000 higher dimensional incarnate beings -12,000 from each of the twelve tribes of Israel. They are souls who were touched by the Christ consciousness during the First Coming mission and have already attained 4th. dimensional awareness. They shared the pain with Jesus of anchoring the Christ Consciousness on Earth over many persecuted life-times between the First and Second Coming. They will rise into the 5th. dimension and above, provided they fulfil their assignment of awakening the rest of humanity at this time. This is the minimum 'critical-mass' number decreed by the Mind of One (God) to be capable of raising the consciousness of that section of the human family that is prepared in these 'Last Days'. Spirit indicates, moreover, that as women are generally more spiritually aware than men at this point in our evolution, the major proportion of this group now manifests as female.

Chapter 11

WHO AM I? -THE GREAT
SECRET REVEALED

"If there is only light, how could you choose that which is sacred, for only in the darkness can you see the sacred light."

Apocalypse Ch 3: v 10

The Christian religion, in furtherance of its separative role, has enshrined the doctrine of 'original sin' It used guilt to control its followers and unbalanced mankind's male/female polarity by disempowering the feminine principle and identifying it as 'the temptress, cause of the downfall of the male'. However, the intuitive wisdom of the feminine, represented by Eve, was not fooled by such patriarchal intrigues and by deliberately plucking the 'forbidden fruit', acquired knowledge that gave hu-mans their rightful status as 'gods, knowing good and evil'. And now the feminine polarity within each one leads us back towards a state of unified (Christ) consciousness, at the end of the human experiment in duality.

The Adam and Eve story tells us how 'the Fall' was the result of a conscious decision to lower the frequency of a portion of the One (God) into a separate state. The process represents the primary division of unity into its dual aspects, which in turn demonstrates how the One becomes the *all*. It was not 'sin', but doubt leading to fear, described biblically as the 'fallen light of Lucifer', that originally dispatched our divine consciousness on a daring mission into dense matter, in order to experience our divinity through the reflection process of duality. Hence the hu-man was created 'a little lower than the Angels, but crowned with honour and glory' and in the exact image of a loving Mother/Father God. It is this creation that is the hybrid God/primate called the hu-man, and fear has no more power over it - provided it doesn't fall prey to the illusion of separation in matter.

Inevitably, Christian conditioning urges us to believe that the Love, both human and divine, that creates an innocent child somehow produces a human being conceived in 'sin' destined for a life of guilt and fear - despite the fact that its soul has just arrived on the planet from the mind of God! Therein lies the pernicious programming that is the chief cause of human suffering and our entrapment in duality. Indeed, if we continue to think of ourselves in this way, then we literally have nowhere to go.

The situation was further exacerbated when at the Council of Constantinople in 553CE in a rigged majority verdict declared that, "It is anathema (an accursed thing) to believe in the mythical doctrine of the pre-existence of the soul or its return to Earth after death." Thus was removed at a stroke, through 'the Articles of Anathema', the central, immutable universal Law governing the ascent of Man. Reincarnation is enshrined in the Ancient Wisdom (source of all religious teaching), is implicit in the original teachings of Jesus the Christ and his early followers, was taught in the Mystery Schools of the ancient world, and is still a foundation stone of the major Eastern religions with billions of followers.

"All will come upon the Earth a hundred, hundred times and still will the spirit be raised by the Father." Ch 6, verse 11 of Apocalypse 3 couldn't be clearer on this subject. It would be a callous and arbitrary arrangement indeed that permitted us only *one* opportunity for expression in physical human form - particularly when some die virtually at birth or soon after, and others live to great ages; some enjoy great fulfilment and acclaim, while others know only pain and deprivation.

As part of the process of Creation and in order to perceive itself in action, so to speak, a portion of the consciousness of One takes on the daunting task of lowering its vibratory rate. Slowly, over aeons of 'time', it integrates into the dense and much lower frequency of time/space in the material Universe. This very risky human mission involving almost total spiritual amnesia has achieved its purpose, and now it is time to wake up and start our return to the source, before the mission dissolves into chaos.

We may ask, "Why should Creation need a mirror at all?" The answer is that anything feeding exclusively on itself without drawing on other revitalising energies must inevitably atrophy and decay. Polarities are the building blocks of Creation and electricity gives us a useful example by showing us that a positive and negative charge are needed to produce energy in the form of light or power. The creative spark of life depends on interaction and all evolving consciousness and physical life-forms in the cosmos, including humanity, illustrate that principle.

Let us now firmly establish the fact of our innate divinity by quoting the man who specifically did *not* come to Earth to found yet another religion, but taught instead an empowering universal truth for all mankind known as 'The Way'. He used 'the Word' and it is well to remember that 'In the beginning was the Word' - the spiritual Law governing the rhythms and cycles of the Universe, which is life. In Logion 3 of the Gospel of Thomas, unearthed in Egypt in 1945 and forming part of what otherwise contains the priceless Naq Hammadi library of Gnostic texts, Jesus said:

"If those who guide your being say to you, Behold the Kingdom is in the heaven, then the birds of the sky will precede you; if they say to you, It is in the sea, then the fish will precede you. But the Kingdom is in your centre and is about you. When you know your selves then you will be known, and you will be aware that you are the sons of the living Father. But if you do not know your selves then you are in poverty and you are the poverty."

Again, Logion 24:

"His disciples said, Show us the place where you are, because it is necessary for us to seek after it. He said to them, He who has ears let him hear: there is light at the centre of a man of light, and he illumines the whole world. If he does not shine, there is darkness."

What more unambiguous statements of human identity and potential could possibly be made? Why is this most basic of all gospels not in the Bible? You've guessed first time! The church, denying the higher self and focusing only on the lower ego, judged it 'heretical' and destroyed all known copies around 600CE. Fortunately for searchers after truth, they missed this edition. Ultimately, it has served us well that it was hidden and was preserved intact during the period when most other texts were heavily edited or burned - as were most of the original Aramaic texts by 300 CE. This and many other recently discovered texts, including the Third Book of the Apocalypse, have restored to us many original teachings on the purpose of human life.

Christianity quickly removed any such references in order to enforce control by denying the divine nature of the hu-man and projecting exclusive divinity instead onto an external figurehead, Jesus. It set up a patriarchal priesthood, ruled by fear and presided over by a succession of high priests or Popes, each presumptuously calling himself 'God's infallible vicar on Earth'! Untold millions of sincere Christians have meekly submitted to this cruel and bloody tyranny - in the name of the One who came in Love. What painful lessons we choose to endure in order to learn through the reflection process of duality! Happily, 'the times are a-changing', as we can see, when Spirit goes so far as to intercede in human affairs by restoring a text that finally removes the last vestiges of credibility from an institution that has now served its gruesome purpose.

If we need further proof - this time from the authorised version of the Bible itself - we need look no further than Psalm 82:

"I (God) have said, ye (Hu-man) ARE GODS; and all of you are children of the most High.. Arise, O God (Hu-man), judge (take responsibility for) the Earth; for thou (Hu-man) shalt inherit all nations."

Jesus himself, accused of the blasphemy of claiming to be God, quotes Psalm 82 and continues:

"If he (God) called them (hu-man) gods, unto whom the word of God came, and the scripture cannot be broken. Say ye of him (Jesus Christ), whom the Father (God) hath sanctified, and sent into the world, Thou (Jesus) blasphemest, because I (Jesus) said, I am the son of God? If I do not the works of my Father, believe me not. But if I do, though ye believe not me, believe the works; that ye may know and believe, that the Father is in me, and I in him."

John 10, 34-38

So, after all that, who *am* I? The answer, in the words of Moses himself, is the sacred name of God: 'I AM THAT I AM.' The great secret is revealed: all that matters is already inside each one of us, and we need no longer give away our power to any outside forces or institutions. In other words, 'Our only responsibility on Earth is to become aware of our Godselves. There is no other quest. That is the Holy Grail.' When we are One, we are the All, and automatically serve the Whole.

We are eternal divine beings, individual facets of a vast diamond, who arrive and depart this planet as pure consciousness - and here it is important to remember that all matter, including our physical bodies, is simply energy vibrating at varying frequencies. As Spirit beings, we have bravely volunteered temporarily to limit ourselves in the duality of matter, to learn during successive incarnations, often through pain, the lessons that ultimately reconfirm us in our original state of unconditional love, which is God. We have collectively decided we need to experience this long, but temporary, separation, which also provides Creation with a vital opposite polarity. Thus we are *all* serving the plan of Creation in some way, whatever we are doing. This is why we are told not to judge others and especially to forgive, however hard! We live in a perfect and just Universe and whether we like it or not everything happens for a perfectly good reason! Our own free will choices and karmic dues create each situation.

Chapter 12

PLANET EARTH,
MOTHER OF CREATION

The human race, as a collective group consciousness, is evolving on a living, sentient being called Earth - or "Heart" if letters are rearranged. Apocalypse 3 has interesting information on this subject too. Ch 3, v 13-18:

> "And the Father will send to the Earth a protector, and she will be clothed with the Sun and ride on a chariot of gold. And her name will be Gaia and she will carry the seed of life and her body will be as a womb for all that live upon the Earth. All will know her, for she is the *Mother of Creation*. But she will not be known until the last days come upon the Earth and there is darkness and decay even as she is known."

We experience physical existence as a trinity. The Father, the first cause or impulse of Will represented in the energy of the Light of the Sun. The Mother, the receptive principle of wisdom and nurturing and 'the comforter' or the Holy Spirit, is focused in the Earth herself, the Goddess Gaia. While the 'only begotten' son/ daughter represents all humanity struggling to regain the consciousness of One. 'The Lord thy God is ONE.'

So, quite naturally, in the nursery of our spiritual development, we are in the care of our Mother, who gave us physical birth out of her own body. She nurtures us, sustains us through Nature and opens our eyes to our own beauty as a reflection of her own. She has a remedy in her medicine cupboard for every disease we ever manifest through distorted thinking, *without* resorting to artificial compounds and methods - if we will only trust her and acknowledge our interdependence with her. We are reflections of each other's consciousness, and Earth is aware of and actively responds to each human thought, emotion and action. A sobering thought - and quite obvious when you see her increasingly angry response to human negativity, delinquency and selfishness. Unless we rapidly 'clean up our act' and become responsible stewards, we can expect an extremely rough passage into the new Millennium. We are in the Revelations time known as the 6th. Seal -

so fasten your seatbelts, all those who still wish to exercise dominion over her!

Since all aspects of being including time and life itself are ultimately represented as a spiral or circle - the symbol of the One - our Mother's very roundness illustrates to us the cyclical nature of reality. We observe the passage of the equinoxes and seasons, the phases of her sister, the Moon, which triggers the ebb and flow of the tides, and influences all growth and human emotion. We observe the cycles of birth, growth and decay followed by rebirth and yet another cycle. All follows the immutable and unchanging laws of Nature and the Universe. This is the evolution of consciousness from animal (primate/ ego) man to God man, from primal, instinctive to conscious, intuitive modes of perception and behaviour.

Earth provides all the means for us to learn whatever lessons we have come to learn. This is the Mother planet of aware consciousness within the cosmos; she is a sanctified place, which projects life-forming patterns through humanity's immensely powerful thought projections to other planets. It is important to know that hu-man consciousness evolved *here* not somewhere else in space - and although at the more advanced levels we have projected our consciousness in both negative and positive forms all over the Universe, we remain nonetheless an integral part of *this* planet's evolution. In the Genesis references (Ch 6, v 2) to the 'Gods marrying the daughters of men', we learn of the process of more evolved life-forms or demi-gods raising the consciousness of lower life-forms through cross-fertilisation. Many have been tempted to interpret this as an external interference of visiting extraterrestrials, but it is in fact a continuing process of 'the returning consciousness of the Hu-man' taking many forms (UFOs, ETs, etc.), yet still contained within Earth's multi-dimensional structure.

We belong to *this* planet and our evolution through the seven dimensions takes place within parallel realities related to Earth. Various levels of human consciousness are indeed located on other planets and in other constellations, and can and do communicate with us in different ways, primarily through projected thought. They are not, however, alien to us, whatever their current motives. As Jose Arguelles, chief initiator of Harmonic Convergence, reminds us in his book *The Mayan Factor:* "The Space brothers are not alien entities, but emanations of being itself. And being is, in essence, light, radiant energy. From Light we came and to Light we shall return."

In other words, the entire human soul-group of some ten billion souls experiences various dimensions within this greater planetary consciousness. As time and space are only an illusion of the lower dimensions, geographical location in 'space' becomes meaningless, since consciousness projects at the speed of thought itself. For instance, the Christ impulse, widely acknowledged to emanate from the Pleiades constellation of the Dove, is instantaneously and continuously beamed to Earth by ascended beings in order to raise the consciousness of 'separated' mankind. The more subtle realms and lifeforms do exist all around us in many different densities, which is why sensitive humans can make contact so easily and naturally.

Misguidedly we spend on space exploration and 'defence' the communal resources that could provide us *all* with the dignity of decent standards of living - which would, in turn, give us the chance to evolve spiritually and fulfil the sole (soul) criterion for incarnating here in the first place! This certainly cannot be achieved in the conditions of degradation and squalor that the rich nations impose on the poor. The fear that makes us believe we need to 'defend' ourselves costs us one million pounds sterling per minute, let alone the expense of space travel! The only exploration of any relevance now is internal, and our rockets must be targeted, not into space, but deep into the vast expanse of our own consciousness, where all the answers are found. We chose to experience physical life on Earth, which we co-created, *to test our capacity to love.* So let's concentrate on what we are supposed to be doing, before we lose this amazing evolutionary opportunity to expand - rather than collapse our collective consciousness.

The Earth herself is now in labour, and about to bring to birth the new dimension, Heaven on Earth (4th onto 3rd dimension). Until the process is complete - in the year 2013, which is widely understood to be the Omega point when we move beyond time and history - Gaia will face birth pangs and convulsions like any mother. These could be expressed as all kinds of earth movements, storms, rising water, etc., representing her moods and emotions. As this process now escalates, her more devoted children are sensing imminent change and preparing to fulfil their roles as cosmic 'midwives' In this way, they assist through terrestrial and personal healing work in this glorious event, when we ourselves and our planet together ascend into a lighter density. Our individual ascension takes place right here, from within, and our task is to be transformers of energy, contributing to the process of infusing Light into all matter.

Clearly, the degree of disruption we face over the next sixteen years will be lessened by each one of us who awakens now. Some say the changes are fixed and inescapable, but if the exponential growth of awareness already taking place around the world continues, the transition will be far less violent than expected. Spirit says that not a hair of anyone's head need be harmed in this transition, if we choose to share *now !* The Love encompassing us in the form of God and our mother, Earth, respects our free choice and will respond positively to our positive thoughts, words and actions. As Homo Sapiens now transforms into Homo Spiritus we need to accept that contrary to our separative and fear-filled conditioning of lack, we live in a safe universe with abundant and constantly renewable natural energy everywhere and forever. Many would think that humanity's greatest obsession is money, but in fact it is habit and it is habit that actually stifles the evolutionary process.

> "Humanity can be compared to a cancer ravaging the Earth and destroying the body on which we depend for existence at all levels. The cancer can heal - *if we heal our malignant attitudes.*"
>
> Peter Russell, creator of the *Global Brain* film

Since we have now explored and colonised the entire planet and have nowhere else to escape to or to infect with our dysfunctional thinking and dis-ease (we shall not be permitted by the higher realms to infect the rest of the Universe in which we live while we function at such low frequency levels either), we are faced with a stark choice: evolve or become extinct!

So there is everything to go for, and once a minimum 'critical mass' awaken, the remainder of mankind will find it much easier to remember, and thus ensure an abundant harvest of souls for the next stage of our journey together. It won't be long now till we see which way the pendulum swings!

Chapter 13

LIVING BY UNIVERSAL LAW

A noted sage once replied to a question by a pupil about
what it feels like to be 'spiritual': "Before enlightenment, chopping wood and lighting fire. After enlightenment, chopping wood and lighting fire."

It will be much easier to talk about practical awareness, now that
we have begun to understand who we are, where we are, what our
collective purpose is here and the traps, glamours and distortions we
have to be aware of in order to grow. Knowing what we do, where
could we possibly start other than with the self? We have explored the
One and found that it is the great dynamo of Creation, the expanding
creative force of which we are all an integral part - and which, for
want of a better term, we call 'God'. Paradoxically, having reached
these sublime and reassuring heights, we immediately run into a rather
a big snag: the human ego or lower primate self!

Our DNA is based on two interlocked spirals which not only serve
their vital functions, but provide the basis for our sense of duality and
separation. Our brain too is divided into two hemispheres with the left
'masculine' half focusing on logical intellectual processes, while the
'feminine' right half is a vehicle for accessing universal wisdom
through our intuitive process linked to the heart. Our task here is to
unite these two apparently warring halves - indeed what is the use of
mere knowledge (left brain) without the wisdom to use it (right brain
and heart)! Traditionally, this is known as 'the mystical union', and
we reach self-realisation when all opposites (light/dark, positive/
negative, male/female, etc.) are finally balanced and reconciled within
us. We have to be alert to the fact that the ego demonstrates its fear
through rigidity and structure, because it doesn't dare let go and seeks
to control by limitation all it thinks it doesn't understand at the personality level.

So our challenge is to tame the tiger called ego and neutralise its
fear-oriented, separative and selfish instincts. We should not, however,

sublimate it altogether, since our individual expression as a physical being is, of course, dependent on it!

We find ourselves in duality because at some stage we doubted perfection and created the illusion of separation through our own thought processes. Everything outside us merely reflects our inner state of consciousness, because our higher selves create and manifest it all for our own learning. Therefore, instead of projecting blame onto others, we have to remember that the persons or situations causing us problems are *perfect* for our soul growth - and are in fact our ideal and personally-selected teachers!

We are asked to take our share of responsibility in any situation, knowing that we ourselves have at least partially created it. The issue will then be resolved and the lessons learned. If we don't learn, we then produce a still harder test, until we do. And we all know from experience just how much discomfort and sheer pain it takes to gain our full concentration! We are even not above committing violence against ourselves in the form of accidents or burdening ourselves with debilitating diseases, if that is what it takes to remember. The test is always one of being fully conscious of what we are creating at every moment, and of whether we respond by blocking and projecting the lesson away from us in fear and anger or accepting it unconditionally and with grace.

We have been told by Spirit that if we all immediately stop judging and blaming others and become fully responsible for ourselves, it would take just three days to lift human and planetary life permanently into the 4th dimension!

Unexpectedly, most of us are remarkably truthful about ourselves without realising it - by subtly projecting our own inadequacies, fears, judgements and blame onto others. So when someone tells us their problems with another person or is angry with us, they are actually expressing their own blockages and exposing more about themselves than they realise. Very revealing it usually is too, to the trained ear! What angers us in another person is more often than not an unhealed aspect of ourselves. If we had already resolved the particular issue, we would not be irritated by its reflection back to us We are all here to help each other grow, and although these insights can be very threatening at first, they are indispensable tools for accelerating our own and each other's development.

The fact that we create our own reality through our past and present thought and behaviour patterns, is often the hardest to accept - especially when situations appear irrational and unfair. In fact, there is no such thing as chance, coincidence, luck or fate! Our higher self knows exactly what we need to fulfil the blueprint of our incarnation. It also monitors another crucial side of our lives: integrating any karmic debts or rewards we have accrued, as a result of our past thoughts, words and actions. It all comes back, positive and negative alike, in whatever form we choose to accept. Contrary to popular thinking, we don't get away with anything down here! The Universal Law states: 'As a man sows, so shall he reap' and this immutable principle is responsible for what we as seemingly eternal victims call accidents, diseases, misfortunes, betrayals, ordeals and frustrations. On the bright side, though, there are the rewards, windfalls and unexpected good fortune that do also come our way.

Before incarnating, we draw up our own blueprint for each specific life with assistance from our higher self and experienced guides. We are surrounded by familiar, group-soul energies from other lives as relations, friends, colleagues, so-called 'enemies' and anyone else with whom we have unfinished karmic business. The family unit is intended as a school of learning in which to nurture the child - who is often an older and wiser soul than the parents, and should be respected accordingly!

Once grown to maturity and pushed out of the nest, our task is to remember the specific purpose of our incarnation. We have all come with unique talents and energies, which are part of the great jigsaw of life, and for the plan of evolution to function, each piece is as important as any other. Unless we opt to leave our chosen path and to cut ourselves adrift, we begin, often painfully, a series of tests to clear some of our old personality defects. These usually manifest in negative behaviour patterns, disorders and disease. When enough of this dross has been shifted, through our own hard work, we start to move inexorably towards our spiritual path. That path is our own personal journey, and provided we haven't been ambushed or distracted in the meantime, we are led towards our goal, and intuitively recognise it as we approach.

Native Americans speak about 'living the passion of the heart' and when we make that connection, our personal plan starts to unfold for the first time: unsuspected talents and abilities surface, doors open and we never look back. The universal law of synchronicity or perfect timing springs into effect - and we never need to exercise our planning and organisational talents again or worry about a parking space! It really is an amazing way to live, but demands total faith and confidence in self, purpose and living in the moment.

We connect with our passion by daring, against all the odds and other people's disapproval, to do the thing we love doing. Why do we love doing that particular thing? Because that is what we are uniquely qualified to do and came here to offer in service to the 'whole'. Often we need no qualifications, as no-one else can match our own skills, whatever they happen to be. When we get into our stride, we become an inspiration to all around us and literally lift other people's spirits! A self-realised human being has absolutely no limit to its power and potential and can effortlessly transmute negativity.

Much is made of 'free will', but in a state of separated consciousness, we only have choice between opposites in order to grow. The will is the will of God, or our collective consciousness as the One. So God's plan, to which all now incarnate at higher-self level subscribe, *will be done* - and it will be as comfortable or uncomfortable for the ego as each of us chooses for our spiritual growth within that master plan.

Living a natural state of spirituality is a process of integrating as much experience as the physical realm of matter can offer. That is why we CO-created it as an arena for our own growth. Many people consider matter to be somehow base or evil, and cut themselves off in one way or another from its less pleasing aspects. They would be wise to remember that all creation is permeated by its Creator including what we deem to be negativity, and was all devised specifically for our experience. Renunciations can be a useful temporary process to help us concentrate on particular issues, but sooner or later whatever is denied has to be faced in order to be released. If we bury issues and suppress our instincts and natural processes, we inevitably develop disease caused by confused and distorted thinking. A brief survey of the inner causes of diseases can be most instructive for identifying the positive thoughts and affirmations needed to prevent them.

It is known that all the cells of the body completely renew themselves once every seven years, so we are in fact physically re-created at regular intervals. If this is so, why do we not rid ourselves of all dis eas‸ at the same time? The answer is that our thought processes are so powerful that they override the natural renewal of cells by imprinting them with the same old thought patterns that caused the problem in the first place. Our brain cells, incidentally, are an exception and atrophy still further through drugs, alcohol, aluminium (Alzheimer's disease), mental inactivity and especially lack of oxygen in the body.

We have become notoriously ineffective breathers, which is rather serious considering oxygen is our lifeline. Once our atmosphere contained 32% oxygen; currently, with increased pollution, it stands at 20%, and in inner cities it can fall as low as 11% . It is, therefore, hardly surprising that one of the biggest current success stories in curing killer diseases is oxygen therapy, including pure ozone and H_2O_2. Most viruses and bacteria flourish only in human blood that is anaerobic or starved of oxygen. By mixing pure oxygen products with the blood, there have already been many well-documented cases showing that viruses and bacteria causing cancers, AIDS, arthritis and numerous other dysfuntions have been eradicated.

Over 2000 doctors in Germany now use these inexpensive natural therapies that have been pioneered there over the last 50 years - and been largely ignored by orthodox medicine. Lets hope the artificial toxic cocktails and panaceas manufactured by the multinational pharmaceutical companies at ruinous cost - yet still endorsed by the medical fraternity - will soon be given a run for their money by more natural remedies. Then, maybe the multi-billion-dollar funds now being spent on largely unproductive symptom research will be reallocated to prevention, rather than cure; to causes, rather than effects.

The Chinese had it right when they paid doctors for keeping people healthy, and fined them for being negligent enough to permit disease to manifest - when they should have read the telltale signs emanating from the patient's subtle bodies! Chakras have actually been photographed to provide proof of their existence. As usual, our material reality is upside down and western 'academic' medicine, though technically ingenious, is nonetheless among the most spiritually primitive on Earth. Intellectual doctoring and natural healing are still at loggerheads!

The quality of what we produce in life is directly related to the cleansing work we have had the courage to tackle within ourselves. We all incarnate specifically to redress certain energy imbalances, which manifest as personality blockages of one sort or another. None

215

of us is exempt, and as we ourselves are the cause underlying our lives, it is up to us to resolve the issues that inevitably arise. We must recognise that life is really a ceaseless dance of intermingling energies that encourages us to let go of our ego-based human perceptions while surrendering in trust to the flow of the divine within us. The steps of the dance are forever changing and we cannot afford to be left behind clinging fearfully to concepts that no longer serve us. Only in this way will we be equipped to face the enormous challenges that confront us now as we prepare for the imminent initiation into higher consciousness. Life is a breeze; once we know the rules of the game!

Since the salvation of the human race is now to manifest through the restoration of the feminine polarity to counterbalance the masculine, it is logical that women and especially mothers will begin to have a major impact on events. Having been used by the patriarchy for millennia to produce the cannon-fodder needed to fight their wars, mothers will now find common cause with each other *across* artificial manmade barriers and join together to restore sanity We shall now witness the power of the divine feminine expressed in determined action, unselfish love and gentle wisdom. We live in a feminine environment on this 'mother' Earth and when humans manifest the truly healed feminine energy here it is , of course, *irresistible!*

Although many may doubt it in the present circumstances, we *are* here also to enjoy life on this abundant garden planet. So lets try, as we are asked, to open the heart and recapture the innocence of the unconditional child; to live in wonder, praise and gratitude for the miracle of life, honouring and preserving it in all its manifold expressions. Only then will we feel joy and know that we, as the One, are worthy, beyond our human comprehension.

* * *

There is nothing but YOU.
Nothing different from YOU.
Nothing to attain other than YOU.
Nothing that can be taken from YOU.
That is all YOU need to understand.
There is nothing to know other than that.

Meditate on your SELF.
Worship your SELF.
Kneel to your SELF.
Understand your SELF.
God dwells with YOU AS YOU.
Muktananda

Chapter 14

WAKE UP OR SHAKE UP!

"Wake up! I sing, for the time of the new is at hand, and all things are to be different from what they have been. See what I have in store, believe nothing any more, for I am the source of eternal knowledge and henceforth I will rise up within you like a spring that will never run dry. In the moment of your need will I inform you of everything you need to know. It has always been thus, but in these days the winds of life blow stronger than before. The Creator approaches. Trust all that is and is to be."

The Starseed Transmissions by Ken Carey

"This is the Second Coming of Christ as spoken of in the Book of Revelations and it is the awakening of a new circle, a new design of energy movement for the whole of humanity. Christ means a circle. So, the Second Coming of the sacred circle is all awakened humans dancing as one consciousness."

American Indian inter-tribal predictions incorporating the Hopi prophecies for the year 1989

Some put all this down to 'millennial madness' and dismiss it out of hand, pointing to evidence of similar unrest and unfulfilled apocalyptic predictions, way back in 1000 CE. They say nothing much happened on that occasion, that a lot of people ran around like headless chickens and generally made fools of themselves - then life went on as usual. It'll be no different this time, they say, however dire the present global situation.

We are all entitled to our opinions, but such people really must have their heads buried deep in the sand. Look around you, dear reader, look around you! And when you have done so, why not shift your focus for a moment, and examine things from a rather wider perspective.

What is known as the 'precession of the equinoxes' through 'the twelve ages of man' or the Zodiac, takes 25,920 years. The sun, from our viewpoint on Earth, moves into a different constellation approximately every 2,000 years. Each of the 12 constellations is represented by one of the signs of the Zodiac and the time the sun spends in each one is referred to as an age. There are 12 ages (or months) in a Solar or Great Year and so we see that approximately every 2,000 and *not* 1,000 years Earth transits from one age to another, with all the upheavals that entails.

History reveals that mankind is thrown into turmoil at such times, when rigid, decaying structures give way to the incoming dispensation. The transition from Aries to Pisces 2,000 years ago supports this view; it heralded the most significant event ever to occur on the planet. Since it was clearly stated at that time that there would be a return of the same energy, to be known as Second Coming, it is not unreasonable to assume that the prophesied event will coincide with the next zodiacal transition. And that is *now*, as we start to move out of the Piscean era into that of Aquarius.

If needed as further evidence, all three religions sharing a common source - Christianity, Judaism and Islam - now await either their Saviour, Messiah or Prophet. Apocalypse 3, Ch 6 v 3-5: "It will be known in the time when all the peoples of the Earth will mourn because of him. But that they mourn the man and not the spirit. And seek not the Father through the son, but the flesh reincarnate. For the priests of the Earth will see the image of the beast (flesh) and lead many into the darkness."

The orthodox and fundamentalist movements are clearly in expectation of some major revelation or manifestation - but they appear to expect it to be an exterior physical event, rather than an inner, spiritual one involving *themselves*. In addition, the Hindus approach the end of their 'Kali Yuga' epoch, and indigenous peoples such as the Hopi Indians and the ancient Mexican Mayan civilisation, to name but a few, all predict that the end of their own current cycles of time coincide at the turn of this Millennium.

At the mundane level, we don't need to look too hard to see the signs of decay and collapse all around us. Deteriorating moral standards, sexual excess and confusion, and a constant stream of hypocrisy and double standards from public figures are the clearest indicators that this age is taking its final gasps of polluted air. The last refuge of sane people is in the few self-contained indigenous communities They alone have preserved and *live* natural law. Yet even now, 'civilised' man refuses to acknowledge the wisdom of his humbler cousins, whom he still calls 'savages'.

In 1990, the obscure Kogi Indian tribe from Colombia emerged from the mountain-top retreats into which they had been driven hundreds of years ago by crusading Spanish Catholics, to commission a poignant and unforgettable television programme. Despite daunting problems of language and lack of contact with the outside world, they chose the BBC to make an impassioned plea to 'the younger brothers' to consider the consequences of their actions on the environment. The ravages of our pollution are threatening even their existence. 'The older brothers' have spoken at the appointed hour, and all among the 'younger brothers' who still obstruct environmental protection, actively or passively, will personally reap the whirlwind they have themselves sown during the 'last days'.

How could the outcome of the 1992 Earth Summit in Brazil have been anything other than ineffectual? Those political delegates who determined its agenda and controlled its outcome - including the then self-confessed anti-ecological President of the USA - represent the very economic forces of First World greed and exploitation that cause the problems to begin with.

Such men, who owe their power and position to the prevailing system, are hardly likely to be motivated by what they would consider 'economically imprudent hysteria'! The unhappy yet somehow appropriate legacy of this most disappointing exercise, was a vast slick of untreated sewage in Rio bay, which polluted the sea and killed the very life the conference had convened to save! Once again the controllers have dumped on the planet. How much longer are our safety and survival, and that of the Earth, to rest in the hands of such people? Yet, we voted most of them into power!

This public relations exercise was mounted by the United Nations which, revealingly, acknowledges no spiritual affiliation and is itself already seriously compromised by the interests of powermongers, profligate waste and corruption. The strings of the UN ambassadors are pulled by politicians blatantly defying the true democratic process through the cynical abuse of the veto system. Many think that this institution with its public facade of respectability could well become the instrument of total control known by the seductive title of 'the One World Government'. Anyone still needing to experience the horror of that ultimate lesson in disempowerment is, as always, free to do so.

Others, having experienced entire lifetimes of repression and subjugation, are now intent on creating a very different society. Gone for good are the days of investing our power in those promising to act in our 'best interests'.

When our institutions are so corrupt that they serve and protect a privileged few at the expense of the many, then eventually the universal Law of balance springs into effect. History reminds us how equilibrium is restored through change, and the closing years of the second Millennium will be no different. This time it is to be accomplished by cosmic forces and Earth energies well beyond the comprehension, let alone control, of 3rd. dimensional man.

The vibrational rate of the planet and awakening humans is increasing exponentially as the dimensional shift progresses, and we shall experience over the next few years an even greater polarisation of human behaviour between love and fear. There will be those who take full responsibility for running their own lives in total confidence and perfect higher-self guidance in a tolerant, forgiving and sharing way. Because they are working in harmony with the prevailing planetary design and thus raising their vibratory frequencies, they will also have at their disposal the dynamics of higher frequencies for the manipulation of all matter. This is achieved through individual or group positive thought projection, a rediscovered art that is now being used for many purposes, including deflection of negative thought-forms such as weaponry and for human and planetary healing.

Aquarius, the age we now enter, is an air sign in the Zodiac and is associated with the development of mind - whereas Pisces, which we are now leaving, is a water sign concerned with emotional growth. Our bodies will gradually become less dense as we move from water to air, while our spiritual growth can no longer be satisfied by the devotional/emotional belief systems of the Piscean era.

In the coming age, mental projection and teleportation will become commonplace, while antigravity and antimatter 'light' technology will be harnessed to production and power requirements. Our new, higher frequency bodies will be increasingly sustained by the energy of air and light or 'prana' as it is known in the East, and we will no longer need frequent intakes of dense foods. The illusion and enslavement of 'earning a living' is a 3rd. dimensional concept, as is money itself, and neither will apply at the higher levels, especially as we shall eventually be able to manifest whatever material object we require! A freer and more fluid multi-dimensional reality now awaits us, centred on the principle of mutual support and sharing, within a less rigidly defined framework of time and space.

Sounds like heaven? It is! Heaven is a term like Paradise, describing the experience of higher dimensions adjacent to our present one:

> "Blessed are they that keep His commandments, that they may have the right to the tree of life. And will share divine Love and know Paradise and Bliss."
>
> *Apocalypse 3, Ch 8, v 14*

Since love vibrates at a much higher frequency than fear, the forces of Earthly control, in their dying throes during the overlap of the two dimensions, will not affect fully-focused human beings, neither will the low-vibration viruses, diseases and radiations, which will only affect those who are unable to sustain the higher frequency that is emerging on Earth. At the deepest level, we all know we are facing a major initiation of one kind or another. No-one is unaware of this fact, and millions are coming into incarnation now in order to experience it. The entire human family, whether incarnate or not, is aware of, and being directly affected by, this momentous event.

Cosmic design works out in perfect sequence, and we must now take responsibility for being part of the process. We have all been given literally thousands of opportunities, and many great souls have sacrificed themselves to raise our consciousness by their very presence here. Nothing can hold back the ever-expanding forces of Creation, and such opportunities do not present themselves at the turn of every 2,000-year age. The gates of Heaven open at the decree of the mind of One - so it might be advisable to take full advantage while we can, rather than risk the grim scenario so graphically described in the Apocalypse and Revelations texts. The sorting of 'the sheep' from 'the goats' in these last days is not a judgement by some patriarchal God, who relishes sending 'sinners' to 'hell'. Far from it: we are now facing ourselves in a mirror - and the reflection cannot lie. This is the time to choose, once and for all.

The next stage of the consciousness shift is to be directed towards the core of materialism, the energy called money. Smug though so many are in the capitalist world about the sudden demise of Communism, little do they realise that their equally corrupt system is now to receive precisely the same explosive treatment. Capitalism and Communism are merely reflections of each other within duality - neither of them 'better' or 'worse' for our growth purposes. Both have been appropriate learning devices, and have now reached the end of their allotted time. Each system contains seeds of value in its original design and purpose, but because ego-centred, separative man is reluctant to share and inclined to hoard power and money through fear, the negative potential within both determined what they became.

The solution to establishing an equitable exchange medium is to see as *energy* what we collectively decide to use as currency, be it paper, precious metal or potatoes. Whatever we use, it represents an energy that is in itself neither good nor bad, but can be used either way. We also have to be very clear that there is more than enough aboard starship Earth for every person's need - as opposed to greed - and that we are all entitled to our fair share. The mind of One is perpetual expansion and flow and we, as part of the One, are that very supply. If we have total trust and can see through this deliberately confused issue, we will attract whatever we need to enable us to fulfil our purpose here.

Usury is the fatal flaw in the capitalist system. Enlightened teachers, including Moses, Jesus, Mohammed, Luther, Zwingli and Gandhi, have all warned us in the strongest terms not to charge each other interest for lending money. Biblical quotations from the old Testament abound, though the practice was well established by the time of the writing of the New Testament, which even endorses the practice!

> "Some charge interest on the loans they make to fellow Israelites and get rich by taking advantage of them. They have forgotten me. The Sovereign Lord has spoken.
> "He refuses to lend money for profit; such a man obeys my commandments and carefully keeps my law."
>
> *Ezekiel, Ch 22, v 12 and Ch 18, v 13*

In the Gospel of Thomas, Logion 95, Jesus said: "If you have money, do not lend at interest, but give it to him who will not return it." Note the emphasis on giving outright rather than loaning, as well as the injunction against usury.

> "To each was given a choinix of wheat according to his labour but many will come and take of the bread and give no labour and they will make starvation upon the Earth and they will cry and their voices will be as the wilderness." *Apocalypse 3, Ch 2: v 7*

This last reference gets to the core of the problem. Interest is an entirely artificial concept defying the universal law of balance and compensation and distorts the only purpose of money, which is to create a fair exchange of energy in payment for labour, goods or services. Banks and governments simply bribe the public with often high rates of interest not to remove the liquidity on which they trade, so that they can fraudulently lend up to 13 times the value of their deposits by creating new credits - and inflation - out of nothing but ink and paper, and charge interest on them too! The public is then brainwashed into believing that their money can work for them by accruing interest. In this way, the entire exchange function of money is manipulated to suit the interests of a small minority, who get rich at the expense of the vast majority and control them through enslavement to debt.

If we imagine money can work as a force independent of its relationship to goods and services, we end up creating a fantasy, which is what usury actually is! It is even more damaging when compounded. *Money is not a commodity, nor does it represent real wealth.* It is in fact nothing more than a useful measure of man's evaluation of goods and services and retains relevance only if it accurately reflects that balance. Otherwise, it becomes the disruptive and inequitable confidence trick on which the present system is based.

Our current financial system was first corrupted in the late Middle Ages by the goldsmiths, who became the first bankers. They realised they could issue more paper receipts for deposited gold than they physically possessed, because of the unlikelihood of all their depositors wanting to take possession at the same time. This valueless 'paper credit' became early money. The 'bankers' then encouraged their clients to maintain their deposits by offering them the inducement of a bribe - interest - to keep it there and thus avoid exposing the fraud already perpetrated. The time-bomb of usury, with its inbuilt explosive exponential growth curve, was thus cunningly planted in the world economies. It is the cancer of capitalism, now in its terminal stage.

Having seen *how* the capitalist system was corrupted, it is easier to identify the resulting abuses and see how they have enslaved rather than freed the vast majority of people within the system. A cursory glance at the history of capitalism will reveal repeating cycles of small groups of the population becoming immensely rich at the expense of the majority. When this reaches intolerable extremes, the Law of balance is triggered and revolution, usually violently, redistributes wealth until the next time. There are endless examples, but the French and Russian revolutions graphically illustrate the point. The major imbalance today is between the First and Third worlds, where, through exorbitant interest payments on loans, already poor nations and their environment are literally beggared by bankers.

Money is energy and energy naturally flows, never being static unless artificially blocked. Usury acts as a blockage, since it encourages money to be saved rather than spent.

Spiritual Law tells us that 'all is provided for our just needs', so 'saving' and incidentally 'insurance,' can only equate to lack of trust, and thus fear. Spending is sharing, flowing and therefore loving. With this approach comes automatic redistribution to the benefit of all, without harming anyone's interests, except those focused on greed.

It is significant that bartering and local exchange trading systems (LETS) operating outside the official economies of the western world are proliferating as people now rapidly lose confidence in this chaotic and palpably rotten system - a system dedicated to a crazy fantasy called economic growth (an indiscriminate measure of all financial movements stimulated even by such negative factors as accidents and disasters!) that if left unchallenged will quickly inundate the planet in a tidal wave of indulgent, ecologically destructive and unnecessary consumerism. Ecological responsibility on which we all depend must now dictate all future levels of economic activity.

"We are living in World War III already. It is an undeclared war: a war of usurious interest rates, ruinous prices and distorted exchange conditions. Remote-controlled interest rates and terms of trade have so far killed millions of people on a plundered planet. They are killed by hunger, sickness, unemployment and criminality. Are revolutions still the only viable solution?"

Interest and Inflation-free Money -a Permaculture publication

"Banking was conceived in iniquity and born in sin. Bankers own the Earth; take it away from them but leave them with the power to create credit, and, with the flick of a pen, they create enough money to buy it all back again. . . If you want to be slaves of bankers and pay the cost of your slavery, then let the bankers control money and control credit."

Lord Macmillan

"If civilisation is to survive, this all-important power of credit creation must revert to the community that produces the *real* wealth."

Lord Stamp, Director of the Bank of England

"Permit me to issue and control the money of a nation and I care not who makes its laws."

Mayer Amschel Rothschild

Rags make Paper. Paper makes Money. Money makes Banks. Banks make Loans. Loans make Beggars. Beggars make Rags.

Anon, 18th century

Only after the last tree has been cut down
Only after the last river has been poisoned
Only after the last fish has been caught
Only then will you find that Money cannot be eaten.

Cree Indian prophecy

The opposite of usury is the spiritual principle of tithing (tenth), which guarantees prosperity by recompensing many times over those who trust enough to give without attachment. The definition is, 'Give freely 10% of our annual income to the person or group that give us spiritual food.' This affirms our trust in abundance, supports evolving consciousness and also activates the spiritual law, which directs us to give in order to receive. Judaism encourages tithing, while forbidding usury between Jews (but curiously not between Jews and Gentiles!) Islam also forbids usury, as did even the Popes of the Middle Ages in Europe. Modern Christianity, enormously rich despite specific biblical injunctions against accumulating wealth, gives no leadership on either and invests its hoard without spiritual direction or conscience. The Anglican Church recently lost almost £1 billion through usurious 'geared' property speculation! Meantime the Papacy seems to have met its match at the hands of the Masonic and Mafia financiers, who have now decimated the once vast treasury of the multinational corporation known as 'Vatican Inc.'. (see *In God's Name* by David Yallop)

Is it now surprising to anyone, seeing the distortion at the core of our spiritual, political and economic institutions, that change is long overdue? Many hard and painful lessons will be experienced by the worshippers of mammon, as the same energy of transformation strikes at capitalism as dealt a mortal blow to Communism. Unpleasant though it is for those emerging from the vice-like grip of Communism, these people never possessed much under any recent regime and are inured to hardship and suffering. A large proportion of capitalists, on the other hand, have grown accustomed to material comfort and the turmoil now approaching will be distinctly uncomfortable, unless they turn around their thinking, which is literally to RE-PENT!

> "And he broke the seal and I heard a new song and there came forth the prayers of the saints. And the Earth fell in half, in one there flowed blood and the half was of red. And the second was white, and knew not God, but provoked his works in greed, and saw conquest."

Apocalypse 3, Ch 2. v 4

This reference depicts Communism as the red half and capitalism as the white. Christianity is equated with capitalism, greed and conquest and is accused of using 'the Word' with utmost hypocrisy to serve its own selfish ends.

One can only marvel at the accuracy of these ancient prophecies.

PART 3

THE NEW HEAVEN AND THE NEW EARTH

Chapter 15

THE AQUARIAN CROSS -
A SYMBOL FOR ALL MANKIND

> "There is no greater happiness than to approach the
> Godhead and bring it down to men"
>
> *Beethoven*

In late 1989, you will recall, Mahatma Gandhi communicated through a trance medium to the Wholistic World Vision group in England that 'a golden Cross' was to be made in Jerusalem. I was to receive a vision of its design during my meditations, and was then to set in motion the process of having it made. The story of the Aeon Shift and subsequent work of the Cross around the world form the major portion of this book. It is a symbol of universal Christ consciousness which, we are told, signals the end of the duality of the Piscean era and heralds the advent of the golden age of Aquarius. It is not a Christian cross, but it does represent the same principle demonstrated by Jesus Christ in his original teachings of 'the Way'.

The symbol of the Aquarian age itself is a chalice, and it will be remembered that Joseph of Arimathea is understood to have brought the archetypal symbol of the chalice in the form of the cup used at the Last Supper to Glastonbury and, as the tradition goes, placed it in the Chalice Well. In so doing, he not only identified the next power centre to be activated, but also the symbol that would replace the Cross during the next Age. It is important to understand, therefore, that the Aquarian Cross is the last Christ-related cross of the Piscean age and serves to project an image of perfect balance and harmony - replacing an era of Christian imbalance and distortion that still crucifies the Christ consciousness. The Aquarian Cross has the function of inspiring a heart response in all mankind and thereby reveals the key to 4th. dimensional reality (heaven), through the integration of opposites. In so doing, it offers great healing potential to all who are prepared to release the abjection and self-denial imposed on them by their religions.

231

In his highly illuminating book *Earthstars*, which depicts the sacred geometry of London (a major planetary power centre), Christopher Street gives a concise description of the symbology at the heart of the Aquarian Cross:

> "The Vesica Piscis is the single most important figure and the most fundamental building block of sacred geometry. Formed by two interlinking circles, it provides a simple base for constructing both a pentagram and a hexagram. These two geometric figures underlie most physical forms - animal, vegetable and mineral. The circle symbolises the eternal spiritual dimensions, and the two circles of the Vesica Piscis represent the primary division of universal unity into its dual aspects. It is the first step towards multiplicity - a graphic illustration of how the One begins to become the all. As a symbol of duality, the vesica is the key to the two primary polarities through which divine energy functions throughout the Universe: the hexagram and pentagram, male/female, yin/yang, positive/negative, lunar/solar etc.
>
> "The equal-armed Cross forms a third energy pattern, operating behind the dual energies of the pentagram and hexagram. This extends from its primary form into a squared grid, and is directly related to the symbolism of the square - the manifestation of spiritual force in physical form, the earthing of divine energy in matter. The underlying principle behind the pentagram, the hexagram and a great many other things may be traced back to something Plato called the *Golden Mean*. This is a proportional relationship guaranteed to imbue any structure or design with symmetrical perfection since it ensures that every individual part relates harmoniously, not just to the complete structure as a whole, but to every other part of it."

The Golden Mean's basic (though variable) ratio is 1:1.618033 and combining it with the Vesica Piscis, it becomes the formula that produced many of our most pleasing buildings such as the Parthenon and Chartres Cathedral. At the points of the intersection of the two circles, the Vesica Piscis framed in the Golden Mean rectangle depicts the archetypal *female* shape of the vulva.

The Vesica Piscis as the centrepiece of an equal-sided cross depicts the perfect interaction of Spirit and matter within balanced opposite polarities. Since Christ, the spark of God in man, is love, and love is a function of the heart, so this Cross of Christ consciousness is its ultimate symbol. In this way, the Piscean era ends with the same as it began by offering the key to the higher dimensions during the 'last days'.

The Aquarian Cross absorbed the remaining energy of the First Coming of the Christ on the Mount of Olives at Easter 1990 and since then has been present at the opening of several power centres by focusing that of the Second Coming of the same impulse all around the world. Spirit informs us that by means of these and similar ceremonies in many countries, Earth herself has received the Christ Light and is now initiating the final series of energy adjustments known as 'the Earth Changes' that will raise her into the 4th. dimension. During this period, the Aquarian Cross and its replicas will continue to move across the planet, acting as a focus for those who intend to awaken their own Christ consciousness. Once we reach the next Millennium, we and the planet will be demonstrating the interdependence of all Creation according to the Law of One, and there will be no further need for Christ-related symbology. The original Aquarian Cross will then be taken to the activation point of the next Aeon, to await whatever initiation is to occur there.

Here are a few of the many references to the Cross that we have received from Spirit sources during the last few years:

"The Cross will heal and teach and is the embodiment of God. It contains the energy of God and is the symbol of the Christ."
"The purest and most energised Cross on Earth, which will heal anywhere."
"We know how necessary it was that the beautiful Cross was fashioned and stored with the great Christ energy and then taken from Israel at this time of change."

Michael Joseph, who wrote the Foreword to this book, was involved in an extraordinary project in the mid-1970s, when he and his group 'worked' two huge interlocking circles imprinted across the southern English landscape. With hindsight, therefore, we can see that, years before the events described in this book, these great circles were *already* being activated, in preparation for the seeding in Britain of the energy of the Second Coming of the Christ consciousness !

Since it would seem that we are both players in this cosmic drama, I am including here an extract from Michael's book describing his part of the story:

CIRCLE OF LIGHT

three years before Merlin's dramatic reappearance in 1974, Simon came to see me, excited about a book he was reading: John Michell's *City of Revelation*. A study of Britain's secret landscape, it is a companion to his classic book, *The View Over Atlantis*.

The passage Simon wanted to show me describes a huge circle that is imprinted on the west of England. Around its perimeter lie such key sites as Stonehenge and Glastonbury Tor. The centre of the circle, John Michell calculated, lies in the Malvern Hills, where the three counties of Herefordshire, Gloucestershire and Worcestershire meet.

I was already hooked:

I knew this place!

At the outbreak of World War II my brother, sister and I had been evacuated to a lodge on an estate at the foot of the Malvern Hills. As children, we had scampered happily up the side of the first of these hills Chase End, and gazed out over the immense surrounding plain.

A close friend, Tony Standcumbe, and I decided to drive down to investigate the place. Late one afternoon we arrived at White Leafed Oak a scattering of white-painted houses nestling between the first two hills, where the three counties meet. Tony's little Saab struggled up the last few yards and pulled up gratefully in the little hollow. We lowered the car windows and sat for a while in the almost supernatural silence.

Towering above us to the right was the grassy flank of Chase End Hill southernmost of the range. In front of us rose the tree-clad slope of Ragged Stone Hill, its summit hidden from view.

It was as if we had left the present day and entered medieval England - Arthur's England. Time has stood still here for centuries, I thought Kings, empires, wars and revolutions have come and gone, but life in this sleepy hollow drifts along at its own sweet pace, unchanged and unchanging. Unknown to most people it is a sacred place lying as it does at the exact centre of a circle around whose perimeter, at equidistant points, are situated such ancient sites as Stonehenge and Glastonbury Tor.

The circle is a wheel of immense power, installed by nameless master builders long before the present race emerged, and now lying dormant.

That autumn, my friends and I decided to celebrate the equinox on Ragged Stone Hill, which, we had since discovered, was the exact centre of the great Circle. A robin welcomed us as we entered the wood at the foot of the hill - a courtesy we have enjoyed every time we return to the place. Half an hour later, breathless after trudging long, steep paths lined by gorse and foxgloves, we climbed onto the summit and stood in a circle round the guardian rock.

We closed our eyes and Jacqueline recited a simple invocation. She looked like an Egyptian high priestess who had stepped out of her own time into another....

I opened my eyes for a moment.

The light had turned silvery blue. Over each of my companions a shimmering angelic figure stood on guard.

And above us all stood the incandescent figure of a woman clothed in light - immense, at least thirty feet high.

Surely this was the Goddess herself !

I shut my eyes again and waited until Jacqueline brought the little ceremony to an end....

Ever since, I have associated that hilltop with the feminine ray or energy. It is unquestionably a place of great spiritual potency, both incoming and outpouring.

P.T. later described this Circle of Light, as I have come to call it, as 'in a sense, the Grail of Britain.' The view from the summit rock at its centre is one of the most breath-taking in all the land.

We were not the least surprised to learn that Elgar, Vaughan Williams and Gustav Holst had all lived and worked on or near the Malverns. Their quintessentially English music no doubt derives much of its power and subtlety from the place. Walk these hills in any weather, and you will know why - if not how - *The Planets Suite* came into being.

One summer, we decided to greet the solstice on the top of Ragged Stone Hill - even though it occurred at sunrise. We drove from London, arrived at the foot of the Malverns in the dark, were guided for two miles by a white owl that flew in the beam of our headlights and led us to a small concealed turning that wound up to the hollow - thanks again, Merlin! - climbed the hill with the aid of torches, and waited.

Far below us the ageless plain waited, breathless and expectant in the pearly half-light. The spine of the hills jutted out of the plain like the ridged back of a giant sleeping dragon, sheltering several villages on either side, and the cathedral town of Worcester to the east.

At our feet, two counties stretched towards the horizon, a chequer-board of greens and ochre studded with toy villages and sharpened-pencil spires. And twenty miles to the west, a faint blue smudge of mountains that was Wales. An invading sea of mist rolled across the plain, breaking against two distant hills like waves in ultra-slow motion. Into the orchestrated silence came a piping woodwind chorus from the birds, and an occasional brassy blare of cattle and sheep.

It was a world at the dawn of Creation.

Or a world awaiting a new dispensation.

So perfect, so immaculate, so complete that, despite ourselves, we started to laugh and shout and dance.

High in the sky above us, two vast pink clouds hung like an archangel's wings upraised to invoke? announce? authorise and bless? the coming day.

Our very next visit to that hilltop was equally memorable, but in quite another way:

To celebrate the midsummer solstice, eight of us revisited Ragged Stone Hill. We stood in a circle around the guardian rock and P.T. recited the Great Invocation. As he reached the last line - 'Let light and love and power restore the Plan on Earth' - we raised our arms in the usual way. Or rather, we *tried* to raise them. But a sudden pillar of energy, glowing gold and silver and pink and blue, was pouring down into the hill from above - and none of us could move!

We all 'saw' and felt this colossal, benevolent power and happily let it flood through us. Then, as suddenly as it had arrived, it was gone. We stepped back from the summit rock, gasping and laughing.

P.T. said quietly, "I think something rather important has just happened." Which for him, who is the soul of modesty and hates pretension of any kind, was really saying something.

Back in London, I decided to ask Wellesley Tudor Pole if he could tell us what had happened. He was one of the initiates who had advised Churchill behind the scenes during World War II. A few days later I had his answer, channelled by Lady Cynthia Sandys and transcribed by a dear friend, Rosamond Lehmann:

"Now for the message I am told to give you. Since the summer solstice, on the very eve of the great power-giving moment, the centre of the Earth opened, releasing many new and hitherto unknown rays and forces onto your plane.

"As seen with the inner sight, it was like a huge earthquake or eruption coming without sound, but with a blinding light, and a scent of flowers unknown to you.

"All this has been engineered by the great Nature spirits in order to parry the manmade forces of pollution. Now these rays are beautiful, vital and God-given but, being neutral they also have their darker side; and I know their effect upon negative minds could be very lowering. So we ask you to envelop these rays with your love, and transmute them into a valuable growing asset for man on the planet.

"The one fact to remember above all others at this moment is that all who are awake to the perils of the hour must *think love* into this great vortex of power which is now being freed into your atmosphere.

"Your scientists will grasp its meaning and use it for all kinds of different tasks. But you must infuse into it the element of love, to shield the young, and those countless unawakened souls from the dangers and imbalances that now threaten the very stability of the world and its peoples."

You can imagine how much *that* gave us to think about!

Throughout the remainder of the 1970s - some years before Peter Quiller and I got down to business with what we called 'Operation Excalibur' - my companions and I continued to visit certain ancient sites whenever we could - particularly at equinoxes and solstices, when the energies seemed to be enhanced or multiplied.

Our aim was simple: not being dowsers or geomancers, we arrived on site, intuited the frequency or 'keynote' of the place, and then invoked healing or some similar energy, either for the planet as a whole, or for the animal and Nature kingdoms, or for some country or region devastated by war, famine or tragedy of some kind.

Our visits to these places were strictly of the 'Thy Will be done' variety. It often occurred to us on these expeditions that we were not going about our own business, but were being sent to these locations for some purpose we could only guess at. We were less knights and ladies on the chessboard than willing messengers or engineers.

Why 'Operation Excalibur'? Because, as Pete once reminded me, "The sword is the emblem of the 'King' energy - the power attributed to Arthur, Saint Michael, Saint George and Christ himself. But remember, this power is spiritual, not temporal: this time round, Excalibur's role is to cut away the dross and illusion that have been holding us all in their thrall, and to reveal the truth."

It is *not* a weapon of war, and yet some people - particularly those who are holding on to ill-gotten power, status and wealth - will feel the sharpness of its blade as acutely as if the Sword *were* being wielded in traditional combat.

THE CIRCLE OF POWER

Do you remember me telling you of the dream I had, back in 1974, in which John Prudhoe took me to meet the Magician? Well, immediately after that scene faded, something else happened which I have been keeping until now:

Merlin and the anteroom vanished. In their place, a map of southern England rose up in front of me. The forefinger of some unseen person - Merlin again, I presume - traced a vertical line from Beachy Head on the south coast to the Saffron Walden area of Essex.

A voice said, "Fifty-two, fifty-two."

Next morning I bought an Ordnance Survey map of south-east England. I already knew that 52 degrees latitude runs horizontally through England, passing close to Ragged Stone Hill, so I traced it eastward and stopped near Saffron Walden - then looked down to the bottom of the map.

There was the figure 52 again! Representing 52,000 metres east of the nearest longitude line.

We did some research, and discovered that the exact spot we were looking for was a small wood near Audley End, a lovely Jacobean mansion which in the reign of William III had been the royal palace of England!

We visited the wood one afternoon.

It was like entering hell.

The trees were blackened and stunted, there was no grass, no flowers or green vegetation. It was the kind of place where you might expect to run into demons or malignant dwarfs, cut-throats or brigands.

We found a small clearing, stood in a circle and decided to do a cleansing operation. Within seconds, a great wind blew up out of nowhere. Soon it was scouring the trees, blowing leaves and twigs and dry bracken horizontally through the air. At last it died, and the wood fell silent.

Wordlessly we left the place.

We picnicked in the grounds of Audley End, and John Prudhoe promised to do a little more research to find out what had prompted this strange expedition - and what had happened to cast such a dreadful spell on the wood.

He turned up trumps:

The wood is the centre of *an identical circle* to our beloved Circle of Light! But this one is a circle of power - hence the royal palace at its centre. And what is more, Oxford, Norwich cathedral and Canterbury cathedral are situated on its perimeter. London is contained by it.

So this was the wheel of power - the unseen dynamo behind Britain's rise to pre-eminence in the world, in time gone by! Whereas the Circle of Light, its counterpart and opposite - with which it is interlocked - is the wheel of Britain's spiritual nature.

But why the terrible atmosphere in that wood?

Because Matthew Hopkins, Witchfinder General at the time of Cromwell, had executed countless victims there; so many, in fact, that the place still bore the scars of his terrible work: his henchmen persecuted, tortured and murdered anyone they could find who knew anything about terrestrial and cosmic energies, who collaborated with Nature, observed her rhythms and cycles, who healed or ministered privately to the sick and the oppressed, or who worshipped older gods. During this bloody epoch, the church claimed not thousands, but *millions* of such victims in Europe alone.

It is probably true to say that if these countless custodians of the Earth had not been ruthlessly culled, but had been allowed to practise their arts and pass them on to their children, we would not be facing the chaos that now confronts us.

It has also been pointed out that the ritual of making the sign of the cross on a person's forehead during baptism and communion is in fact an insidious method of closing the person's 'third eye'. If this is so - and I pray that it is not - if a concerted attempt has been made to deprive entire generations of their inner sight, then another monstrous crime must be added to those already heaped at the Church door.

All this, thanks be, is a hideous nightmare of the past - *a nightmare of our own choosing*. Now, our only task is literally to re-create ourselves, our communities and our world. And to guide and protect the young - who *are* the future - from the horrors we brought on ourselves.

If we cannot bequeath to our children a perfect world, at least we can encourage them to recognise their own and each other's capabilities, and to make the utmost use of their combined talents and energies. If that is all we ever give them, we can rest assured that they, at least, will be setting out with growing confidence, self-knowledge, compassion and perspective towards the limitless horizons of the new Millennium.

Chapter 16

THE THIRD BOOK
OF THE APOCALYPSE -
THE PROPHECY OF
THE SECOND COMING

This remarkable text was received by Wholistic World Vision direct from Spirit through a word-processor in early 1990, just before the Aquarian Cross was brought to Glastonbury from Jerusalem during the Aeon Shift ceremony. I have already described the miraculous circumstances of its arrival earlier in the book and so shall use this chapter to reveal its long-suppressed, but now most relevant, prophecies. The full text and guidance notes may be found on page 297.

The transmission was initiated by the spirit of John the Elder, pupil of John of the Revelation. The identity of the many Johns is confusing because the disciple John later established his own community in Asia minor, where all participants used the name 'John' to signify their allegiance to his spiritual mastery. Whether the disciple actually received the Revelation vision or whether it was the experience, as some think, of another member called John who was banished from Effesus to Patmos for two years. Whoever it was, the vision obviously derived from the same high source that overlighted each member of the community.

Its provenance, as explained by John the Elder, is as follows: he was charged by his Master to summarise the existing Revelation vision and at the same time 'to project thought into the future', in other words 'to prophesy'. The summary is in effect a simplification of the entire Revelation vision to assist wider comprehension, using some of the original text of the first two books (22 chapters), known as the Judgement of the Jews (Book 1) and the Judgement of the Gentiles (Book 2). 22 is a significant number, representing the number of letters in the Hebrew alphabet and the major Arcana of the Tarot. Since 22 also represents 'the gateway to the new', it suggests that there is more to come! How fitting that this miraculously-restored text should relate specifically to what was in those days seen as the future time of Second Coming.

John the Elder states that "it was all the inspiration of my Master and I summarised his words so that others might understand his mind." It would appear that the by now elderly John passed on, just after he received the final vision as described in Ch 7, v 3:

"Quickly I am to be taken unto the throne of the Father. I place into your keeping the vision given to me by the Father in the years of my life. That the vision may be made safe unto the time of the second coming of our Lord Jesus the Christ that the prophecy may be revealed."

Then he continued to overlight his pupil from Spirit, who 'channelled' the summary that became the Third Book of the Apocalypse. Those readers who are now familiar with the reality of communication with Spirit dimensions, will not find it difficult to understand how the two Johns worked together, first in the physical and then through Spirit.

The subsequent lives of John the Elder, one of which was the entity known as Galileo, have been used to accumulate knowledge on all aspects of the evolution of the Earth, including its shape! He retained the wisdom of the Apocalypse prophecy, 'as bidden by his Master', until the last days of 3rd. dimensional Earth and then chose a most ingenious way to share the inspiration of their joint work! In Spirit, he is considered by Gandhi and Churchill to be a 'teacher of teachers' and is held in the highest regard. Certainly, we have been privileged to receive some exceptional material ourselves, much of which is contained in these pages.

The text of the Third Book of the Apocalypse was written at the time of the Emperor Domitian (81-96CE). As a summary of the vision of the higher levels of human existence, it has always posed a major threat to religious leaders intent on subverting spiritual truth. With the realisation that 'the Word' has been changed all too frequently in the many 'authorised' versions of biblical texts, the 3rd. Book becomes an indispensable asset and reveals the basic inconsistencies and distortions in current Christian theology.

Being a work of higher dimensional wisdom, the Book of Revelation is not easily understood, and so simplification by John the Elder in this summary will help many to understand humanity's place within

Creation as inheritors of the Christ consciousness and stewards of this planet. There are warnings for those continuing to follow an exclusively materialistic or destructive path, but a promise is also given of lasting world peace for those 'sharing Divine Love and entering the garden of Paradise and Bliss.' Those acknowledging the Christ *within* themselves are directed to prepare for 'a New Heaven and a New Earth' at this time of Second Coming, just before the end of the second Millennium.

Loving beings in higher dimensions guide our destiny and by restoring this long-lost text just as with the Ten Commandments, give us due warning and such assistance as they can to stimulate our awakening and avert personal and planetary disaster. We at Wholistic World Vision guarantee the circumstances and timing of the text's arrival and our suggestion is not to be overly concerned with the details of how it happened, but rather to concentrate on *why* it should have appeared at this time and, above all, *what* it says.

Chapter 1

We see immediately that the chapters forming this book were dispatched to the Seven Christian Communities in Asia Minor for safekeeping as part of the main body of *Revelations* material. The fate of this particular text was decided by the early Christian movement, which quickly fell under the influence of Paul's teachings. *Revelations* in its original composition was unlikely to have survived his and subsequent patriarchal influence intact! In verse 2, John clearly explains that he is channelling from spirit through use of the 'inner ear' of his pupil John the Elder:

> "Having the ear, I John write in the spirit, for there came a loud voice like a trumpet behind me, and turned did see the light and fell at his feet as though dead."

The chapter then describes the proclamation of Second Coming, the nature of the city, New Jerusalem, and the experience of living in higher-dimensional reality:

> "For the beast will be slain and his sign will lie down with the Lamb. A great trumpet will sound from a high place and a great star set on a staff will be carried into the midst of the crowd. And the Lord will bless this place and make it a Holy City, and it will be called the new Jerusalem.

"And they will bare their feet and bow their heads, for all nations and kings of the Earth will see no other splendour. And the temple gates will not shut by day, and there will be no night there. And the city will be borne on a cloud of light, not set upon the Earth, but carried by the spirit."

Note that those not of the Light will be clearly identified by the visibly contaminated energy of their subtle bodies. The first reference to 'the Priests of the Earth', or non-spiritual leaders of world religions, makes abundantly clear their anti-Christ role in these end times:

"Thus the word will be revealed by the spirit of the light. But the Priests of the Earth will not see the word, but make witness to the defiled word, which came out of the mouths of angels, but fell into the hand of the beast."

The minimum critical mass number for raising human consciousness is 144,000. These are the souls 'sealed' as the 12,000 within each of the 12 tribes of Israel:

"And the Priests of the Earth will come forth and call the book evil and make pain of the 144,000 who are of the light."

They are already 4th.dimensional beings, who volunteered for this work, and are now in the process of awakening spiritually. They were all incarnate on Earth at the time of Harmonic Convergence in 1987.

Chapter 2

In this chapter we are led through the breaking of the seven seals, or the releasing of information, starting with the identification of the characteristics of the capitalist and communist systems. The 2nd Seal refers to the demise of Communism under the influence of Mikhail Gorbachev and his successors, and the raising of the spiritual consciousness of Mother Russia as a profound influence on the world in the last days. (per the Fatima prophecies)

Members of the 'First world responsible for denying food and sustenance to the 'Third' world and failing to *share* their good fortune will have to transmute all the suffering they created through their selfishness:

"When I cut off your supply of bread, they will dole out the bread by weight."

Closely linked to this is the imminent collapse of the corrupt capitalist system. Many in the West will learn hard lessons as material values collapse around them and "they will cry and their voices will be as the wilderness, for even the oil and the wine will be scarce for there will be no rain and from the sun none will find cover." Global warming will cause scarcity of essentials to sustain physical life.

Inevitably, the pale horse of 'death' takes his toll among the weakened and diseased, but it is pointed out that this misery is of man's own creation through the misuse of his free-will. Even man's advanced technology will not assist at this stage, because it will merely create more terror. The long-predicted devastation of the former Yugoslavia is an early example of this revelation. These times are to be the final test of mankind, but simultaneously the Light is restored and the reincarnated saints and martyrs, the 144,000 souls touched by the Christ consciousness at First Coming, reappear to lead those so choosing among humanity into the next dimension:

> "And he gave charge to his servants to walk abroad and to carry the message, so that all may be prepared for the age that will be as gold, and when all will know their brothers and sisters by the light of their being."

The breaking of the 6th seal (occurring currently) unleashes spiritual and physical changes on Earth and a sure sign of this is the unpredictable weather and seasons now being experienced world-wide. In verse 18 much blame for the chaos is laid squarely at the feet of the Priests of the Earth for what they have perpetrated. This is why there can be no effective cleansing on the planet until basic spiritual truth such as that contained in the 3rd Book of Apocalypse is widely re-established.

In verse 19, God's covenant with humanity is reaffirmed at the moment of the raising of the Cross at Glastonbury Tor, when half an hour's silence was observed to unite Heaven and Earth. Jesus, as the seventh Angel, then endows the disciples of the Light with universal knowledge at the time of the Second Coming of the Christ spirit. The chapter ends with a vision of the re-birthing of the Earth and the sending of the trusted messengers to all parts of the Earth to 'lead the nations to Light.'

Chapter 3

This chapter starts with a most illuminating description of the process of 'channelling' spirit information, confirming that it is an ancient and approved method of interdimensional communication, used over the ages by most cultures and traditions. Christianity obviously did not want the higher realms to cast doubt on its distorted teachings and used its well-tried and tested method of condemning the practice as devilry and witchcraft, with the severest penalties for those caught at it! No wonder mankind in the West has long forgotten this invaluable link to higher sources of knowledge and, even worse, now denies the very existence of Spirit!

> "And the seven angels spoke in one voice, for as they came to walk upon the land, they took many forms that were man, but though the form was man, the spirit was not man, for they entered into man as one entering into a Holy place. But when they were gone, the man was made singular again. And while they were with man, they told of the secrets of the Father, that all signs may be understood, even as is written in this prophecy. For nothing will be as it is seen."

There are then references to the positive/negative polarities governing our lives, our free choice and the need to look for hidden meaning, as things in this dimension are never what they first appear to be!

Warnings are given about discernment in 'this Earthly classroom' of duality, where Light and dark both manifest. Without first experiencing the dark, we would be unable to distinguish the Light, because it is only in the dark that Light can be perceived. By recognising one, we shall know the other! "If you know not the darkness, how can you understand the light?"

The rest of the chapter is devoted to the restoration of the feminine principle through the acknowledgement of the Earth Goddess in the last days. Our mother is about to give birth to the new dimension, while her children face a spiritual reawakening:

> "And the Father will send to the Earth a protector and she will be clothed with the sun and ride on a chariot of gold. And her name will be Gaia and she will carry the seed of life and her body will be as a womb for all that live upon the Earth. But she will not be known until the last days come upon the Earth and there is darkness and decay."

We are reminded to trust in Spirit and outgrow our dependency on material security. Through the selfishness of materialism, the few have failed the vast majority by enslaving them in poverty and so denying them the opportunity of spiritual growth.

Chapter 4

The Archangel Michael ministers to those now awakening, as many are still unsure. As he opens their inner sight, they become all-knowing and -seeing and gather at a 'high place' - a reference to the symbolical meeting of heaven and earth on Glastonbury Tor.

Then there is a description of the great Light of the comet Austin or Star of Bethlehem alerting the 'known and unknown' Spirit masters of the planet returning at this time. Michael presents the 144,000 to them and explains how they, as representatives of all tongues and nations, are the 'critical mass' to lift human consciousness:

> "And the angel Michael said, "These are they who have walked with the Father and are ascended, even to the throne. They are the 144,000 children of the first born and are of every tongue and of every nation. For the risen Christ is in their heart, that the word may be fulfilled." "

Verses 11-13 go on to make it abundantly clear that the Christ is a consciousness which has descended at this time, and that it is to be accessed within each human heart:

> "And you will know the Christ, which is descended and made one with all who are of the sign. And they will make the sign one to another and they will know themselves pure in the blood of the Lamb. And they will rejoice, for the Christ is descended from the higher planes even to the darkest corner of the Earth. For none will know fear, *for the Christ is within.*"

The old 3rd.dimensional cycle apparently ends at the instant of the declaration of the Second Coming, when the gates of Paradise are opened for all who wish to enter:

> " And the cherubim will stand guard no more. And the gates of Paradise will be opened and all will dwell there in the purity of Love. Thus will end the cycle at the instant of the second coming of the Christ consciousness."

The higher dimensions are not open, however, to those who 'stray from the teachings of the Christ' or those who receive 'the mark of the beast'. It is thought that the controllers on this planet will attempt to force humanity to accept a laser mark on their hands or forehead as an identification to enable them to participate in the computerised debit/credit exchange system of the 'One World Government', after money is withdrawn.

Compliance with this or any other conspiracy precludes participation in the higher dimensional initiation:

"For those who would worship the beast and his image and anyone who receives the mark of his name...."

Finally, when it is too late, people will realise their mistake - but by then they will be trapped in their own and the surrounding negativity.

Chapter 5

The chapter starts with the validation of the Aquarian cross:

"And the seven angels sat in a circle with the twelve and the one who holds the golden cross that is the mark of the Christ.'

It then goes on to describe the many blessings bestowed on man to assist him through his earthly experiences. Bowls, as concepts of our consciousness and facets of our Being, are used to illustrate how Nature in an undefiled state of purity is designed to provide man's basic needs. In terms of planetary ecology trees create oxygen and the clouds they make above them produce moisture to stimulate growth. All building materials are provided so we can also make transport vessels to distribute and share our common produce. Skills in arts and crafts are given to us as a glorification of God and are to be shared for the inspiration and upliftment of everyone. Gold is described as 'a base metal of man's treasure upon Earth' - which suggests that it should have remained the foundation for all our exchange systems and that abandoning the gold standard was inadvisable. Crystal is equated with the intellect we are given to discern truth and beauty. In verse 11 all these gifts are mingled with the Earth, so that all man's needs may be met.

It is made clear in verse 12 that there are sufficient resources on the planet to feed all mankind, unless the balance is disturbed by greed. There then follows a startlingly accurate prophecy concerning the processes of human abuse of all these gifts, culminating in the crisis we now face. The wholesale destruction of trees and forests reduces our oxygen supply and directly causes pollution and disease in humans and the animal and vegetable kingdoms. As we try to solve the problems of our own making without the indispensable tools of truth and wisdom, we merely compound the problems and cause more disruption. Financial greed and fear of each other, resulting in the obscenity of 'defence budgets', turn us into locusts that cause famine. Food mountains then graphically illustrate the paranoia of the greedy through hoarding rather than sharing.

Art is the inspiration of God, and if public access is denied to it by collectors who use it only as an investment, then the people starve spiritually. Verse 17 gives a graphic illustration of the chaos in our financial institutions controlled by avaricious speculators manipulating commodities, metals, currencies and finances without knowing what they are doing and without any benefit to the human race. Such people are described as 'incessantly and meaninglessly croaking, clothed in gold and looking wise and learned, yet underneath naked.'

Through the unbridled intellect of world leaders, the blind lead the blind into ever-growing chaos, towards Armageddon. The age-old pattern of alternating roles as controllers and victims, neither taking personal responsibility, became such an entrenched format that it has been extremely hard to break this vicious spiral. Now, however, corrupt dictators and rulers are being removed in ever-increasing numbers, and their people are at last being set free.

Chapter 6

Christian priests now lead people astray by proclaiming the Second Coming of Jesus as a physical reappearance. Yet it is the spirit or essence of the Christ and not the body of Jesus that has now returned:

> "It will be known in the time when all the peoples of the Earth will mourn because of Him. But they mourn the man and not the spirit. And seek not the Father through the son, but the flesh reincarnate. For the Priests of the Earth will see the image of the beast (flesh) and lead many into the wilderness."

Verse 6 makes it clear that we can expect many signs and phenomena, such as crop formations, to prepare everyone for the coming initiation. The original teachings of Jesus Christ will now be restored and those who follow them are given access to 'heaven'.

Resurrection and immortality appear to us as mysteries. However, the repeated process of discarding the body, raising the spirit and then returning for another incarnation is clearly explained:

"All will come upon the Earth a hundred, hundred times, and still will the spirit be raised by the Father. For the sign of the resurrection of the Son, is the sign of life eternal."

There is then timely guidance on balancing the male/female polarity within each one of us and honouring divine love as the essence and purest expression of God. The loving energy generated between two compatible people can then express itself in any creative capacity - procreation (contrary to some of the most damaging of all current religious distortion) being only ONE of many possibilities and NOT the sole objective! Women are thus also liberated from the enslavement of reproduction and enabled to fulfil roles other than motherhood.

"And this gift did He give all creatures, even to the lowest form that in their union they would touch the Divine spirit."

Those expressing selfish sexuality without a loving basis, abuse the divine gift and unleash the seven plagues currently manifesting on Earth. We are reminded that unconditional love - or compassion, kindliness and understanding - is the key to 'Paradise and Bliss'.

Chapter 7

The first six verses describe how John received the final vision through an altered state of consciousness, so that his pupil, John the Elder, could complete the writing and send it to the seven churches for safe keeping. Verse 4 assures us that the Spirit of John will live and 'know my brethren in the time foretold', meaning he will assist those currently working in the vision on Earth, as 'he knows them of old'. Verse 7 is a powerful directive to those in the vision to communicate the truth wherever opportunities present themselves:

"Forasmuch as you have made faithful declaration of these things that are and will come to pass, let my Word be known that all will hear."

The remainder of the chapter describes the comet Austin known as the Star of Bethlehem returned, signifying the time and place of the Declaration of Second Coming. All who attuned to this great moment anywhere on Earth were equally blessed and joined those bathed in Light around the Golden cross in receiving wisdom and knowledge, enabling them to teach and communicate everywhere.

Verse 15: "For the spirit will talk through the prophets." Here is unequivocal confirmation that 'channelled' spirit guidance will play a leading role in initiating humanity into the new consciousness at this time. 'The pure spirit is not touched by the darkness of the Earth and comes to Earth in pure form, so that all may drink of its nectar.'

The New Bride referred to in verse 15 is the Gaian consciousness and those involved in the vision will be concerned with responsible husbandry on the planet. In verses 18 & 19, we have the prediction of the full awakening of the 144,000 'chosen of God', their role of raising human awareness, and that in this they will not be restricted by mortal form and will have the ability to manifest at 5th.dimensional levels:

> "And their spirit will inherit the Earth. And they will have dominion over the stars even to the tenth planet."

Once raised into a higher dimensional 'octave', we will live in a state of permanent love, joy and harmony.

Chapter 8

This is basically a repeat of chapter 22 of the biblical *Revelations*, but on reading it carefully, it soon becomes clear that the 'authorised' version has been significantly and rather crudely abridged. Furthermore, on comparing the two we discover that a poor attempt has actually been made to disguise the complete withdrawal of ALL 7 chapters of this book from the 'official' *Revelations* vision! By bringing forward this concluding chapter to make it appear that the 'authorised' version is complete at the end of Book 2, the church fathers long ago deprived humanity of indispensable spiritual wisdom and the part of the prophecy that is MOST relevant to these times. Chapter 8 has three clear references to the time period of Second Coming (verses 7,12 & 20): 'until the second millennium is nigh and to the return of the 'guiding star' of Bethlehem - while the restored text throws much more light on the sublime, mystical vision of John's Revelation:

> Verse 16: "And there was great light and there stood before me Jesus the Christ. And he spake thus, that I may know the authority of the angel. And bade - Watch for the star that was foretold by the prophet Jacob, that you will know the time of the second coming, when I will enter all hearts."

Inevitably, the controversy will rage over which is the original work - but knowing the Church's infamous track record of tampering with material it considered threatening to its authority, I know which version *I* trust!

The chapter starts with a description of our entry into the higher dimension (Paradise), where we find perfect peace and exist beyond time. In this state, we reflect divinity to one another and, knowing we are all equal, worship the One who permeates us all - that is, from now on, we align with the God force internally rather than worship it as an external projection. Once restored to our Christ consciousness, as exemplified by Jesus, we rise permanently out of the duality and follow where he led.

> Verse 10: "Hide not the sayings of the prophecy of this book, neither let no man do likewise, for the time is at hand that all wisdom shall be known."

Here, in one relatively simple text, we have a summary of all the instructions we need to lift ourselves into full awareness, free forever from fear, self-denial, guilt and separation. The time period and process of Second Coming is explained, reincarnation and communication with spirit realms are authenticated, the restoration of the Feminine principle is confirmed, most religious priests and leaders are exposed as spiritually ignorant or devious, while humanity's divine origin and potential is reaffirmed.

The passport to heaven is a loving heart and open mind focused on the Law of One and a willingness to share. We need nothing more to guarantee us safe passage against all adversaries, as we set out on our exhilarating journey home.

Chapter 17

SPIRIT ON THE LINE

WHOLISTIC WORLD VISION

"Wholistic World Vision was born with the Christ Light for a supreme purpose beyond anything which we even now can visualise. Ultimately, we shall be walking bathed in the Light of the Sun. Our aim is the restoration of the planet and the purification of the soul of man. Those working for this cause are ambassadors of a new universal consciousness leading to a world consensus through harmony."

Mahatma Gandhi 1990

Since this noble inspiration was first channelled in 1990. WWV has indeed begun to develop into a global communications network attracting to it on all continents those who take full responsibility for empowering themselves to make this interdimensional partnership a practical reality.

OBJECTIVES

To promote the understanding that humanity and all other lifeforms are an inseperable part of **one** evolving unit of consciousness - the Supreme Intelligence called 'God".

To explain the true nature and timing of the Second Coming of the Universal and Unified (Christ) consciousness, using the miraculously restored Third Book of the Apocalypse as the only biblical authority for this event. This encoded and challenging text is a crucial 'missing' section of the Revelation of St.John that was placed onto the WWV computer screen in 1990 through direct Spirit intervention. WWV is charged with the distribution and promotion of this sacred work

To increase the awareness of the subtle dimensions of Spirit that now play a vital part in communicating both new and suppressed information capable of freeing us from ignorance, superstition and fear. 'Direct intervention' by Spirit through our modern electronic communication technology is on the increase and WWV seeks to encour age acceptance and creative partnership for this all-important interdimensional initiative.

To restore harmony on Earth by re-educating humanity spiritually in the principles of the immutable Universal Laws and Ancient Wisdom, so that we are enabled to trigger a 'critical mass' response through living an *expression* of unconditional love, sharing, forgiveness, non-judgement, service and respect for each other and all kingdoms of nature.

To raise awareness of Earth's natural power sites and subtle energy grids, and the fact that spiritually awakened humans with open hearts have the ability to activate and realign them. In this way our social and political reality will continue to be rapidly and effectively tranformed without opposition.

Let us now hear from the spirit sources who are guiding much of this practical work. First, the words of Gandhi, himself a supreme example of Christ consciousness in action:

"There is in our life a perfect truth. We were all created equally by God, the Father. He did not place in our hands at birth a bible or a Koran or any other religious book and did not tell us to seek any particular religious path. He sought only that we would be enlightened, that our intuition, which is part of the reincarnated purpose of our life, should have in itself some spiritual conviction. This should not isolate us, but instead unify us with our brothers and sisters. We should rejoice, for we have been given life by the Father, God - the spark of life which no scientist can find. What we cannot find is the divinity given by God, which is part of us all. Inside us is the great love and light, which is the droplet of the Father. We are all part of his Love and Light and part of his flesh in spirit.

"He has created us to find harmony and love in this world of ours, to share and not cause greed. To be as One, giving Light to one another, not taking Light away. He has made on this planet sufficient food for all our needs and *none* should starve. Yet how many starve because of greed in Western society. You must seek to find a new way of living, for this way will not continue for much longer.

"I have come to speak to you from those in the Spirit realm, who seek to find those who are of a kindred spirit to us. We have no hands or feet but yours. We seek that you will be the instrument of the work and the Light. We do not desire to take you over, but simply to walk beside you. One day, we will be in the body again *and you will be here!* We change so rapidly, but at this moment I greet you in the Spirit! My message is simply that we must together change this world. No easy task, you will say, but I know it can be done with a great effort. There must be a great unity of purpose and linking throughout the world with those who carry Light on the many continents. We must remove all barriers of language, nationality and religion. We must share our Love equally with our brothers and sisters, regardless of who they are.

"The whole banking system is corrupt and money has been used as a power source, which has caused so many people to enter into poverty. Poverty of the material is as much a poverty of the spirit and the spirit must be free to unite with the father in the ecstasy of meditation and Light. Therefore, we must conceive through a new way to create an economic system which is viable in your world.

"In all things there is an influence beyond that which can be endured by the small majority which controls nations and that is what you call people power. In India, it was not I who brought the British Raj to its knees. I was simply a little man who humbly followed the path I saw as right. But hundreds of people in the same vision came and walked beside me and we as a mass changed the history of India. We removed the British Raj. You also can remove those who offend the true light and who should not be in the government of countries. Government should have compassion on the people, and not as has so clearly come to be that they work to restrict power into the hands of the few and beggar the people, to indulge its military aggrandisement. I am not talking about either capitalism or communism, but about a lifestyle that is sustainable in which all can share. What is the point of making wealth, if it is not shared as the Spirit is shared?

" I want to bathe the world in Light. I seek the great inventions of your age, the satellite that moves across the sky, and through the energy made from the beam of the satellite, to enter into little homes and large institutions, so that the Word can be manifest.

Not the Word of spirit, but the Word unified between spirit and man, which is in every sense, common sense. If we are going to survive on this planet, we must do it *now*.

"As we sit here, I can hear the multitudes of cars that are moving along your street; it sounds like Bombay! It is making so many fumes, which you are forced to breathe, and these pollutants increase daily the people suffering the disease you call cancer. Also the pestilence of the farms causes water pollution and so you drink poison from your taps. I could read you a long list of how you are carelessly destroying your bodies. When you come to spirit and look back on the world and see what is causing the death of so many of your brothers and sisters, you find yourself bewildered as to why you did not make an issue of it there, when you had a body.

"Why do our scientists not start to work for rather than against us? They bleed the economy by creating things we cannot afford and do not really need. What they should be doing is working towards an environment which does not take from Nature, but which gives to Nature and is safe for us and our fellow creatures. We here in Spirit know that it is perfectly possible to create machines that do not pollute. We know that in Nature the most important element created by God is the atom, but it was not intended to be misused. It is a structural part of your whole being. All things are made of the interaction of atoms and are made by Nature as elements to be contained in one piece, *not* to be spun off for use in destructive purposes. In the process of making electricity you also create destructive elements and chemicals which pollute the Earth and will cause distress to future generations. You must turn away from these evils and use what Nature intended you to use instead.

"The sun not only warms the body, but can also produce all the electricity needed for all machinery on Earth! The silicone chip is made of sand and can be adapted to do a great deal for us without polluting the environment. There are billions of tons of sand, so why don't the scientists work with this transformational technology?

"We must find a way to solve our conflict with non-violence and avoid the sudden death of so many souls, who will in a short time come back again and have to work extra hard to enable them to find their own perfection in spirit. We must seek to remove the weapons which cause violence on Earth. All this can be achieved if you draw down the Light of God into many circles like this meeting. Let God work through you, through the Love that you share with other people. In this part of the world, you create great mountains of food that you will never use, which continue to perish and cost so much money. In my own country of India, you can walk down the road any day and you will find many people dead of malnutrition. Why is it that in what you call a civilised part of the world you store food till it rots - and deny your brothers and sisters in India? Is *this* civilised behaviour?!

"We give to you great Love, great Light and perseverance. We need to walk with you for you to be our vision on the Earth.

"Let us bring to you the inspiration of how this planet should be and let us work together to restore it. God created you to be happy, healthy and to love one another. Your Christian holy book commands you to love one another as you love yourself. A simple ideal, but how many people try to follow it? Please think upon my words and walk with me as I walk with you and together in the Light of God, we shall restore this beautiful world and be proud of it. God bless you."

> *Mahatma Gandhi speaking at the first*
> *WWV International Symposium in October, 1990*

In May 1992, Winston Churchill himself made the following observations:

"I long believed that democracy was clearly upheld by our British Parliament. My own thoughts were that this could be a pattern for the whole world and if that could be achieved, we would have a country, States and a globe, whose harmony and peace would require nothing more than the assistance of the occasional conference to air ideas. Now, in this part of the last decade of the 20th century, my dreams are like shadows long since spent, for the politicians of today have as little power as any individual walking in the street. The controlling influence now rests with a few people held under the title of 'Cabinet', who abuse the responsibility given to them by the British people.

"The banks now control the government, because it requires so much money to sustain the many ideas and schemes it reflects in its manifestos. This then interacts, so that you find a large number of important persons in government, who are also on the boards of various banks. The banks have through their own influence contained most of the 3rd World in bondage and suffering, through enormous debts and through the ability to exploit from those countries their wealth in the course of what we would term interest. We must change this situation. I'm not going to suggest a revolution; *not half!"*

We are told that the soul of the personality we know as Winston Churchill previously incarnated as that champion of Hellenistic democracy, Pericles. This was followed in Roman times by his role as Pompey the Great, the celebrated general, orator and lawmaker, who successfully reduced the power of ruling families exactly as Pericles had done before him in Greece. His involvement in the formative stages of English history as the warrior King Alfred the Great, enabled him to organise a navy as Pompey had done, translate scriptures into English and to continue in his law-making capacity. After this, he incarnated into the Churchill family as the 1st. Duke of Marlborough. This time round he was born in the 1st. Duke's bed and became one of the most highly-acclaimed war leaders ever known.

The themes of this redoubtable soul are consistent throughout his lives as a pioneering democrat, naval strategist and patriot with a brilliant gift for language. Such a powerhouse of energy is not always easily assimilated into human affairs, and he often faced isolation and rejection. When it most mattered, however, this noble champion and protector of democracy was at the helm for his greatest victory: the defeat of the negative forces in the first stage of the final conflict between Light and dark, known as the Great World War of 1914 to 1945. The issues at stake can only be grasped when the full spiritual dimension of the struggle are taken into account.

Mistakes or not - and none of us is perfect in this dimension - he was no appeaser and knew far better than latterday 'historians' the real nature of the threat that faced the free world in 1939. I am grateful to the authors of *The Mark of the Beast* for some of this research and am in a position to confirm that it has been authenticated by the great man himself ! (refer to the *Spear of Destiny*)

It is a remarkable experience to watch the old familiar habits manifesting as Churchill takes over Robert's body, his fingers still clutching the famous cigar and swirling the imagined cognac in a glass of what is now, to his disgust, only orange juice to lubricate Robert's throat! The deep, resonant tones of that inspiring voice in full flight are very demanding on the vocal chords, and the contrast with the much gentler Gandhi energy that usually follows him in our channelling sessions is quite marked.

Both souls are aware that they will reincarnate during the middle 1990s to fulfil still more decisive functions in the human evolutionary process. Churchill makes it plain he can't wait to leave what he calls 'this desolate realm of spirit for more action in the physical! Especially to challenge what he describes as 'monstrous politicians' currently in his beloved forum of the House of Commons. Many there who profess to admire him would be rather dismayed by his opinion of them; he particularly abhors the corruption that now permeates all levels of national and local government. Real statesmen of his stature are virtually an extinct species, very rarely spotted among the herds of unashamed power-seekers and manipulators, who have in all too many cases abused the privileges of public service and betrayed those whom they represent.

Churchill regrets his own lack of spiritual awareness during the war years, when the advice of attuned leaders like Lord Dowding and Sir Victor Goddard was all too often ignored by sceptical colleagues. He now knows that many in the Spirit realms are capable of giving valuable advice to humanity from a more detached perspective - if only we would trust our own intuition.

He is fascinated by interdimensional communication between Spirit and the physical plane and is a regular contributor to our sessions, whenever he is not otherwise occupied in attempting to influence politicians at international peace negotiations! He is even known on occasion to 'jump the queue' of intended contributors, if he has something of importance to say, and the humble, gentle Gandhi - whom he once called 'a half-naked fakir' - usually gives way! They are now, however, despite minor indications to the contrary, totally committed as a partnership with us all in guiding the destiny of humanity towards the Light.

Churchill has spoken of the occasion when an Air Vice Marshal told him during the war that, "One day you will realise that life is not as we perceive it from here and you will know the enigma of war." Now that he is in the realms of Spirit, he *knows* that it is only an illusion to think we can kill anyone, and that such acts only accumulate karmic debts that must eventually be paid in full. He, like Gandhi, is now convinced that non-violence and the focused projection of tolerance and love are the most potent weapons in humanity's armoury, and that these are the only keys to our survival.

Projection of positive thought will transmute all negativity and ensure the triumph of the Light in our time. The speedy curtailment of the recent Iraq war and the lone woman who turned a crowd against the dictator Ceaucescu of Romania and, single-handed, triggered a revolution, are but recent examples. Churchill has confirmed that it is up to us to hold the balance and that, contrary to much contemporary 'New Age' disinformation, we will *not* be rescued and removed by some miraculous outside force from whatever fate we have selected for ourselves!

This, then, is the long-promised 'giant leap' that mankind is about to make. For thousands of years, we have been programmed to think of ourselves as 'sinful, guilty and unworthy' subjects of this deity or that. But now, having at last rediscovered our real identity, we are ready to reclaim our birthright - as fully-accredited co-creators with God in all His/Her enterprises!

Chapter 18

OUR SAFE, JUST AND ABUNDANT UNIVERSE

"So I have waited for you yesterday, and will wait again tomorrow, if there is a need. But the wave of which I speak rides upon a tide that spans only a few circlings of your world around this star, and some of those circlings have already passed. The limited human concepts adrift in this rising tide of consciousness are not suitable craft in which to confine your understanding. They will never carry you beyond sight of history's shore. The ships of my understanding navigate eternal seas. You cannot board them if you cannot perceive them – and you perceive naught from behind the doors of yesterday. My ships, light ships of understanding, sail. They will not long remain. I am a moving being, and this is not my final port of call. I come now to knock upon the door of your *heart*. There are those with me of the angelic realms who, though they cannot open the door for you - you alone must do that - will illuminate the doorway and encourage you in Spirit. Once you reach forth your will to move through the opening, be assured that many luminous beings will help you hold the opening while you pass through into the new awareness, the awareness that will make my light ships, my ships of vision, your own."

From *Starseed, the Third Millennium* by Ken Carey

My own understanding of the initiation into higher dimensional reality is that it can happen in two ways, once we have fully awakened to our unseparated state and demonstrated the principles of love and sharing on Earth. The majority will pass as usual from the physical plane into spirit and, in due course, take on a much less dense physical body for their first higher-dimensional incarnation. Others will be able to raise not only their consciousness, but their physical form too, by increasing their vibration rate sufficiently to become what is known as a 'light body'. This is the 5th.dimensional initiation, which is attainable by the

'144,000 with the Christ in their hearts' and any others able to reach the frequency of their light bodies. At this level we simply project an image of how we wish to appear in the physical realms - if indeed we wish to appear there at all!

At this point in our evolution, all dimensions are accessible to those qualified, but very few at present have the ability to integrate with the highest frequencies. Once clear of the 3rd dimension, however, the borders between the higher states of consciousness are much less defined. Those of us who succeed in raising ourselves into the 4th dimension will very quickly be able to reach the 5th and transcend the cycle of physical life, 'death' and rebirth altogether.

The light body is so named because light literally infuses and separates the densely packed molecules and atoms that form physical structure, giving it a luminous quality. This would explain some of the many recorded appearances by angels and other exalted beings throughout history. Indeed, the resurrection and ascension of Jesus is probably the best known example. He came in human form specifically to demonstrate everyone's ability to assimilate Christ consciousness while in the body, and thereby to transcend death and the grave. As we all know, his physical body vanished and it was transformed into a 'light body' that was seen by many witnesses around the world long after his 'Ascension'. We have no reason to doubt his promise:

> "He that believeth in me, the works that I do shall he do also; and greater works than these shall he do."

John 14: 12

As we are made in the image of a Creator of wisdom, power, freedom and love, it follows that our natural state is one in which we manifest all these qualities ourselves, totally unrestricted by matter. Having reached this state, any of us can manipulate matter and perform so-called 'miracles' of healing, materialisation and dematerialisation of objects and astral projection/teleportation/bilocation wherever we choose. At these levels, we travel at the speed of thought and appear at will. In this way we express the total freedom that is our birthright and can use an ideal light body of perfect youth, health and beauty that never deteriorates through negative thought-forms of ageing, sickness and death.

It was only by doubting our real identity in the first place that we "fell" into duality. By doing so, we created the illusion of death, fear, pain and misery that, ever since, have become our harshest teachers. It is these negative thought patterns that remorselessly age the physical body - usually well before the span of 120 years for which it is currently designed to last.

There is a widespread misconception fostered largely by religions that our bodies and indeed all matter are somehow unworthy. The truth is that *all* creation is of God, and our bodies are no exception, being made of light. Hence our ascension into life eternal is the natural progression for us, while the very concept of 'death', inspired by the preponderance of the negative, conditioned thought we hold about the body and our presumed unworthiness, is 'evil' or 'live' spelt backwards.

Consider the sheer magnificence and ingenuity of the human body, with its countless functions, which are still well beyond the understanding of physicians and scientists - and are the inspiration behind all our technology. Gandhi spoke of the mystery of the 'spark of life', which is God within, that no-one can prove or locate. We walk the Earth in a body that is a veritable miracle of complexity, and instead of being grateful for the privilege of its use, we exploit and abuse it with an ignorance and arrogance that almost defy belief. Filling it with regular toxic doses of microwaved junk food doesn't help either!

They are quite amazing, the positive changes we can make when we start to honour our bodies as the vehicles we chose to manifest. Let us start to see ourselves at our physical peak of health, youth and beauty - rather than complaining about the body when it reflects the abuses we inflict on it, or when the subject of physical incorruptibility is raised. As we begin to reacquaint ourselves with universal Law, perhaps the thought of perpetuating the form we created in the first place will seem less outlandish, less disconcerting!

There are many advantages to ascension, not least of which is the ability to dispense with the often painful and distressing birth process as we know it. Why bother to go through all the forgetting and re-learning, parental and cultural conditioning and so on, in an unending cycle, when we can remain with our awareness intact in a perfect light body of our choosing? Why endure an often protracted and painful transition to Spirit after long periods of disease, when such a miserable state doesn't even exist where consciousness is unified?

In the ascended state we are free to serve all Creation by doing what we love to do, so our existence can only become an ever greater expression of perfection. Love and creativity shared are always rewarded many times over, and in that state we attract all the beauty, fulfilment and magnificence that is our rightful heritage.

Ascension is a state of mind, so it is through our thought processes that we prepare for it. This starts with the absolute conviction that the Force is manifesting within us and that we are in fact gods walking on Earth, the moment we achieve a unified consciousness. Love is the indispensable fuel of ascension, and with enough of it, we can create everything we need, everywhere. It is also vital to release judgement, anger, criticism, resentment, envy, prejudice and other negative attitudes, because they poison our minds, contort our emotions, and contribute directly to the ageing and dysfunction of our bodies. Growth, health and peace of mind only come from tolerance and forgiveness - first of ourselves as we are, then of others.

Knowing the Law of Reincarnation and Karma, and that we have specifically chosen certain people and situations to assist us in our growth, we need to release the past and history entirely, to the point where it no longer imprisons us or prevents us from moving forward. Soul lessons have to be indelibly imprinted on us; if not, other sharper situations are created, to ensure they do sink in! The past only plays on emotions and like death, it is not the place to project an ascending consciousness. Neither is preoccupation with the future, which is in fact formed *in the present moment* by our current thought processes! Acceptance of a situation as the best we can manage at any one time and knowing we can always improve on it, rather than continual self-reproach, is also important. *We* have created it all, so we might as well make the best of it, and learn from both the positive and negative repercussions.

I am grateful to Joanna Cherry's inspiring booklet *Ascension for You and Me* for some useful guidelines. (Available from PO Box 1018, Mt. Shasta, California 96067 USA.)

Another key to ascension is the process of reversing the 'clockwise spiral' of life in cell structure that I have briefly touched on in the context of Time shift 26/7/92.

Linda Goodman's book Starsigns has an excellent chapter on ascension, among much other fascinating information, from which I take the following quotes:

"We are all built of right-handed corkscrews."

Sir Lawrence Bragg Nobel prize winner

"All spirals of living matter twine around in the same direction, although everything would work equally well the other way around."

Linus Pauling Nobel prize winner

"Because the spiral is used to convert radio waves into electrical impulses, it is evident that the capacity exists to move from one level to another, or from one vibration to another."

John Nelson, electronic scientist

All of which suggests that we can consciously reverse the spiral of our cell structure, in an anti-clockwise direction. The clockwise, right-handed spiral draws us into physical and mental gravity, and the conditioning of ageing and decay leading to the grave - seen as the 'out-breath' of creation. Whereas the anti-clockwise spiral reverses that programming and through *levity* regenerates the cells causing youthing rather than ageing. By reprogramming our cellular memory and visualising the reversal of the corkscrew spiral in all our cells, we embark on the 'in-breath' of creation - and a journey that finally conquers the insidious programming of 'the grave', replacing it with the long-promised 'life everlasting'.

We have reached a time when we are all being challenged to go beyond our conditioning and self-imposed limitations, and only those brave enough fearlessly to trust the evolutionary process by overcoming their own ego resistance will soon be shouting, "We have lift-off!"

"And ye shall be changed to immortality without the separation of death, in the twinkling of an eye."

It is not only willing humans who are candidates for ascension, but Earth too. I have already mentioned that groups acting as 'planetary midwives' have for several years been activating the subtle power centres of the planet in preparation for this process. However, we need to look briefly at the celestial as well as the terrestrial energy changes now manifesting to form a complete picture. It appears from a wide variety of research that we shall now experience a form of heightened energy that will be the means by which both we ourselves and the Earth will be raised into a higher dimension.

"There is presently occurring a space-time overlap with the higher evolution as the Earth's solar system enters an electromagnetic null zone, a vacuum area which will change the magnetic forces of Creation. Upon entering the lip of this zone, the whole solar system will be picked up and re-seeded in a different vibratory dimension of the galaxy."

The Keys of Enoch by J.J. Hurtak

In 1989 we received channelled guidance that this heightened energy was being directed by a 'photon beam':

"It is a selective energy that only interacts with those attuned to its vibratory level and does not affect those of other frequencies. This energy is powerful enough to alter the whole balance on Earth. These energies are created for the spontaneous motivation of the spiritual work, but they cannot be stored. As you use the energies, so you will retain them, but this needs constant discipline and attention."

What seems likely is that our Sun and solar system are to enter a wall of charged particles during the 1990s, which might explain the enigmatic biblical prophecy, "All stars will fall from Heaven and the sky will be no more." Our interaction with these particles could produce some spectacular atmospheric effects and might also give meaning to this description of higher dimensional reality:

"And the city will be borne on a cloud of light, not set on the Earth, but carried by the Spirit. And the temple gates will not shut by day, and there will be no night there. They need no torch, neither light of the sun, for the Father giveth them light, that they may abide in the light forever."

Apocalypse 3, Ch 1 v 7 and 11 and Ch 8, v 5

With all these changes, we will rapidly adapt to new forms of energy. Among these will be free AC electrical power, as pioneered by Nikola Tesla, but ruthlessly suppressed by those with profit in mind. Free natural electrical energy can easily and inexpensively be harnessed for domestic and commercial use - only tax greedy governments stand in the way! There will also be free power through the 'water fuel cell' technology, which splits water efficiently into its component parts of hydrogen and oxygen, without producing carbon during combustion.

Environmentally unfriendly fossil fuels will be adapted to non-combustive uses, such as the manufacture through carbon technology of synthetic wood, which is infinitely more practical and adaptable than the organic variety. Coal will be processed into organic soil conditioner/fertiliser containing humic acids and humates, capable of transforming vast tracts of infertile land.

Among other new sources will be the photon, operating in the still largely unexplored fields of anti-gravity and anti-matter. I now quote a brief description of the nature of the photon adapted from an article by Vincent Selleck, the Australian mystic and initiator of the Earth Link 1988 event at Uluru. (Earth Link, PO Box 677, Byron Bay, NSW Australia):

"The key to the jigsaw puzzle is an atom and a small group of electrons which orbit around it. Everything that we can see or touch is made up of atoms. For reasons our scientists have not yet fathomed, the electrons around the atom move out a little and emit a photon - a particle of light. The English physicist Paul Dirac said that "for each type of particle, an anti-particle will exists". In 1932 Carl David Anderson discovered the anti-electron and called it a positron. In 1956, the anti-proton and anti-neutron were discovered. When an anti-particle is formed, it comes into existence in a Universe of ordinary particles, and it is only a matter of time, a millionth of a second, before it meets and collides with an electron. The charges cancel, the mass of the pair is converted into energy which will partially be in the form of photons. This offers a new and unprecedentedly powerful source of energy.

"The photon is about to become the way of life in the very near future. As the Earth comes increasingly under this influence, all atoms will become excited and their electrons will move out a little to emit those particles of Light. As long prophesied, *all things will change*. All things will become slightly luminescent and there will be constant light everywhere, whether in the human body or in the deepest cave.

"The Light is to come from the beam, not the sun, and we will exist in a new vibration. If the concept of the photon beam can be accepted, then the need to raise our consciousness, to be spiritually aware, as well as to make ourselves physically, emotionally and mentally more healthy, takes on new meaning as we prepare to enter the era of the light body.

"I see the influence of the beam growing gradually through the 1990's. This joining of energies between spiritual substance and illumination is the most powerful influence for transformation this century. Harmonic Convergence and all the many other human planetary link-ups since 1987 were in preparation for this major activation."

Meantime, we are experiencing the break-up of the ozone layer, mainly through huge, but natural, emissions of chlorine from volcanic eruptions. This layer has, until now, protected Earth and ourselves from harmful rays and energies coming towards us, but as we now grow in awareness, collective human consciousness is attracting powerful influxes of light radiations. These include photons, which will now transmute the negative human thought-forms that *are* the main pollution on the planet, and raise all those vibrationally prepared and the Earth into permanent light:

"And if we could really be surrounded by this forcefield of divine magnetic power, we would have complete protection perhaps the only protection we would ever need - to enable us to grow to fulfilment."

Sir George Trevelyan

Photon-infused, 4th.dimensional Earth has her protection, but this is not to say that humanity still hasn't an absolute duty to avoid unnecessary pollution. It is well to remember that all life forms, including human that have not reached the required vibration, by expressing love will be unable to absorb the new frequency and be incapable of lifting into the new dimension. There will be a *new* Heaven and a *new* Earth, and Revelations tells us that all will be changed. Whatever happens - and it seems likely that just about everything *will* happen as this century hurtles to its climax - the ultimate responsibility lies with us to take charge of ourselves, to respect each other, and to fulfil our designated role as stewards and custodians of the Earth.

And when that happens - when we start giving to life and each other, rather than taking, as we have for so long been conditioned to do - we will all become fantastically wealthy overnight: just imagine six billion people, most of them strangers, working for you . . . !

This, then, is the new Earth that, despite all appearances to the contrary, is almost within our reach. But remember, these riches will not be dropped into our laps: we are going to need all our powers of concentration, confidence and one-pointed will as we run the gauntlet of our own apathy, cynicism and doubt, in our final dash to the gates of Heaven!

"The world is a bridge - pass over it, but build no house upon it."
Attributed to Jesus

Chapter 19

LIFE EVERLASTING
- INNER PREPARATION

**'We are but one stupendous whole,
whose body Nature is and God the soul'.**
Alexander Pope

In answer to the question "What is it that enslaves humanity?" Merlin's response, channelled by Isabelle Kingston in 1995, was as follows:

"Fear, for it chains the soul and stops growth. Fear is the most negative aspect within your planet, as it prevents your enjoyment of the love and light that is your true heritage. The greatest mission of those who work in the light is to negate fear by healing the planet and the souls of those who walk in the darkness of their own fear. Do not buy into fear and create a negative reality, but rather perceive and release magic that is beauty and a healed world".

Having absorbed the material in this book, the reader will be in no doubt that humanity has reached an awesome point of no return, when its collective freewill choices will determine the future not only of this race, but also of the planet on which we are all attempting to evolve spiritually. In the words of the late Sir George Trevelyan in his review of this book, "the choice is now between love or fear". We separated originally from the source in order to experience soul individualisation and personal freedom - the freedom eventually to choose freely the path of Love which alone leads us back to that Divine source. The Love we withhold is the pain and fear we carry, lifetime after lifetime. Fear is actually separation, which is caused by the denial of our divinity and our connection to the source.

The Earth's vibrational frequencies at spiritual levels are now being significantly raised by such events as the 1995 comet impact on Jupiter, the arrival of many other consciousness-shifting comets - especially Hale-Bopp "the Blue Planet" in 1997 - the highly significant and challenging withdrawal of the ozone layer and human-inspired Earth energy activations, grid re-alignments and mass mind-linking. All this and much more has led to the fulfilment of the "sorting of the wheat from the chaff" prophecy in Revelations, which is none other than the polarisation of human consciousness between the diametrically opposing forces of love and fear. Some look on it as 'The day of Judgement', but it is really only the long-appointed time for us to face our own reflection. The spiritual mirror cannot lie and from it we see whether our thoughts, words and deeds are of a sufficiently high vibration (loving) 'to qualify us for Universe function and continuance on board this planet' as Buckminster Fuller has said. We are given Divine freewill choice, but if we persist in negativity and the low vibrational path of fear after all the warnings, both human and divine, that are now saturating this planet, then we must accept the consequences.

Jesus Christ himself said: "Suppose ye that I am come to give peace on Earth? I tell you, nay, but rather division" (Luke 12:51). I have found an extract from Ken Carey's book "Visions" most helpful in clarifying the challenging concept of the now imminent 'separation' and the destiny of those who freely choose to 'sleep the long sleep':

"Whatever form the healing of the human world takes during the next few years, know that it is for the good of all. Do not be concerned with the fate of those who reject my spirit. Their story is far from over. I am caring for each one in the manner of his or her greatest need. The human world is in good hands. When you and much of the Earth's present biological life have been sprinkled throughout the stars, and the oceans have changed places with the land, after the poles have shifted and new mountains have come to look out over the plains, then will these slow-learners be recalled from the *mineral realms where they slumber*, to learn of intelligence again and to come again to choose between love and fear. If there is one, even one, that shall choose fear, then that one shall sleep while the rest journey on, but in the fullness of a new time, I will awaken the one again - and again - and again if need be - until that which was designed to be conscious takes up my love and joins me in joy and gladness.

"For though in creating human beings I create a creature that must choose of its own will to accept the freedom that Love's Spirit alone can convey, in the end that creature will choose the best. Not because

272

I have given it no choice, but because I will give it choice, and choice, and choice again, until it learns the nature of love and comes to prefer consciousness over the sleep of ignorance and fear.

"**You** have incarnated at this time specifically to help ease this transition. Help me guide the human lives that are disorientated as the old temple topples. Direct them to the new organisation that is taking place everywhere human beings love."

What seems abundantly clear and entirely logical is that the lower frequencies of fear are to be cleared from the planet in order that the new dimensional 'Heaven' can manifest here undistorted. Since it is humans that hold and proliferate the fear, it must be within the human species that this 'sorting' takes place. Hence the current polarisation of human consciousness so that, through the now accelerating chaos, each individual is obliged to make this final decisive choice.

There are many theories about Second Coming, the Rapture, Ascension, the dimensional shift and how it is all to manifest. As we have seen, Christianity is incapable of preparing us, and perhaps it is as well that we do not have to rely for inspiration on what has become an increasingly self-indulgent and separative 'New Age' cult. Unquestioning acceptance of often patronising and controlling ET, Alien and so-called 'Ascended Master' channellings, together with all kinds of ascension escapism, psychic phenomena, abduction and conspiracy theories and violent and unsurvivable upcoming Earth changes aren't contributing to anyone's spiritual development! Quite the reverse in fact, because these alluring distractions are usually fear-orientated and subtly designed to divert our focus from the real and much more challenging work of inner personal growth and assuming responsibility for the Earth. The problem is that all this ungrounded New Age hype inevitably damages the genuine spiritual cause by increasing the scepticism of the general public, thereby retarding their awakening.

The negative forces desire nothing more than to prolong humanity's disempowerment and to see us fall into the trap of abandoning responsibility for this planet. By all accounts, it wouldn't be the first time such a scenario, with disastrous consequences, has occurred in this solar system. Of course, there are many levels of Being in our multidimensional reality, some well disposed towards humanity and others still determined to subjugate and disempower us. None of them, however, are going to 'save' us, and as we now have the potential to lift ourselves beyond the reach of the negative elements among them by attaining the love vibration, our time is far more productively spent concentrating on personal transformation here into the truly loving beings that we are supposed to be. In this way alone do we finally break the endless cycle of karma and rebirth that chains us to third-dimensional reality.

Intellectually-oriented and therefore only partially awake New Agers are too easily blinded by spiritual glamour to notice that their movement has been subtly subverted by Luciferic and Ahrimanic forces. These forces made devastating inroads into all the world's religions and were long ago predicted to be the greatest tests of discernment for these times. With the human awakening process well under way, it is hardly surprising that they have shifted their attention from the disintegrating religions to a more productive arena by now attempting to destabilise the gullible New Age commercial industry. Reliable spiritual discernment is only available to us once we have each tackled our inner work, and are able to open the heart and live without fear so that we can recognise Truth. It will never come through intellectual theory and the mere accumulation of knowledge. Only by bringing our thinking and feeling faculties into alignment, are we able to discern between the true spiritual path of unconditional love and service and the illusions of intellect and ego that have all too evidently been the motivating factors of many of the first wave of western New Age teachers - and plenty of oriental gurus too!

The true heart-centred spirituality is to be manifested through personal example - literally 'living the loving' and 'walking the talk' - by the emerging breed of selfless Aquarian World Servers that was long ago predicted to replace the valiant, though still Piscean-orientated pioneers. It is indeed interesting to observe how the established high priests of intellectual spirituality are now facing the challenge of the razor-sharp frequencies of the new consciousness - love in action. The sorting of the posturers from those who have really worked on themselves is now well and truly underway. Those who 'surf the interdimensional wave' with confidence, poise and perfect inner balance are, of course, far more effective through the quality of their practical example than those who can only intellectualise what for them is still an unattainable dream.

The 'anything goes' attitude of many unfocussed people caught up in the current 'explosion of possibility' is responsible for the subtle subversion of the movement. There has always been available to evolving members of this race a structure of Universal Law that governs the evolution of all creation at every level. In these unstable times, it particularly behoves the 'cosmic anarchists' amongst us to study this body of information. They too can then discern what is actually relevant to this particular moment in our evolution and allow it to take precedence over glamorous, but otherwise distracting, material that through their influence delays the true awakening of so many others. The latest New Age fantasy is a powdered substance derived from gold that apparently when ingested automatically raises us into the new dimension! A sufficient realisation of Love is the **only** immortal elixir that guarantees our ascension, and certainly never mere 'substances' which are available to any human regardless of their spiritual attainment. Just another example of the subtle influence of negative forces that keep us externally rather than inwardly focused.

It must be said that there are also many aware people committed to the principles of the unified consciousness, who nonetheless make the mistake of denying individual free choice by assuming that all humans will automatically qualify for higher dimensional reality. Once critical mass is reached - meaning that when a specific proportion of mankind starts thinking the same way, others will be automatically influenced by the same expanding thoughtforms - it will be easier for the masses to become aware. It is however, the freewill choice of each individual that is the deciding factor. All we can do is to focus on raising our own consciousness, pray and envision that the whole human family will freely choose the path of light and remember that ultimately it is only by our example that we give others the opportunity to empower themselves.

Since it is clear that we shall only participate in this shift if we have transformed ourselves inwardly and raised our vibrational frequency, let us now look at the all too often overlooked process of preparation.

> The longest way to God, the indirect,
> is through the intellect.
> The shortest way is then through the heart,
> the journey's end, and also its start.

Not the greatest poetry perhaps, but a catchy couplet nonetheless for the majority of humans still afflicted by the infectious human disease called 'headology'! Let's remember that it is the sheer cleverness of human intellect, unqualified by wisdom, that has brought this race and planet to their knees. When one considers the abysmal lack of body awareness these days, perhaps it won't be long before humans just give birth to big heads attached directly to two small feet! Joking aside, we do co-create miraculous physical and etheric bodies for each of our Earthly incarnations and yet, once here, we promptly ignore their reasonable needs and maintenance.

The only way we can fulfil the spiritual missions for which we each came here is through a healthy body and so it follows that they must be considered our single greatest investment and asset here on Earth. Where, for God's sake, would we be without them? Anyway, who would be foolish enough to put the cheapest grade of fuel into a Rolls-Royce car engine? It wouldn't get very far and repairs and maintenance would be inconvenient and costly. The magnificently engineered Rolls-Royce of a body with which most of us started life, and which no human yet fully understands, is no different.

Yet most of us are more than happy to economise by relying entirely on the dead, inorganic, 'refined', sprayed, toxic 'fast' and 'junk' substances that pass for food in our mad, mad world. We are prepared to cram almost anything down the throat that temporarily satiates us without even stopping to think that it is only through live, nutritious, organic fresh food that we receive the vital energy that fuels our physical vehicles, sustains our life force and gives balance to our behaviour. One only needs to pick up roadside litter on a regular basis to observe that much of it derives from snacks and drinks, and deep-fried 'fast' food. Those relying on such a diet prove just how detached from reality they have become when they despoil the environment we all have to share in such insensitive and irresponsible fashion. All pollution, cruelty and disrespect for one another and the planet is initially caused by human psychological imbalance resulting from inappropriate eating habits.

After all this abuse of our magnificent bodies, we are not only surprised when they collapse, but all too often expect State intervention to treat us at other people's (taxpayers') expense! A debilitating life of chronic ill health then prevents us from fulfilling our spiritual blue prints and consigns us to an untimely grave. We are what we eat and what we think, and on both counts the human race urgently needs to reassess its reality levels.

A truly healthy body, of course, depends more than anything else on whether we understand in spiritual terms exactly how it is constructed. Contrary to flawed, secular and mechanistic thinking, what we call 'the spark of life' is housed within, but is not of the physical flesh. This divine spark, which no one has yet been able to identify scientifically, is in fact infused into us through the agency of 'soul' and 'spirit'.

At the moment of conception, the embryo is spiritually permeated with 'life' and throughout the pregnancy, the fully conscious soul of the entity seeking incarnation observes and encourages the birthing process through the aura (subtle bodies) of the mother. However, the soul is not committed to the foetus **until the first breath after birth** and at any stage during the pregnancy it may still choose **of its own free will** not to proceed to birth. This is because the energy of the incoming soul is sometimes being used only to infuse the prospective parents with a specific energy frequency at subtle spiritual levels - without the need to complete the birthing process. Challenging though it may be for many, we must remember that all pregnancies terminated by either miscarriage or abortion and even cot deaths are pre-agreed at the soul level of all those participant. Here on Earth we seem to learn mainly through pain and traumatic events such as these need to be seen primarily as opportunities for soul growth.

The spiritual dynamic of natural conception - and in these times of artificial interference it is well to remember it - is that the soul is magnetised towards the compatible energy generated by the bonding and loving interaction of a male and female, who choose to create a birth opportunity for an incoming being. Just as importantly, a male and female simply wishing to consummate their love for each other - the most elevated and creative act of which a human is capable when conducted in full spiritual awareness - are free to do so **without** risk of unwanted conception by mastering the life force energies flowing through their bodies. This is known as the ancient oriental art of Tantric breathing and needs to be understood by us all.

Those involved in the ever fiercer debate on pro- and anti- abortion need to understand the **facts of life** before they jump to emotional and

277

usually irrational conclusions that are formed without the benefit of spiritual awareness. Anyway, if we entered into sexual union with greater knowledge about and skill in handling our expression of the life force within us, then the need for artificial abortion would be largely eliminated and we would avoid the worst and most degrading of all human misery - planetary overpopulation.

Spirit is the divine essence permeating all aspects of creation, and soul is that which unites Spirit with our mental, emotional and other subtle bodies within the individual unit of consciousness that we each represent. Both, of course survive so-called 'death' fully intact and continue to evolve through many and varied experiences in new bodies on the Earth and in the wider universe.

When these simple facts are understood, one can only look at pathetic human antics like cryonics in utter despair. To imagine we can deep-freeze the dead physical body so as to be able to reignite 'the spark of life' once within it whenever we feel like it, is the height of arrogance born out of a level of spiritual ignorance that defies belief. Are we to believe, then, that during this lengthy and indeterminate process, the soul sits in a neighbouring deep-freeze, anxiously awaiting developments?! It's about as mad as the still prevalent Christian belief that after only one permitted life here on Earth, we then sit around the feet of Jesus and his father, God, bored out of our tiny minds and playing interminable harp-music until judgement day! Rather more macabre, is another crazy Christian notion that we moulder in our coffins until the 'great and awful day', when the graves yawn open and deliver us in skeletal form for judgement. As they say these days; **get real!**

Then there is the indignity of artificial interference with fertility that sees mothers giving unnatural multiple births that resemble sows with litters rather than human beings. It is categorically **not** everyone's right to have children and there are many reasons for not being able to conceive, including karmic lessons after abusing the process in previous lives. Motherhood is **not** in every woman's destined life path, contrary to the reproductive enslavement imposed on them by church authorities for so long and many have set themselves very different and fulfilling agendas, once they come to terms with being unable to conceive. We need to be far more aware of the spiritual dimension before allowing medical technicians with test tubes and scal-

278

pels to interfere with our natural processes **and above all** the blueprint we have set for ourselves.

Anyway, what's wrong with adoption, now that we know we are all **one** great family? So much sexual incontinence, bred of spiritual ignorance, has produced literally millions of unwanted children desperately needing genuine love and affection. When we finally realise that spirit and soul are our true common bond rather than blood, which is in fact their vehicle for penetrating the physical body, then the healing of the human family with its endlessly divisive blood-feuds will really begin.

Jesus Christ himself came specifically to destroy the old blood lines, which is why the Jews could never accept him as their Messiah. This fact also undermines the notion, beloved of certain New Agers who still seek blood lines to worship, that Jesus produced physical children. Jesus' energies were balanced with scrupulous care by Mary Magdalene - his opposite polarity - and the other women around him without the need (despite the obvious desire) for sexual union in order to prepare him to be the vehicle for the Christos. The task was to raise his consciousness from the lower bodily energy centres, where most humans are still trapped, into the sublime frequencies of the heart and higher mind. The three year mission here of Jesus the Christ was to infuse the human race and the planetary consciousness with an immensely high vibrational frequency - **carried in the blood he shed** - in order to liberate us all from entrapment in third dimensional duality. Begetting physical children was certainly **not** part of it! Mary Magdalene had children, but they were not fathered by our redeemer.

We in the western culture are not exactly helped by an intellectual medical system that has the dubious distinction, despite photographic proof, of failing to acknowledge the existence of our many subtle, higher vibrational bodies - Spirit and Soul. Our academic medicos, often under the influence of multinational pharmaceutical companies, have long been content to resort to toxic, synthetic drugs with such serious side effects that they eventually kill more than they cure. No wonder even official statistics show that ever larger numbers of disillusioned and damaged patients are transferring to the healing arts, natural medicine and 'leading edge' vibrational healing technology. This is where the real progress is being made at causal levels in curing the major killer diseases that orthodox medicine has only succeeded in turning into the 'AIDS and Cancer Corporation' - a vast multinational industry trading in death. Considering that our bodies are constituted of the food we eat, the air we breathe, the water we drink and the Light that we are, it only compounds the problem that our doctors are not even educated in basic nutrition, let alone high-frequency vibrational treatment.

With the rapidly deteriorating quality of sprayed food, BSE-contaminated meat and possibly milk, poisoned drinking water, air polluted by lethal carbon emissions, highly toxic mercury used in dental filling amalgam, toxic aluminium used for food storage and preparation contributing the Alzheimer's disease, microwave ovens destroying the life force in food and often leaking radioactivity, and portable telephones frying our brains with radiation - to mention just a few of our daily tests of survival, we obviously need to be more discerning about what we ingest and bring into contact with our bodies!

In a survey conducted between 1939 and 1991, the astounding fact emerges food has actually lost some 50% of its nutritional value - and flavour! (Source: McCane and Widdowson 'Composition of Foods 1939 - 91'). Clearly, the farming community too has betrayed the public's trust through its greedy exploitation of the land and livestock in its care. This means that deriving required levels of vitamins and minerals etc from available food is impossible without resorting to daily natural, nutritional supplements - including strong anti-oxidants to counteract free radicals and general toxicity in our systems.

We then find that bureaucrats and their taskmasters in governments - usually under the influence of the pharmaceutical corporations - attempt to control the unrestricted scale of non-prescription food supplements by making nutritionally untrained orthodox doctors responsible for their dispensation. There was such a huge public outcry in the USA and Europe recently that legislation was shelved, but already in 1996 further attempts at control are being attempted in the EEC and the USA. For instance, the 'Codex Alimentation Commissions Committee on nutrition and foods for special dietary uses' (meeting in Germany in October 1996) is made up of unelected, government-appointed representatives, who are mainly connected with pharmaceutical interests and are once more untrained in nutrition. This is how these mighty corporations attempt to eliminate competition from the dietary supplements industry.

This situation again so graphically illustrates the whole battle between the 'alternative' causal healing of disease and the drug-dominated suppression of symptoms favoured by orthodox medicine. Most people, given the choice, would rather prevent disease in their bodies than cure it once it developed. However, unless we are very vigilant indeed and prepared to stand up for our preference, the excessively rich and powerful pharmaceutical lobby will soon see to it that we **all** become dependent on their toxic synthetic substances.

> *"Man is born free, but everywhere he is in chains".*
> J.J. Rousseau.

One of my slogans for public talks is "Enemas before ET's". It usually gets an embarrassed laugh! My aim, though, is not only to bring ungrounded New Age space cadets back to Earth with a bump, but also to focus attention on the specific location of the first real step on the spiritual path. The inner work actually starts, as all great spiritual teachers down the ages including Jesus Christ have emphasised, with cleansing and detoxifying of the physical body. Since bowel and colon cancer are among the main western killer diseases, it is clear that our overstressed, nutritionally under-nourished and highly toxic bodies need all the help they can get to survive. At a spiritual level, we cannot hope to make progress unless we have a clean and efficient bodily vehicle. The subtle frequencies emanating from our glands and organs are designed to support the proper functioning of our intuitive potential and without this connection to the source, we are truly lost.

In the AIDS epidemic, once the misleading causal theories are dismissed, what we are actually witnessing is the collapse of the severely compromised human immune system. The proliferation of ME, identified as the burn-out of the central nervous system- is yet another example of this collapse. In a devastating attack on the fallacious orthodox hypothesis identifying HIV as the viral cause of AIDs, Dr Robert Willner points out in his book 'Deadly deception: The Proof that sex and HIV absolutely **do not** cause AIDS' and that the many diseases causing 'Acquired Immune Deficiency' have been known about for centuries and listed in medical textbooks for at least 60 years. All that is new is the name 'AIDS' itself and the false assumption that it is an epidemic caused by a virulent virus.

281

Revealingly, the many well-known diseases attacking the immune system are somehow not categorised as AIDS related unless the HIV retrovirus happens to be identified. So for example pneumonia without HIV is just pneumonia, but pneumonia with HIV present mysteriously becomes AIDS! Willner has frequently had himself injected with the harmless HIV retrovirus in public, to raise awareness of the 'pharmacological homicide' perpetrated by a particularly sinister and highly lucrative medical / pharmaceutical / political conspiracy.

Over 500 of the world's leading scientists are now challenging this false hypothesis that has actually never even been proven. According to Dr Willner and Professor Peter Duesberg, who has just published his own strong indictment of the conspiracy, what is actually killing large numbers of otherwise perfectly healthy HIV positive people is a combination of the most toxic drugs ever administered into the human body and the devastating daily barrage of psychological attack inflicted on them by misinformed and retributive public opinion. It is somewhat akin to 'pointing the witchdoctor's bone' at someone - they die of sheer fright. The world's media points the bone every day and thousands of disempowered people obediently die, needlessly.

Project AIDS International states: 'If action is not taken immediately against those who are directly or indirectly responsible for these crimes against humanity through the practice of profit over life, **the drug-induced AIDS deaths** will most certainly reach proportions unparalleled by any natural catastrophe in human history'.

The average length of survival for those unfortunate enough to have trusted the orthodox system is two years, in which the patient paradoxically dies of the very destruction of the immune system that these drugs are supposed to remedy. AZT, an experimental drug devised originally for cancer treatment and long ago discarded for its extreme toxicity by the US authorities, is now somehow back in use as the main weapon in the phoney HIV epidemic - 'to prolong life'! Yet few people realise that no one has ever survived its lethal assault on the human body. According to Willner and Duesberg 'AZT is a DNA chain terminator with so many fully-acknowledged lethal side effects that it actually causes acquired immune deficiency and can **only hasten death itself**'.

Having unleashed this mass killer into the human system, the experts then attempt to counteract its ravages by saturating the body with the new generation of equally lethal antibiotics.

When will we wake up to the truth, stop trusting 'experts' and put an end to this pharmacological slaughter? The whole ghastly drama, like so many others we are creating to test ourselves at this critical time of choice, is precisely to strengthen personal empowerment. **We** now become the experts in our own lives, with no need to depend on those conditioned in the old, separative ways of dysfunctional thinking and behaviour. We have allowed the least aware among us to influence the way we think and run our lives, so the transformation must logically be initiated from the grass roots by those 'ordinary' individuals who intuitively know a better way!

The message to all those healthy people who happen to have HIV in their blood - estimated at over 12 million in the USA alone - is the same as for everyone else wishing to maintain optimum health:
1.Boost the immune system with 'living' food and natural support substances
2.Detoxify the body with enemas, colonics, intestinal cleansing, regular fluid fasting and anti-oxidants
3.Breathe as much fresh, unpolluted air as possible and drink plenty of fresh, energised water not polluted with chlorine and fluoride (fluoride contains quantities of bromide, which is a strong tranquilliser that dulls our senses!)
4.Eat a light, balanced, organic food diet, ever less dependent on red meat and (cow) dairy products
5.Release any remaining addictions as soon as possible
6.Exercise daily in fresh air sufficiently to raise the heart beat so that the blood can flush the system of toxins
7.Regular refreshing, deep sleep is essential, as is rest and relaxation whenever necessary
8.Never economise on your health! Spend an ever greater proportion of your budget on life-sustaining food and products and cut back elsewhere
9.Treat others as you would wish to be treated yourself
10.Reduce all unnecessary stress and live a healthy, balanced, love-filled, harmless existence in pursuit of happiness!

Above all, avoid the lethal drugs of a medical system that is itself in a chronic state of disease and watch closely as it now promotes half-baked, pseudoscientific theories to disguise the fact that - barring toxic drug interference - HIV simply is **not** the cause of Acquired Immune Deficiency.

I have devoted considerable space to the AIDS debate because we all need to awaken to the fact that ignorance of spiritual laws and all kinds of intolerable abuse have created the deep crises in human mental, physical and emotional health.

Collapsing immune system-related deaths - whatever fancy names we give them - will continue to spiral beyond all control while we continue living unhealthy and unnatural lifestyles. This, together with the rapidly-falling male sperm count - a sure sign of impending crisis that has occurred in the final stages of all known previous civilisations - couldn't be a clearer warning for those with ears to hear that a drastic change in attitude is long overdue, if we are to avoid imminent decimation of the population.

Since the heart is to be the organ of our transformation and the ability to activate its subtle but dynamic potential is central to the raising of mass consciousness, it is important that we look at its multiple functions. We must, however, remember that at the energy levels we are concerned with, the heart cannot be effective until the rest of the physical body is first cleansed - **only then does it reveal its hidden secrets.**

In a 1995 article published in Australia, Glenn Krawcyk of POB 1504, Burleigh Heads, Qld 4220 wrote, "It is now scientific fact that when we generate the energy of love in our hearts, we resonate with the Earth's electromagnetic field at approx. 7 cycles per second (currently rising fast!). In turn, by releasing the right frequencies in the heart, we create positive feedback within our environment and among our fellow beings. These high frequencies then travel around the world at the speed of light and are recorded forever in the morphogenic fields beyond time and space. We can literally bring body, mind and spirit into resonance with Earth's heartbeat!"

Now we can see how attuned humans in the appropriate heart energy can interact so effectively with Earth's power sites and her many energy grids. This is exactly what I seek to demonstrate by using ex amples of consciousness-raising work carried out during my travels that would appear to change social and political reality soon afterwards.

Krawczyk goes on to point out that "the strongest electromagnetic signal and loudest sound in the body emanates from the heart, causing waveforms that directly influence the brain, nervous system, endocrine glands and immune system. It is where we reconcile our thoughts with our experience of the outer world and, as the centre of emotion, it is also where we make our most important decisions and discernment's. Our minds and bodies soon detach from the reality and become both destructive to ourselves and our environment, if we ignore the feelings of the heart. Remember the brain analyses, processes and makes distinctions, whereas the heart makes 'wholes'!

"Apart from being the primary co-ordinating organ of the body, few people know that the heart actually releases important secretions, one of which is a powerful peptide hormone (ANF) that accesses the hypothalamus and pituitary glands. These in turn play a critical role in the release of growth hormones to the body and the control of metabolic function among much else. In esoteric terms, the pituitary gland is the Seventh Seal and contains a hormone structure that, with the right heart signals, flows to the brain and activates a higher thought frequency called 'unlimitedness'. It seems, therefore, that the correct waveform signals from the heart can open the doorway for consciousness to increase the range and quality of its experience.

"Finally, to prove the point, ECG experiments by the Institute of Heart Math in the USA demonstrate that the emotion we call love is the most beneficial one to hold in the heart for true health in body and mind. They show that, when we think about and feel love, care and appreciation, there is a far more coherent ECG frequency distribution than when thoughts of worry, anger, frustration and fear predominate. Heart frequencies create an electromagnetic field which is distributed throughout the body. The degree of coherence in the heart is the major determining factor for coherence in the rest of the body, suggesting the possibility that ECG frequencies have profound effects on overall health and well-being.

"Psychological evaluation has confirmed that subjects who produce higher percentage of coherent ECG frequencies are far better adjusted and able to manage their mental and emotional natures and their reactions to stressful events in life."

It would be hard to accumulate more evidence to show why as a species we so urgently need to access and open 'the thinking heart' in order to achieve the Love Initiation that is the current spiritual goal of all our striving. Once we are truly functioning in the heart's higher vibrational qualities of wisdom, intuition, spontaneity and unconditional love - all feminine, right brain attributes - we then synchronise with the Earth's own heightening energy field and automatically 'ascend' with her. Exactly how this is to happen is the subject of endless and unproductive intellectual debate and opinion, but ultimately all that matters is that **we are prepared energetically**. We will then be ready to participate in whatever the next wondrous stage of evolution holds in store for us - right here, on a New Earth healed by our love.

Having worked on ourselves in order to open the heart, we then access our life's spiritual blueprint and contribute the particular expertise with which we were born to the greater unfolding picture. In this way, through clear motivation, intention and total commitment to our purpose here, we not only serve the greater plan through the Aquarian ideal of co-operation, but also contribute directly to the mysterious scale of 'critical mass'.

Critical mass has already been reached subconsciously, thanks to the millions of people who sincerely yearn for peace in our world. However, in our physical reality, yearning alone is not sufficient to turn the tide. We are required to put our higher aspirations into action and set an example to inspire others. Dulled by our obsession with passive entertainment and fear of change, we tend to forget that we specifically incarnated to **participate** in the 'dance of life'!

The transformational, fully conscious 'critical mass' number (144,000 in Revelations) will only be activated for the greater benefit of all, if those who have the courage stand up for their truth, despite the cynicism and scorn of the less aware, commit themselves fully to being the pillars of the new consciousness on which others can build and rise in confidence.

In view of the inaccuracies of the Gregorian calendar, which I have already pointed out, and of the fact that we actually passed into the new millennium in 1993, it is important to remember that most western prophecy culminated at the year 2,000. From that time onward we need to understand that we ourselves are creating the new reality for which there is no precedent. It is literally up to aware humans with their every thought, word and deed to dream, focus and anchor the New Heaven onto the New Earth. This is why it is so vital to hold only positive and constructive thoughts about what we are creating and not to fragment our energy by giving power unnecessarily to the many disturbing aspects of the collapsing third-dimensional reality around us. The clearer and more committed our focus on the new reality we have come to create, the sooner will it manifest on Earth and release those levels of consciousness that are becoming increasingly uncomfortable here.

Considering that the spiritual quality of what we produce in life is entirely dependent on the success of our inner transformational achievements, it becomes ever clearer that our preparation work also needs to include a daily discipline of meditational attunement, prayer, affirmation, invocation, gratitude and as much silence as possible. However else in this noise-polluted world of ours are we to hear the 'still small voice' of our higher self expressed in our innate wisdom and intuition that is the only reliable source of guidance through the uncharted waters we now navigate?

And finally, in this ever more troubled world, let those with awareness be humble and truly grateful that the priceless jewel of spiritual truth has been made available to them. Those with a firm grasp on the nature of reality can access the higher planes of consciousness now open to them - and count themselves blessed indeed to have the ability to rise above the fear-filled reality of the less aware amongst humanity.

Chapter 20

THE UNIVERSAL CHURCH OF LOVE

**"Thou art Peter, and upon this rock I will build my
church, and gates of hell shall not prevail against it".**

Matthew ch.16 v.18

The 'church' represents the unified consciousness. The 'rock' is the
planet Earth and the time is now. It is actually at the end of the second
millennium that each incarnate human has the opportunity to bring Jesus
Christ's Universal mission to its fulfilment. In other words, we are destined
to create 'Heaven on Earth' right here and now!

Many have been confused and alarmed by the glaring contradictions
within Christianity over the centuries since the Master first gave this task
to his disciple Simon called Peter. With the benefit of hindsight, it is clear
that the attempt by the apostle Paul together with various Roman Emperors
and politically rather than spiritually motivated male priests to found a
church based on a physical structure, was **not** at all what the Master had in
mind! In fact, the imbalance and distorted belief system they concocted
and called 'Christianity' was light years away from the original teachings
of Jesus known as 'The Way'. He taught the Universal Laws and Ancient
Wisdom in the tradition of the Essenes. Had the human race abided by
these timeless and immutable truths, it would have been spared the rivers
of blood resulting from 'holy' wars, inquisitions and the many other
historically documented atrocities perpetrated by this first 'church' - all
apparently in the name of the one who came in **love**! Is it any wonder at
the dawning of our New Age of Enlightenment that Christianity doesn't
make sense to most people and that ever larger numbers are repelled and
deeply offended by the horror of its ongoing sectarian divisiveness?

Jesus Christ did **not** come to impose yet another religion on humanity.
He knew as well as any spiritually aware person that truth can never be
accessed through emotionally focused, second hand belief structures. Truth
can only be experienced and known within as a living reality. Jesus the
man came as an innocent vessel of redemption. By painstakingly preparing

289

himself through total commitment, discipline and many initiations, he became - during his three year mission - the physical vehicle of the Christos or 'that aspect of the Creator that enters into conscious relationship with his / her creation'. At the crucifixion, by mingling his immensely high vibrational blood with the water and earth substance, he anchored the supreme frequency of the Unified (Christ) Consciousness onto this planet. The Cosmic Christ, as it is known, is actually 'The Spirit of the Sun' - representing 'the Father' - and it is through this alchemical infusion of light that the Master raised the vibratory frequencies here. It was in this way and **not** by 'vicarious atonement' through blood sacrifice 'for our sins', that he liberated (redeemed) the living consciousness of the Earthmother and all evolving life forms here (including human) from entrapment through fear within the dense third dimensional realms of matter. This in turn permitted those humans so choosing after lifetimes of preparation to reach spiritual maturity now at the end of the second millennium. The 'Fall' from the divine source of our origin or the 'out breath of God' - was caused initially by our doubt, which led through (low vibrational) fear to our long confinement within this dense realm of matter. Nonetheless, this process was our chosen reality and did give conscious expression to the overall creative impulse - despite the heavy price of inevitable human spiritual amnesia in the process!

Now at the Second Coming, we are invited to raise our individual and collective consciousness by re-educating ourselves spiritually and completing our creative cycle by evolving back to 'the source' - the 'in breath of God'.

Gaia (the Earth) in her restored and rightful role as 'Mother of Creation' is now ready, after a gestation period of 2,000 years, to give birth to the new frequency with which Jesus Christ impregnated her. **This** is what is known as the Second Coming of the Christ consciousness for which his mission long ago opened 'The Way' for each human should to participate. Now, if we so choose and having prepared ourselves entirely through our own efforts, we are empowered to 'Christ' ourselves and 'ascend' into a higher dimensional frequency known as 'Heaven'.

In order to evolve spiritually within the duality of this third dimensional plane of existence, humans needs to experience 'soul growth' through their many lives on Earth gaining direct experience. We learn in this duality by the process of reflection through the interaction of opposites. Thus,

290

wherever 'light' manifests, so the 'dark' will automatically challenge it. It is by careful discernment between these opposing forces that we 'grow', though it is important to remember that every aspect of creation is an inseparable part of the Divine 'Wholeness', including even what we with our limited understanding judge to be 'dark' or 'evil'. We have co-created it **all** specifically to test ourselves and of course, one of the greatest tests of all over the past 2,000 years for millions of reincarnating souls has been the distinctly un-Christlike example and direction of the Christian religion itself.

Where intolerance and fear-based fundamentalism raises its ugly head in any religion, it is a sure sign that spirituality has been sacrificed to the blind and rigid dogma of limited human intellect. But, it is within Christianity, with its dysfunctional influence on the controllers of the world's most technically powerful nations, that it poses the greatest immediate danger to the safety of this race and planet. For this reason alone, it is incumbent on all free-thinking people of goodwill to carefully investigate the origins of this flawed belief structure from a strictly historical and non-emotional perspective. After centuries of flagrant abuse, we can now all too clearly see that 'man-made' Christianity has manifested the exact reverse of the Master's teaching and demonstration. As surprising as it may seem, this flawed religion has actually represented our collectively chosen path through darkness, in order that by careful discernment through many incarnations we could attain spiritual maturity at the current time of the Second Coming of the Christ consciousness.

Although Jesus gave Peter the task of consolidating the new level of consciousness on the Earth, it was actually the apostle Paul who initially took up the challenge. It was he, not Peter, who is responsible for the foundation of what became the physical structure of the gentile church and eventually the Roman 'Christian' religion. He established it on an inspired, but nonetheless intellectual interpretation of the Master's teachings - what in today's imbalanced world might be termed a 'head-trip'! In so doing, he bequeathed humanity two millennia of dire theological confusion and mayhem at the hands of clever, but all too often unwise, male political priests. It will be remembered that Jesus Christ himself never preached in a building, preferring instead 'the Temple of the Father, whose roof is the Heavens and foundation the Earth'. The Master never envisaged his church as a physical structure, but rather the presence of the Christ wherever 'two or more are gathered in my name'. We can only come to the 'Father' (self-realisation) by experiencing the 'Christ' (unified consciousness) within our hearts as unconditional love.

Paul also failed to give equal emphasis or personal expression to the heart-centered demonstration of Jesus Christ based on healing and compassion. The exemplification of 'Living the Loving' was, of course, the mainstay of the Master's mission. Furthermore, by denying the vital spiritual role of women, Paul managed to unbalance the human male / female polarities, for which this race has ever since paid a heavy price. It is well to remember that women were only acknowledged as even having souls at the Council of Trent in the 16th century - and then only by a majority verdict of one vote! Their right to vote in the western democracy came only in the 20th century.

Progressively, over the next three hundred years, the foundations of 'The Way' were then systematically destroyed. Iranaeus, Bishop of Lyons, known as the 'Father of the Bible', wrote his 'Five books against heresy' in 180CE. His highly selective inclusion in the construction of the Bible of what he deemed 'sacred' texts from the wealth of documents available totally rejected the Essene, Gnostic and Manichean paths. This led to all Aramaic texts containing the truth of the original teachings being burned. Then, at the Council of Nicea in 325CE, the human entelechy of body, soul and spirit was broken, with the individual human spirit being denied and relegated to an intellectual quality of the soul. This infamy thus closed the gates of the spiritual worlds to the uninitiated masses, making them easy prey for unscrupulous priests. From then on priests denied the guidance of the unseen realms that had till then inspired the direction of whole nations through oracles, mediums and sensitives. Now, only 'the demented and unintelligible prattling known as 'talking in tongues' was to permitted, with interpretation monopolised, as usual, by Christian clerics!

Through the "Articles of Anathema" at the Council of Constantinople in 550CE, the most serious assault of all was made against the immutable Universal Laws that govern creation and ensure human soul growth. Under the malign influence of the Empress Theodora - wife of the Roman Emperor Justinian - the then Pope (Vergilius) was prevailed upon to declare invalid the Laws of Reincarnation and personal karmic responsibility (for our every thought, word and deed). The church quickly substituted the doctrine of 'vicarious atonement', claiming falsely that Jesus Christ would henceforth atone for all human sin. Thus, at a stroke, personal responsibility was replaced with the profitable sale of church-dispensed 'indulgences' for the pardoning of sin!

Having successfully emasculated the original teachings, the church fathers now exercised control over their flock through fear of Divine retribution, guilt, self-denial and the illusion known as 'death'. At this point, the ignorance of 'man-made theology' replaced the spiritual enlightenment of the great Greek philosophers. Europe was plunged into the abyss known as the 'Dark Ages' of unprecedented blood-letting through distinctly un-holy wars, inquisitions and the destruction of some 9 million wise-women as so-called witches. With them was lost the precious knowledge of the ways of Nature, which included natural birth-control and healing also taught by Jesus through the Essene wisdom. There then followed the wholesale genocide of the Amerindian population at the hands of the 'Christian Conquistadors', adding tens of millions more to the account of this bloody religion's long reign of terror. Man's unbridled intellect and sheer 'cleverness', untempered by wisdom, as always brought us terrible misery. Today we face even greater dangers, with religious fanatics manipulated by priestly intellectuals only too willing to use the weapons of ultimate mass destruction now available to justify their unloving and non-universal religious mis-interpretations.

So, we have reached the end of the Second Millennium. A time when the entire human race faces the long-prophesied 'Second Coming' - yet we are virtually unprepared spiritually! The church, after millennia of confusion and an inability still to comprehend the universal nature of Jesus Christ's original mission, is hardly the place to look for spiritual guidance now. Its lack of understanding has in any case led to a vacuum in its authority, which has largely been usurped by fundamentalists invoking the Revelation of St John to support their narrow and catcysmic understanding of that, until recently, incomplete prophetic text.

It is perhaps as well that the long-suppressed, missing chapters of Revelations known as the Third Book of the Apocalypse, were restored to humanity in 1990 by the direct intervention of the unseen realms. History shows us how our partners in Spirit intervene whenever humanity strays too far from the spiritual path - the miraculous physical manifestations of the Ten Commandments themselves and the Golden Tablets of Mormon are but examples. This time intervention was accomplished through the great advances we have made in communication technology and right over the heads of the church fathers, so that no more controls or subversions of 'the Word' could again occur in their hands. The text, launched with *Rising out of Chaos* in 1994, is now safely in the hands worldwide of those who, through its pages, are indeed remembering 'The Way' and that they are here to bring enlightenment to this weary and confused race. Revelations 3 will now act as a laser beam within the Christian Church to expose those divisive and negative forces that have always hidden within it. Furthermore, it will isolate them from those of genuine Christ consciousness, who know no other way of expressing their spiritual devotion than through the church. Here is but a brief summary of a most enlightening text that merits detailed study.

Second Coming is the awakening of the unified consciousness in all human hearts that understand the interconnection and inseparability of all life. Such people live a practical demonstration of unconditional love, forgiveness, sharing and non-judgement, tempered by careful spiritual discernment. Only such Beings will automatically raise the vibratory frequencies of their physical bodies into the highest harmonic of love (the fuel of creation) that alone guarantees their 'ascension' of consciousness or 'rapture' in these times. Neither Jesus, nor any other messiah figure that humans could again mistakenly worship will reincarnate now in flesh. Humanity is required to sit an exam to see if we have learned what all the great Masters came to teach us - and obviously the teacher won't be sitting the exam for us! There is to be a 'sorting of the wheat from the chaff' as humans individually choose between love and fear. The higher frequencies of energy that daily increase this planet's vibratory rate will simply reject and remove all life forms (including human) that fail to raise themselves to the required level. There is to be a 'New Heaven and a New Earth' open to those who freely choose such a reality and we are told that all will change on this planet during the upcoming dimensional interface. The 144,000 humans, who have incarnated this time embodying the higher consciousness, are here to trigger a 'critical mass' response. This is an exponential raising of mass human consciousness that will assist all those choosing love over fear to raise their frequencies in order to be part of what is known as 'the harvest of souls.' Yes, we have indeed reached the 'Last Days', **not** of the Earth, as fundamentalists so misguidedly suppose, but of the old third-dimensional, dualistic reality and all its fear-based institutions of human disempowerment and control.

Free will is ours by Divine decree and with full awareness of the significance of these times now restored to us, we must each make our own spiritual preparations and take full responsibility for whatever final choice we make. We are unlimited Beings with infinite evolutionary potential, but only if we surrender to the Divinity that has always been **within** us.

REVELATION III

The Third Book of the Apocalypse

The Prophecy of the Second Coming of the Christ Consciousness

The Complete text with notes

(Also available on the World Wide Web at:
http://www.globalvisions.org/cl/wwv, and
Compuserve's Religion Forum)

The following guidance notes are inspired by the same source as the main text, and are intended to promote a better understanding of the divine inspiration encoded in this work.

Chapter One

1: Seven spirits represent the first seven Christ-inspired communities in Asia minor (listed in Ch 7 v 1). Each received part of the complete Book of Revelations, including this work, in the form of letters for safe-keeping. "Kopos" is the early Greek word for work/labour, and "Dynamis" means spiritual path. Spiritual work is thus seen as a "calling", rather than mere labour, and represents a release from the yoke with which mundane work is usually associated.

2: "Having the ear" is a reference to the subtle communication known as "channelling" between the spirit of the author of the Book of Revelations and his pupil still then incarnate on Earth, John the Elder.

3: John, in spirit, is guided to complete the Revelations vision by transmitting this, the summary of the whole work including the Second Coming prophecy, to his pupil in the flesh. John oversaw the writing of the first two books of the Revelation himself, but was unable personally to complete the vision he had received about the 3rd book before he passed on.

4: The "beast" denotes the worldly illusions of the flesh, while the Lamb refers to the higher levels of consciousness embodied by Jesus the Christ. The "sign" is an emblem and, after a battle, the victor traditionally laid the "sign" of the vanquished down to show that it no longer held any power. Here, it does not mean that the beast lies down with the Lamb, but that the beast is slain and will never rise again, as his symbolic emblem is removed by the Lamb. The trumpet is the voice of proclamation that sounded when the Aquarian Cross, made in "old" Jerusalem and brought from there, was raised on Glastonbury Tor at midday April 21st, 1990.

5: New Jerusalem signifies a higher dimensional state of awareness. which is usually described as an archetypal "city of light". Glastonbury Tor has a special historical association with the Second Coming of the Christ consciousness and many feel that the New Jerusalem has its initial Earthly anchor point there.

The "twelve foundations" is a symbol of the communion between the higher and lower realms and this was represented by those who gathered that day on Glastonbury Tor. All those in the vision will be the vehicles for communicating spiritual truth at this time of "Second Coming"

6: The thirteenth, or Cross bearer, embodies the Christ consciousness. Some are destined by past reincarnational associations with the Master Jesus to participate in the work of raising consciousness - the

THE THIRD BOOK OF THE APOCALYPSE

Prayer of Dedication

*May the light of God, whose perception of the human soul has so sur-
mounted the centuries, enlighten your mission and at this, the moment
of its rebirth, pour love and light into this work of passion and glory,
so that each book so ordained to go forth upon the Earth and once
more restore the secret message be lifted into the heart and from the
heart be ever cherished!*   The Spirit of John. Received in 1993

Chapter One

1: To the seven spirits in the province of Asia, your brother John bore
faithful witness to your deliverance from kopos, being known that dynamis is the pure soul.

2: Having the ear, I John write in the spirit, for there came a loud
voice like a trumpet behind me, and turned did see the light and fell at
his feet as though dead.

3: Out of the light came forth the voice saying, "John, Be not afraid, I
hand you a key that transcends death and Hades, for you have not for-
saken your first love, do all things that you did at first".

4: For the beast will be slain and his sign will lie down with the
Lamb. A great trumpet will sound from a high place and a great star
set on a staff will be carried into the midst of the crowd.

5: And the Lord will bless this place and make it a Holy City, and it
will be called the new Jerusalem. And the city will come out of heaven
from God and be of jasper and of crystal. And the wall of the city will
have twelve foundations and the gates will bear the names of the apostles.

6: And the Lamb will sit in the midst and will number thirteen. For
seven will be called and five will be chosen The city will be measured
by a rod of gold and to its measure will be added every kind of precious stone.

Others, though not historically connected, are not excluded either and they are those now "chosen" to join the vision - the 5.

"Rod of gold" means the "city's" value will be measured by the high quality of work performed there. Precious stone denotes "jewels of wisdom" that represent not only the word, but all associated energies.

7: The "city" will be recognised by everyone. Limitless energy will be available to this place and the spiritual light will shine, so that no other form of light will be needed. Peace will come to all nations.

8: All will be seen for what they are and those not of the light will be identified by the clearly visible contamination of their subtle energy bodies. The enlightened among nations will gather at the throne of God in the city of New Jerusalem. "Seed of iron" means without life.

9: Our third eyes will be opened to psychic perception. Aristeas - an old Testament reference to one who remained steadfast, when all others denied the truth. One of many warnings not to change the received word, in order that people now seeking genuine spiritual truth are not misled again.

10: Those who freely accept the word will be raised in consciousness. while those denying it must accept the dire consequences described here. The "frog" is a reference to the plagues of Egypt.

11: A description of New Jerusalem and higher dimensional consciousness. People will be united by the common bond of the one truth they all share.

12: "Priests of the Earth" spiritually ignorant religious officials incapable of comprehending higher dimensional reality. The "144,000" are those souls originally initiated as the 12,000 in each of the twelve tribes of Israel. Re-incarnated, they now awaken spiritually and become the "critical mass" catalyst for raising mass human consciousness. The words of priests may sound inspired, but as they have no truth, they cannot sustain the inner spirit.

13: The true word will be revealed through "Spirit", but the priests and their flock are too spiritually blind to recognise it and will remain trapped in the sterile dogma of "the defiled word" - the misinterpreted word of the bible.

14: Once truth is released, it will not be silenced again. Any religious priest still persisting in the distortion, will not participate in the general upliftment of consciousness.

Chapter Two

1: The seven Archangels select John as the only one found worthy at that time to receive the divine word and convey this prophecy.

7: And they will bare their feet and bow their heads, for all nations and kings of the Earth will see no other splendour. And the temple gates will not shut by day, and there will be no night there.

8: And the impure will burn as transparent glass and the pure as gold. The glory of nations will sit by the throne of the temple that is within the city. And any that come in shame or deceit will bear no fruit, and their seed will be as iron.

9: Each will know the prophecy of the other, and each forehead bear the sign. For the words of prophecy must not cause false witness, for Aristeas knew his Lord, for the word is solemn and cause it not to be tampered with, for the Spirit said, "Come, whoever is thirsty, take the gift of the water of life".

10: Anyone who receives the word from the temple of light will be born again and those who make false witness will walk naked as a thief. They will carry no name and their mouths will be as the mouths of the beast, for they will sit with the spirit of demons and lie with the frog.

11: And the city will be borne on a cloud of light, not set upon the Earth, but carried by the spirit. Through the gates will come many peoples and languages and they will speak with a single tongue and read of the book of life.

12: And the Priests of the Earth will come forth and call the book evil and make pain of the 144,000 who are of the light. But the Priest will read of the book and the word will turn the stomach sour, but in the mouth it will be as sweet as honey.

13: Thus, the word will be revealed by the spirit of the light. But the Priests of the Earth will not see the word, but make witness to the de-filed word, which came out of the mouths of angels, but fell into the hand of the beast.

14: What the spirit opens, no-one can shut; and what he shuts, no-one can open. The defiled priest will lie with the beast.

Chapter Two

1: And the vision changed and I saw seven angels come from heaven and they bade me, for no-one was found worthy to receive the word.

2: The "right hand" is usually the "working" hand and represents the outworking of intellect. John's faith ensures he will be "raised".

3: "Written on both sides" means full of knowledge, in the sense that all wisdom is to be given at this time. This great vision of spiritual uplift- ment is entrusted to the seven communities, which are charged to protect its original purity.

4: "Breaking the seal" is releasing information at the appropriate time. "New song" means the restored knowledge of this prophecy. The "red half" is bloodstained communism, which forbade spiritual teaching. The "white half" represents Christianity, which is equated with capital- ism, greed and conquest. Led by the church, it used "the word" with utmost hypocrisy to serve its own selfish, political and commercial ends.

5: The "red horse" is communism and the new flow of cleansing blood will herald rapidly changing spiritual concepts as it transmutes the old order. The horse represents fast movement with a rider (leader) who is a messenger of peace.

6: The black nations of the "third world" are badly treated by the indus- trialised nations, who refuse to share properly. Karmic judgement will be made on those responsible exactly according to the measure of deprivation they have inflicted.

7: A "choinix" is an ancient measurement. This describes the practice of usury, which is receiving money without labour through bank inter- est. Money will cease as an exchange mechanism and cause much distress.

8: Reference to "global warming". Essentials on the planet will become scarce.

9: Death is "Pale" and without life-force. Disease and misery are ram- pant. Even the spirit realms are disturbed by occurrences now on earth, knowing that they themselves are due to reincarnate here.

10: God knows not "death", as it is man's own creation. Conditions on earth now are the consequences of our misuse of freewill.

11: This refers to man's misuse of energy and technology. He will not find God through them, but only make more terror on Earth. Unbridled intellect and scientific knowledge applied without wisdom are among the main causes of our misfortune.

2: And I bowed my head and wept, for I saw the light came from the right hand of Him who sat on the throne. And He said, "Have no fear, for I know my servant and will lift you above all Kingdoms and priests and give authority over every tribe, people, language and nation."

3: And the first angel came forth and in the hand held a scroll, written on both sides. And said, "Pure are the seven eyes for they are as the seven spirits of God sent out to give wisdom to the Earth".

4: And he broke the seal and I heard a new song and there came forth the prayers of the saints. And the earth fell in half, in one there flowed blood and the half was of red. And the second was white and knew not God, but provoked his works in greed, and conquest.

5: And the second angel came forth and broke the seal. And there appeared a fiery red horse, for the blood would cleanse and its rider was given power to take peace to the earth.

6: And the third angel broke the seal. And there came forth a black horse and the rider was called Famine and carried a pair of scales, for the Lord said, "When I cut off your supply of bread, they will dole out the bread by weight".

7: To each was given a choinix of wheat according to his labour but many will come and take of the bread and give no labour and they will make starvation upon the earth and they will cry and their voices will be as the wilderness.

8: For even the oil and the wine will be scarce for there will be no rain and from the sun none will find cover.

9: And the fourth angel broke the seal. And there came forth a pale horse and the rider was Death. And the sky was filled and I saw unrest, misery, pestilence, scarcity, war in all forms, and was full of fear.

10: And the angel said, "Be not afraid, for death is of man and God does not know me, for I bare the fruits of free-will, which is the gift of God, but of all those signs, they are made of man.

11: They will walk upon the waters, and fly with the creatures of the sky and go to the depth of the sea. They will lift their body into the stars, but they will find not God, for of these gifts they will make terror upon all the nations of the earth.

12: Humanity will be tested in this time.

13: The gathering of light at Glastonbury during the declaration of the New Jerusalem. The Lamb and the reincarnated souls of martyrs now return to be one with humanity in the new light on planet Earth.

14: The martyrs are already purified and now volunteer to spread the word once more. This also includes those in past lives who were once persecuted for their work with spirit.

15: Refers to the gathering of the 144,000, who trigger the transformation of consciousness at this time. We shall recognise each other as "light", beyond all illusory divisions.

16: An indication of the inevitable physical and spiritual changes coming now. Those in the vision will need to hold to their convictions to survive.

17: There is much unusual activity in the heavens and consequently the seasons become unpredictable.

18: The distorted teachings of religious priests are initially responsible for the dysfunctional thinking and behaviour of humanity, which in turn has dire consequences for the Earth and our Universe. There can be no effective cleansing on the Earth until there is a restoration of spiritual truth.

19: This is the vision of the moment when the light touched Glastonbury Tor on April 21st, 1990 and is also a reaffirmation of the divine plan to support mankind .

20: This emphasises that the expression here in flesh of pure, unconditional love is the *only* key to accessing the next dimension. It is the supreme harmonic of love alone that has the ability to raise the vibratory frequencies of our physical bodies.

21: This refers to the period of deep meditation after the Cross was raised and is an understanding of the peace when heaven and earth are united.

12: And they will hand out pestilence and they will make evil upon all that was made by the hand of God. For God has tested His people even to the fourth seal".

13: And the fifth angel broke the seal. And the angel wore a robe of white. And he held out his hand and said, "Come, for I am the breath of life". And from the cloud came forth the Lamb and around and in a circle came forth the souls of martyrs.

14: For they all have lain on the altar of knowledge and received the baptism of life eternal. And the martyrs cried in a loud voice, "Sovereign Lord, may we go abroad even as the spirit that all will know the time of Your coming". And there came a loud trumpet from heaven and all bowed their heads.

15: And He gave charge to His servants to walk abroad and to carry the message, so that all may be prepared for the age that will be as gold, and when all will know their brothers and sisters by the light of their being.

16: And the sixth angel broke the seal. And there came a great wind from heaven, and the earth shook, every mountain and island moved for the stars knew not their place in the sky.

17: And there came from the sky many stars that did fall towards the earth and the time was seen, for late were the figs that dropped from the tree.

18: And all stood in fear, for great was the wrath of the Lamb. And his servants threw out all the priests of the earth who had given false prophecy, for they had laid bare the earth and caused the stars in the sky to move.

19: And there came a great light from heaven and the wind was still. And the Lord said, "Though the mountains be shaken and the hills be removed, yet My unfailing love for you will not be shaken nor My covenant of peace".

20: And those of the light will make the sign, which is of love and will share comfort in the pure spirit.

21: And the seventh angel came forth and broke the seal. And there was silence in heaven for half an hour for the time of the prophesy was

22: Jesus, as an individual being distinct from the "Christ", is the seventh angel and hands down universal knowledge to the disciples of the light at this, the time of his "Second Coming" in spirit. These are not physical manifestations, but symbols of the purity of the light that entered the planet as the Cross was raised.

24: The re-birthing of the Earth.

25: The seven archangels are directed to different parts of the Earth to lead the nations to light.

Chapter Three

1 & 2: This is an explanation of the subtle process used by spirit over the aeons in all known civilisations to channel wisdom and guidance into the conduct of human affairs.

3: The word needs to be studied for hidden meaning.

4: Reference to our free choice within the third dimension of duality in which we currently live and learn our lessons.

5 & 6: An example of polarity. All that is negative is also positive and vice-versa, but it requires a shift in the structure of our perception to realise it. In this way, we see that all things that are and ever have been remain the same.

known. And there appeared the seven angels standing before God and seven trumpets were sounded.

22: And the names of the angels were, Uriel, Raphael, Michael, Saraqael, Gabriel and Remiel. And the seventh angel took the final scroll and filled it with fire from the altar, and hurled it onto the earth and there were peals of thunder, rumblings, flashes of lightning and an earthquake.

23: And all were bathed in the light and walked in the knowledge of love and of spirit.

24: And where there was desert there came forth grass and where there was murky water it was made clear and in the sky there were no clouds and all the stars were made bright.

25: And the Lord directed His angels to walk amongst all the nations that they may know the prophesy and make the sign, so that at that day they may freely enter the age of Gold.

Chapter Three

1: And the seven angels spoke in one voice, for as they came to walk upon the land, they took many forms that were man, but though the form was man the spirit was not man, for they entered into man as one entering into a Holy place. But when they were gone, the man was made singular again.

2: And while they were with man, they told of the secrets of the Father, that all signs may be understood, even as is written in this prophesy.

3: For nothing will be as it is seen.

4: All things will have two heads, that which gives to the man the knowledge of death and that which gives the knowledge of life eternal.

5: And you will know the sign from the staff that is pointed to the Heavens and touches the earth. For if the staff was turned upside down, would not the lower part be to heaven and the top to the earth?

6: For as I have seen the visions of the Father, my visions have touched both the earth and heaven, for each is the same, though they are opposite.

307

7: The angel saw that John was confused by this.

8 -12: God created darkness to contrast with the light for our own growth, as we can only perceive the light by first experiencing the dark. Only careful discernment will protect us from enslavement to material illusion and spiritual distortion. God permeates *every* aspect of His/Her creation, whether we with our limited understanding perceive it as good or evil, right or wrong. It is through the interaction of opposites that we learn our lessons and grow at soul level here in the Earth school.

13 & 14: The female aspect of God known as "Gaia" the ancient Greek name for mother Earth at the time this book was written.

15: The consciousness of the living Earth is "the Mother of Creation" - the Goddess. She is the creative aspect of deity.

16: She will have dominion over all realms.

17: The Earth is not recognised as an aware Being and Mother of Creation until now, when the "Last Days" of our decaying material reality are upon us.

18 & 19: The Earth mother is now in the process of birthing the next dimension of consciousness at the outworking of the divine will, or masculine principle of deity.

20: We have to give up material security and trust in the higher dimensional reality of our own spirit essence. This is an illustration of the true re-birth and the need to remain constantly open to spirit, despite worldly diversions.

21: Historically, we have not brought enlightenment to the Earth. Like everyone else born human, Jesus himself had to struggle with the temptations of matter and ego in order to demonstrate our individual potential to attain Christ consciousness while in the flesh

7: And the angel saw that l was vexed and sat with me.

8: "For is not the Father the maker of all things? And has He power even over that which makes darkness of the light".

9: If you know not the darkness, how can you understand the light?

10: If there was only light, how could you choose that which is sacred, for only in the darkness can you see the sacred light.

11: Even as the prophesy has been given in these visions, the hand has written on both the dark and the light scrolls. For there will be spirits of light and spirits of darkness and only by knowing one will you know the other.

12: Therefore, you will receive all knowledge that in choosing, you will not fear that which is hidden within the dark chambers of the earth.

13: And the Father will send to the earth a protector and she will be clothed with the sun and ride on a chariot of gold.

14: And her name will be Gaia and she will carry the seed of life and her body will be as a womb for all that live upon the earth.

15: She will know every creature and be lifted onto every mountain. She will ride across the flat land and enter into the depth of the sea. And all will know her, for she is the Mother of creation.

16: And they will see Her clothed with the sun, with the moon under Her feet and a crown of twelve stars on her head.

17: But She will not be known until the last days come upon the Earth and there is darkness and decay, even as She is known.

18: And She will be, as a woman with child and about to give birth who writhes and cries out in her pain.

19: So were we in the presence of the Father.

20: We were with child, we writhed in pain, but we gave birth to wind.

21: We have not brought salvation to the earth; we have not given birth to the people of the world.

Chapter Four

1, 2 & 3: The "twelve" is a symbol for all those now opening to the new awareness. Many are still unsure, but with the restoration now of un-distorted spiritual knowledge, they will be given clarity.

4: He raises their spiritual perception so they can again hear the guid-ance of the inner voice and fulfil their purpose on Earth. The Glaston-bury ceremony symbolised this awakening.

6: Those in the vision become all knowing and all seeing.

7: Reference to the comet Austin which returned in 1990. "Known and unknown" refers to the spiritual Masters of the planet attracted by the light of the Second Coming.

8 - 12: The 144,000 are higher dimensional initiates, who have incar-nated throughout the planet specifically at this time to lift human con-sciousness. They represent the minimum focus of energy capable of transmuting the negativity and spiritual ignorance currently permeating the human race. The realisation of the "Christ within", has opened their hearts so that they now embody the Second Coming of the Christ con-sciousness as their living demonstration.

13: The Christ consciousness will now penetrate and transmute all remaining negativity on Earth. Love will replace fear as humans awaken to the truth that each of us is an expression of God and that, beyond the illusion of separation, we are in reality united as one con-sciousness in a "safe, just and abundant" universe.

Chapter Four

1: And the angel Michael came forth and sat with the twelve. But they were troubled and some hid their face.

2: And he bade them uncover their face that they may have vision. But some of the twelve were blind and could not see the light.

3: Then the angel Michael placed his hand upon their eyes and they were with sight. And they rejoiced, praising the name of the Father and making the sign.

4: And he took them to a high place and their ears were open to the voice and they knew their Father and were made newly born.

5: And there was a great voice from Heaven and they saw visions of that which was to be.

6: And they saw all the land and it was without boundary. And all the sea even to the furthest star.

7: And the sky was filled with a great light and out of the light came forth many beings known and unknown. And they marvelled and asked, "What is this that fills our eyes?"

8: And the angel Michael said, "These are they who have walked with the Father and are ascended, even to the throne".

9: "They are of the 144,00 children of the first born and are of every tongue and of every nation. For the risen Christ is in their heart that the word may be fulfilled".

10: And they carry the sign of the second coming of the Lamb, which is the prophesy of the resurrection. And all will be gathered unto the sacred city, being of one consciousness and of one family".

11: And you will know the Christ, which is descended and made one with all who are of the sign.

12: And they will make the sign to one another and they will know themselves pure in the Blood of the Lamb.

13: And they will rejoice, for the Christ is descended from the higher planes even to the darkest corner of the earth. For none will know fear, for the Christ is within.

14: The portals to the fourth dimension are now open to all who wish to enter.

15: Heaven is drawn down onto Earth and merges with it. So is born the new Aquarian age. The declaration of Second Coming at Glastonbury in 1990 ended the old Piscean cycle. Now we enter the overlap period, when the inspirational energy overlighting the New Dispensation becomes established.

16: Although harsh and unforgiving language for our times, this is nevertheless an unequivocal statement. Those still persisting in separative rather than integrative thinking and behaviour must now face the consequences of being out of step with the next phase of mankind's evolutionary progress.

17: Those who persist in material delusion and its demands will realise their mistake too late. Having uttered so much negativity, they will find themselves trapped and unable to reach the light. "Eternal darkness" or "hell" represents a lower dimension of consciousness, where individual human soul expression can no longer be sustained. It would seem that failure to sufficiently maintain the inner spiritual light over many lifetimes leads in this initiation to absorption into an inanimate energy force that only at some future stage starts a new evolutionary process. This is a description of "the sorting of the wheat from the chaff" in the "last days". Those not prepared now "sleep the long sleep."

Chapter Five

1: This is the authority for the Aquarian Cross being the symbol of Christ consciousness at Second Coming. The chapter is a teaching on how man abuses the gifts he has been given.

2: "Bowls" are concepts of our consciousness and facets of our being at this time.

3: A description of nature in an undefiled state of purity before man interferes with her.

4: Ecology - Trees provide oxygen and wet conditions which stimulate growth.

5: Resources for building in the world of matter.

6: Transportation to enable man to distribute and share.

7: Arts and crafts for man to glorify the Divine.

14: And the Cherubim will stand guard no more. And the gates of paradise will be opened and all will dwell there in the purity of Love.

15: And the boundary of paradise will be the boundary of the City which is of gold. Thus will end the cycle at the very instant of the second coming of the Christ consciousness.

16: But whosoever strays from the teachings of the Christ will know not love, but be cast out and will burn. And they will not receive the sign, but will lie with the beast that is in the land that is desert.

17: For those who would worship the beast and his image and anyone who receives the mark of his name will be forever cast out and their sign will be the sign of the beast and their resting place eternal darkness. Out of the abyss of darkness will come the moaning of men who gnawed their tongues in agony.

Chapter Five

1: And the seven angels sat in a circle with the twelve and the one who holds the golden cross, that is the mark of the Christ.

2: And before each was set a bowl. And the bowls were made of reeds, of wood, of iron, of copper, of silver, of gold, and of crystal.

3: And the angel poured from the bowl of reeds all the gifts of nature that is fulfilled by the seasons. None had touched the hand of man, but all were known to his spirit.

4: And the second angel poured from the bowl of wood. And there came forth great forests, covered in clouds, which did make rain upon the earth.

5: And the third angel poured from the bowl of iron. And there was fashioned all the tools for man's labour upon the earth, even to the great cities and the wonders of man.

6: And the fourth angel poured from the bowl of copper. And there came forth all manner of vessel for the carrying of man's possessions while on the earth.

7: And the fifth angel poured from a bowl of silver. That was made bright and pleased the eye of man.

8: Money and finance based on the purity of gold.

9: Intellect to discern truth and beauty.

11: The process of feeding ourselves from nature.

12: Only failure to share resources causes starvation and poverty on the Earth.

13: Large scale destruction of trees leads to pollution and disease.

14: If man tries to solve the problems he has created without spiritual awareness, he will merely compound them and cause turmoil.

15: Failure to distribute. There is sufficient abundance to feed all on Earth, but through fear of each other, financial greed and hoarding, we become like locusts and cause famine. This leads to such absurdities as "defence budgets" (a euphemism for arms manufacture and trading) and "food mountains", while much of humanity starves.

16: Hoarding treasure - Art is the inspiration of God and is not a commodity to be traded commercially. If this approach to the Divine is denied through greed and selfish indulgence, then the people starve spiritually.

17: Stock markets and financial institutions. These are in the control of extravagantly paid and apparently wise people, who manipulate commodities, metals and finance for greed without any real understanding or benefit for mankind in general.

8: And the sixth angel poured from a bowl of gold. Which is a base metal of man's treasure upon the earth.

9: And the seventh angel poured from a bowl of crystal, which did sparkle and was fashioned in great beauty.

10: And they were pure and untouched by man.

11: Then the first angel took a staff which had been held by man and touched it upon the bowl of reeds and they did wither. And all that was contained fell to the ground and was made one with the earth. And there came forth from the rich seed all the needs of man, even until the last day.

12: And the first angel said, "Your Father will feed all his children, for none will go in hunger other than by the greed of man".

13: And the second angel smote the bowl of wood with the staff of man. And the forest shook and the sky was turned to blood. And the blood covered one third of the earth, the sea, and the waters. And the beast walked through the sky of blood and there were ugly and painful sores on the beast.

14: And the third angel took the staff and touched the bowl of iron. And there came forth a multitude of man's implements to defend him against the sky of blood. And man cast down many demons with his tools, but as they were slain so they multiplied.

15: And the fourth angel took the staff and touched the bowl of copper. And the bowl was filled to overflowing, and there appeared a great number of locust that darkened the sky and consumed all that was in sight and tortured the people with pain and scorching heat.

16: And the fifth angel smote the bowl of silver and there was seen a great city with much treasure. And there came upon the city a severe earthquake and it was shattered. For the nations of the earth knew not the Father but rendered a cup filled with the wine of the fury of His wrath.

17: And the sixth angel touched the bowl of Gold. And there came forth seven frogs that were slimy and ugly. And from their mouths came forth incessant and meaningless croaking. And they were clothed in gold and looked wise and learned, but underneath they were naked.

18: Through the disempowerment of the people and their own unbridled intellect, politicians and world leaders cause increasing chaos culminating in wars for which Armageddon is the archetype.

19: Mankind continually reincarnates without taking personal power or responsibility for self and thus repeats the same mistakes. Rulers become so used to domination through this pattern of mass self-disempowerment, that they do not recognise the ego imbalance they are creating within themselves lifetime after lifetime and continue to manipulate the masses into war.

20: Now, however, corrupt rulers and dictators, who have become slaves of negativity, fall from power in ever-increasing numbers.

21 & 22: Spiritual truth is restored to the people and through self-empowerment based on the principles of unconditional love and sharing, they see the light and are set free. Wisdom will flow from their intuitive centre - the heart, symbolised by the golden sash.

Chapter Six

1 & 2: Confirmation by the author that the information he imparts here is a divine inspiration and an accurate prophecy.

3 & 4: Conventional Christianity still awaits a physical reappearance of Jesus and mourns the flesh image. It does not comprehend the spiritual significance of the Christ consciousness and is therefore incapable of understanding the event as a personal initiation open to all humans able to access the divinity of their own higher nature.

5: Spiritually unaware Christian priests lead the people astray by proclaiming "Second Coming" as another messianic mission. Many individual teachers have come to initiate the planet and humanity in the past, but now is the time of testing to establish whether we each remember the lessons we have so often been taught and are living according to Universal Law.

6: Unusual signs (like symbolic crop formations in the UK) enable all people to understand that a significant event is occurring in these final days of third dimensional reality. This is an opportunity for all to prepare themselves for the initiation through the Universal, as distinct from Christian, teachings of Jesus Christ. His spirit restores the purity of the teachings as the 7th angel (Ch 2 v 22). The fourth dimension on Earth is only open to those wishing to enter in love and live in harmony.

7: Resurrection is a mystery of God - here it is symbolised by the destruction of the physical Jerusalem and its current etheric reconstruc-

18: And the seventh angel touched the bowl of crystal and there were gathered all the kings and rulers of the earth to a place called Armageddon. And they found no peace but caused war among their people even to the mountain called Megiddo.

19: And they counted their dead to one third of all the peoples of the Earth. And the bodies were consumed by demons and made again alive. But the kings and rulers saw not the Demons but commanded the great host to make war.

20: And the Demons mounted the kings and rulers and made slaves of them. And they were driven into dark caverns and lay with the beast.

21: And the people came forth into the light and rejoiced that they had been set free.

22: And they were clothed in clean shining linen with golden sashes around their chests. And the sky was filled with light from the glory of God.

Chapter Six

1: All these visions were made unto me by the angels that were from the Father, that all may bear witness to the word of God.

2: That all will know the sign of the final days, when Him who is, and who was, and who is to come will signify the prophesy.

3: It will be known in the time when all the peoples of the earth will mourn because of Him.

4: But that they mourn the man and not the spirit.

5: And seek not the Father through the son, but the flesh re-incarnate. For the priests of the earth will see the image of the beast and lead many into the wilderness.

6: Yet will your Father make many signs, that all will bear witness to the final days when all have washed their robes and made them white in the blood of the lamb. And the gates of paradise will be opened and they will come in the power of Divine love and live in bliss.

7: For did not Jesus the Christ become dead, and sprang to life again. And was not the Holy City laid waste and now lives once more. These

tion as a higher-dimensional thought form. Such mysteries are the source of all wisdom.

8: So long as we don't doubt and despite being tested to the limit, all so choosing will be initiated into the new consciousness now prevailing on Earth.

9 - 12: This is a detailed reconfirmation of the all important reincarnational process to which everybody is subject on this planet. The resurrection of Jesus Christ was specifically enacted to prove that our individual consciousness survives the transition from flesh intact. In spirit, it continues to "dwell in many cities and mansions" beyond time i.e. to experience other dimensions of consciousness, as well as to frequently return to the Earth.

13: This denotes the equality of all nations and peoples.

14 & 15: A restatement of the Law of One (Christ consciousness), emphasising the qualifications of unconditional love and sharing necessary for participation in the new dispensation.

16: The male/female polarity balance, first within ourselves and then externally between the sexes, is critical to the unfoldment of the plan.

17: A symbol of the male reproductive seed.

18: Unselfish human lovemaking, either leading to procreation or not as decided both consciously and at soul level by all the participants, including the incoming soul, is the essence and purest expression of the Divine. The energy produced in such an act is never wasted, whatever the outcome, as it always energises other aspects of our creativity. Understanding this, women are freed from reproductive enslavement and can choose to fulfil themselves in roles other than motherhood - rather critical on an overpopulated planet and a direct challenge to patriarchal disempowerment of women particularly by the Roman church. In sexual union all creatures experience this exalted state and touch the Divine.

19 & 20: Christ consciousness can only be attained through the purity of unconditional love for one another. This is the path we are encouraged to follow in order to now experience the new level of consciousness described as "Paradise and bliss".

things were made by the Father, and his mystery is the source of all wisdom.

8: Be therefore faithful, even to the point of death, and He will give you the crown of life.

9: For the body will die and be as the earth was whence it came, but the spirit will live and dwell in many cities and not know time.

10: For the body is mortal and will decay, but the spirit is eternal and knows not death.

11: All will come upon the earth a hundred, hundred times, and still will the spirit be raised by the Father.

12: For the sign of the resurrection of the Son is the Sign of the life eternal.

13: For the Father will spread his tent over all His kingdom and they will number every people, tribe, language and nation.

14: And all that live in the seal of the living God, will be baptised in the gift of Divine Love, and be known through the mark of the purity of the spirit.

15: For as the Father shares His Divine presence through the sharing of the spirit, all will be made one in the baptism of Divine Love. And they will know each other and share the gifts of paradise and bliss.

16: For the Father saw His work and was well pleased. For Adam did He conceive Eve. And for Eve did He conceive Adam, that all may have balance in the Divine plan.

17: And he touched the side of Adam and there sprang forth a spring.

18: And he touched Eve that she would know the sign of His Divine love and bear forth from the spring all the offspring of the earth. And this gift did He give to all creatures, even to the lowest form that in their union they would touch the Divine spirit.

19: And this made He the sign of purity, that all may bathe in the water of life. And through the gift of Divine Love will the Christ spirit enter.

20: For blessed are they that come in purity to the spring of life and are baptised in the spirit. For they will live in paradise and share bliss.

21: The abuse of love through selfish sexual gratification, having no divine foundation, leads to the seven plagues now starting to manifest on Earth.

22: Only those who have prepared themselves by expressing unconditional love without judging individual people, will qualify for "life eternal" in the higher dimensions.

Chapter Seven

1 - 5: John's vision is witnessed by the seven communities. Knowing he is soon to pass into spirit, John is temporarily taken out of the body and, in an altered state of consciousness, is given this, THE PROPHECY OF THE SECOND COMING. On his return, he shares the vision briefly with John the elder and then finally passes on. However, he remains in contact with his pupil (see Ch 1 v 2/3 "having the ear") and together, using channelled communication, they complete the Third Book of the Apocalypse and what John calls "the Revelation of Jesus the Christ". Verse 4 indicates that, even in these times, John still works directly with those in this vision and assists them, because "he knows them of old". The miraculous reappearance of this text alone is proof enough of this promise!

6: John is taken in spirit to a "Tabernacle" - a tent or Holy place where he is bathed in light.

7: A powerful directive to all aware people to commit themselves to communicate spiritual Truth in these times of great change.

8: Comet Austin was visible from Earth during the declaration of Second Coming in April 1990, and having fulfilled its purpose on Earth, will not return. "Its two appearances were designated to link the perfect union of energy between the time when the Master Jesus took on the Christ consciousness and now, when it is given to the people of Earth."

21: But any who come with unclean spirit will be made desolate and naked. And waters of the spring will dry up. And they will walk with demons and be beset by seven plagues.

22: But the pure spirit will bathe in the river of Paradise. And those who have washed in this spring have the right to the tree of life and they may go through the gates into the city of Paradise and bliss.

Chapter Seven

1: My brothers in spirit in Ephesus, in Smyrna, in Pergamum, in Thyatira, in Sardis, in Philadelphia, in Laodicea, bear faithful witness to the revelation of Jesus the Christ, which angels and visions have shown unto his faithful servant.

2: I, John being of great age, lie down in the certain knowledge of resurrection of the spirit.

3: Quickly I am to be taken unto the throne of the Father. I place into your keeping the vision given to me by the Father in the years of my life. That the vision may be made safe unto the time of the second coming of our Lord Jesus the Christ that the prophesy may be revealed.

4: Though weary are the eyes of His servant, they still know the spirit. And the spirit will live that I will know my brethren in the time foretold.

5: Though I am bidden quickly to finish my witness, that the wisdom of the prophesy may be fulfilled. For I was raised from sleep, and there came three angels clothed in white robes, that lifted me onto a cloud that took me to a high mountain.

6: And there was a multitude of host praising the Father. And before me was set a tabernacle. And in the tabernacle came forth a great light.

7: And a voice spoke, saying, "I am Alpha and Omega, the Originator and Completer of all things. Forasmuch as you have made faithful declaration of those things that are and will come to pass, let my Word be known that all will hear.

8: For the days of the prophecy are to be fulfilled. And you will know

9: All those in the vision across the planet who observe these teachings are also blessed.

10 - 14: The Aquarian Cross, symbol of Christ consciousness is raised on a staff at Glastonbury. All in the vision of the Second Coming of the SPIRIT of Jesus Christ are raised into the new awareness, where they receive wisdom and knowledge enabling them to teach and communicate throughout the planet.

15: The new consciousness will be initiated on Earth through **spirit communication**, in whatever form of subtle, intuitive contact is appropriate. Christ conscious humans will work in close attunement with the spirit and the subtle energy body of Mother Earth, in order to promote healing and responsible husbandry. Sudden and inexplicable political and social transformation also occurs as the Earth energy frequencies are raised by spiritually aware groups, who in this way "starve" of energy the negative forces of control and fear.

16: The mark of the beast is any symbol denoting our allegiance to mammon and its decaying financial structures. A clear warning to develop a more equitable exchange trading system to replace capitalism.

17: A symbolism of purity. Those in the vision will recognise each other by the light in their auras.

18: Reference to the full awakening of the 144,000 to their true purpose. They will spread the word, realign the energy grid of the Earth and thus restore the divinity of mankind and the planet.

the place by the bright star that was sent as a messenger to Bethlehem.

9: And the bright star will appear over the Holy City and all that abide within will be baptised in the light. And all that sit in high places and observe the light from afar, they also will be made one with the light.

10: And they will raise the sign of the cross that will be carried on a staff and all will bow their heads in the presence of the Father. For the old will be made new, and the city abide for ever. For all who share this vision will enter through the gates of the city of paradise and bliss.

11: And I will search in all hearts and in all minds, that they may be pure. For I will send the spirit of My son, Jesus the Christ, that all will be made one with His spirit.

12: And a great light will circle them and they will know each other. And they will rejoice and share the Sign. And they will be given vision and light. And wisdom will be revealed to them, that they will know their task.

13: And there will be a new Heaven and a new Earth. And everything will be made new. And they will walk in the light of the Christ returned.

14: And the light will go out to every nation from their mouth. And to every king and leader and to every nation, tribe and language, they will know the will of the Father.

15: For the spirit will talk through the prophets. And there will be a new bride. And the Bride and the Spirit will talk with one voice. And the Bride will bless the Earth.

16: But those who see not the light will be full of torment and have no rest day or night. And those that worship the beast and his image and anyone who receives the mark of his name, will be cast into eternal darkness.

17: The redeemed will be known to one another, for they will be dressed in white robes. And the Christ light will lead them to the springs of living water.

18: And they will make the sign to the newly born and baptise one another. And their riders will be given power to take peace to all the

19: Spiritually aware humans will not be restricted in this work by mortal form and will use the "miraculous" powers of the spirit to fulfil their purpose. The tenth planet is the symbolic source of wisdom to the Earth - it is hidden, just as wisdom has been hidden from the Earth.

20: Those qualifying to remain on Earth will be guided by Beings in the higher realms to live in total love and harmony in the garden of Eden restored.

Chapter Eight

For this chapter a verse by verse comparison with Ch 22 of the authorised version of the Book of Revelations in the bible is recommended

1: Knowing ourselves as spiritual beings in order to enter the higher dimensions.

2: Paradise is the garden of Eden, where there is no Earthly time, because no darkness or night exist there (verse 5). It is permanently illuminated by the spiritual light, so we shall only be aware of time in relation to monthly cycles of nature. The Tree of Life refers to the state of bliss within paradise and it is this which will keep the peace of nations.

3: As we move beyond duality, we shall realise that the Christ is the essence of God within man and that the Divine infuses every atom and molecule within the consciousness of ONE. Ch 22 verse 3 omits any reference to "being ONE in the glory of the Father".

4: We shall recognise the face of God in each other.

6: Final directions to those in the vision to be faithful and true.

7: First reference to the timing of "Second Coming".

9: All are equal, whether in a spiritual or physical body, so only the common factor uniting us all - the GODFORCE - is to be venerated. We are not to worship each other, but instead to be "at one" with one another and all creation.

people. And they will rejoice in the light and be trustworthy and true in the gift of the Divine Love of the Father.

19: And their spirit will inherit the earth. And they will have dominion over the stars even to the tenth planet.

20: For His angels will show His servants all things to come, that all will bathe forever in the river of Divine Love which flows through the city of paradise and bliss.

Chapter Eight

1: And the spirit led me forth and showed me a pure river of the water of life, clear as crystal, proceeding out of the throne of God.

2: And the river and the land were one, and on every side of the river there was the tree of life, which was in paradise. And the tree bore twelve manner of fruits, and yielded up fruit every month, for the leaves of the tree were for the healing peace of the nations.

3: And there will be no more anger, for the throne of God and of the Christ are there, and his servants will rejoice and be one in the glory of the Father.

4: And they shall see the face of God and know their Father and His sign shall be on their foreheads.

5: And there shall be no night there, and they need no torch, neither light of the sun, for the Father giveth them light, that they may abide in the light forever.

6: And He said unto me, "All will be faithful and true, for the Lord God of the holy prophets sent His angel to shew unto His servants the things which must be done.

7: A millennium will pass, then near another and behold, I come quickly, blessed is he that keepeth the sayings of the prophecy of this book".

8: And I John saw these things, and heard them. And when I had heard and seen, I fell down and worshipped before the feet of the angel which showed me these things.

9: Then the angel saith unto me, "Why do you worship at my feet? Know that I am as you, for I am thy fellow servant, and of thy brethren

10 & 11: A clear directive to all those resonating with the information in this work to take personal responsibility for communicating it far and wide. However, conversion of people in the manner of religious evangelism is unnecessary, as those drawn to the light will need no coercion.

Ch 22 verse 10 significantly omits "that all wisdom shall be known", while verse 11 excludes "That we shall know our brethren by their sign".

Note that Ch 22 verse 12 says . . . and, behold, "I" come quickly. Whereas the original version presented here states clearly "The Christ" come quickly. Christianity explains the Second Coming in terms of the physical reappearance of the Jesus Christ personality, whereas throughout Chapter 8 this text emphasises his presence at the present time of Second Coming as an "internal" and not "external" experience.

12: A second reference to the timing of Second Coming and the announcement of the comet's presence overhead (both references omitted in Ch 22). There will be great rejoicing in spirit as all those working in the vision on Earth are raised up.

15: Those initiated into Divine love, will remain in the higher dimensional reality. Ch.22 omits the first half of the verse.

16: A clear explanation that the Second Coming of the Spirit of Jesus is the acceptance of the Christ consciousness in all open human hearts at this time. Ch 22 verse 16 bears no resemblance, and refers only to Jesus without reference to the Christ.

17: Ch 22 verse 17 omits all reference to sharing Divine love with the Father in paradise.

the prophets, and of them which keep the sayings of this book, that we worship only the Father".

10: And he saith unto me, "Hide not the sayings of the prophecy of this book, neither let no man do likewise, for the time is at hand that all wisdom shall be known.

11: And be it known that he that is unjust, let him be unjust still; and he which is filthy, let him be filthy still; and he that is righteous, let him be righteous still; and he that is holy, let him be holy still. That we shall know our brethren by their sign.

12: And behold, the Christ come quickly, for a millennium will pass and near another and there will be made a sign in the heavens. And you will know this star that called the wise and all-knowing to Bethlehem. Seek there the star at the appointed time, and all spirit will rejoice in the reward, even unto those who come out of the body, that every man according as his work shall be".

13: For the Father saith, "I am Alpha and Omega, the beginning and the end, the first and the last".

14: Blessed are they that keep His commandments, that they may have the right to the tree of life. And will share Divine Love and know paradise and bliss.

15: For I tell you, none who do evil will come into this paradise, neither will they know the power of Divine Love. For only the sacred will live in the temple and make to each other the sign. And they will not leave paradise. For without are dogs, and sorcerers and whoremongers, and murderers, and idolators, and whoever loveth and maketh a lie.

16: And there was great light and there stood before me Jesus the Christ. And He spake thus, that I may know the authority of the angel. And bade "Watch for the star that was foretold by the prophet Jacob, that you will know the time of the second coming, when I will enter all hearts".

17: And the spirit and the bride say, Come. And let him that heareth say come. And let him that is athirst, Come. And whosoever will, let him take of the waters of life freely that they will live with the Father in paradise. And they will be baptised with the sign and share the Divine Love that comes from the spring of life.

327

18 & 19: A directive, long ignored by Christianity, **not** to change the "received" word. To have included this stern directive in a chapter that has otherwise been so abridged is extraordinarily deceitful! Ch 22 verse 19 omits reference to "not sharing the eternal gift of paradise and bliss".

20: The third and final warning as to the timing of Second Coming. All three references in this chapter were withdrawn by the church. Chapter 22 ends "Even so, come Lord Jesus", whereas this text invokes the Christ Light.

18: For I testify unto every man that heareth the words of the prophecy of this book. If any man shall add unto these things, God shall add unto him the plagues that are written in this book.

19: And if any man shall take away from the words of this book of prophecy, the Father shall take away his right to the tree of life and he will be cast out of the Holy City and will share not the eternal gift of paradise and bliss.

20: He which testifieth these things saith, "Surely I come quickly. Even as night follows day, so shall century follow century, until the second millennium is nigh". Amen. Even so, come, Christ light.

21: Let the grace of our Father and the Lord Jesus the Christ be with you all. Amen.

PASSPORT TO PARADISE

Inspirational readings, meditations, prayers and invocations to prepare us for our release into 'the Great Beyond':

THE ARAMAIC LORD'S PRAYER

Original transliteration and translation from the Syriac-Aramaic version of the Peshitta by Neil Douglas-Klotz. These are the words in the language Jesus actually used, preserved by the Sufi tradition of Islamic mysticism:

1. ABWOON D'BASHMAYA (O birther! Father-Mother of the Cosmos, you create all that moves in Light.)
2. NETQADDASH SHMAKH.(Focus your light within us - make it useful as the rays of a beacon show the way.)
3. TEETE MALKUTAKH (Create your reign of unity now through our fiery hearts and willing hands.)
4. NEHVWEY TZEVYANNACH AYKANNA D'BASHMAYA APH B'ARHA (Your one desire then acts with ours, as in all light, so in all forms.)
5. HAVLAN LAHMA D'SUNQANAN YAOMANA.(Grant what we need each day in bread and insight.)
6. WASHBWOQLAN HAUBVAYN WAHTAHAYN AYKANA DAPH HNAN SHBVOQAN L'HAYYABAYN. (Loose the chords of mistakes binding us, as we release the strands we hold of other's guilt.)
7. WELA TAHLAN LE'YNESYUNA. (Don't let surface things delude us.)
8. ELA PATZAN MIN BISHA. (But free us from what holds us back.)
9. METUL DILAKHIE MALKUTA WAHAYLA WATESHBUHTA L'AHLAM ALMIN. (From you is born all ruling will, the power and the life to do, the song that beautifies all, from age to age it renews.)
10. AMEYN.(Truly, power to these statements, may they be the source from which all our actions grow. Sealed in trust and faith. Amen.)

This prayer is not only spoken - but sung and danced as part of the Universal Peace Dance programme being introduced worldwide. The energy around it is immensely powerful and many people experience personal transformation on hearing it.

THE INVOCATION OF THE OMEGA POINT

Know, O Universe, that I love You with All the Grace,
And with All the Power of the Love of Messiah . . .
That my awareness is Eternally caressing all Forms of Reality,
sharing this Bliss in the most Beautiful and Creative Manifestations . .

Let my Heart be possessed by the Spirit of Truth.
Let my Existence be Dedicated to the enlightenment of All
Consciousness throughout the Universe! Let my Enthusiasm be
a Light of Love and Truth for all to Feel. Oh Let my Touch
Be the Highest Manifestation for the Will Divine.

Let my every Action transform this Reality into Greater
And more Loving Perfections! Let my body be
the Most Sacred Temple of Truth! The Omega Point is Here!
Clarity of Vision has been Redeemed throughout the Universe.

This invocation was given to Robert Coon by elders of the Melchizedek priesthood who materialised on Mt. Tamalpais, California at Rosh Hashanah (Jewish New Year) 1975. It was used to open the Earth's heart chakra on Glastonbury Tor at Easter 1984 and the elders indicated that it is to replace the Great Invocation given by the Master D.K. to Alice Bailey in 1945, invoking the now manifested Christ consciousness back to Earth. *Affirmations and evocation of the presence of Christ on Earth in all open hearts are now more appropriate.*

WORLD HEALING MEDITATION

This event is now observed by over 50 million people every December 31st at noon GMT for one hour, and is the largest annual focus of Light on the planet. You are invited to join in wherever you are, to speak the meditation aloud and link your valuable energy to the ever-growing grid of Love. This is the power that will soon transmute negative forces on the planet - IF enough of us make the effort to participate in this and other global linking events:

"In the beginning.
In the beginning GOD.
In the beginning God created Heaven and Earth,

and God said let there be Light and there was Light.

Now is the time of the New Beginning.

I am a co-creator with God and it is a new Heaven that comes,
as the good will of God is expressed on Earth through me.

It is the kingdom of Light, Love and Peace and Understanding.
And I am doing my part to reveal its Reality.

I begin with me. I am a living soul and the spirit of God dwells
in me, as me.

I and the Father are One, and all that the Father has is mine.

IN TRUTH, I AM THE CHRIST OF GOD.

What is true of me is true of everyone, for God is all and all is God.

I see only the spirit of God in every soul.

And to every man, woman and child on Earth I say:

I love you, for you are me. You are my Holy Self.

I now open my heart, and let the pure essence of Unconditional Love
pour out.

I see it as a Golden Light radiating from the centre of my Being
and I feel its Divine vibration in and through me, above and below me

I am one with the Light. I am filled with the Light.

I am illumined by the Light. I am the Light of the world.

With purpose of mind, I send forth the Light.

I let the radiance go before me to join the other Lights.

I know this is happening all over the world at this moment.

I see the Lights. There is now One Light. We are the Light of the
world.

The One Light of Love, Peace and Understanding is moving.

It flows across the face of the Earth.

Touching and illuminating every soul in the shadow of illusion.

And where there was darkness, there is now the Light of Reality.

And the radiance grows, permeating, saturating every form of life.

There is only the vibration of one Perfect Life now.

All the kingdoms of Earth respond and the planet is alive with Light
and Love.

There is total Oneness, and in Oneness we speak the word.

Let the sense of separation be dissolved. Let mankind be returned to
Godkind.

Let peace come forth in every mind. Let love flow forth from every
heart.

Let forgiveness reign in every soul. Let understanding be the common
bond.

And now from the Light of the world, the One Presence and Power of
the Universe responds.
The activity of God is healing and harmonising Planet Earth.
Omnipotence is made manifest.
I am seeing the salvation of the planet before my very eyes,
as all false beliefs and error patterns are dissolved.
The sense of separation is no more;
the healing has taken place, and the world is restored to sanity.
This is the beginning of Peace on Earth and Good Will toward all,
as love flows forth from every heart, forgiveness reigns in every soul,
and all hearts and minds are one in perfect understanding.

It Is Done. And It Is So.

John Randolph Price

CHILDREN OF THE LIGHT

The time of the great awakening is come. You who have chosen to lift
your eyes from the darkness to the light are blessed to see the advent of
a new day on the Earth. Because your heart has yearned to see the real
peace where war has reigned, to show mercy where cruelty has dominated, and to know love where fear has frozen hearts, you are privileged to usher real healing to your world.

The Planet Earth is blessing you. She is your friend and your mother.
Always remember and honour your relationship with her. She is a
living, loving, breathing being, like unto yourself. She feels the love
that you give as you walk upon her soil with a happy heart.

The Creator has chosen your hands to reach the lonely, your eyes to
see innocence in the guilty, and your lips to utter words of comfort to
the wounded. Let pain be no more! You have wandered in dark
dreams for too long; now you must step into the light and stand for
what you know to be true. The world has suffered not from evil, but
from the fear of the acknowledgement of good. That fear must be
ended now, forever, and it is within your power to do so.

No-one can find yourself but you. All of your answers are within. You
must now teach the lessons you have learned. Your understanding has
been given not only for yourself, but to guide a sore and tired world to
a place of rest in a new consciousness.

Here before you is your vision come true. Here is your answer given
you, a song to soothe a weary soul and make it new again. Here is a

bridge that joins you to your brothers and sisters. Here is your Self. Look gently upon your Self, and allow yourself to be filled by the light you have been seeking. True love comes from yourself, and with such a power your every thought is a blessing to the entire Universe.

All areas of your life will be healed. You will shine with a golden splendour that speaks of the One who created you in wisdom and glory. The past will dissolve like a dark dream, and your joy will be so brilliant that you will have no recollection of the night.

Go forth then, and be a messenger of hope. Point the way to healing by walking in gratefulness. Your brothers and sisters will follow, and as you pass beyond the portal of limitation you will be united and re-united with all who seemed to be lost. There is no loss in the Creator. Choose the path of forgiveness, and you will weep tears of joy for the goodness you find in all.

Go forth and live the life of the radiant soul that you are. Glorify the Creator in your every deed. You are important, you are needed and you are worthy. Never allow the dark cloak of fear to hide the light from your view. You were not born to fail you are destined to succeed. The hope of the world has been planted in your breast, and you are assured of success as you stand for the One who created you.

This then is the healing of the Earth. All of your doubts and fears can be set aside as you know the healing will come through the love of your heart.

Network 2012 - Michael Lightweaver

The speech of Chief Seattle in 1854 on the taking of his tribal lands by the white settlers in America, adapted for the Australian continent by Burnham Burnham, the Aboriginal elder and statesman, who laments the same behaviour of the white settlers in his own land:

"This land of the Dreamtime was given to us and we love it very dearly. The idea of it being taken is strange to us. If we do not own the freshness of the air and the sparkle of the water, how can you buy them? Every part of this land is sacred to my people. Every shining gum leaf, every sandy shore, every mist in the eucalypt forest, every clearing and insect is holy in the memory and experience of my people. The sap which courses through the trees carries memories of the black man. The shining water that lives in the billabongs and rivers is not just water, but the blood of our ancestors.

"If you take our land, you must remember that it is sacred, and you must teach your children that it is sacred, and that each ghostly reflection in the clear water of the lakes tells of events and memories in the life of my people.

"Our dead never forget this beautiful land, for it is the Mother of the black man. We are part of the land and the land is part of us. The perfumed flowers are our sisters; the koala, the kangaroo and great eagle, these are our brothers. The rocky crests, the juices of the forest, the body heat of the dingo, and man - all belongs to the same family.

"There is no quiet place in the cities. No place to hear the crackling of leaves or the rustle of an insects wings. What is there to life if we cannot hear the lonely cry of the curlew or the mopoke, of the archetypal arguments of the frogs around the billabong at night?

"The air is precious to us for all things share the same breath - the animal, the tree, the man; we all share the same breath. Since you have already taken our land, you must remember that the air is precious to us, that the air shares its spirit with all the life it supports. The wind that gave grandfather his first breath, also receives his last sigh, and the wind must also give our children the spirit of life.

"Teach your children as we have taught our children, that the Earth is our Mother. Whatever befalls the Earth, befalls the sons and daughters of the Earth. If men spit upon the ground, they spit upon themselves. This we know; the Earth does not belong to us, we belong to the Earth. This we know; all things are connected. Whatever befalls the Earth, befalls the people of Earth.

"Man did not weave the web of life, he is merely a strand in it. Whatever he does to the web, he does to himself. Men come and go, like the waves of the sea. Love your land as we loved it; care for it as we have cared for it. Hold in your mind the memory of the land as it was when you took it. And with all your strength, with all your mind, with all your heart, preserve it for your children - and love it."

January 25th, 1990

THE CATHAR PROPHECY
OF 1244 CE

The last of the Cathars was burnt by the Inquisition of the Roman Catholic Church at Montsegur, Languedoc, France in 1244, but they left this prophecy: that the Church of Love would be proclaimed in 1986.

It has no fabric, only understanding.

It has no membership, save those who know they belong.

It has no rivals, because it is non-competitive.

It has no ambition, it seeks only to serve.

It knows no boundaries for nationalisms are unloving.

It is not of itself because it seeks to enrich all groups and religions.

It acknowledges all great Teachers of all the ages who have shown the truth of Love.

Those who participate, practise the Truth of Love in all their beings.

There is no walk of life or nationality that is a barrier. Those who are, know.

It seeks not to teach but to be and, by being, enrich.

It recognises that the way we are may be the way of those around us because we are that way.

It recognises the whole planet as a Being of which we are a part.

It recognises that the time has come for the supreme transmutation, the ultimate alchemical act of conscious change of the ego into a voluntary return to the whole.

It does not proclaim itself with a loud voice but in the subtle realms of loving.

It salutes all those in the past who have blazed the path but have paid the price.

It admits no hierarchy or structure, for no-one is greater than another.

Its members shall know each other by their deeds and being and by their eyes and by no other outward sign save the fraternal embrace.

Each one will dedicate their life to the silent loving of their neighbour and environment and the planet, while carrying out their task, however exalted or humble.

It recognises the supremacy of the great idea which may only be accomplished if the human race practises the supremacy of Love.

It has no reward to offer either here or in the hereafter save that of the ineffable joy of being and loving.

Each shall seek to advance the cause of understanding, doing good by stealth and teaching only by example.

They shall heal their neighbour, their community and our Planet.

They shall know no fear and feel no shame and their witness shall prevail over all odds.

It has no secret, no arcanum, no initiation save that of true understanding of the power of Love and that, if we want it to be so, the world will change but only if we change ourselves first.

ALL THOSE WHO BELONG, BELONG; THEY BELONG TO THE CHURCH OF LOVE.

Acknowledgement to the Fountain Group, UK

THE CATHAR MANTRAM

I am the fountain of Light
I am the Universe
I am all Consciousness
I am all Being
I am the spirit of Love, deep unconditional and forever
My gift to the Light which is around me is the spark of life
I carry it freely, generously, in purity of the Soul
And thus it shall be for ever and ever.

LOVE

There is no difficulty that enough love will not conquer;
No disease that enough love will not heal;
No door that enough love will not open;
No gulf that enough love will not bridge;
No wall that enough love will not throw down;
No sin that enough love will not redeem . . .

It makes no difference how deeply seated may be the trouble;
How hopeless the outlook;
How muddled the tangle;
How great the mistake;
A sufficient realisation of love will dissolve it all.
If only you could love enough you would be the happiest
and most powerful being in the world.

Emmet Fox

FEELING LOVE

I realised that the heaven
to which we aspire, is here and everywhere.
The hell we fear, is only failure to see our heaven.
The ecstasy we crave, is our permanent state.
The answers we search, we know.
The love of God or godhood which we desire is permanently ours.
The God or Godhood whose presence in this infinite cosmos
we cannot sense, is our pure being,
the God or Godhood which we are.
Not to see this every moment is our only sin.
Not to understand that it is all our mutual game, our blindness.
Not to see the love, the pain and poignancy in each other's eyes,
in every atom, star, flower and tree is our absurdity.
Not to see our eternity in every moment of our feeling lives is our
     foolishness.
Not to exult over our own glory, is to insult the glory of our universal
     nature.
Not to love it all is to miss the point entirely.
Not to embrace and celebrate life, is our only misery,
but it is also part of our game.

To strangle life with our theories, to distort our majesty
by limiting our Godhood to ascetic rules and tragic airs,
is to insult our God and Godhood.
It is all an infinite blessing,
including the tears that wash away our pain,
and the forgetfulness that limits our memory.
We range through the entire manifest and unmanifest worlds,
through a kaleidoscope of indescribable experiences
of 'mansions', miracles, light, sound and music
that transcend our wildest imagination.

The death we feel is our own intent.
The purpose we seek is our very purpose.
The meaning we deny, is the meaning that is everywhere.
The idiocy we indulge, is the notion that this blissful cosmos,
trillions of stars, endless change and ultimate enchantment
is an accident of blind matter.
We are all gullible fools
And we are all gods!

                                                              Milton Ward

ROSEMARY FOR REMEMBRANCE

"O Lord, remember not only the men and women of good will,
but also those of ill will. But do not only remember all the suffering
they have inflicted upon us; remember the fruits we bore,
thanks to this suffering - our comradeship, our loyalty, our humility,
the courage, generosity, the greatness of heart which has grown out of
    this.
And when they come to judgement, let all the fruits
that we have borne be their forgiveness."

*This was found written on a scrap of wrapping paper
in the Ravensbruck concentration camp in Germany
at the end of the second World War.*

MY LAW - TIEME RANAPIRI

The sun may be clouded, yet ever the sun
Will sweep on its course till the Cycle is run.
And when into chaos the system is hurled
Again shall the Builder reshape the new world.

Your path may be clouded, uncertain your goal:
Move on - for your orbit is fixed to your soul.
And though it may lead into darkness of night
The torch of the Builder shall give it new light.

You were. You will be! Know this while you are:
Your spirit has travelled both long and afar.
It came from Source, to the source it returns
The Spark which was lighted eternally burns.

It slept in a jewel. It leapt in a wave.
It roamed in the forest. It rose from the grave.
It took on strange garbs for long aeons of years
And now in the soul of yourself It appears.

From body to body your spirit speeds on
It seeks a new form when the old one has gone
And the form that it finds is the fabric you wrought
On the loom of the Mind from the fibre of Thought.

As dew is drawn upwards, in rain to descend
Your thoughts drift away and in Destiny blend.
You cannot escape them for petty or great,
Or evil or noble, they fashion your Fate.

Somewhere on some planet, sometime and somehow
Your life will reflect your thoughts of your Now.
My law is unerring, no blood can atone -
The structure you built you will live in - alone.

From cycle to cycle, through time and through space
Your lives with your longings will ever keep pace
And all that you ask for, and all you desire
Must come at your bidding, as flame out of fire.

Once list' to that voice and all tumult is done
Your life is the Life of the infinite One.
In the hurrying race you are conscious of pause
With love for the purpose, and love for the Cause.

You are your own Devil, you are your own God
You fashioned the paths your footsteps have trod.
And no one can save you from Error or Sin
Until you have hark'd to the Spirit within.

Attributed to a New Zealand Maori

COMMITMENT

Until one is committed
there is hesitancy, the chance to draw back,
always ineffectiveness.

Concerning all acts of initiative (and creation)
there is one elementary truth,
the ignorance of which kills countless ideas
and splendid plans:
that the moment one definitely commits oneself,
then Providence moves too.
All sorts of things occur to help one
that would otherwise never have occurred.
A whole stream of events issues from the decision,
raising in one's favour all manner
of unforeseen incidents and meetings
and material assistance,
which no man could have dreamt
would have come his way.
I have learned a deep respect
for one of Goethe's couplets:

"Whatever you can do, or dream you can . . . begin it.
Boldness has genius, power and magic in it."
W.N.Murray The Scottish Himalayan Expedition 1951

ON THE CROP FORMATION PHENOMENON

The human mind will search Death's face for love
And will see roses where brittle thistles grow -
'Twill see bright Order where nought but Chaos reigns
And e'en feel peace though it hears War's trumpets blare
Great Goddess MA, Queen of the tumbling worlds -
Ishtar of old, Pacha-Mama of the West
Bright, green Fetish that bore the Race of Man
Though bright mirages will oft delude my eyes
And lies by missionaries told confuse my tumbled mind
Though tales mistold will oft lead me astray
This do I know - GREAT GODDESS YOU ARE THERE!
Yours is the mind that whispers from the corn
Yours are the hands that shape the circles there -
Tis You warn us "Sons and daughters beware
The fiery missiles born on dark wings of SPACE!
I am in peril - and so are you -BEWARE!"
You listen to the hidden thoughts of men
and closely watch the symbols that they draw -
And then, smiling, using the living grain,
You send these symbols as messages for us!
Mother, you exist, and all these wondrous things
Are shining proof, undoubted that you are there
No alien being, spawned on some distant world -
Can know us, and so understand our minds!

by Credo Mutwa, spiritual leader of the Zulus, on seeing my slides of
the 1996 Crop formations in UK during the 'Prophecies of the Andes'
conference at the Sacred Valley, Cusco, Peru September 1996

Mahatma Gandhi speaking to supporters of Wholistic World Vision,
September 1990:

"We are not creating a new religion. We are not creating a new beginning. We have been illuminated by the Christ Light, and our vision is
as old as the planet herself. We seek to restore all mankind to that
moment of conception, when harmony was so all-engulfing; where
man saw no evil, for no evil occurred; when man saw love and felt
love, for love was the divine light of God. We must strive back in

simplicity. We have taken a long road together. Now we must see the destiny from which we came, to which we go.

"The circle is complete."

ESSENE MORNING AND EVENING ANGEL ATTUNEMENTS

These are said each morning and evening, preceded by the Prologue before entering into meditation. They make us conscious that we are surrounded and penetrated by cosmic forces and Earth energies which we can use for balance, integration and healing. The full meditation wording is available from the Essene Network (see p.348)

Prologue

"Let us enter the eternal and infinite Garden of Mystery, our Spirits in Oneness with the Heavenly Father; our bodies in Oneness with the Earthly Mother; and our hearts and minds in Oneness with each other and with all of creation."

EVENING	MORNING
Friday *The Heavenly Father and I are one.*	*Angel of Air, enter me with my breath and give the Air of Life to my body*
Saturday *Angel of Eternal Life, descend upon me and give eternal life to my spirit.*	*The Earthly Mother and I are one. Her breath is my breath; her blood is my blood; her bone her flesh, her bowels, her eyes and ears are my flesh, my bowels, my eyes, my ears. Never will I desert her, and always will she nourish and sustain my body*
Sunday *Angel of Creative Work, descend upon earth and give abundance to all the sons of men*	*Angel of Earth, make fruitful my seed, and with your powers give life to my body.*
Monday *Peace, peace, peace, Angel of Peace, be always everywhere*	*Angel of Life, enter with strength the limbs of my body.*

Tuesday Angel of Power, des-
scend on me and fill with power
all my deeds.

Angel of Joy, descend upon
Earth, pouring forth beauty and
delight to all the chldren of the
Earthly Mother and the Heavenly
Father.

Wednesday Angel of Love, descend on me and fill with love all
my feelings.

Angel of Sun, enter my body and
let me bathe in the fire of life.

Thursday Angel of Wisdom, descend on me and fill with wisdom
all my thoughts.

Angel of Water, enter my blood
and give the Water of Life to my
body.

TRAVELLING COMPANIONS

Books that have directly inspired this work and have given us food for thought - and action! - along the way:

CENTRAL TO THIS BOOK

The Drama of the Lost Disciples	Jowett	*Covenant*
The Invisible Hand	Dunstan	*Megiddo*
The Spear of Destiny	Ravenscroft	*Sphere*
The Mark of the Beast	Ravenscroft	*Sphere*
The Dead Sea Scrolls Deception	Baigent/Leigh	*Corgi*
In God's Name	Yallop	*Corgi*
The Gospel of Thomas	McGregor Ross	*Element*
The Earth Chronicles (6 volumes)	Sitchin	*Avon(USA)*
Glastonbury and the Planetary New Jerusalem	Coon	
Spheres of Destiny	Coon	
Conversations Beyond the Light by Electronic Means	Kubris/Macy	*Griffin (USA)*
Interest and Inflation Free Money	Kennedy	*Seva Int.*

PRACTICAL GUIDANCE

You can have it All	Patent	*Celebration*
The White Hole in Time	Russell	*Harper/Collin*
The Road less Travelled	Peck	*Rider*
You can Heal your Life	Hay	*Hay House*
Creative Visualisation	Gawain	*Whatever*
The Fifth Dimension	Alder	*Rider*
Adventure in Meditation	Parrish	*SparrowHawk*

CHANNELLED WISDOM

Starseed, the Third Millennium	Carey	*Harper/*
Visions	Carey	*Collins*
The Return of Merlin	Dean	*Global Communication*
The Spiritual Connection	Hagen	*Prism*
Christ consciousness speaks	Finch	*Revelation*
Revelation - Birth of a New Age	Spangler	*Findhorn*

Why on Earth	Hodgson	*White Eagle*
A Course in Miracles		*Arkana*
The Sleeping Prophet (Edgar Cayce)	Stearn	*Muller*

HEALTH AND WELLBEING

Healers on Healing		*Rider*
Quantum Healing	Chopra	*Bantam*
Hands of Light	Brennan	*Bantam*
Taoist Secrets of Love	Chia	*Healing Tao*
Sexual Energy & Yoga	Haich	*Aurora*
Deadly Deception (re.HIV/AIDS)	Willner	*Peltec*

EARTH ENERGIES/GEOMANCY

The Dimensions of Paradise	Michell	*Thames & Hudson*
Earthstars	Street	*Hermitage*
Crop Circles: Harbingers of World Change		*Gateway*
The Sun & the Serpent	Miller	*Pendragon*

GENERAL INTEREST

Autobiography of a Yogi	Yogananda	*Rider*
Star Signs	Goodman	*Pan*
More Lives than One	Iverson	*Pan*
Summons to a High Crusade	Trevelyan	*Findhorn*
Life and Teaching of the Masters of the Far East	Spalding	*DeVorss*
Surfers of the Zuvuya	Arguelles	*Bear & Co*
The Light in Britain	Cooke	*White Eagle*
The Mists of Avalon	Bradley	*Joseph*
Initiation	Haich	*Aurora*
The Secret Teachings of All Ages	Hall	*Philosophical Research Soc. LA (USA)*
The Gnostic Gospels	Pagels	*Penguin*
The Universe is a Green Dragon	Swimme	*Bear & Co.*
The Star of Bethlehem Mystery	Hughes	*Dent*
The Christian Conspiracy	Moore	*Pendulum*
Mass Dreams of the Future	Snow	*DCS Prod'ns*

CONTACTS

WWV welcomes enquiries from anyone with skills, contacts or resources who is interested in assisting or supporting the growing worldwide communications network that has been described. All mail to WWV requires a stamped, addressed envelope to save scarce resources. We also operate regular local Celtic Odyssey tours of sacred power sites in the UK each summer. Apply for details. Small Aquarian Cross pendants in gold, silver or nickel, as well as audio and video cassettes about WWV and Simon Peter Fuller are available. The WWV Home Page is at: http://www.globalvisions.org/cl/wwv.

WWV U.K.
P.O. Box 1046
Eastbourne
E. Sussex BN21 3HN
UNITED KINGDOM
e-mail to:
106160.235@compuserve.com

WWV New Zealand
P.O. Box 97111
South Auckland Mail Centre
NEW ZEALAND

WWV U.S.A. (Mainland)
Sancta Sophia Seminary,
Sparrow Hawk Village
Tahlequah
OK74464

WWV Hawaii (Pacific Basin)
c/o Spiritual World Network
#332, 150 Hamakua Drive
Kailua, HI 96734

WWV South Africa
C/o Rosemarie Crosson
P.O.829
KLOOF
3640

Tel/fax +2731-7644082

WWV Australia
P.O.Box 1409
Ballarat Mail Centre
VIC3354

OTHER CONTACTS ASSOCIATED WITH THIS BOOK

ZUVUYA LAND
A Lake Taupo sanctuary dedicated to Nature, Spirit and Earth energies; also a natural meeting place for Maori and white citizens intent on healing divisions:
Silbury Crystal
Zuvuya Land, Acacia Heights Drive
RD1, Taupo, New Zealand
(north island)

MOTHER MEERA Avatar of the Divine Feminine
Mother Meera
Oberdorf 4a
65599 Dornburg-Thalheim
Germany

PATTAYA ORPHANAGE
This inspiring initiative is maintained entirely by donations:
Father Raymond Brennan
PO Box 15
Pattaya City
Cholburi 20150
Thailand

AGNI HOTRA FIRE RITUAL
The ancient Vedic sunrise and sunset fire ritual for cleansing negativity at all levels, both inner and outer:
Fivefold Path Inc.
Parama Dham
RFD #1 Box 121C
Madison VI22727
USA

ROBERT COON
A writer and visionary, and one of the fore-runners of the great adventure on which we are now all embarked:
Robert Coon
c/o 7 Landmead,
Glastonbury, Somerset. BA6 9DB UK

THE TRADITIONAL HOPI INDIAN COUNCIL

Global Purification Messenger
c/o Roy Little Sun
P.O.Box 1
Flagstaff
AZ 86001
USA

THROUGH THE HEART TO PEACE
Dandelion Trust
41, Limehouse Cut
46, Morris Road,
London E14 6NQ
United Kingdom
tel.+44(171)5385633 Fax +44(171)5377099

THE ESSENE NETWORK
c/o Windwood
22, Avenue Road,
Christchurch
Dorset BH23 2BY
United Kingdom

Angel Power Int P/L (Makers of Aquarian Cross Jewelry)
P.O.Box 1041,
Box Hill,
Vic 3128
Australia
Tel. +61(0)3987-66062
Fax +61(0)3987-66044

NETWORKING IS THE LIFEBLOOD OF THE NEW AWARENESS

If you resonate with the material in this book, please take personal responsibility for ensuring its widescale distribution. This will also greatly assist the WWV communications strategy.

WE CAME TO INITIATE CHANGE!

CURTAIN CALL

My gratitude and boundless love to:

Irma - the mother I never knew.

Norrie - the father who found me.

'Omi' - the granny every child should have!

Stuart and Catherine - who nurtured me.

Elaine and Rex - who recognised me.

Isobelle, Tumi and Robert - who reminded me.

My human and spirit partners in WWV - for their loving guidance and support.

Bob - whose exceptional mediumistic skills helped lay the foundation of WWV.

Louise, Mary and Sophy - who shared the vision of the Cross.

Robyn, Philip and friends - for anchoring the Aeon shift in Australia and in South Africa.

Michael Joseph - whose skill, enthusiasm, dedication and good humour transformed the presentation of this, my first book!

Gilian Cotterell - for her long commitment to the cause and so enthusiastically co-ordinating WWV Australia.

Carol Parrish - for opening her nation-wide mystery school to facilitate my own work in the important American arena.

Sir George Trevelyan - for his unfailing generosity to those who aspire to the glorious vision he so long championed.

Ken Carey - for communicating the purest and most lucid insights into these dramatic times.

Gordon - for giving me the freedom to write in such glorious and elevating surroundings.

Martyn and Catherine, *and* Guy and Mitzi - for your enduring friendship.

Father Ray - who is the embodiment of unconditional love in action.

Robin and Renché - my publishers - for the courage in taking on this project after so many had refused it.

And all those, too numerous to name, whom I have met and worked with in joyful common cause, on our journey to the New Horizon.

INDEX